Ad Oculos
Digital Image Processing
Student Version 2.0

Ad Oculos
Digital Image Processing
Student Version 2.0

Henning Bässmann
Philipp W. Besslich

INTERNATIONAL THOMSON COMPUTER PRESS
I ⓉP An International Thomson Publishing Company

London • Bonn • Boston • Madrid • Johannesburg • Melbourne • Mexico City • New York • Paris
Singapore • Tokyo • Toronto • Albany, NY • Belmont, CA • Cincinnati, OH • Detroit, MI

Ad Oculos Digital Image Processing
Student Version 2.0

 A division of International Thomson Publishing Inc.
The ITP logo is a trademark under licence

British Library Cataloguing-in-Publication Data
A catalogue record for this book is available from the British Library

First printed 1995
Reprinted 1995
Printed in the UK by The Alden Press, Oxford
Commissioning Editor: Samantha Whittaker

ISBN 1–85032–132–9

International Thomson Computer Press
Berkshire House
High Holborn
London WC1V 7AA
UK

International Thomson Computer Press
20 Park Plaza
14th Floor
Boston MA 02116
USA

http://www.thomson.com/itcp.html

Imprints of International Thomson Publishing

Contents

Preface

Unfortunately the preface has to start sadly. Prof. Besslich died during the preparation stage of this book. As with all his colleagues, I deeply regret that he did not live to see his work completed. I have done my best to realize the project as he would have wished.

The project's name is Ad Oculos which means 'to the eyes'. It is intended to give any interested beginner a clear demonstration of digital image processing which is used for such tasks as the enhancement of noisy images, for identifying characters, for checking the measurements of workpieces, for inspecting the garnishment of cookies, for analyzing cellular substances (for example, biopsies), for detecting environmental pollution from aerial photographs, and so on.

Since the mid-sixties such digital image processing has become an increasingly important subject of scientific research. Due to the enormous computing power required by image processing algorithms, for several years it remained a research area of very few specialists but with the dramatic increase in desk top computing power over the last few years, more and more people have become interested in 'making the computer see'. Thus, the number of publications concerning image processing has risen considerably in recent years. This development has been paralleled by the entry of digital image processing into the industrial arts: the number of companies trying to make money from industrial image processing has risen sharply due to optimistic market prognoses. Nevertheless, digital image processing still seems to be a 'playground' for specialists, when compared to other new techniques such as CAD. Consequently, it is not at all easy for beginners to enter this discipline. The aim of this book is to give a helping hand to those who want to get started.

The central idea behind this book is to demonstrate classical image processing algorithms regarding

- their basic idea from an application-oriented point of view,

- their realization from the programmers point of view,

- and (if necessary) their background from a theoretical point of view.

Consequently the basic intention of this work is by no means to be complete or scientifically up-to-date but to give the reader the seed for fruitful applications. The prerequisite for a good harvest is to fully grasp the subject material. It is no coincidence that to grasp means to touch it and to understand it. Thus the book is accompanied by Ad Oculos, a Windows 3.1 program which contains the algorithms discussed in the book. Due to its graphical user interface it allows you to grasp the individual algorithms easily and to combine these algorithms to form complex processing chains.

Since this book aims to be relevant for practical utilization it was very important to illustrate the gap between the theoretical possibilities of digital image processing and the harsh realities of industrial image processing. For this purpose the appendix contains a chapter illustrating examples of industrial applications. I wish to thank the companies DST Deutsche System-Technik GmbH, Innovationstechnik Gesellschaft für Automation m.b.H., Atlas Elektronik GmbH, and O.S.T. Optische Systemtechnik GmbH & Co. KG, which form the Bremer Arbeitskreis Bildverarbeitung (working group for image processing in Bremen), for kindly placing these examples at my disposal.

I wish to extend a very special note of appreciation to Rolf Bollhorst, Hans-Jürgen Oertwig and Heiner Suhr from DBS Digitale Bildverarbeitung und Systementwicklung GmbH, Bremen not only for producing the Ad Oculos Software but also for their support for the publication of this book.

The realization of the book was supported by fruitful discussions with M.Sc. and Ph.D. students. Thanks are especially due to Christian Backeberg for his contribution to region oriented segmentation, Wolfgang Bothmer for his work concerning morphological image processing and region segmentation and Siegfried Meyer for his support in the field of pattern recognition.

I am indebted to Dr John Illingworth of the University of Surrey, Dr Tim Morris of the University of Manchester and Dr George Wolberg of

City College of New York for their help with the development of the manuscript.

Without Ian Campbell and Lucy Etherington the English of this book would have been very 'German'. I greatly appreciate their help. Thanks are also due to Bettina Schmalfuss and Christine Stinner for preparing parts of the drawings.

I am especially grateful to Jonathan Simpson and Samantha Whittaker from International Thomson Publishing for their supportive assistance and to Hans-Dieter Rauschner and all of his colleagues at Logotechnics C.P.C. for their excellent typesetting and printing work.

Finally, I would like to dedicate this book to my colleagues at n.e.t.z software-partner gmbh and Neuhimmel Consulting GmbH for their encouragement of my 'hobby' – the Ad Oculos project.

Henning Bässmann

1

Introduction

1.1 What can image processing be used for?

The first step in answering this question is to structure the subject of digital image processing into its applications. Five typical areas of application are (Figure 1.1):

- **Computer Graphics** deals with the generation of images in such domains as desktop publishing, electronic media and video games.

- **Image Transmission** describes the transportation of images via cable, satellite or any kind of data highway. One important topic of image transmission is image compression to reduce the enormous amount of data required for digital images.

- **Image Manipulation** performs such tasks as the enhancement of noisy images, the enhancement of blurred images (for example, caused by bad focussing or jumping), geometrical correction (especially of satellite images), the improvement of contrast, and changes for artistic purposes.

1

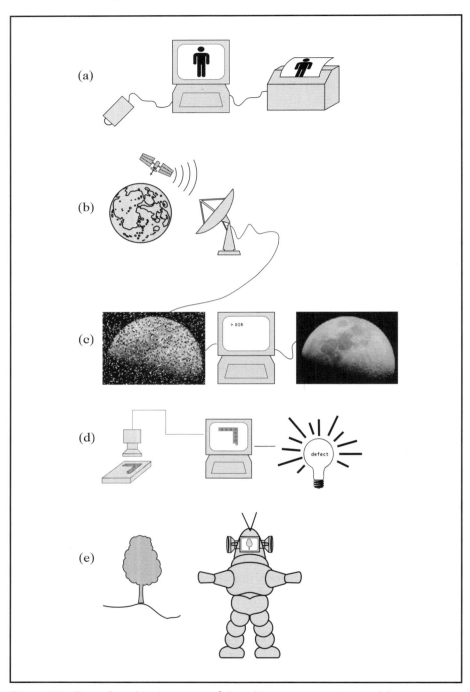

(a)

(b)

(c)

(d)

(e)

Figure 1.1 Typical application areas of digital image processing are (a) computer graphics, (b) image transmission (c) image manipulation, (d) image analysis and (e) scene analysis.

- **Image Analysis** is used for such tasks as identifying printed or hand-written characters, for checking the measurements of workpieces, for checking the accuracy of PCB manufacture, for classifying wooden panels with respect to surface failures, for inspecting the garnishment of cookies, for analyzing cellular substances (for example, biopsies) and for detecting environmental pollution from aerial photographs.

- **Scene Analysis** is one of the most fascinating facets of image processing. A typical application is the 'electronic eye' of autonomous vehicles (that is, exploratory robot space craft). Scene analysis is however particularly difficult to implement and is one of the topics the scientific community must continue to work hard on to obtain useful systems.

Inevitably, these areas of application are not clear cut and tend to overlap. Nevertheless, this book is devoted to the subjects *image manipulation* and *image analysis*. The examples of these subjects mentioned above are only a few typical areas of application. In principle, image analysis procedures are applicable in those tasks where human beings have to perform monotonous visual inspection duties or where accurate measurements at a glance are required. Moreover, these procedures offer new *functionalities* for visual inspection. For instance, they allow inspection problems to be solved with extreme speed.

In contrast to the theoretical possibilities, many serious obstacles arise when practical implementation is called for. To estimate these requires adequate expert knowledge which can only be acquired from long standing experience. However, there are many books which introduce digital image processing. The reference list ([1.1] to [1.28]) is a selection of some recent books.

1.2   Back to basics

The aim of this section is to illustrate the special aspects of image analysis which (in contrast to image manipulation) tries to extract information from an image. This illustration is based on the roots of image analysis, namely the camera. Figure 1.2(a) shows a light sensitive device as a very simple form of camera. This sensor only responds to 'light' or 'no light'. It provides a binary output.

Figure 1.2(b) shows a more sophisticated light meter which measures the degree of brightness or intensity (which is called a *graylevel* in the context of image processing) of a light source. Simple animals (such as snails) use such a light meter as a protective indicator of excessive sunlight which would dry them up. Thus biological as well as engineering systems are able to use such simple sensors in order to analyse their world.

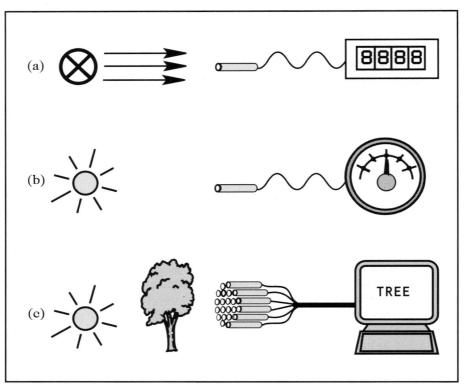

Figure 1.2 Different forms of light sensors: a light sensitive device (a), a light meter (b) and a camera/retina (c).

Bundling a lot of light meters together as shown in Figure 1.2(c) produces a camera, or referring to biology, a retina. It is very important to understand that the measurements which this sensor provides are only the individual light intensities measured by each of the light meters together with their relative positions. Based on these measurements, computers and brains have to extract useful information about the environment in which they are located.

Humans easily derive and express information in symbolic qualitative statements, such as 'the tree in front of the cabriolet is an oak'. They do not easily produce precise numeric statements of the form 'the rod at position (x,y) measures the light intensity z'. However, the latter form of statement is precisely that derived from artificial sensor systems.

To get a feeling for the problems faced by specialists, consider Figure 1.3. It shows a satellite image of Cologne. Asking a geologist, a hydrologist and a botanist to deliver an interpretation of the satellite image would yield three fairly different results, since the image has different *meanings* to each of these experts. But what does an image mean to a PC? Nothing! The image is only an array of numbers.

Figure 1.3
A satellite image of Cologne. Asking a geologist, a hydrologist and a botanist to deliver a line drawing of the image would yield three fairly different results, since the image has different meanings to each of the experts.

This problem is well-known in the technical community, and it leads to the development of so-called *knowledge-based systems*. The knowledge is entered (or better: is forced) into the system with the aid of a knowledge engineer, that is, a person, who tries to put as much *human* knowledge and understanding into the computer as is necessary for the task (for example, analyzing a scene).

Although such systems are sophisticated, they are not very successful in comparison with biological systems. They suffer from what is known as the *frame problem*, that is, they are engineered for a very specific set of circumstances and are not able to adapt themselves autonomously to other situations. They need to have explicit knowledge concerning an environment as well as their own possible behavior (for example, for obstacle avoidance). Their learning strategy is predetermined and externally controlled. Their understanding of the world is not their own, but only a small fraction of the knowledge engineer's.

To overcome these problems of this classic artificial intelligence approach, scientists have suggested new ones with names such as Instinct-Based Systems, Motivational-Based Systems, Artificial Life and Animates (which is the short form of Animal-automate, *see* [1.17]).

1.2.1   Summary

- Processing images with computers when precise measurements are needed (for example, in the context of industrial image processing) is a good choice. Computers execute their tasks fast and precisely if the tasks are fully defined. This book has been written from this point of view, focussing on realizable systems.

- Processing images with computers when these images are to be used to enable autonomous robots to 'see' has been much less successful. Investigations to improve this situation often try to use autonomous biological systems (animals) as models. Autonomous in this sense is used to mean that the system is only controlled by internal parameters (ultimately, pleasure and distress).

1.3   The basic components of image processing systems

Figure 1.4 shows a typical scenario for an industrial image processing system the task of which is to inspect components and to classify them as complete or defective.

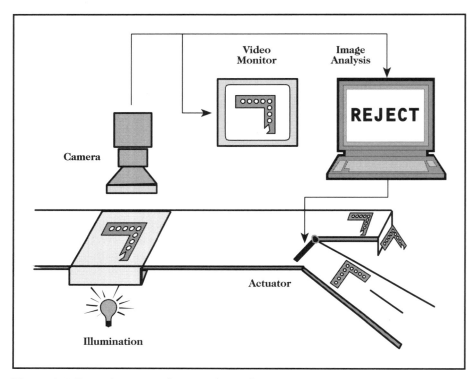

Figure 1.4 Typical scenario for an industrial image processing system.

- **Illumination**
  The success of most existing industrial image processing systems is fundamentally based on adequate illumination. There are several standard alternatives for illumination (Figure 1.5):

  (a) Uncontrolled light is a particular challenge.

  (b) The object is positioned between camera and light, so that the camera yields a silhouette of the object.

  (c) The relative positions of object, light and camera play an important role: imagine inspecting a surface in order to check it for scratches (for instance a disc). Typically one orientates the object so that the scratches have a high contrast relative to their background.

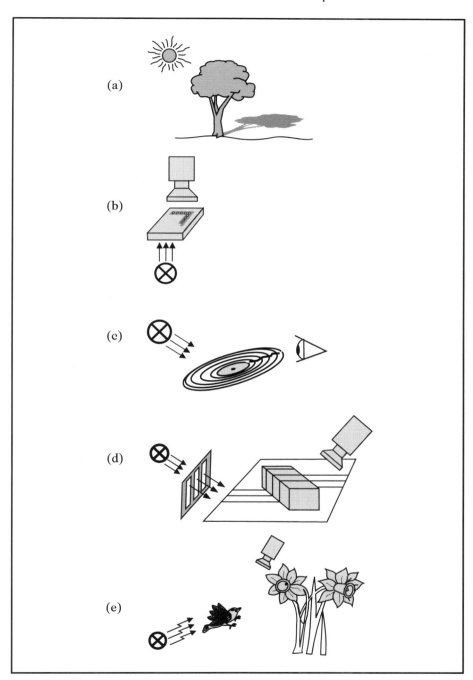

Figure 1.5 These are examples of typical forms of illumination: (a) uncontrolled light (typical for outdoor scenes), (b) analysis of an object's silhouette, (c) checking a disc for scratches, (d) 3D analysis with the aid of light strips (structured light), (e) freezing movement by a flashing strobe.

(d) Surfaces may be illuminated homogeneously or with special patterns of light (structured light).

(e) In the case of moving scenes, flashing strobe light is used to 'freeze' the image.

Besides visible light, other types of radiation such as X-rays, infra-red light and ultrasonic sound sources may be used.

- **Acquisition**
CCD array cameras are the sensors most commonly used to acquire images. Their light sensitive area consists of a matrix-like structured chip. Since the chip is small, it is possible to build extremely small cameras. These chips do not usually produce a standard video signal and do not have a power supply 'on board'. These tasks are fulfilled by external devices. If the camera size and weight are not critical parameters, it may be more convenient and cheaper to use a normal commercial video camera.

  If very high resolution of an image is required, the standard video norm is insufficient. High resolution CCD array cameras would be very expensive. One-dimensional CCD arrays are a more appropriate alternative. A typical application of such arrays can be found in scanners. They are normally used to digitize paper documents, but it is evident that this principle need not be confined to scanning paper. Clearly, workpieces may be treated in the same way, for example, in order to inspect their measurements. The cameras used in this way are called line-scan cameras.

  Apart from these special cameras, CCD cameras yield a standard video signal. The first step in achieving this is to digitize the signal. Figure 1.6 shows a camera with a CCD chip consisting of 604 rows and 576 columns (this is a common format). The camera's electronics 'squeezes' the CCD output into a standard video signal. A *frame grabber*, plugged into a computer, samples and digitizes the incoming video signal and puts the digital image into the computer memory. From a technical point of view the whole process is a folly. The CCD chip produces an electronic signal which measures the light intensity. It would be more sensible to shift the CCD contents via a quantizer directly into the computer memory. The stage of producing a standard video signal is redundant and using an intermediate frame grabber only serves to degrade the original measurement.

  From an economic point of view, the folly makes sense, due to the internationally accepted video standards. One disadvantage of using these standards however is that their synchronization mechanisms are based on rows. For measuring applications, the synchronization of the transport of every picture element with a so-called *pixel clock* (pixel = picture element, *see* Section 1.4) is commonly recommended. The camera is usually triggered by the pixel clock of the frame grabber.

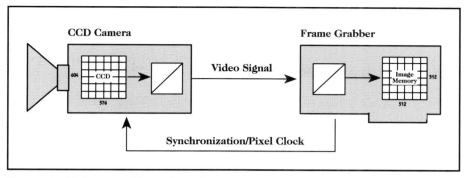

Figure 1.6 A frame grabber, plugged into a computer, samples and digitizes the video signal of a camera or another video source and 'collects' the incoming picture elements in the image memory.

- **Processing**
  The task for the computer is to acquire and process images and, should the occasion arise, to control any kind of actuator. In a simple case, the computer is a PC with interfaces to a camera and to an actuator. However, special image processing computers are often used. These computers need not be expensive, because it is often possible to realize a sophisticated configuration with the aid of standard components (hardware and software). Alternatively, using components which have to be custom developed for special applications (for example, in the context of real-time image processing) leads to drastic cost increase.

  In the context of a complex production process, the image processing computer is usually part of a large computer network and its integration may require considerable effort.

  In an industrial environment 'turn-key' systems which lack a keyboard and a monitor are often found. However, use of video monitors is advisable for diagnostic purposes, such as checking the system's image acquisition capability.

  A typical software development system for image processing algorithms consists of a library of standard procedures, tools for realizing new algorithms (high-level language, debugger, and so on) and a comfortable user interface.

- **Action**
  The type of actuator is highly dependent on the type of application. Actuators range from simple systems which control valves to complex robots. In any case, the image processing computer must be able to control the actuator(s) efficiently.

The description of these four components illustrates that 'pure' image processing plays only a minor role in the context of visual inspection in an industrial environment. This is a fact which is often ignored or underestimated.

This book focuses on the algorithms of image processing. Thus, one only needs a PC running Ad Oculos (Section 1.5) to become familiar with this subject. For further experiments, it is advisable to use a frame grabber supported by Ad Oculos in order to obtain images from a standard video source.

1.4   Digital images

Figure 1.7 shows a typical digital image. It is represented by an array of N rows and M columns. Usually, the row index and the column index are labeled with y and x, or r and c. In many cases (but not all) the image array is square that is, $N=M$. Typical values for N and M are **128, 256, 512** or **1024**.

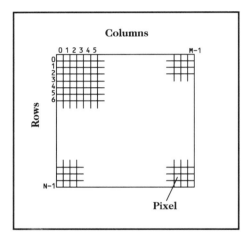

Figure 1.7
Basic structure of a digital image.

The elements of the image array are called pixels (picture elements). In the simplest case, the pixels merely take either the value 0 or 1. Such pixels constitute a *binary image*. Usually, the values 1 and 0 represent light and dark regions or object and background, respectively. In order to obtain a finer quantization of the video image's light intensity, it is usual to use one byte per pixel, leading to integer values ranging from 0 (black) to **255** (white). Between these limits the values are gray and therefore, the integer value associated with a pixel is called its *graylevel*.

Clearly it is also possible to process color images. In this case, an image requires an $N*M$ array for each of the primary colors red, green and blue. Thus, the 'graylevels' of each of the arrays determine the 'strength' of the red, green and blue components of the image at the position of the pixel in question.

Processing *real* colors must not be confused with the *pseudo-color* visualization of images which were originally gray. Pseudo-color representation is sometimes useful to emphasize graylevels or graylevel ranges of interest, in order to facilitate image analysis by a human observer.

Digital image processing usually requires large resources of computing power and memory. A typical graylevel image of 512*512 pixels and 256 graylevels (8 bits) per pixel needs 256K bytes of memory. This is approximately equivalent to 100 typewritten pages. Suppose that one has to deal with realtime processing of 10 images per second. Then the amount of data to cope with exceeds 150 Mbytes or 60,000 typed pages per minute. This corresponds to a heap of paper 3 meters (10 feet) high.

Figure 1.8 shows a graylevel image of 128*128 pixels, each with 256 graylevels. It represents the image of simple geometrical objects cut out of cardboard. A black piece of cardboard serves as the background, while the objects are gray or white. A human observer is able to identify the objects and their position in the image without any problems (Section 1.2), but the computer only 'sees' an array, the elements of which are integers within the range 0 to 255. This fact is illustrated by a section of the source image shown in Figure 1.9. Algorithms which enable a computer to identify the contents of an image are the main subject of this book.

Figure 1.8
Example of a graylevel image.

	0	1	2	3	4	5	6	7	8	9	10	11	12	13	14	15	16	17	18	19	20	21	22
0	1c	1b	1a	1b	1c	1b	1c	1b	1a	1a	1a	1c	1b	1c	1c	1c	1c	1f	1e	1f	1d	20	21
1	1a	1a	1b	1a	1b	1b	1a	19	1a	1c	1a	1c	1d	1b	1b	1c	1c	1c	1e	1e	1e	1e	1f
2	1b	1b	.1a	1b	1b	1b	1c	1c	1c	1c	1a	1c	1c	1c	1c	1c	1b	1d	1d	1e	1e	1f	20
3	1a	1a	1b	19	1c	1a	1c	1b	1b	1b	1b	1a	1c	1a	1a	1b	1d	1e	1f	1d	1e	20	1f
4	1a	1a	18	18	1a	1a	1a	1a	19	19	1a	1b	1b	1b	1c	1a	1c	1b	1d	1e	1e	1e	20
5	19	18	1a	18	1a	19	1a	19	19	19	1a	1a	1a	1a	1a	1b	1d	1c	1d	1f	1f	1f	20
6	19	1a	1a	19	1a	1a	1b	1a	1a	19	1b	1a	1a	1b	1b	1c	1c	1e	1e	1e	1d	1f	1d
7	1a	19	1a	1a	1a	1b	1a	1a	1b	1a	1b	1b	1c	1c	1c	1a	1c	1e	1f	1e	20	21	20
8	1b	1a	1a	1a	1c	1a	1a	1a	19	1b	1b	1b	1a	1b	1c	1e	1c	1e	1f	1e	1f	1f	21
9	1c	1a	1b	1b	1a	1a	1a	1b	1b	1b	1b	1c	1b	1c	1b	1d	1b	1e	20	1f	1f	20	21
10	1b	1b	1a	1a	1b	1b	1b	1b	1a	1a	1c	1b	1c	1d	1d	1d	1d	1e	1e	1e	1e	20	20
11	19	18	1a	1a	18	19	19	1b	1a	1a	1b	1b	1a	1c	1c	1d	1c	1d	1f	1e	1f	21	20
12	19	1a	19	1a	1a	19	1a	1b	1a	1a	1c	1b	1c	1b	1c	1d	1c	1d	1c	1f	20	1f	1f
13	1b	19	1a	1a	1a	1b	19	1b	1a	1d	1b	1c	1a	1e	1b	1d	1d	1e	1e	1f	20	1f	22
14	1a	1b	1a	1a	1a	1a	1c	1a	1c	1a	1c	1c	1d	1c	1c	1c	1e	1e	1e	1d	20	1f	20
15	1a	19	1a	1b	1b	1a	18	19	1a	1b	1b	1c	1c	1d	1c	1c	1e	1e	1e	1f	21	21	22
16	19	1a	1b	1a	1a	19	1b	1a	19	1b	1b	1b	1c	1e	1c	1c	1e	1e	1e	1f	21	23	20
17	1b	19	1a	1b	1b	1c	19	1a	1c	1c	1d	1b	1b	1c	1e	1e	1e	20	1f	21	20	21
18	19	19	19	19	19	1a	1b	1b	1b	1c	1c	1b	1d	1c	1b	1d	1e	1e	1f	21	20	21	22
19	19	1a	1a	1a	1a	1a	19	1b	1b	1b	1b	1b	1c	1d	1e	1d	1b	1e	1f	21	21	21
20	1b	19	1b	19	1b	1c	1d	1b	1a	1c	1d	1d	1e	1c	1c	1f	1f	20	20	21	21	23	22
21	1b	1c	1a	1a	1c	1c	1d	1c	1d	1c	1d	1d	1f	1f	1f	1f	20	21	21	22	23	23
22	1c	1b	1c	1b	1b	1d	1c	1d	1c	1e	1c	1d	1d	1d	1f	1f	22	20	1f	1f	22	23	24
23	1c	1a	1b	1e	1c	1c	1d	1c	1d	1c	1d	1d	1d	1e	1b	20	20	20	20	22	24	22	24
24	1c	1d	1b	1c	1c	1c	1c	1d	1d	1d	1e	1e	1f	20	1e	1d	1f	20	23	21	23	23	24
25	1b	1c	1a	1b	1b	1b	1c	1a	1c	1d	1e	1d	1e	1f	1f	1e	20	21	20	22	21	23
26	1b	1a	1b	1b	1b	1d	1a	1c	1b	1c	1b	1d	1e	1e	1f	1f	1f	1e	21	20	21	22	25
27	1b	1b	1c	1d	1b	1c	1c	1c	1d	1d	1e	1f	1e	1e	1f	1f	1f	21	21	22	23	25
28	1d	1b	1c	1c	1b	1d	1c	1f	1d	1d	1f	1e	1f	1e	20	22	23	20	22	23	25	27
29	1c	1a	1c	1d	1b	1d	1e	1d	1c	1d	1d	20	1e	1f	20	1f	22	22	22	22	24	24	25
30	1b	19	1b	1d	1b	1c	1d	1e	1d	1f	1e	1d	1f	20	21	20	21	22	24	23	24	25
31	1b	1b	1c	1b	1b	1c	1c	1d	1e	1e	1e	1e	1e	20	20	20	20	23	22	23	24	24	25
32	1c	1c	1b	1d	1c	1d	1e	1e	1e	1e	1f	1e	1f	20	20	21	21	22	23	23	26	f
33	1c	1c	1b	1e	1e	1d	1d	1d	1e	1d	20	1f	1f	1f	1f	20	22	21	22	25	24	26	38
34	1e	1c	1d	1c	1c	1d	1f	1d	1e	20	1e	1f	20	20	23	23	22	26	21	ab
35	1c	1c	1c	1d	1c	1d	1e	1e	1d	1f	1d	1f	1f	1e	21	20	22	22	24	24	24	a	d4
36	1b	1b	1c	1d	1d	1d	1e	1e	1c	1e	1d	1e	1f	1f	21	22	22	22	25	24	62	e0
37	1c	1a	1b	1b	1c	1b	1c	1c	1b	1c	1d	1e	1e	1d	20	1f	20	21	22	25	16	bf	e0
38	1a	1b	1b	1b	1a	1c	1b	1c	1c	1a	1e	1d	1d	1f	1e	20	20	22	21	23	13	d9	e0
39	1b	1a	1a	1a	1b	1c	1b	1d	1c	1c	1b	1e	1e	1e	20	1f	21	22	23	21	87	e1	e1

Figure 1.9 Hexadecimal representation of a section of the graylevel image shown in Figure 1.8.

The example image shown in Figure 1.8 highlights two other fundamental problems which occur in the context of digital images:

- The elliptic object in the middle of the image was originally a circular area. Its distortion is due to the geometry of the pixels. Usually a pixel has the form of a rectangle. In a standard video system, the ratio of the size of the pixel edges is four to three. This leads to the distortion shown in Figure 1.8.

- The edges of the objects are not smooth, but have 'digital teeth'. This problem decreases with higher image resolution. However, in the example shown, the ratio of pixel size to the size of the objects are such that problems may arise with some applications, such as measuring the size of the object.

Figure 1.7 shows the pixels as an arrangement of tiles. This common representation of an image is inconvenient from the point of view of signal processing. Thinking in terms of signal processing, a digital image is a rectangular array of sampling points. Figure 1.10 shows a circle in an 'analog' image with an overlay of a 4*4 sampling grid. If the circle and the background are uniform (for example, the background may be black while the circle is white or vice versa), then the corresponding 4*4 digital image is shown in Figure 1.11. Note that in practice the sampling grid of a CCD-camera consists neither of infinitely fine 'needles' nor of tiles with infinitely fine joints, but of tiles and joints processing similar dimensions.

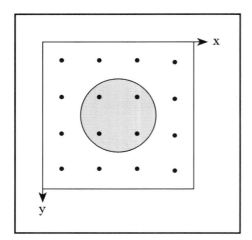

Figure 1.10
This is a circle in an 'analog' image (an image not yet sampled). To get a 4*4 digital image, the image has to be sampled at the marked points.

The previous example dealt with the arrangement of the samples of a digital image. But what about the 'behavior' of the individual samples? Figure 1.12(a) depicts a cut through an image whose intensity varies as a sinusoidal signal. Figure 1.12(b) shows 8 samples taken at the individual positions. Extending this sample over the whole sample space leads to the 'tile representation' in Figure 1.12(c).

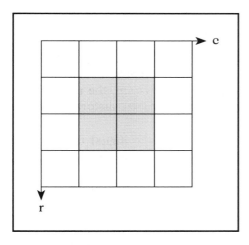

Figure 1.11
Digitized circle image (Figure 1.10)
with a resolution of 4*4 pixels.

The subject of 'digital images' has already been extensively discussed by many authors. For example, Ballard and Brown [1.1], Jähne [1.12], Jain [1.13], Netravali/Haskell [1.19], and Schalkoff [1.24] deal with many of the detailed problems presented by digital images. These problems range from the geometry of a single pixel to Moiré effects.

1.5 Getting started with Ad Oculos

The Ad Oculos Digital Image Processing software comes in two versions:

- The *Student Version*, which is an excellent educational tool for visualizing and experimenting with digital image processing. The shell program provides Ad Oculos with a comfortable user interface which allows the user to combine image processing algorithms to form complex processing chains.

- The *Professional Version*, which offers the following additional features:
  - Functions which have been specially prepared as measurement tools (such as automatic counting, measuring, calibration,...).
  - Drivers for several frame grabbers.
  - The inclusion of the complete source code of the Windows DLLs (Dynamic Link Libraries) representing the image processing algorithms.
  - A *Technical Reference Guide* which clearly describes the application programming interface, allowing new image processing algorithms written by the user to be easily integrated into the Ad Oculos environment.

Please contact your local bookstore or the Publisher for information concerning the distribution of the *Professional Version*.

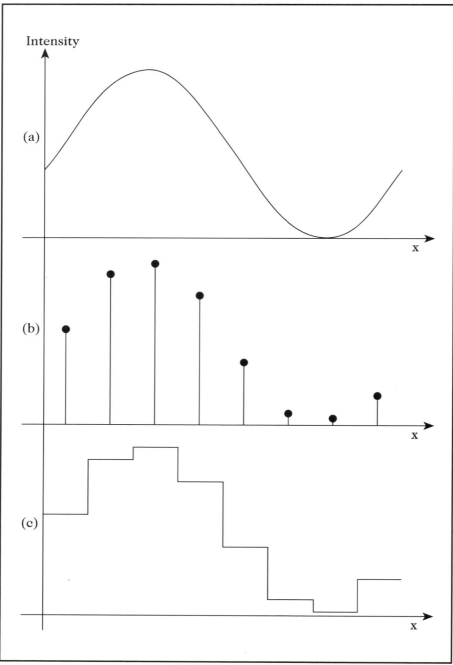

Figure 1.12 This is a cut through an image the intensity of which varies as a sinusoidal signal (a). (b) shows 8 samples at an infinitely small width. Extending this sample over the whole sample space leads to the 'tile representation' (c).

One of the benefits of Ad Oculos is its simplicity. The demonstration given in this section is sufficient to grasp the basic function of Ad Oculos. It is easy to explore further details simply by working with Ad Oculos or by using the help facilities. The prerequisites of understanding this section are:

- familiarity with any Microsoft Windows application (for instance word processing),

- the successful installation of Ad Oculos.

Ad Oculos' start-up screen shows the Symbol Window which appears in the main window (Figure 1.13). The following steps demonstrate the application of a simple image processing algorithm to an input image:

1.   Select **New Image** from the **File** menu (Figure 1.14). An empty image appears in the main window while a corresponding Image Icon is located in the Symbol Window (Figure 1.15).

2.   Double click on the empty Image Window to load an image. The sample images used throughout the book are to be found in the **images** subdirectory (the path leading to this subdirectory depends on the choice made during installation). Select **PLIERS.128** from the images subdirectory. The result is shown in Figure 1.16.

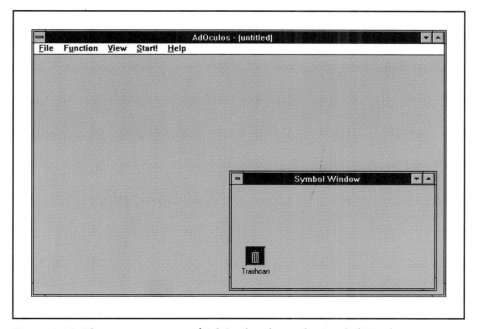

Figure 1.13 The start-up screen of Ad Oculos shows the Symbol Window appearing in the main window.

16   Ad Oculos: Digital Image Processing

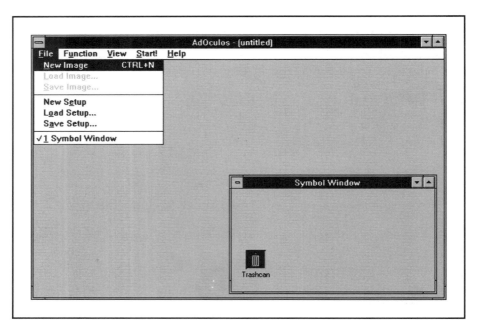

Figure 1.14 Selecting New Image from the File menu leads to an empty image appearing as shown in Figure 1.15.

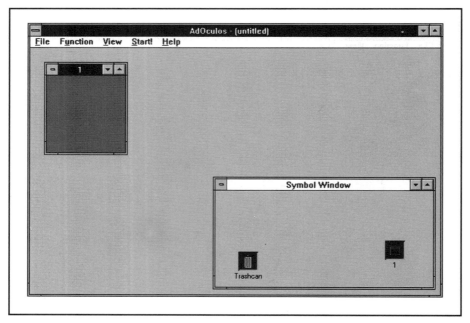

Figure 1.15 Double click on the empty Image Windows to load an image. Figure 1.16 shows an example.

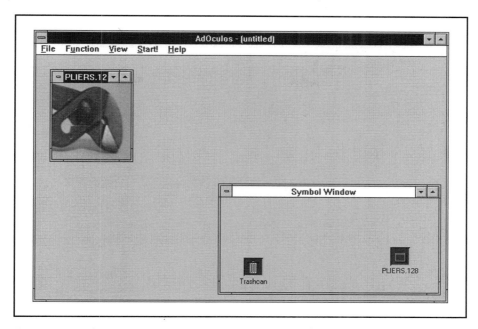

Figure 1.16 The PLIERS.128 image has been selected from the images subdirectory.

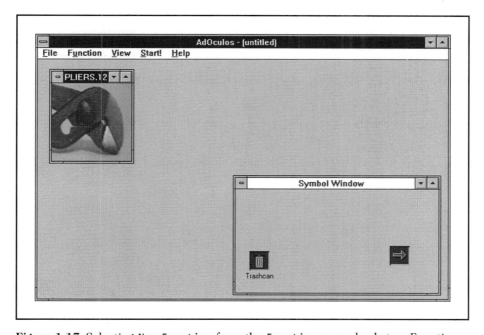

Figure 1.17 Selecting New Function from the Function menu leads to a Function Icon covering the Image Icon.

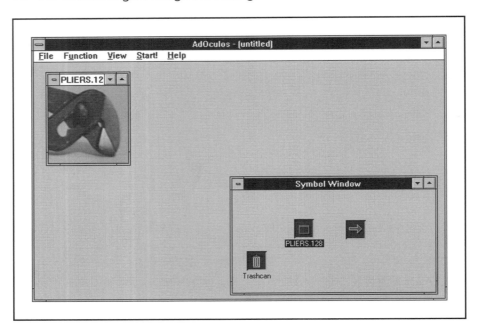

Figure 1.18 Icons may be moved by clicking on them, depressing the mouse button and moving the mouse.

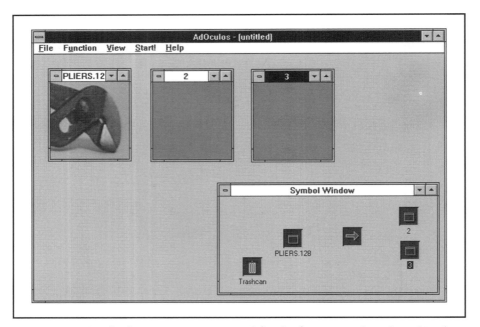

Figure 1.19 Two further images are required for the function to be selected in the following steps. Image Windows may be moved by clicking on their title bar, depressing the mouse button and moving the mouse.

3. Select **New** Function from the **Function** menu. Figure 1.17 shows that a Function Icon covers the Image Icon in the Symbol Window.

4. Rearrange the icons as shown in Figure 1.18 (To move the icons, click on them and hold the mouse button down while moving the mouse).

5. Select **New Image** from the **File** menu to obtain two further images. Arrange the empty Image Windows and the corresponding Image Icons as shown in Figure 1.19. (To move the Image Windows, click on their title bar and hold the mouse button down while moving the mouse).

6. Double click on the Function Icon to select a function (Figure 1.20).

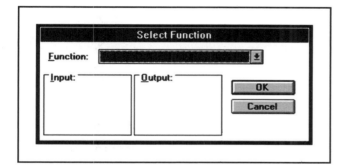

Figure 1.20
This window appears due to a double click on a Function box.

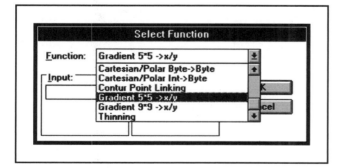

Figure 1.21
Clicking on the down arrow reveals the function list.

7. Click on the down arrow (placed above the OK button) to obtain the function list and select **Gradient 5*5 -> x/y** (Figure 1.21). The gradient operator is explained in detail in Chapter 3 and Chapter 6.

8. The empty input fields indicate that the gradient operator needs one input and two output images. To fill the input field as shown in Figure 1.22, first click in this field and then click on the Image Window **PLIERS.128**. Repeat this process to enter the output images.

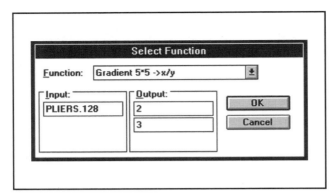

Figure 1.22
To enter
PLIERS.128 into
the input field, first
click in the input
field and then click
on the Image
Window
PLIERS.128.
Repeat this process
to enter the output
images and click
on OK.

9. Click on OK. The connection of the images to the function is visualized in the Symbol Window (Figure 1.23).

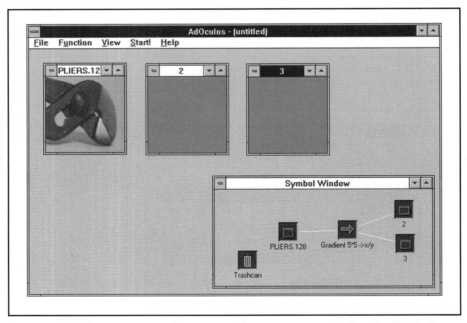

Figure 1.23 The connection of images and function is visualized in the Symbol Window.

10. First click on the Function Icon in order to activate it (Figure 1.24) and then on Start! to start the process. The result is shown in Figure 1.25.

11. The current connection of images and functions is named Setup. Save it by selecting Save Setup from the File menu (Figure 1.26).

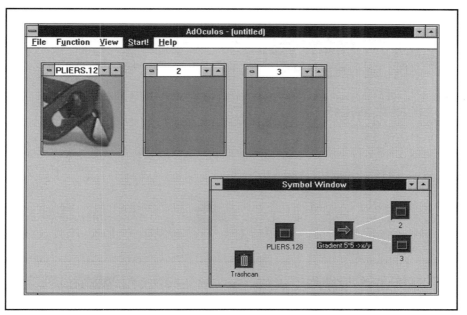

Figure 1.24 First click on the Function Icon in order to activate it and then on Start! to start the process.

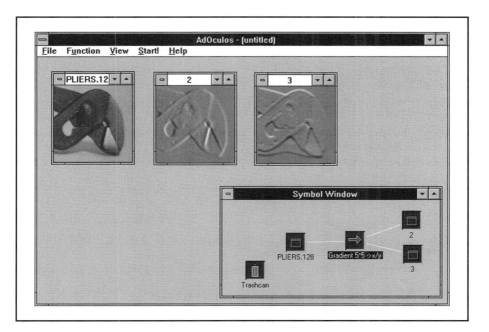

Figure 1.25 This is the result of the gradient operation.

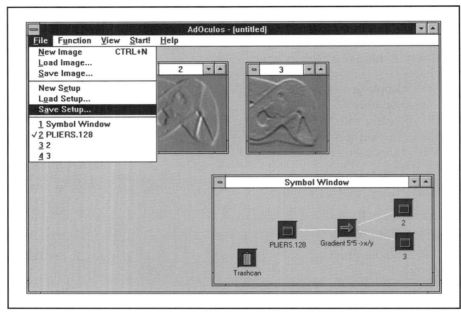

Figure 1.26 Save the current processing chain by selecting `Save Setup` from the `File` menu.

Load a few **setups** from the Ad Oculos setups subdirectory to see that larger processing chains are easy to handle. Each of the setups is associated with one of the following chapters of this book.

Ad Oculos offers various facilities which are easy to explore by navigating through the menus. One of the most important facilities is `Image Attributes`. Use the *right* mouse button to click in the `PLIERS.128` image. A window as shown in Figure 1.27 reveals the image attributes. Editing `Min. Graylevel` and `Max. Graylevel` manipulates the range of graylevels displayed for the current image. Note that this manipulation only influences the way an image is displayed on the screen. The image itself remains unchanged. It is a basic principle of Ad Oculos to change images only with operators selected from the `Select Function` menu.

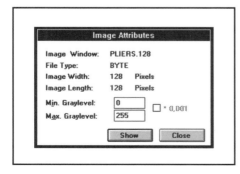

Figure 1.27
Click with the right mouse button on the `PLIERS.128` image to obtain the `Image Attributes`. Editing `Min. Graylevel` and `Max. Graylevel` manipulates the range of graylevels displayed for the current image.

1.6   Remarks on the example procedures

Each of the succeeding chapters contains a section with example procedures. Concerning these procedures, the following remarks are appropriate:

- The example procedures are intended to be a means of knowledge transfer. They may only be used as a core for applications if they are 'wrapped up' well. Usually this 'wrapping up' is the most expensive part of programming. The authors disclaim any responsibility for the use of the example procedures used in any of the applications.

- The example shown in Figure 1.28 uses function prototypes. For the sake of simplicity, they are omitted in all succeeding examples.

- In Appendix B, 'service procedures' which are often used, as well as some special data types are defined.

- The example procedures are independent of any hardware or operating system.

Usually, the development of image processing algorithms is based on high-level programming languages. Figure 1.28 shows a simple C program which may serve as a frame for further developments. For the sake of simplicity, the input image INFILE and the output image OUTFILE are predefined. Furthermore, they are assumed to be squares of size IMSIZE. The main procedure main merely consists of a sequence of subroutines. The procedures ImAlloc and ImFree organize the memory management required for the images. They are described in Appendix B. GetImage reads an image file from the disk, while PutImage writes an image to the disk. ShowImage is a procedure which manages the presentation of an image. The realization of the last three procedures depends on the respective host machines. Therefore, they have not been described in this book.

ProcessImage serves as an example to demonstrate the basic elements of an image processing procedure. Such a procedure starts with the initialization of the output image (here OutIm). Actually, this would not be necessary in the current example, since the following operation only works on single pixels. However, it is a good working habit to always initialize any variable. The operation already mentioned above scales the graylevel down by 50%. Since this is a pixel operation, the output could be written directly to the input. However, this is a rare exception: usually the result of an image processing procedure must not be rewritten into the input image. To do so would destroy data which are required in their original form. Surprisingly, this error is made by many beginners in the image processing field, even when they have been previously warned. An obvious explanation for the phenomenon might be the early experience of 'image processing' with pencil and eraser, which actually takes place in one and the same image.

```
#define  INFILE   "c:\\image\\in.128"
#define  OUTFILE  "c:\\image\\out.128"
#define  IMSIZE   128

void ** ImAlloc (int,int,int);
void ImFree (void **, int);
void GetImage (int, char[], BYTE **);
void ProcessImage (int, BYTE **, BYTE **);
void ShowImage (int, BYTE **);
void PutImage (int, char[], BYTE **);

/*********************** MAIN ****************************/
void main (void)
{
   BYTE ** InIm;
   BYTE ** OutIm;

   InIm  = ImAlloc (IMSIZE, IMSIZE, sizeof(BYTE));
   OutIm = ImAlloc (IMSIZE, IMSIZE, sizeof(BYTE));

   GetImage     (IMSIZE, INFILE, InIm);
   ProcessImage (IMSIZE, InIm, OutIm);
   ShowImage    (IMSIZE, OutIm);
   PutImage     (IMSIZE, OUTFILE, OutIm);

   ImFree (InIm,  IMSIZE);
   ImFree (OutIm, IMSIZE);
}

/******************* ProcessImage ***********************/
void ProcessImage (ImSize, InIm, OutIm)
int  ImSize;
BYTE ** InIm;
BYTE ** OutIm;
{
   int   r,c;

   for (r=0; r<ImSize; r++)
      for (c=0; c<ImSize; c++)
         OutIm [r][c] = 0;

   for (r=0; r<ImSize; r++)
      for (c=0; c<ImSize; c++)
         OutIm [r][c] = InIm [r][c] / 2;
}
```

Figure 1.28 Frame of a simple image processing program. The procedures ImAlloc, ImFree and the data type BYTE are defined in Appendix B. The realization of the procedures GetImage, ShowImage and PutImage depends on the computer used.

1.7   Exercises

1.1   A 512*512 satellite image shows an area of 10*10 km (6*6 miles). How large is the area represented by a pixel?

1.2   A typical transmission rate of a serial link between two computers is 9600 baud. How long would it take to transmit a 512*512 image with 256 graylevels?

1.3   Assuming 24 bit, 1280*1024 pixel color images, what baud rate is required to transmit a stream of 25 images/sec over a serial link?

1.4   Figure 1.10 and Figure 1.11 show an example of the application of a 4*4 sampling grid to an 'analog' image. Repeat the sampling with a 8*8 and a 16*16 grid.

1.5   In contrast to the solid circle used in Exercise 1.4, a finer structure is now to be digitized. Figure 1.29 shows two rings. Digitize this image based on a 8*8 sampling grid.

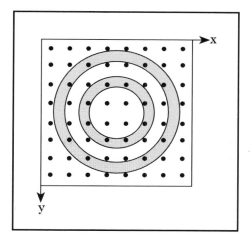

Figure 1.29
What happens if a structure which is finer that the sampling grid is to be digitized?

1.6   Figure 1.30 depicts a cut through an image whose intensity varies like a noisy sinusoidal. Apply the same quantization process shown in Figure 1.12 to this curve.

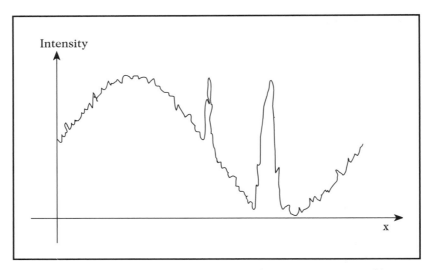

Figure 1.30 This is a cut through an image whose intensity varies like a noisy sinusoidal.

1.7   Explore the following Ad Oculos functions for image handling: Change Size, Cut, Hex Image and Noise.

1.8   Explore the Ad Oculos View Menu.

1.9   Load a *.128 image from the Ad Oculos images subdirectory. Save this image using the TIFF option. Activate any DTP tool and try to import the saved image.

1.10   Implement the program depicted in Figure 1.28. Create a development environment which makes it easy to realize your own image processing procedures whose results may be evaluated with the aid of Ad Oculos. Use the sample images from the Ad Oculos images subdirectory.

1.11   Write a program which transforms an 8-bit graylevel image into a binary image and outputs it to a file. Minimize the file size by grouping 8 pixels to a byte.

1.12   To save more disk space write a program which compresses the binary images generated in Exercise 1.11 without loosing information. Write a second program to decompress the compressed images.

1.13   Write a program which decreases the resolution of a 128*128 graylevel image, to a size of: 64*64; 32*32 and so on.

1.14   Write a program which decreases the number of graylevels from 256 to 128, to 64 and so on.

1.8   References

[1.1]   Ballard, D.H.; Brown, C.M.: *Computer vision*. Englewood Cliffs: Prentice-Hall 1982

[1.2]   Boyle, R.D.; Thomas, R.C.: *Computer vision – a first course*. Oxford: Blackwell Scientific Publications 1988

[1.3]   Braggins, D; Hollingum, J.: *The machine vision sourcebook*. Berlin, Heidelberg, New York, Tokyo: Springer 1986

[1.4]   Freeman, H.: *Machine vision – algorithms, architectures and systems*. New York: Academic Press 1988

[1.5]   Freeman, H.: *Machine vision for inspection and measurement*. New York: Academic Press 1989

[1.6]   Gonzalez, R.C.; Wintz, P.: *Digital image processing*, 2nd ed. Reading MA, London: Addison-Wesley 1987

[1.7]   Gonzalez, R.C.; Woods, R.E.: *Digital image processing*. Reading MA: Addison-Wesley 1992

[1.8]   Grimson, W.E.L.: *Object recognition by Computers*. Cambridge, Massachusetts: The MIT Press 1990

[1.9]   Hall, E.L.: *Computer image processing and recognition*. New York: Academic Press 1979

[1.10]   Haralick, R.M.; Shapiro, L.G.: *Computer and Robot Vision, Vol. 1 & 2*. Reading MA: Addison-Wesley 1992

[1.11]   Horn, B.K.P.: *Robot vision*. Cambridge, London: MIT Press 1986

[1.12]   Jähne, B.: *Digital Image Processing. Concepts, Algorithms, and Scientific Applications*. Berlin, Heidelberg, New York, London, Paris, Tokyo: Springer 1991

[1.13]   Jain, A.K.: *Fundamentals of digital image processing*. Englewood Cliffs: Prentice-Hall 1989

[1.14]   Levine, M.D.: *Vision in man and machine*. London: McGraw-Hill 1985

[1.15]   Low, A.: *Introductory computer vision and image processing*. London: McGraw-Hill 1991

[1.16]   Marion, A.: *An introduction to image processing*. London: Chapman and Hall 1991

[1.17]   Meyer, J.A. and Wilson, S.W. (eds.): *From animals to animates*. Cambridge, Mass.: MIT-Press 1991

[1.18] Morrision, M.: *The magic of image processing.* Carmel: Sams Publishing 1993

[1.19] Netravali, A.N.; Haskell, B.G.: *Digital pictures.* New York, London: Plenum Press 1988

[1.20] Niblack, W.: *An introduction to digital image processing.* Englewood Cliffs: Prentice-Hall 1986

[1.21] Pavlidis, Th.: *Graphics and image processing.* Rockville: Computer Science Press 1982

[1.22] Pugh, A. (Ed.): *Robot vision.* Berlin, Heidelberg, New York, Tokyo: Springer 1984

[1.23] Rosenfeld, A.; Kak, A.C.: *Digital picture processing, Vol.1 & 2.* New York: Academic Press 1982

[1.24] Schalkoff, R.J.: *Digital image processing and computer vision.* New York, Chichester, Brisbane, Toronto, Singapore: Wiley 1989

[1.25] Shirai, Y.: *Three-dimensional computer vision.* Berlin, Heidelberg, New York, London, Paris, Tokyo: Springer 1987.

[1.26] Torras, C. (Ed.): *Computer Vision: Theory and Industrial Application.* Berlin, Heidelberg, New York, London, Paris, Tokyo: Springer 1992.

[1.27] Young, T.Y.; Fu, K.S. (Eds.): *Handbook of pattern recognition and image processing.* New York: Academic Press 1986

[1.28] Zuech, N.; Miller, R.K.: *Machine vision.* Englewood Cliffs: Prentice-Hall 1987

2

Point operations

2.1 Foundations

The requirements for understanding this chapter are:

- to be familiar with basic mathematics,
- to have read Chapter 1.

In point operations, a new graylevel for each of the pixels in an image is calculated exclusively from its original graylevel. Some authors therefore use the term *pixel value mapping* [2.4], while others talk of *gray scale modification* [2.5]. Point operations are mainly used for image manipulation (Chapter 1), such as contrast enhancement of an image.

Figure 2.1 shows an image which will be used as the source image during the first part of this section. The graylevels of this image are supposed to lie between 0 and 250. A *graylevel histogram* which reflects the distribution of graylevels in the source image is depicted in Figure 2.2. Such a histogram helps to evaluate the image from a global point of view. For instance, the low contrast of the image is obvious since the highest graylevel is **160** instead of **250**.

20	20	20	20	20	20	20	40
160	60	60	60	60	60	60	40
160	60	70	70	70	70	60	40
160	60	70	80	80	70	60	40
160	60	70	80	80	70	60	40
160	60	70	70	70	70	60	40
160	60	60	60	60	60	60	40
160	120	120	120	120	120	120	120

Figure 2.1
This image will be used as the source image during the first part of this section. The graylevels of the image lie between the values 0 and **250**.

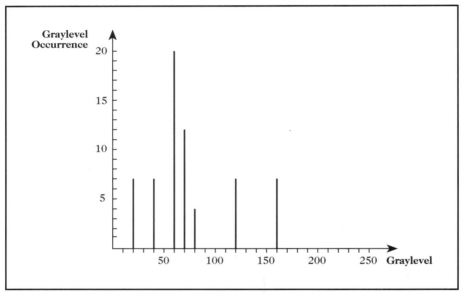

Figure 2.2 A graylevel histogram reflects the distribution of graylevels in an image. This is the histogram of the source image shown in Figure 2.1. Among other things it highlights the low contrast of the source image, since its highest graylevel is **160** instead of the potential **250**.

Another representation of the graylevel histogram is the so-called cumulative histogram shown in Figure 2.3. Here the number of graylevels is summed up resulting in a staircase curve. Sometimes, this form of histogram is more convenient for evaluation than the conventional histogram.

There are several methods of enhancing the source image with the aid of point operations. The actual choice depends on the desired application. In the next part of this section, four interactive and one automatic method of image enhancement are introduced.

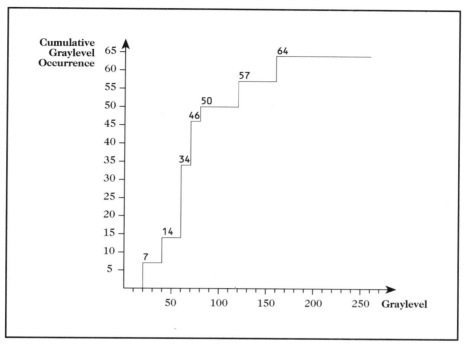

Figure 2.3 This is an alternative representation of the graylevel histogram depicted in Figure 2.2. Here the number of graylevels is summed up yielding a new insight into the source image.

The first method 'amplifies' the original graylevels GV_{in} using

$$GV_{out} = GAIN*GV_{in} + BIAS \tag{2.1}$$

GAIN is directly defined by the user, while *BIAS* may be determined by the mean graylevel of the original image ($MEAN_{in}$) and the mean desired by the user ($MEAN_{out}$)

$$BIAS = MEAN_{out} - GAIN*MEAN_{in}$$

For the example shown in Figure 2.1, $MEAN_{in}$ is 74. Assuming $MEAN_{out}$ = 125 and *GAIN* = 1.5, the relation between the input and the output graylevel is

$$GV_{out} = 1.5*GV_{in} + 14$$

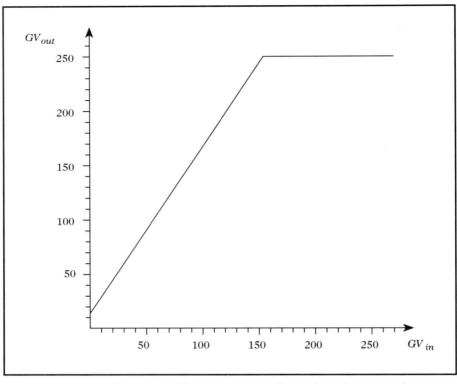

Figure 2.4 This is the mapping of the original graylevels from the image shown in Figure 2.1 (GV_{in}) to the new graylevels GV_{out}. The resulting image is shown in Figure 2.6.

Figure 2.4 shows the mapping of the graylevels according to this formula. Usually, this mapping is performed with the aid of a *look-up table* (LUT), such as that depicted in Figure 2.5. In practice, such a LUT is realized by an array whose index is equivalent to the graylevels to be changed (GV_{in}), while the contents of the array is equivalent to the new graylevels GV_{out}.

Applying the LUT to the source image, the result shown in Figure 2.6 is obtained. The histograms of the resulting image are depicted in Figure 2.7 and Figure 2.8. Comparing them with the original histograms (Figure 2.3 and Figure 2.2), the stretching of the graylevels is obvious. The result is a higher contrast in the new image.

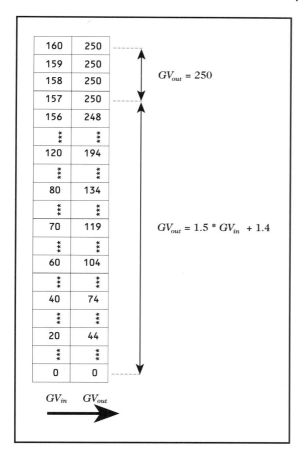

GV_{in}	GV_{out}
160	250
159	250
158	250
157	250
156	248
***	***
120	194
***	***
80	134
***	***
70	119
***	***
60	104
***	***
40	74
***	***
20	44
***	***
0	0

$GV_{out} = 250$

$GV_{out} = 1.5 * GV_{in} + 1.4$

Figure 2.5
The mapping shown in
Figure 2.4 is performed with
the aid of this look-up table.

44	44	44	44	44	44	44	74
250	104	104	104	104	104	104	74
250	104	119	119	119	119	104	74
250	104	119	134	134	119	104	74
250	104	119	134	134	119	104	74
250	104	119	119	119	119	104	74
250	104	104	104	104	104	104	74
250	194	194	194	194	194	194	194

Figure 2.6
Mapping the graylevels of the original image
(Figure 2.1) to new ones according to the
function shown in Figure 2.4 leads to this
new image. When compared with the original,
the contrast can be seen to have improved.

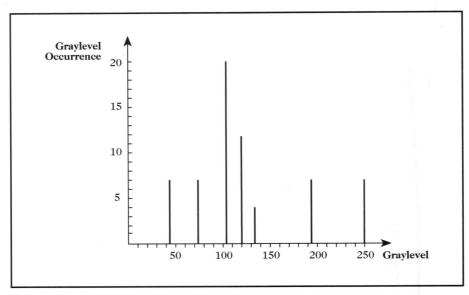

Figure 2.7 This is the histogram of the processed image shown in Figure 2.6. The comparison of contrast between this histogram and the original one (Figure 2.2) is much easier than the comparison between the images. See also the cumulative histogram in Figure 2.8.

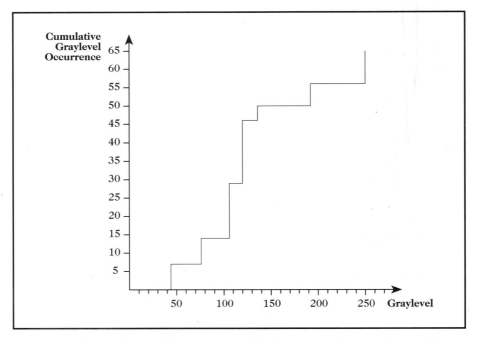

Figure 2.8 This is the cumulative version of the histogram shown in Figure 2.7. The counterpart of the original image is shown in Figure 2.3.

2.1.1 Automatic graylevel mapping

This part of the section begins with a new source image that is shown in Figure 2.9. For the sake of simplicity, the graylevels of this image only range from 0 to 15. Relating to the histogram of the new source image (Figure 2.10), it is useful to emphasize the separation between the graylevels 7 and 8. This can be done by replacing the original graylevels by the frequency of their occurrence which is taken from the cumulative histogram (Figure 2.11):

$$
\begin{aligned}
0 &\rightarrow 28 \\
7 &\rightarrow 48 \\
8 &\rightarrow 60 \\
15 &\rightarrow 64
\end{aligned}
$$

Since only graylevels ranging from 0 to 15 are valid, the mapping is rescaled so that values fall within these limits:

$$
\begin{aligned}
28 &\rightarrow 0 \\
48 &\rightarrow 8 \\
60 &\rightarrow 13 \\
64 &\rightarrow 15
\end{aligned}
$$

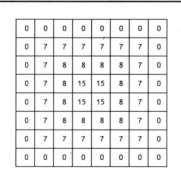

Figure 2.9
This is a new source image comprising graylevels which only range from 0 to 15. According to its histogram (Figure 2.10), it is useful to emphasize the separation between graylevels 7 and 8.

The resulting image is shown in Figure 2.12. The histograms depicted in Figure 2.13 and Figure 2.14 show the new graylevel distribution.

Since there was no need for user definitions during the whole process of graylevel mapping, it is possible to realize it as an automatic process. This is known as *histogram equalization*. Note that the classical definition of equalization refers to a re-mapping of the input image graylevels, so that the output image has an equal number of pixels at each graylevel.

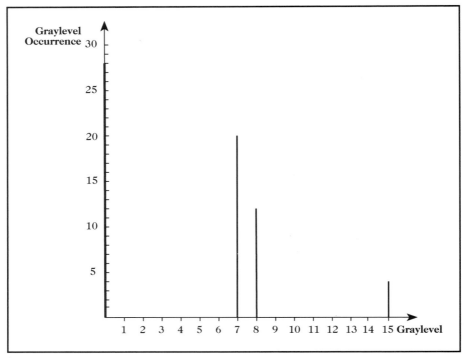

Figure 2.10 The graylevel histogram of the new source image (Figure 2.9) shows that it is useful in emphasizing the separation between graylevels **7** and **8**.

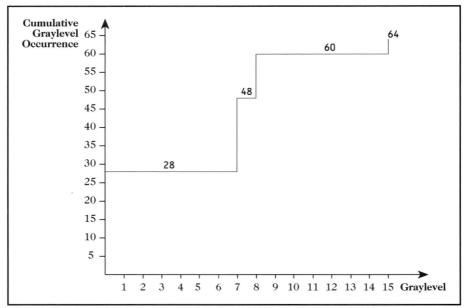

Figure 2.11 The cumulative histogram taken from the new source image (Figure 2.9) has its steepest rise between the graylevels of interest, **7** and **8**.

0	0	0	0	0	0	0	0
0	8	8	8	8	8	8	0
0	8	13	13	13	13	8	0
0	8	13	15	15	13	8	0
0	8	13	15	15	13	8	0
0	8	13	13	13	13	8	0
0	8	8	8	8	8	8	0
0	0	0	0	0	0	0	0

Figure 2.12
Result of re-mapping the graylevels according to the cumulative histogram.

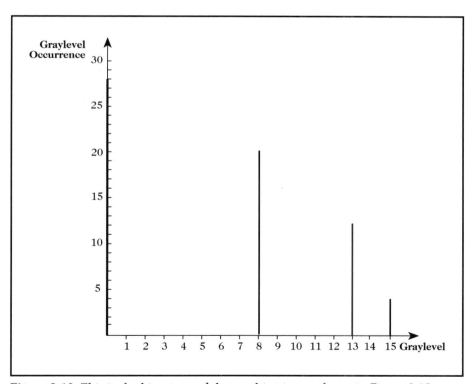

Figure 2.13 This is the histogram of the resulting image shown in Figure 2.12.

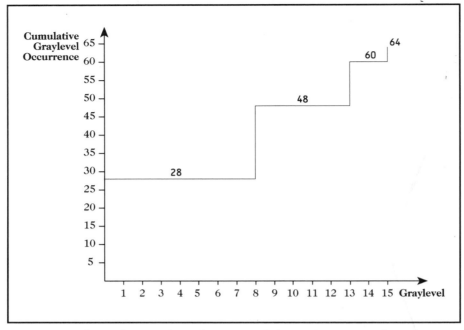

Figure 2.14 This is the cumulative histogram of the resulting image shown in Figure 2.12.

2.1.2   Binarization

The binarization of graylevel images is the most popular method of segmentation. This applies especially to industrial image processing. This subject is discussed in detail in Chapter 5. The following paragraphs are for the sake of completeness, since binarization is also a subject of 'Point Operations'.

The simplest form of binarization is achieved by applying a threshold to a graylevel image, thereby mapping graylevels below this threshold to 0 and the remaining graylevels to 1. Applying a threshold of 65 to the source image shown in Figure 2.1 leads to the binary image shown in Figure 2.15.

An alternative binarization procedure is the so-called *bit-plane slicing* which offers a special view into the 'interior' of an image. Figure 2.16 shows a new source image (whose graylevels range from 0 to 15) and additionally row 3 of the image with its graylevels in binary representation. If the graylevel image is thought of as a stack of bit-planes (slices), then the current example has 4 of them. The 'membership' of a pixel within a slice depends on the highest bit of its graylevel (circled in Figure 2.16). So pixel (3,0) belongs to no slice, pixel (3,1) belongs to slice 2 and so on.

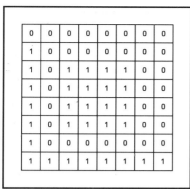

Figure 2.15
This binary image is obtained by applying a threshold of **65** to the source image shown in Figure 2.1.

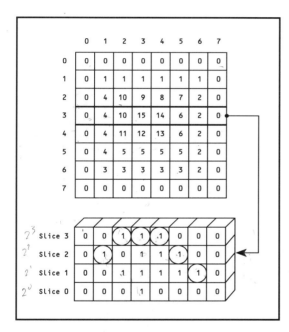

Figure 2.16
The graylevels of this image range from **0** to **15**. Thus it consists of 4 bit-planes (slices). The 'membership' of a pixel in a slice depends on the highest bit of its graylevel (circled). Hence pixel (3,0) belongs to no slice, pixel (3,1) belongs to slice 2 and so on.

2.1.3   Varying graylevel mapping

So far graylevel mapping has been applied homogeneously to the whole image. In this section, the necessity of having different graylevel mappings depending on the position of the pixels to be processed is considered.

Figure 2.17 shows a very simple line scan camera consisting of only 8 pixels. Suppose this camera is used in an application with inhomogeneous illumination. To keep things simple, the example is somewhat extreme: at the position of pixel 7 the original luminosity is only 50% of the luminosity at pixel 0.

Shadows are a frequent cause of inhomogeneous illumination. It has therefore become customary to talk about *shading* instead of inhomogeneous illumination. Consequently, a shading correction has to be performed.

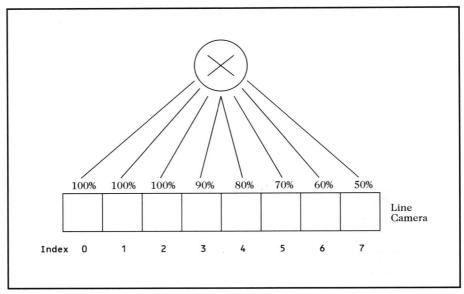

Figure 2.17 This is a very simple line scan camera consisting of only 8 pixels. This camera is used in an application with an illumination decreasing from left to right. To compensate for this effect, different graylevel mappings for pixels 3 to 7 are required.

2.1.4 Arithmetic operations on two images

Until now, point operations have been applied to single images only. The next step is to combine two or more images pixel by pixel.

Figure 2.18 (*left*) shows two images consisting of 2 regions whose graylevels are almost homogeneous (graylevels 1 and 10), except for a few disturbed or 'noisy' pixels. Taking the mean of the graylevels of equivalent pixels diminishes the impact of the disturbance (Figure 2.18).

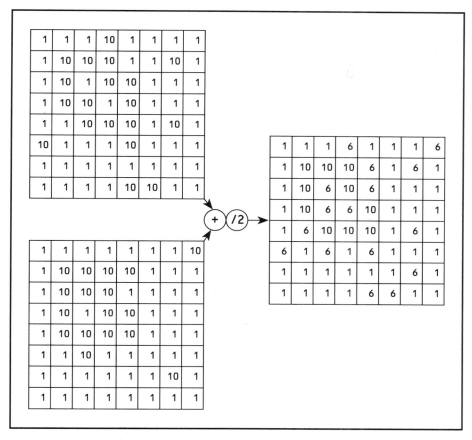

Figure 2.18 On the left are two images consisting of 2 regions whose graylevels are almost homogeneous (graylevels **1** and **10**), except for a few disturbed 'noisy' pixels. The image on the right-hand side shows that the averaging of both images diminishes the noise. (**+**) means: sum two graylevels. (**/2**) means: divide the sum by two.

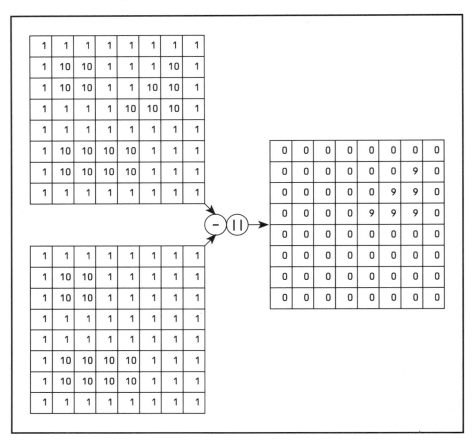

Figure 2.19 The subtraction of two images yields the differences between the gray-level patterns. (−) means: subtract two graylevels. (| |) means: use the absolute value.

This remedy works if the original ('clean') graylevel pattern is consistent from image to image and the noisy pixels change from image to image. The cleaning effect of the additions increases with the number of images.

The complementary operation to addition is subtraction. Subtracting two images leads to an emphasis of the differences. Figure 2.19 (*left*) shows two images whose graylevel patterns differ in a triangular small area. In the difference image, this small area becomes more prominent or 'pops out'.

2.2   Ad Oculos experiments

The aim of the first experiment is to become familiar with the Invert, Stretch and Mark functions. As described in Section 1.5, realize the New Setup shown in Figure 2.20. The source image (which has to be loaded into image (1)) used in this experiment originates from a medical application of image processing. Figure 2.21 (TUMSRC.128) shows a tomographic reconstruction of a skull. The ear-like objects in the lower part of the image are supports for the patients head. Image (2) shows the result of Invert. This image does not disclose any new information which is useful for medical analysis. However, stretching the original graylevels emphasizes the details of the brain structure (Image (3)). More importantly, a pathological disorder appears which was not previously visible. A tumor which contrasts with the healthy brain structure becomes clearly visible. The parameters of Stretch were:

```
min. graylevel:    100
max. graylevel:    105
```

These parameters may be varied by clicking the right mouse button on the function symbol Stretch.

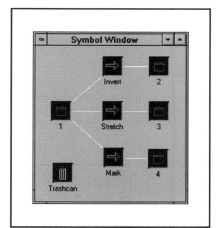

Figure 2.20
The aim of the first experiment is to become familiar with the Invert, Stretch and Mark function. This New Setup is realized according to the steps described in Section 1.5. The results are shown in Figure 2.21.

Image (4) shows the result of Mark in which the graylevel range of interest is marked white and superimposed on the original image. In practice, such marking is performed by pseudo-color, that is, the original gray levels within the range of interest are colored.
The parameters of Mark were:

```
min. graylevel:    105
max. graylevel:    107
mark value:        255
```

These parameters may be varied by clicking the right mouse button on the function symbol Mark.

After having started Histogram Equalization, the dialog box depicted in Figure 2.23 appears. The histogram of the input image (TUMSRC.128) is shown on the left, while the right histogram is that of the output image. Between them, the cumulative histogram controlling the equalization process is located (Figure 2.11). After clicking on OK, the output image appears (Figure 2.25 (2)).

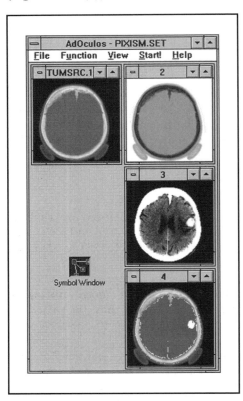

Figure 2.21
The source image (TUMSRC.128) shows a tomographic reconstruction of a skull. (2) is the result of Invert. (3) is the result of Stretch with the parameters min. graylevel: 100 and max. graylevel: 105. (4) is the result of Mark with the parameters min. graylevel: 105, max. graylevel: 107 and mark value: 255. These parameters may be varied by clicking the right mouse button on the corresponding function symbol.

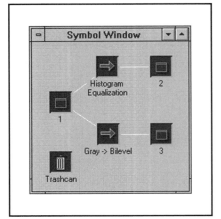

Figure 2.22
This is the New Setup of the second experiment involving histogram manipulation and analysis with the aid of Histogram Equalization and Gray -> Bilevel. The results are shown in Figure 2.25.

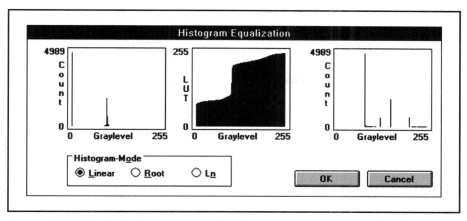

Figure 2.23 This dialog box appears after Histogram Equalization has been started. On the left, the histogram of the input image (TUMSRC.128) is shown, while on the right the histogram of the output image is illustrated. Between them, the cumulative histogram which controls the equalization process is located. After clicking on OK, the output image appears (Figure 2.25 (2)).

The second experiment deals with histogram manipulation and analysis with the aid of Histogram Equalization and Gray -> Bilevel. The New Setup is shown in Figure 2.22. The source image (TUMSRC.128) needs to be loaded into image (1).

Figure 2.24 shows the dialog box which appears on the start of Gray -> Bilevel. The small bar in the middle of the input image histogram (TUMSRC.128) represents the current threshold which may be varied by entering another value for Threshold. After clicking on OK, the output image appears (Figure 2.25 (3)).

The last experiment demonstrates the Slice function. The New Setup is shown in Figure 2.26. The source image (TUMSRC.128) should be loaded into image (1). The results are collected in Figure 2.27. The slice to be extracted may be defined by clicking the right mouse button on the function symbol Slice. The slices and the resulting images correspond as follows:

```
Slice 7: Image (2)
Slice 6: Image (3)
Slice 5: Image (4)
Slice 4: Image (5)
Slice 3: Image (6)
```

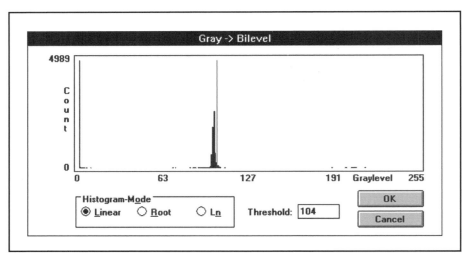

Figure 2.24 This is the dialog box appearing at the start of Gray -> Bilevel. The small bar in the middle of the histogram of the input image (TUMSRC.128) represents the current threshold which may be varied by entering another value for Threshold. After clicking on OK, the output image appears (Figure 2.25 (3)).

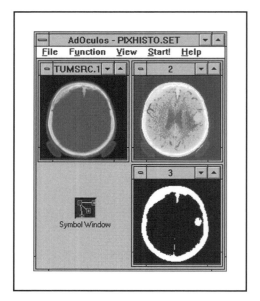

Figure 2.25
The source image (TUMSRC.128) is again the tomographic image. (2) is the result of Histogram Equalization with the parameters shown in Figure 2.23. (3) is the result of Gray -> Bilevel with the parameters shown in Figure 2.24.

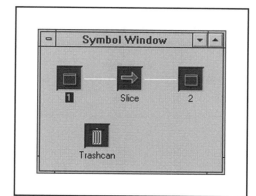

Figure 2.26
This is the New Setup of the last experiment demonstrating the Slice function. The results are shown in Figure 2.27.

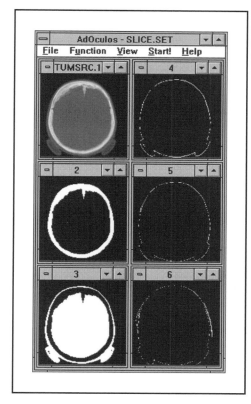

Figure 2.27
Here the results of Slice are collected. The slices and the resulting images correspond as follows: Slice 7: Image (2), Slice 6: Image (3), Slice 5: Image (4), Slice 4: Image (5) and Slice 3: Image (6). The slice to be extracted may be defined by clicking the right mouse button on the function symbol Slice.

2.3   Source code

Figure 2.28 presents four C procedures useful for executing point operations. The base for all these operations is the look-up table. It is generated by the procedures Invert, Stretch and Mark. The procedure LutOp performs the actual image manipulation.

```c
void LutOp (ImSize, Lut, Image)
int   ImSize;
BYTE *Lut;
BYTE **Image;
{
   int r,c;
   for (r=0; r<ImSize; r++)
      for (c=0; c<ImSize; c++)  Image[r][c] = Lut [Image[r][c]];
}

void Invert (MaxGV, Lut)
int   MaxGV;
BYTE *Lut;
{
   int  r,c, gv;
   for (gv=0; gv<MaxGV; gv++)  Lut [gv] = (BYTE) (MaxGV-gv-1);
}

void Stretch (LoGV, HiGV, MaxGV, Lut)
int   LoGV, HiGV, MaxGV;
BYTE *Lut;
{
   int  r,c, gv;
   long gvn;

   for (gv=0; gv<MaxGV; gv++) {
      if (LoGV<=gv && gv<HiGV) {
         gvn = gv - LoGV;
         gvn = (gvn * (MaxGV-1)) / (HiGV-LoGV);
         Lut [gv] = (BYTE) gvn;
      }else
         Lut [gv] = (BYTE) ((gv<LoGV) ? 0 : (MaxGV-1));
} }

void Mark (LoGV, HiGV, MaxGV, Color, Lut)
int   LoGV, HiGV, MaxGV, Color;
BYTE *Lut;
{
   int  r,c, gv;
   for (gv=0; gv<MaxGV; gv++)
      if (LoGV<=gv && gv<HiGV)  Lut [gv] = (BYTE) Color;
                          else  Lut [gv] = (BYTE) gv;
}
```

Figure 2.28 C realization of point operations.

Formal parameters are:

ImSize:	image size
Lut:	current look-up table
Image:	image to be manipulated

Like the following procedures LutOp is very simple and self-explanatory. The procedure Invert inverts the graylevels of an image. Formal parameters are:

MaxGV:	maximum graylevel to be inverted
Lut:	current look-up table

The procedure Stretch enhances the contrast of an image within a user-defined graylevel range. Formal parameters are:

LoGV:	lower limit of the graylevel range
HiGV:	upper limit of the graylevel range
MaxGV:	maximum graylevel permitted
Lut:	current look-up table

The purpose of the procedure Mark is to color those pixels whose graylevels fall into a user-defined graylevel range. Formal parameters are:

LoGV:	lower limit of the graylevel range
HiGV:	upper limit of the graylevel range
MaxGV:	maximum graylevel permitted
Color:	color as desired
Lut:	current look-up table

2.4   Supplement

Further applications of point operations as well as theoretical reflections are described by Jähne [2.1], Jain [2.2], Marion [2.3], Niblack [2.4] and Rosenfeld and Kak [2.5].

2.5   Exercises

2.1   Suppose the graylevels of interest in Figure 2.1 only range from 60 to 80. This range should be mapped from 0 to 250 forcing the lower graylevels to 0 and the higher ones to 250.

Draw the mapping function (similar to that shown in Figure 2.4), the look-up table that realizes the mapping function (similar to that shown in Figure 2.5), the resulting image (similar to that shown in Figure 2.6) and the two histograms (similar to those shown in Figure 2.7 and Figure 2.8) for this transformation.

2.2   Rather than completely suppress the lower and higher graylevels as shown in Exercise 2.1, the contrast of these graylevel ranges may be diminished and the contrast of the range of interest between 60 and 80 may be increased. The advantage of this approach is that the graylevel range of interest is emphasized without losing the impression of the complete image.

Compress the original graylevels between 0 and 60 to a range between 0 and 30, stretch the original graylevels between 60 and 80 to the new range between 30 and 230, and compress the upper range from 80 to 160 to the new range between 230 and 250. Draw the mapping function, the look-up table realizing the mapping function, the resulting image and the two histograms.

2.3   In some applications (that is, manipulation of medical images) it is useful to mark a certain graylevel range. Mark the graylevels of the source image which range from 70 to 80 as shown in Figure 2.1, by mapping them to 250 (white), while mapping the remaining graylevels to half of their original value. Draw the mapping function, the look-up table realizing the mapping function, the resulting image and the two histograms.

2.4   Apply histogram equalization to the source image shown in Figure 2.1. Draw the resulting image and the two histograms.

2.5   Draw the complete bit-planes (slices) of the source image shown in Figure 2.16.

2.6   Figure 2.29 shows an image taken with a line scan camera operating under the bad illumination conditions shown in Figure 2.17. For a shading correction, 5 different graylevel mappings are required. Draw them together with the corrected image.

10	10	10	9	8	7	6	5
10	10	10	9	8	7	6	5
10	10	100	90	80	70	60	50
10	10	100	90	80	70	60	50
10	10	100	90	80	70	60	50
10	10	10	90	80	70	60	50
10	10	10	9	80	70	60	50
10	10	10	9	8	70	60	50
10	10	10	9	8	7	60	50
10	10	10	9	8	7	60	50
10	10	10	9	8	7	60	50
10	10	10	9	8	7	60	50
10	10	10	9	8	7	60	50
10	10	10	9	8	7	60	50
10	10	10	9	8	7	6	5
10	10	10	9	8	7	6	5

Figure 2.29
This image, taken with the line scan camera shown in Figure 2.17 under bad illumination conditions, has to be corrected.

2.7   Average the images shown in Figure 2.30, Figure 2.31 and the resulting image shown in Figure 2.18.

1	1	1	1	1	1	1	1
1	10	10	10	10	1	1	1
1	10	10	10	10	1	1	10
1	1	10	10	1	1	1	1
1	10	10	10	10	1	1	1
1	1	1	1	1	1	1	1
1	1	10	1	1	1	1	1
1	1	1	1	1	1	1	10

Figure 2.30
Average this image, the one shown in Figure 2.31 and the resulting image shown in Figure 2.18.

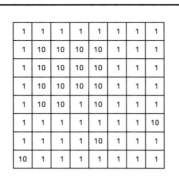

Figure 2.31
See Figure 2.30.

2.8   Write a program which applies Equation 2.1 to an input image.

2.9   Write a program which applies a mapping function (Figure 2.4) to an input image. The mapping function should be user-definable by entering the breaks of the curve.

2.10   Write a program which makes it possible to experiment with gray-level mappings which are dependent on pixel locations in the image. Try a contrast diminishing mapping, the influence of which increases near the border of the image.

2.11   Acquire images showing objects on an inhomogeneous background and acquire the background images without the objects. Write a program which is able to isolate the objects from their inhomogeneous background.

2.12   Acquire an image with an ensemble of objects. Write a program which is able to detect a missing object after it has 'seen' the complete ensemble.

2.13   Become familiar with every point operation offered by Ad Oculos (Ad Oculos Help).

2.6   References

[2.1] Jähne, B.: *Digital Image Processing. Concepts, Algorithms, and Scientific Applications.* Berlin, Heidelberg, New York, London, Paris, Tokyo: Springer 1991

[2.2] Jain, A.K.: *Fundamentals of digital image processing.* Englewood Cliffs: Prentice-Hall 1989

[2.3] Marion, A.: *An introduction to image processing.* London: Chapman and Hall 1991

[2.4]   Niblack, W.: *An introduction to digital image processing.* Englewood Cliffs: Prentice-Hall 1989

[2.5]   Rosenfeld, A.; Kak, A.C.: *Digital picture processing, Vol.1 & 2.* New York: Academic Press 1982

Local operations

3.1 Foundations

The requirements for understanding this chapter are:

- to be familiar with terms such as derivative, gradient and convolution,
- to have read Chapter 1.

The global aim of local operations is to emphasize or to suppress graylevel patterns of neighboring pixels. Figure 3.1 (*left-hand side*) illustrates the idea: the graylevels of an input image in an arbitrarily defined neighborhood around a central pixel (also called the *current pixel*) are processed by a given algorithm. The result of this procedure is a new graylevel which is assigned to the current pixel in the output image. The position of the current pixel in both images is identical. The neighborhood is called a *mask* or a *window*.

In order to process the whole image it has to be 'scanned' by shifting the mask step by step. Usually, this procedure starts in the top left-hand corner of the image (Figure 3.1, *right-hand side*). After the new graylevel has been calculated, the mask must be shifted *one* pixel to the right, followed by a new calculation, and so on. When the end of the current row is encountered, the whole procedure must be started again at the beginning of the next row. Note that masks are not placed side by side like tiles.

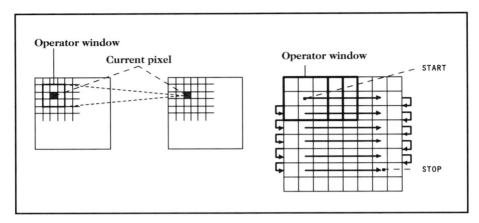

Figure 3.1 *Left:* The graylevels in the mask are processed by a given algorithm. The result of this procedure is a new graylevel which is assigned to the current pixel in the output image. *Right:* To process the whole image the mask (centered around the current pixel) skips from pixel to pixel. Usually, this procedure starts in the top left corner of the image.

1	1	1	1	10	10	10	10
1	1	6	1	8	10	2	10
1	3	1	1	9	10	7	10
1	1	1	2	8	9	10	10
1	1	1	1	10	10	10	10
1	4	1	2	9	10	2	10
1	2	1	8	10	10	10	10
1	1	1	1	10	10	10	10

Figure 3.2
This is the input image used by the examples and exercises of Section 3.1.1 (Graylevel smoothing).

Clearly, the current pixel never reaches the border of the image. Thus the image 'shrinks' as a result of a local operation. Usually, this shrinking is not important, but it must be ensured that the border pixels are not given an accidental graylevel. To simplify matters, the whole output image should be initialized to 0.

Two important rules of image processing have now been highlighted:

- Separate the output image from the input image.
- Initialize the whole output image to 0, before starting an operation.

It is said that 'there are exceptions to every rule', and this applies to image processing as well as to life in general (Section 3.4).

So far, the algorithms for processing the local graylevel patterns have not been discussed. The following section demonstrates three classical applications of local operations, namely graylevel smoothing, emphasizing graylevel differences and sharpening graylevel steps. Further applications are discussed in Section 3.4.

The following sections discuss various well-known local operations. Note that these are only the 'mainstream' in a wide spectrum of possible local operations.

3.1.1   Graylevel smoothing

The examples in this section employ the image shown in Figure 3.2 as input image. This image mainly consists of two graylevel regions, a 'dark' one (graylevel 1) and a 'light' one (graylevel 10). Interpreting the other graylevels as noise, one obvious task is to remove it or, in other words, to obtain two smooth regions. A very simple smoothing method is the mean operation. Figure 3.3 shows the output image resulting from a mean operation applied to the input image (Figure 3.2). The mask size was 3*3. The graylevels of the pixels in the mask were summed up and divided by 9. Obviously, the graylevels of the noisy pixels have been brought closer to the desired graylevel. On the other hand, the formerly steep graylevel step between the two regions in the input image has been flattened. The assessment of this as a positive or negative effect depends on the application. Some of the following examples demonstrate smoothing methods which preserve the graylevel steps.

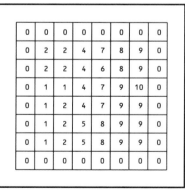

Figure 3.3
Result of the application of a 3*3 mean operator to the input image shown in Figure 3.2.

An alternative to the normal mean operator is the weighted mean. In this case, the graylevels in the mask are multiplied by certain weights (also known as *coefficients*). Figure 3.4 (*right-hand side*) shows the weights of the *Gaussian low-pass*. On the left-hand side the weights of the normal mean (also known as *box filter*) are set against the Gaussian low-pass.

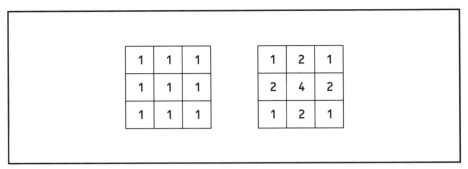

Figure 3.4 *Left:* In the case of a normal mean operation (3*3 mask), the graylevels in the mask are equally weighted with 1. Due to the shape of this mask, a filter using it is called a box filter. *Right:* This mask represents a Gaussian low-pass. Since (in comparison with the box filter), the weights realize a smoother filter characteristic, the resulting image has fewer harmonics.

The smoothing effect of the Gaussian low-pass is only slightly better than that of the box filter. Furthermore, the problems of flattened graylevel steps remain.

A very simple smoothing operator which preserves graylevel steps is the *min operator*. As the name suggests, the min operator yields the minimum graylevel within the mask as the new graylevel. Figure 3.5 shows the result of a 3*3 min applied to the input image (Figure 3.2). Now the dark image region (graylevel 1) is clean, but, on the other hand, the former light region is destroyed. The complementary *max operator* cleans light regions, but destroys dark regions.

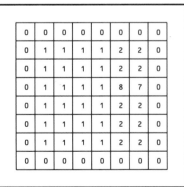

Figure 3.5
The 3*3 min operator cleans the dark region of the input image (Figure 3.2), but unfortunately also corrupts the former light region.

Thus, an operator is required which combines the functions of the min and max operators and avoids their disadvantages. Figure 3.6 shows the solution: the idea of the *median operator* is to sort all graylevels within the mask according to their values. The one in the middle of the list is used for the current pixel of the output image. This strategy removes peaks of both high and low graylevels, without flattening graylevel steps separating graylevel regions. The disadvantage of the median: computing time is high since the graylevels of the neighboring pixels must be sorted.

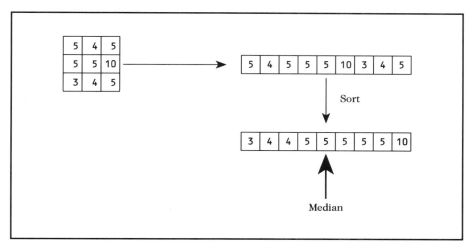

Figure 3.6 The median operator combines the functions of the min and max operators but avoids their disadvantages. The idea is to sort all graylevels within the mask, according to their values. The one in the middle of the list is the resulting graylevel.

Another edge preserving smoothing method is the *k nearest neighbor* approach. This is a normal mean operation (box filter) which does not work on all pixels of the mask, but only on those *k* pixels whose graylevels are closest to the graylevel of the current pixel. Figure 3.7 shows the result of a 3*3 nearest neighbor operator with *k=3* (including the current pixel) applied to the input image (Figure 3.2). Since only 3 graylevels were used to compute the mean, the smoothing effect is less than that of the median. Usually *k* should be greater than half of the number of pixels in the mask.

0	0	0	0	0	0	0	0
0	1	3	1	9	10	6	0
0	2	1	1	9	10	9	0
0	1	1	1	9	9	10	0
0	1	1	1	10	10	10	0
0	2	1	1	10	10	7	0
0	1	1	9	10	10	10	0
0	0	0	0	0	0	0	0

Figure 3.7
This is the result of a 3*3 nearest neighbor operator with *k=3* (including the current pixel) applied to the input image shown in Figure 3.2. The nearest neighbor operator performs a normal mean operation on those *k* pixels of the mask whose graylevels are closest to the graylevel of the current pixel.

3.1.2 Emphasizing graylevel differences

Emphasizing graylevel differences is the classical first step of contour-oriented segmentation [3.2]. This subject is discussed in detail in Chapter 6. What follows has been included for the sake of completeness, since emphasizing graylevel differences is also often achieved by a 'Local Operation'.

For the examples of this section, a new input image is to be used, shown in Figure 3.8. Like the input image before, this image consists mainly of two graylevel regions, a 'dark' one (graylevel 1) and a 'light' one (graylevel 10). In contrast to the former image this is not a noisy image which is to be smoothed. Now the aim is to emphasize the graylevel step between the dark and the light region. A classic method is based on the *Laplacian operator*. Figure 3.9 (*left-hand side*) shows the weights of this local operator. Applying a Laplacian operator to the input image shown in Figure 3.8 leads to the output image shown in Figure 3.10. Omitting the sign of the resulting graylevel differences yields the desired emphasizing.

One disadvantage of the Laplacian operator (which is an approximation of the second derivative) is that even graylevel differences caused by small peaks are emphasized. If these peaks are a result of undesirable noise, then the Laplacian operator makes the noise problem worse. To avoid this problem an operator based on the first derivative should be used. Figure 3.9 (*right-hand side*) shows the weights of the *Prewitt operator*. Applying the top mask (in which vertical graylevel transitions are emphasized) first, results in the output image shown in Figure 3.11. Apart from the absolute magnitudes, it is similar to the image achieved by the Laplacian operator. However, a closer look reveals that it is smoother than the output of the Laplacian. This is the effect which is intended when applying an operator based on the first derivative.

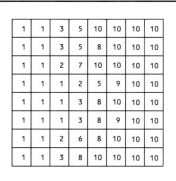

Figure 3.8
This is the input image used by the examples and exercises of Section 3.1.2 (Emphasizing graylevel differences).

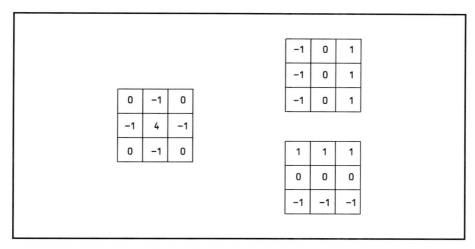

Figure 3.9 In contrast to the weights shown in Figure 3.4, which give rise to smooth out graylevel differences, the weights in this figure realize masks which emphasize graylevel differences. *Left:* The Laplacian operator emphasizes graylevel differences by using only one mask. *Right:* In contrast, the Prewitt operator utilizes two masks. The top mask emphasizes vertical graylevel transitions, while the bottom mask emphasizes horizontal ones.

0	0	0	0	0	0	0	0
0	-2	1	-3	1	2	0	0
0	-1	-4	9	10	1	0	0
0	0	-2	-8	-9	1	1	0
0	0	-2	-2	10	4	0	0
0	0	-3	-6	8	-2	1	0
0	-1	-3	3	2	3	0	0
0	0	0	0	0	0	0	0

Figure 3.10
Result of the application of a 3*3 Laplacian operator to the input image shown in Figure 3.8.

0	0	0	0	0	0	0	0
0	5	14	20	13	2	0	0
0	3	11	17	15	7	1	0
0	1	9	19	17	7	1	0
0	0	5	18	20	9	2	0
0	1	9	20	17	6	1	0
0	3	14	20	12	4	1	0
0	0	0	0	0	0	0	0

Figure 3.11
Result of the application of the Prewitt mask emphasizing vertical graylevel transitions (Figure 3.9, *top right*) to the input image shown in Figure 3.8.

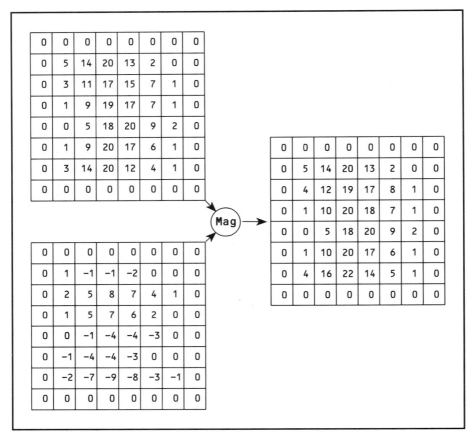

Figure 3.12 This is the result of the complete Prewitt operation. *Top left:* the result of the first Prewitt mask has already been computed (Figure 3.11). *Bottom left:* this is the result of the second Prewitt mask. Since the main graylevel transition in the input image (Figure 3.8) is horizontal, there are only fragmented vertical graylevel steps in it. Consequently, the output of the second Prewitt mask is consistently small. *Right:* the magnitude image yields the maximum graylevel change at every pixel.

The Prewitt operation is not yet complete. The second mask has to be applied to obtain the horizontal graylevel transitions. Having the results of both masks, it is obvious that the Prewitt operator approximates a *gradient operation*. That is, it will yield for each pixel of the input image (apart from the border pixels) the direction of the maximum graylevel change and the magnitude of this change. To achieve this information explicitly, the Cartesian representation of the gradient has to be changed into a polar representation. Figure 3.12 shows the result of the complete Prewitt operator. The gradient magnitude is computed using $\sqrt{(\Delta x)^2 + (\Delta y)^2}$, where Δx is the horizontal graylevel difference and Δy is the vertical graylevel difference. The direction of the maximum graylevel change is an important subject in the context of contour-oriented segmentation and (together with further aspects of gradient operators) is discussed in detail in Chapter 6.

As Section 3.1.1 has shown, min and max operations (which are very attractive due to their simplicity) yield interesting smoothing results. They are also suitable for emphasizing graylevel differences, as demonstrated by the example shown in Figure 3.13, which shows the results of a min (*top left*) and a max operation (*bottom left*) applied to the source image (Figure 3.8). The absolute difference between the min and the max values yields the emphasized graylevel transition between the dark and the light region.

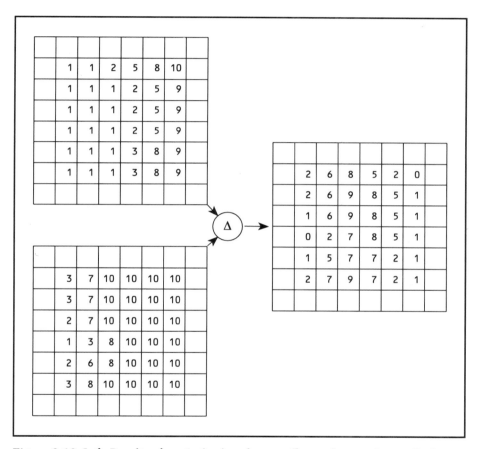

Figure 3.13 *Left:* Results of a min (*top*) and a max (*bottom*) operation applied to the source image (Figure 3.8). *Right:* The absolute difference between the min and the max values yields the emphasized graylevel step between the dark and the light regions.

3.1.3 Sharpening graylevel steps

The transition from the dark to the light region of the input image shown in Figure 3.8 is flat. The aim of this section is to demonstrate approaches which change the flat graylevel transition into a steeper step. The first task is to add one of the output images from Section 3.1.2, which emphasizes the graylevel transition, to its input image. As an example, Figure 3.14 shows the result of adding the input image shown in Figure 3.8 to its output image obtained by a Laplacian operation (Figure 3.10).

0	0	0	0	0	0	0	0
0	-1	4	2	9	11	10	0
0	0	-2	-2	20	11	10	0
0	1	-1	-6	-4	10	11	0
0	1	-1	1	18	14	10	0
0	1	-2	-3	16	7	11	0
0	0	-1	9	10	13	10	0
0	0	0	0	0	0	0	0

Figure 3.14
This is the result of adding the input image shown in Figure 3.8 to the output image obtained by a Laplacian operation (shown in Figure 3.10).

In principle this idea works. However, the negative values and the very high graylevels are far from ideal. They may be diminished by adding the Laplacian image with reduced difference values. An alternative is to clip the extreme low and high graylevels.

Another approach is again a variation of the well-known min and max operators. The result of the *closest of min and max* operation is either the minimum or the maximum graylevel in the current mask. The decision depends on the difference between the graylevel of the current pixel and the minimum and maximum graylevel in the mask. If the difference from the minimum is less than that from the maximum, the operator outputs the minimum graylevel, and vice versa. Figure 3.15 shows the result of a 3*3 closest of min and max operator applied to the input image (Figure 3.8). The result is obviously better than that demonstrated in Figure 3.14.

1	1	1	3	10	10	10	10
1	1	1	2	10	10	10	10
1	1	1	10	10	10	10	10
1	1	1	1	2	10	10	10
1	1	1	1	10	10	10	10
1	1	1	1	10	10	10	10
1	1	1	10	10	10	10	10
1	1	1	10	10	10	10	10

Figure 3.15
This is the result of a 3*3 closest of min and max operator applied to the input image (Figure 3.8). This operator returns the minimum (maximum) graylevel in the mask if the difference between the graylevel of the current pixel and the minimum (maximum) graylevel is less than the difference between the graylevel of the current pixel and the maximum (minimum).

So far the min and max operators have performed well. The idea of this operator is based on the observation that a transition from a dark to a light region is formed by graylevels lying between the low and the high graylevels representing the dark and the light regions. But what happens if the graylevel transition from dark to light is very wide and gradual so that it consists of areas with identical graylevels, and the low (min) and high (max) graylevels do not lie within the spatial scope of the operator?

1	1	1	3	10	10	10	10
1	1	1	3	3	10	10	10
1	1	3	3	3	10	10	10
1	1	3	3	3	10	10	10
1	1	3	3	3	10	10	10
1	1	1	3	3	10	10	10
1	1	1	1	3	3	10	10
1	1	1	1	1	1	3	10

Figure 3.16
To learn about further aspects of the closest of min and max operator, this image is used as a source for new experiments.

To find an answer to this question, a new input image (shown in Figure 3.16) is used for an example. Figure 3.17 shows the result of a 3*3 closest of min and max operator applied to the new input image. The aim of obtaining a step between the dark and the light region has not been achieved.

1	1	1	1	10	10	10	10
1	1	1	1	3	10	10	10
1	1	3	3	3	10	10	10
1	1	3	3	3	10	10	10
1	1	3	3	3	10	10	10
1	1	1	3	1	10	10	10
1	1	1	1	1	1	10	10
1	1	1	1	1	1	1	10

Figure 3.17
This is the result of a 3*3 closest of min and max operator applied to the new input image (Figure 3.16). The aim of obtaining a step between the dark and the light regions has not been achieved.

Applying two iterations of the 3*3 closest of min and max operator to the output image resulting from the first iteration (Figure 3.17) yields the images shown in Figure 3.18 and Figure 3.19. Step by step a 'channel has been dug' by the operator to separate the disturbed region (graylevel 3) and the light region. Further iterations would have no effect. Obviously, the alternative to the iteration approach is the enlargement of the operator mask.

1	1	1	1	10	10	10	10
1	1	1	1	1	10	10	10
1	1	3	3	1	10	10	10
1	1	3	3	3	10	10	10
1	1	3	3	1	10	10	10
1	1	1	3	1	10	10	10
1	1	1	1	1	1	10	10
1	1	1	1	1	1	1	10

Figure 3.18
The result of the second iteration of the 3*3 closest of min and max operator, applied to the result of the first iteration shown in Figure 3.17.

1	1	1	1	10	10	10	10
1	1	1	1	1	10	10	10
1	1	3	3	1	10	10	10
1	1	3	3	1	10	10	10
1	1	3	3	1	10	10	10
1	1	1	3	1	10	10	10
1	1	1	1	1	1	10	10
1	1	1	1	1	1	1	10

Figure 3.19
The result of the third iteration of the 3*3 closest of min and max operator, applied to the result of the second iteration shown in Figure 3.18.

3.2   Ad Oculos experiments

3.2.1 Graylevel smoothing

The first experiment deals with the local **Mean Operator**, **Min Operator**, **Max Operator** and **Median Operator** which are aimed at removing noise. Realize the **New Setup** as shown in Figure 3.20.

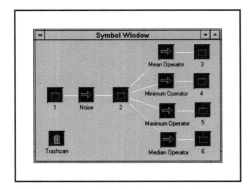

Figure 3.20
The first experiment deals with the local **Mean Operator**, the **Min Operator**, the **Max Operator** and the **Median Operator** which are aimed at removing noise. This **New Setup** is realized according to the steps described in Section 1.5. The results are shown in Figure 3.21.

Figure 3.21 (PLIERSRC.128) shows the source image for the current experiment. It needs to be loaded into image (1). In order to demonstrate noise suppressing operators, we need a noisy version of the original image (1). For this purpose, salt-and-pepper noise is applied to the source image with the aid of the Noise function: the graylevels of randomly selected pixels were assigned either as black or as white.

The parameters of Noise were:

```
No. of Random Pixel: 1000
Salt & Pepper:       on
```

These parameters may be varied with a click of the right mouse button on the function symbol Noise. Similarly, the parameters of the four local operators should be determined. Each of these operators is controlled by the parameter Window Size:. it should be 3 to obtain the results shown in Figure 3.21.

A straightforward solution to the noise problem can be achieved by employing an averaging operator. Using a 3*3 mask, output image (3) (Figure 3.21) is obtained. Obviously the disturbance is not entirely removed. Furthermore, the image is blurred, which is usually an undesirable side effect.

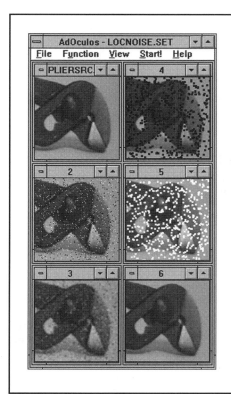

Figure 3.21
In the first step, the Noise function adds salt-and-pepper noise to the input image (PLIERSRC.128). Image (2) shows the result. The parameters of Noise were No of Random Pixels: 1000 and Salt & Pepper: on. These parameters may be varied by clicking the right mouse button on the function symbol of noise. Similarly, the parameters of the four local operators can be specified. Each of these operators is controlled by a parameter Window Size:. it should be 3 to obtain the results shown here: (3) is the result of the Mean Operator, (4) is the result of the Min Operator, (5) is the result of the Max Operator and (6) is the result of the Median Operator.

Min and max operators avoid blurred output images and they consume little computing time. However, inspection of the resulting images (4) and (5) reveals their obvious disadvantages. Since the min operator yields the minimum graylevel of the current mask, it completely removes white peaks, while, on the other hand, enlarging black peaks. The result is achieved by using a 3*3 mask. Assuming the disturbance has been caused by only one black pixel, the min operator generates 8 additional black pixels around the original one. The max operator behaves in a complementary way.

For the removal of these point-like disturbances, the median operator performs really well. Image (6) shows the result of a 3*3 median applied to the noisy image. The salt-and-pepper noise is completely suppressed. The blurring effect of the median is negligible. Unfortunately, a high price is paid for this performance: the sorting procedure requires a lot of computing time.

3.2.2 Emphasizing graylevel differences

Section 3.1.2 described the *Laplacian operator* and the *Prewitt operator* as representatives of gradient operators. Experiments with the Laplacian are demonstrated in Section 3.2.3. Chapter 6 (*Contour-oriented segmentation*) is based on gradient operators, so that experiments with these operators are discussed there.

3.2.3 Sharpening graylevel steps

The aim of the second experiment is familiarization with the Laplace function. As described in Section 1.5, the New Setup shown in Figure 3.22 is used.

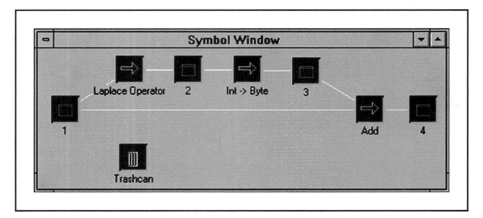

Figure 3.22 The aim of the second experiment is familiarization with the Laplace function. This New Setup is realized according to the steps described in Section 1.5. The results are shown in Figure 3.23.

The Laplacian operator performance is complementary to the averaging operator. Image (2) in Figure 3.23 shows the emphasis of the graylevel differences of the input image (DIGIM.128, loaded into image (1)). The resulting graylevels of a Laplacian may be negative. The dark regions of the output image represent negative 'graylevels', while the light regions are assigned positive graylevels. Their maximum magnitudes are colored black and white, respectively. If the Laplacian operator yields zero, the pixel in question is represented by a medium gray.

For further processing, the resulting image (2) which is an integer type, has to be converted to a byte image with the aid of the Int -> Byte function. As image (3) shows (Figure 3.23), the region's borders are emphasized by positive graylevels. Adding this result to the original image (DIGIM.128) yields a resulting image with sharpened graylevel steps. Note that the Add function divides the graylevel sum by 2 to avoid any overflow. Thus the mean graylevel of the resulting image (4) is lower than that of the input image. For the current case this effect is compensated with the aid of the Image Attributes option (Section 1.5 and Figure 1.27).

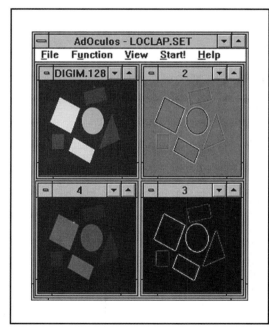

Figure 3.23
Image (2) shows the emphasis of the graylevel differences of the input image (DIGIM.128) by a Laplacian. The dark regions of the output image represent negative 'graylevels', while the light regions are assigned positive graylevels. Their maximum magnitudes are colored black and white, respectively. If the Laplacian operator yields zero, the pixel in question is represented by a medium gray. Image (3) is the 'byte version' of image (2). Image (4) is the sum of the input image and image (3). Note that the Add function divides the graylevel sum by 2 to avoid any overflow. Thus, the mean graylevel of the resulting image (4) is lower than that of the input image. For the current case, this effect is compensated with the aid of the Image Attributes option (Section 1.5 and Figure 1.27).

3.3   Source code

Figure 3.24 shows a procedure which realizes an averaging operation. Formal parameters are:

```
ImSize:   image size
WinSize: size of the mask
InIm:     input image
OutIm:    output image
```

In the first step of the procedure, an initialization of the parameters n and Area and the output image OutIm takes place. n represents half the mask size WinSize, while the number of pixels in the mask is assigned to Area. r and c are the coordinates of the current pixel.

The averaging that follows is simple. The graylevels in the neighborhood of the current pixel InIm[r][c] are summed up in Sum. The value of Sum is then normalized by the number of mask pixels Area and assigned to the current pixel of the output image OutIm[r][c].

```
void Average (ImSize, WinSize, InIm, OutIm)
int  ImSize, WinSize;
BYTE ** InIm;
BYTE ** OutIm;
{
    int    r,c, y,x, n, Area;
    long   Sum;

    n = (WinSize-1) >> 1;
    Area = (2*n+1) * (2*n+1);

    for (r=0; r<ImSize; r++)
       for (c=0; c<ImSize; c++)  OutIm [r][c] = 0;

    for (r=n; r<ImSize-n; r++) {
       for (c=n; c<ImSize-n; c++) {
          Sum = 0;
          for (y=-n; y<=n; y++)
             for (x=-n; x<=n; x++)
                Sum += InIm [r+y] [c+x];
          OutIm [r][c] = (BYTE) (Sum/Area);
} } }
```

Figure 3.24 C realization of the averaging operator.

Figure 3.25 shows the procedure for the Laplacian operator. Formal parameters are:

```
ImSize:   image size
InIm:     input image
OutIm:    output image
```

```
void Laplace (ImSize, InIm, OutIm)
int  ImSize;
BYTE ** InIm;
int  ** OutIm;
{
    int   r,c, y,x, Sum;

    static int Mask [3][3] = { { 0,  1, 0},
                               { 1, -4, 1},
                               { 0,  1, 0} };

    for (r=0; r<ImSize; r++)
        for (c=0; c<ImSize; c++)  OutIm [r][c] = 0;

    for (r=1; r<ImSize-1; r++) {
        for (c=1; c<ImSize-1; c++) {
            Sum = 0;
            for (y=-1; y<=1; y++)
                for (x=-1; x<=1; x++)
                    Sum += InIm [r+y] [c+x] * Mask [y+1] [x+1];
            OutIm [r][c] = Sum/9;
} } }
```

Figure 3.25 C realization of the Laplacian operator.

The procedure starts by initializing of Mask with the coefficients of the Laplacian operator, and with the output image OutIm set to 0.

The frame of the procedure is similar to the one used for averaging. However, in the case of a Laplacian operator, Sum stores the products of the graylevels InIm[r+y][c+x] and of the coefficients Mask[y+1][x+1]. This operation realizes the local convolution (Section 3.4). Another difference from the averaging operation concerns the data type of the output image OutIm. Since the results may be negative, signed data is required, that is, an int image.

Figure 3.26 and Figure 3.27 show procedures realizing the min and the max operator, respectively. Formal parameters and initialization correspond to those of the averaging procedure. The procedures themselves are also similar. However, the core of the algorithm consists of a procedure which searches for the minimum or maximum graylevels within the mask, that is, a non-linear operation which cannot be reversed.

The realization of the median operator is shown in Figure 3.28. Formal parameters and initialization are the same as before. The array Lst serves for the sorting procedure. It needs the allocation of memory to be appropriate to the mask size. The core of the algorithm starts by loading Lst with the graylevels of the current mask. The next step sorts the graylevels in Lst based on a standard algorithm (bubble sort). Finally the median value is assigned to the current pixel of the output image OutIm[r][c].

```
void MinOp (ImSize, WinSize, InIm, OutIm)
int  ImSize, WinSize;
BYTE ** InIm;
BYTE ** OutIm;
{
    int   r,c, y,x, n, Area;
    BYTE  Min;

    n = (WinSize-1) >> 1;
    Area = (2*n+1) * (2*n+1);

    for (r=0; r<ImSize; r++)
      for (c=0; c<ImSize; c++)  OutIm [r][c] = 0;

    for (r=n; r<ImSize-n; r++) {
      for (c=n; c<ImSize-n; c++) {
        Min = InIm[r][c];
        for (y=-n; y<=n; y++)
          for (x=-n; x<=n; x++)
            if (InIm[r+y][c+x] < Min)  Min = InIm [r+y] [c+x];
        OutIm [r][c] = Min;
} } }
```

Figure 3.26 C realization of the min operator.

```
void MaxOp (ImSize, WinSize, InIm, OutIm)
int  ImSize, WinSize;
BYTE ** InIm;
BYTE ** OutIm;
{
    int   r,c, y,x, n, Area;
    BYTE  Max;

    n = (WinSize-1) >> 1;
    Area = (2*n+1) * (2*n+1);

    for (r=0; r<ImSize; r++)
      for (c=0; c<ImSize; c++)  OutIm [r][c] = 0;

    for (r=n; r<ImSize-n; r++) {
      for (c=n; c<ImSize-n; c++) {
        Max = InIm[r][c];
        for (y=-n; y<=n; y++)
          for (x=-n; x<=n; x++)
            if (InIm[r+y][c+x] > Max)  Max = InIm [r+y] [c+x];
        OutIm [r][c] = Max;
} } }
```

Figure 3.27 C realization of the max operator.

The procedures shown in Figure 3.24 and Figure 3.25 are based on local convolution (Section 3.4). In the case of the averaging operator, an explicit mask is not necessary because all the coefficients are 1. The realization of the Laplacian operator is based on a static definition of the mask *in* the procedure.

It is obvious that both operations can be performed by a single procedure which realizes a local convolution. In this case, the mask must be a formal parameter. Note that the convolution procedure should be able to work with any mask size and any coefficients.

```
void Median (ImSize, WinSize, InIm, OutIm)
int  ImSize, WinSize;
BYTE ** InIm;
BYTE ** OutIm;
{
    int   r,c, y,x, i,j, n, Area;
    BYTE  Buf;
    BYTE  *Lst;

    n = (WinSize-1) >> 1;
    Area = (2*n+1) * (2*n+1);
    Lst = (BYTE *) malloc (Area*sizeof(BYTE));

    for (r=0; r<ImSize; r++)
       for (c=0; c<ImSize; c++)  OutIm [r][c] = 0;

    for (r=n; r<ImSize-n; r++) {
       for (c=n; c<ImSize-n; c++) {
          i=0;
          for (y=-n; y<=n; y++) {
             for (x=-n; x<=n; x++) {
                Lst [i] = InIm [r+y] [c+x];
                i++;
          } }

          for (i=0; i<Area-1; i++)   /**** bubble sort ****/
             for (j=Area-1; i<j; j--)
                if (Lst[j-1] > Lst[j]) {
                   Buf       = Lst[j-1];
                   Lst[j-1]  = Lst[j];
                   Lst[j]    = Buf;
                }
                OutIm [r][c] = Lst [Area/2];
} } }
```

Figure 3.28 C realization of the median operator.

3.4   Supplement

Human beings try to extract something meaningful from an image. For them, an image has a 'content'. To give only one example, consider the constellation in the night sky. People talk about the Big Dipper (the Great Bear in England, the Great Wagon in Germany), even though there is clearly only an accidental alignment of some stars. They have no meaningful relationship other than to human observers on earth.

It is extremely important to understand that a local operator merely processes (two-dimensional, discrete, spatial) signals which are meaningless to it. Thus, one should be cautious in choosing words to describe an image or the processing of an image. For instance, local operators which emphasize graylevel differences (Section 3.1.2) are sometimes called 'edge detectors'. This is misleading, since the correspondence of these differences to the edges of the objects in the image is generally not guaranteed (Chapter 6).

The classical local operation is based on the well-known convolution of two signals, $h(m)$ and $f(n)$:

$$h * f(n) = \int h(m) f(n - m)\, dm$$

In practising image processing, a small 'image' containing the weights (of the processing mask) is convolved with the input or source image. Let $w(i,j)$ be weight at position (i,j) related to the origin of the mask and $f(x,y)$ the graylevel at position (x,y) related to the origin of the source image. Then

$$w * f(x,y) = \sum_i \sum_j w(i,j) f(x - i, y - j)$$

is the local convolution of the image f with the mask w. Although it is incorrect from a formal point of view, it is useful to talk about a cross-correlation between the image f and the mask w. $w * f$ yields a measure for the similarity between the weight pattern of the mask and the graylevel pattern of the image part which is currently overlaid by the mask.

Local operations which are not based on convolution are often more interesting. In Section 3.1, these included the min, max and median operations. They are typical representatives of the so-called rank filters. The general idea of rank filters (Figure 3.29) is to sort out the graylevels overlaid by the mask, to put them into a list, to weight the list entries and to sum up the weighted entries. This sum is the new graylevel. That is, for the median operator all weights except the medium one (which is 1) are 0. In the case of the min (max) operation, only the weight corresponding to the lowest (highest) graylevel is 1.

Other interesting alternatives to the convolution approach are the so-called morphological image processing operations (morphology = science of shape) which are discussed in detail in Chapter 8. The basic idea here is to exploit knowledge regarding the shape of those graylevel regions of interest.

The large amount of literature concerning local operations reflects the broad spectrum of applications and the corresponding problems. A few examples are: Ballard and Brown [3.1], Horn [3.4], Jähne [3.5], Niblack [3.7], Rosenfeld and Kak [3.8] and Schalkoff [3.9]. Since local operations are an important tool of image manipulation (Chapter 1), literature from the desktop publishing domain can be of interest for further reading. Morrison [3.6] offers a magical gateway to image processing.

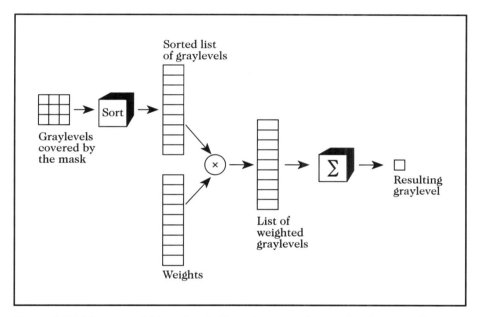

Figure 3.29 The general idea of rank filters is to sort the graylevels covered by the mask, to put them into a list, to weight the list entries and to sum up those weighted entries.

3.5   Exercises

3.1   Apply the Gaussian low-pass operator depicted in Figure 3.4 to the input image (Figure 3.2).

3.2   It is not hard to guess that the complement to the min operator is the *max operator*. Apply a 3*3 max operator to the input image (Figure 3.2).

3.3   Apply a 3*3 median operator to the input image (Figure 3.2).

3.4   Apply a 3*3 nearest neighbor operator with $k=6$ (including the current pixel) to the input image (Figure 3.2).

3.5   In Section 3.1.2, the min and max operations were used to emphasize graylevel transitions. Apply the second lowest and second highest graylevels to obtain a similar result.

3.6   Apply a 3*3 closest of min and max operator to the output image resulting from the first iteration of the example shown in Figure 3.15.

3.7   Apply a 5*5 closest of min and max operator to the source image shown in Figure 3.16.

3.8   Let B be a blurred version of image I. Implement an image sharpening filter by subtracting B from I, scaling that result, and adding it back to I. Show that this is equivalent to adding the output of a high pass filter (*see also* Section 4.1) back to the original. Explain how this serves to sharpen the image.

3.9   Write a program which realizes k nearest neighbor operators of various sizes.

3.10 Write a program which realizes closest of min and max operators of various sizes.

3.11 Write a program which realizes a general rank filter.

3.12 Ignore the rule of separating output images from source images, and experiment with local operators which work on the source image itself.

3.13 Try to find local operators which yield aesthetically interesting outputs. For instance, realize an operator which mimics looking through rippled glass.

3.14 Become familiar with every local operation offered by Ad Oculos (Ad Oculos Help).

3.6   References

[3.1]   Ballard, D.H.; Brown, C.M.: *Computer vision*. Englewood Cliffs: Prentice-Hall 1982

[3.2]   Bässmann, H.; Besslich, Ph.W.: *Konturorientierte Verfahren in der digitalen Bildverarbeitung*. Berlin, Heidelberg, New York, London, Paris, Tokyo: Springer 1989

[3.3]   Haralick, R.M.; Shapiro, L.G.: *Computer and robot vision*. Reading, Massachusetts: Addison-Wesley 1992

[3.4]   Horn, B.K.P.: *Robot vision*. Cambridge, London: MIT Press 1986

[3.5]   Jähne, B.: *Digital image processing. Concepts, algorithms, and scientific applications.* Berlin, Heidelberg, New York, London, Paris, Tokyo: Springer 1991

[3.6]   Morrision, M.: *The magic of image processing.* Carmel: Sams Publishing 1993

[3.7]   Niblack, W.: *An introduction to digital image processing.* Englewood Cliffs: Prentice-Hall 1986

[3.8]   Rosenfeld, A.; Kak, A.C.: *Digital picture processing, Vol.1 & 2.* New York: Academic Press 1982

[3.9]   Schalkoff, R.J.: *Digital image processing and computer vision.* New York, Chichester, Brisbane, Toronto, Singapore: Wiley 1989

4

Global operations

4.1 Foundations

The requirements for understanding this chapter are:

- to be familiar with complex arithmetic/numbers,
- to have a basic understanding of Fourier analysis (this chapter is intended to refresh that knowledge),
- to have read Chapter 1.

Global operations require all the pixels of the input image to calculate the graylevel of one output pixel. A typical global operator is the Fourier transform. This transformation is well-known in the context of one-dimensional continuous and discrete time signals. Digital images are two-dimensional discrete spatial signals. The formal roots of the corresponding two-dimensional Discrete Fourier Transform (DFT) do not differ from the one-dimensional case and are described in many books dealing with digital signal processing or image processing. Thus, the following sections offer the opportunity of brushing up basic understanding with the aid of a few examples.

Figure 4.1 depicts the basic idea of the Fourier transform: by summing sinusoidal signals, a non-sinusoidal waveform can be synthesized and vice versa; by applying Fourier analysis to a waveform, information concerning the individual sinusoidal signals (comprising the non-sinusoidal waveform) is obtained. Figure 4.2 shows the non-sinusoidal waveform synthesized in Figure 4.1 and its representation in the spatial frequency domain which has been generated by Fourier Analysis. The spatial frequency domain reveals the sinusoidal 'components' (Figure 4.1) f_0, $2f_0$ and $4f_0$ of the non-sinusoidal signal.

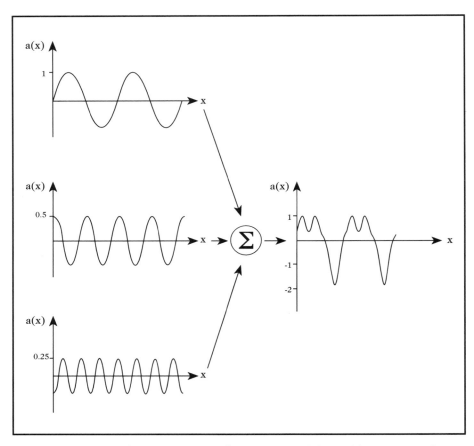

Figure 4.1 Example for the synthesis of a non-sinusoidal signal by summing three sinusoidal signals. Usually, this representation is known as *time domain* and the x-axis is therefore labelled with a *t*. Image processing deals with spatial signals. Thus, we talk about a spatial domain and label the x-axis as *x*. $a(x)$ means the amplitude of the spatial signal at position *x*.

The example depicted in Figure 4.2 and Figure 4.1 is based on continuous signals. In the case of discrete signals (such as digital images), Fourier Analysis is performed by the Discrete Fourier Transform (DFT). An application-oriented discussion of its formal foundation is given in Section 4.4. Figure 4.3 outlines the application of a DFT which has been simplified by using only a period of eight samples $a_0, a_1, \ldots a_7$ of a real input signal (that is, the signal has no imaginary component).

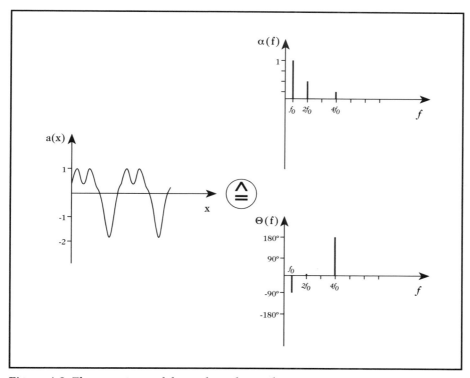

Figure 4.2 The non-sinusoidal signal synthesized in Figure 4.1, represented in both the spatial domain and the spatial frequency domain, as yielded by Fourier Analysis. The spatial frequency domain reveals the magnitude $\alpha(f)$ (which corresponds to the amplitude of sinusoidal signals in the spatial domain) and the phases $\Theta(f)$ of the sinusoidal 'components' f_0, $2f_0$ and $4f_0$ of the non-sinusoidal signal. f_0 is the fundamental (spatial) frequency.

The DFT yields a Cartesian representation of the spectrum. The real part consists of the coefficients $A_0, A_1, \ldots A_7$ while $B_0, B_1, \ldots B_7$ form the imaginary components. The Cartesian representation is useful for computers, but not very illustrative. Changing the Cartesian representation to a polar representation clarifies the spectrum: $\alpha_0, \alpha_1, \ldots \alpha_7$ are the magnitudes, while $\Theta_0, \Theta_1, \ldots \Theta_7$ are the phases of the sinusoidal signals revealed by the DFT. The sign of the phase is defined in Figure 4.4. Accordingly, a positive real component A and a positive imaginary component B yield a phase angle between 0° and 90°, a positive real and negative imaginary component a phase angle between –0° and –90°. A negative real component leads to a phase angle between ±90° and ±180° (depending on the sign of the imaginary component).

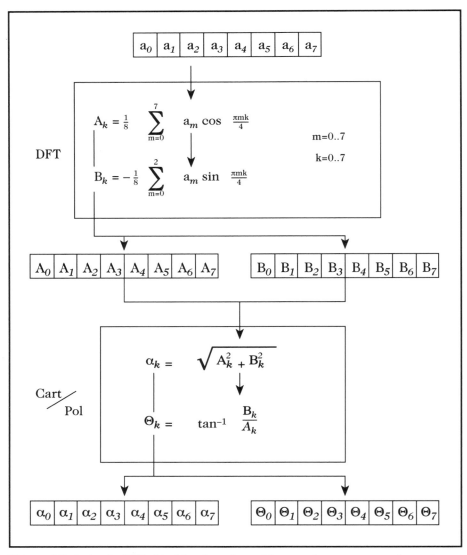

Figure 4.3 A simple DFT algorithm based on eight samples $a_0, a_1,...a_7$ of a real input signal yielding a Cartesian representation of the spectrum. Its real component consists of the coefficients $A_0, A_1,...A_7$. The imaginary coefficients are $B_0, B_1,...B_7$. The polar representation yields the magnitudes ($\alpha_0, \alpha_1,...\alpha_7$) and the phases ($\Theta_0, \Theta_1,...\Theta_7$) of the sinusoidal signals revealed by the DFT. The sign of the phase Θ_k is defined in Figure 4.4.

Figure 4.5 demonstrates the application of the DFT on eight samples taken from a sinusoidal signal. Computing by hand is easy, using the expanded DFT sums shown in Figure 4.6 and Figure 4.7 (*see also* Figure 4.3).

According to Figure 4.2, a spectrum is to be expected which consists of only one peak whose magnitude is **1**, since the signal is a pure sinusoidal.

However, the actual spectrum shows two peaks (Figure 4.5), each with a magnitude of 0.5. Figure 4.8 shows the structure of the spectrum of the simplified DFT. Except for the restriction to 8 samples, this structure is valid for the general DFT.

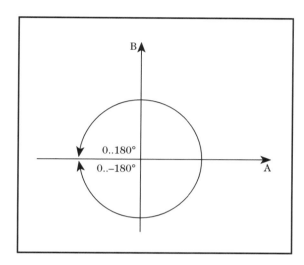

Figure 4.4
Definition of the phase: A positive real component A and a positive imaginary component B yielding a phase angle between 0° and 90°, a positive real and negative imaginary component yielding a phase angle between -0° and -90°. A negative real component leads to a phase angle between ±90° and ±180° (depending on the sign of the imaginary component).

At first glance, the coefficients generated by the DFT are ordered in an unusual way (for example, why are the coefficients divided into positive and negative parts, and what is a negative frequency?). This ordering has no special significance, it is due to the definition of the DFT and only a question of getting used to it. The DC coefficient indicates the average value of the sample period $a_0, a_1, \ldots a_7$. The fundamental frequency is the reciprocal of the period ($f_0 = 1/T$), and therefore the lowest frequency that the DFT reveals. The Nyquist frequency is the highest frequency the DFT is able to handle (in the current case $4f_0$). The remaining coefficients are integer multiples of f_0, the so-called harmonics.

Figure 4.9 shows the first harmonic to be treated by the simple DFT (remember the support of Figure 4.6 and Figure 4.7). As expected, coefficients 2 and 6 indicate this harmonic with a magnitude of 1 and a phase angle of ±90°.

Trying to transform the third harmonic as shown in Figure 4.10 leads to problems: the signal is sampled at the zero-crossing points, so that the digitized signal is always 0. The problem is due to the violation of the rule of using sample rates which are greater (and not equal to) than double the Nyquist frequency (Figure 4.8).

A more difficult everyday problem of DFT applications is the so-called leakage effect: at first glance the DFT example shown in Figure 4.11 is similar to that depicted in Figure 4.5. However, although the input signal is a 'pure' sinusoidal signal, the spectrum indicates various harmonics. The spectrum can be said to 'leak'. The answer to this apparent contradiction is that the actual sinusoidal signal is *not* 'clean'. One of the most important properties of the DFT is that it assumes periodic signals. From this point of view, the sinusoidal signal looks like that in Figure 4.12. It is the step which causes the harmonics.

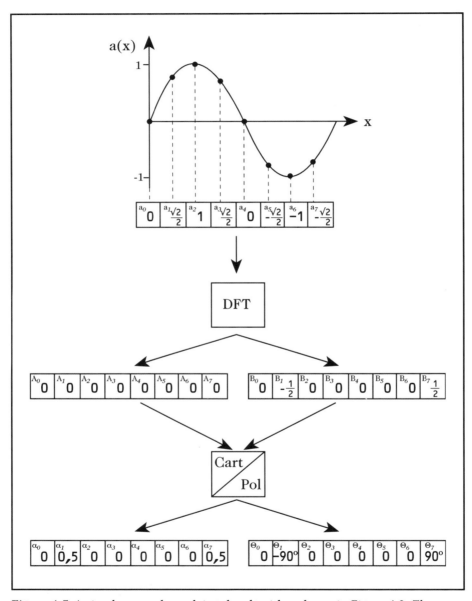

Figure 4.5 A simple example applying the algorithm shown in Figure 4.3. The expanded sums in Figure 4.6 and Figure 4.7 support the computing of the DFT algorithm by hand.

$$A_0 = \tfrac{1}{8}(a_0 + a_1 + a_2 + a_3 + a_4 + a_5 + a_6 + a_7)$$

$$A_1 = \tfrac{1}{8}(a_0 + \sqrt{\tfrac{2}{2}}\,a_1 + 0 - \sqrt{\tfrac{2}{2}}\,a_3 - a_4 - \sqrt{\tfrac{2}{2}}\,a_5 + 0 + \sqrt{\tfrac{2}{2}}\,a_7)$$

$$A_2 = \tfrac{1}{8}(a_0 + 0 - a_2 + 0 + a_4 + 0 - a_6 + 0)$$

$$A_3 = \tfrac{1}{8}(a_0 - \sqrt{\tfrac{2}{2}}\,a_1 + 0 + \sqrt{\tfrac{2}{2}}\,a_3 - a_4 + \sqrt{\tfrac{2}{2}}\,a_5 + 0 - \sqrt{\tfrac{2}{2}}\,a_7)$$

$$A_4 = \tfrac{1}{8}(a_0 - a_1 + a_2 - a_3 + a_4 - a_5 + a_6 - a_7)$$

$$A_5 = \tfrac{1}{8}(a_0 - \sqrt{\tfrac{2}{2}}\,a_1 + 0 + \sqrt{\tfrac{2}{2}}\,a_3 - a_4 + \sqrt{\tfrac{2}{2}}\,a_5 + 0 - \sqrt{\tfrac{2}{2}}\,a_7)$$

$$A_6 = \tfrac{1}{8}(a_0 + 0 - a_2 + 0 + a_4 + 0 - a_6 + 0)$$

$$A_7 = \tfrac{1}{8}(a_0 + \sqrt{\tfrac{2}{2}}\,a_1 + 0 - \sqrt{\tfrac{2}{2}}\,a_3 - a_4 - \sqrt{\tfrac{2}{2}}\,a_5 + 0 + \sqrt{\tfrac{2}{2}}\,a_7)$$

Figure 4.6 Expansion of the DFT sums yielding the real component of the spectrum (Figure 4.3).

$$B_0 = -\tfrac{1}{8}(0 + 0 + 0 + 0 + 0 + 0 + 0 + 0)$$

$$B_1 = -\tfrac{1}{8}(0 + \sqrt{\tfrac{2}{2}}\,a_1 + a_2 + \sqrt{\tfrac{2}{2}}\,a_3 + 0 - \sqrt{\tfrac{2}{2}}\,a_5 - a_6 - \sqrt{\tfrac{2}{2}}\,a_7)$$

$$B_2 = -\tfrac{1}{8}(0 + a_1 + 0 - a_3 + 0 + a_5 + 0 - a_7)$$

$$B_3 = -\tfrac{1}{8}(0 + \sqrt{\tfrac{2}{2}}\,a_1 - a_2 + \sqrt{\tfrac{2}{2}}\,a_3 + 0 - \sqrt{\tfrac{2}{2}}\,a_5 + a_6 - \sqrt{\tfrac{2}{2}}\,a_7)$$

$$B_4 = -\tfrac{1}{8}(0 + 0 + 0 + 0 + 0 + 0 + 0 + 0)$$

$$B_5 = -\tfrac{1}{8}(0 - \sqrt{\tfrac{2}{2}}\,a_1 + a_2 - \sqrt{\tfrac{2}{2}}\,a_3 + 0 + \sqrt{\tfrac{2}{2}}\,a_5 - a_6 + \sqrt{\tfrac{2}{2}}\,a_7)$$

$$B_6 = -\tfrac{1}{8}(0 - a_1 + 0 + a_3 + 0 - a_5 + 0 + a_7)$$

$$B_7 = -\tfrac{1}{8}(0 - \sqrt{\tfrac{2}{2}}\,a_1 - a_2 - \sqrt{\tfrac{2}{2}}\,a_3 + 0 + \sqrt{\tfrac{2}{2}}\,a_5 + a_6 + \sqrt{\tfrac{2}{2}}\,a_7)$$

Figure 4.7 Expansion of the DFT sums yielding the imaginary component of the spectrum (Figure 4.3).

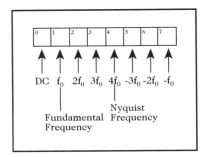

Figure 4.8
One needs to get accustomed to the order of the DFT coefficients. The coefficient DC indicates the average value of the sample period $a_0, a_1, ... a_7$. The fundamental frequency is the reciprocal of the period, while the Nyquist frequency is the highest frequency the DFT is able to handle. The remaining coefficients (harmonics) are integer multiples of f_0.

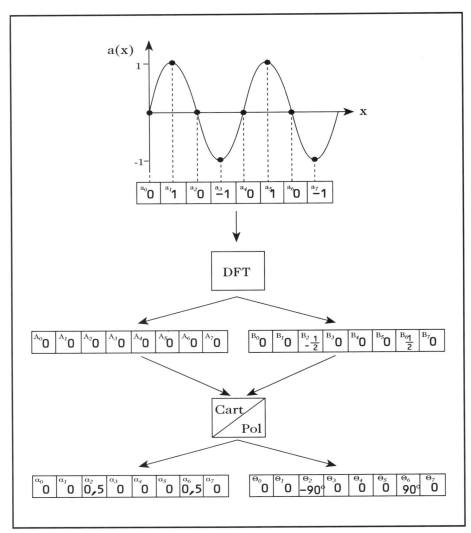

Figure 4.9 This example shows the DFT analysing the first harmonic.

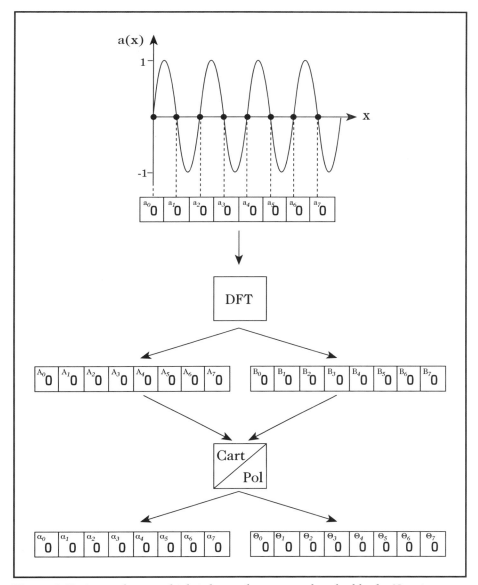

Figure 4.10 A sample rate which is lower than or equal to double the Nyquist frequency leads to errors.

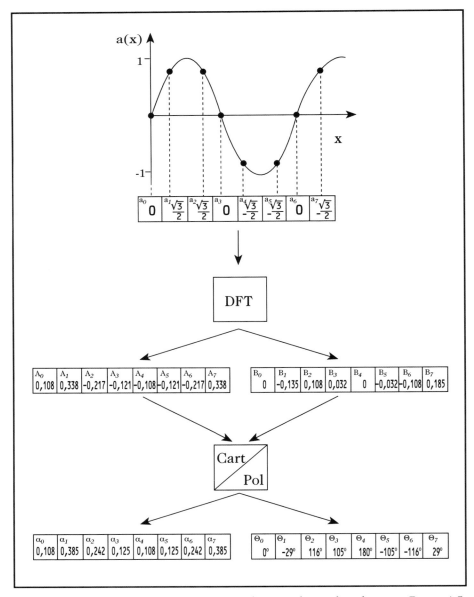

Figure 4.11 At first glance, this DFT example is similar to that shown in Figure 4.5. However, although the input signal is a 'pure' sinusoidal signal, the spectrum indicates various harmonics. It can be said that the spectrum 'leaks'.

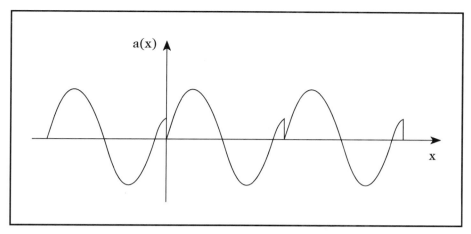

Figure 4.12 For the DFT, the sinusoidal signal shown in Figure 4.11 looks like this.

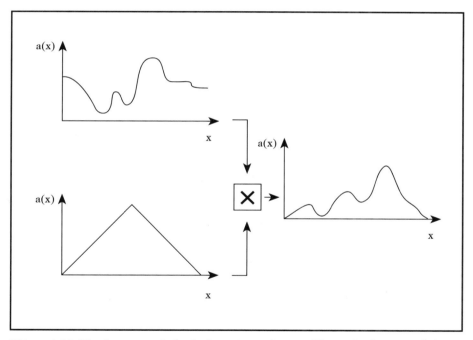

Figure 4.13 The best remedy for leakage is windowing. The multiplication of the original signal (*top left*) and a roof function (*bottom left*) yields a signal with flattened edges.

One way of reducing leakage is to try to choose the sample period so that the height of the steps is minimal. Unfortunately, in practice the repositioning of the sample period is difficult (if not impossible) to implement.

The practical solution is *windowing*. The principle is demonstrated in Figure 4.13, where the multiplication of the original signal (top left) and a roof function (bottom left) yields a signal with flattened edges. The roof function used in this example may be replaced by other windowing functions (for example, bell-shaped) which are able to flatten the original signal.

So far, the DFT has been executed by hand. Obviously it is a fairly time-consuming process even for computers (floating point matrix operations). The so-called Fast Fourier Transform (FFT) is the most efficient algorithm for performing the Discrete Fourier Transform. Compared to the straight-forward implementation of the DFT, the FFT saves time and memory since it performs the transformation on the input vector, hence needing no extra output vector. Figure 4.28 shows the source code of the FFT.

4.1.1 The 2-dimensional case

Usually, anyone who is interested in signal processing is familiar with the 1-dimensional DFT. However, this is not so for the 2-dimensional case. The first hurdle is the idea of a 2-dimensional sinusoidal signal. The example shown in Figure 4.14 demonstrates its generation. The two 1-dimensional cosinusoidal signals depicted in the top illustration are repeated in every row and column. The mean of these two images (superposition) yields a 2-dimensional cosinusoidal signal. It looks a little bit like the underside of an egg box. The spectrum of this 'pure' cosinusoidal signal consists of 4 peaks.

Fortunately, the computing of a 2-dimensional DFT is simply realized with the standard 1-dimensional DFT, by transforming the single rows first, and then transforming the single columns of the resulting image (or vice versa). This algorithm is shown in Figure 4.29.

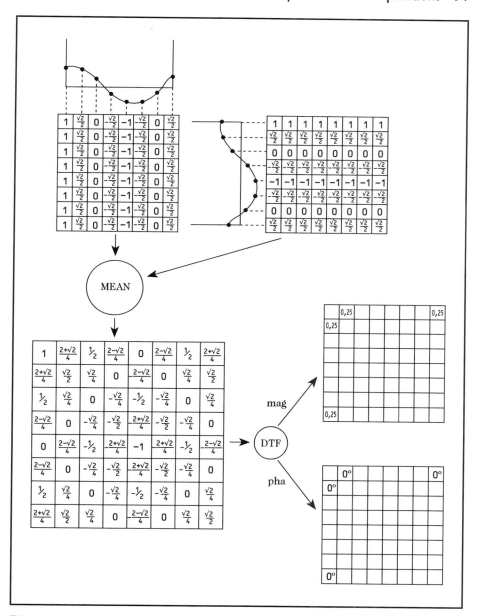

Figure 4.14 We obtain a 2-dimensional cosine signal by superposing two 1-dimensional cosine signals. The 2-dimensional signal looks like the underside of an egg box. The spectrum consists of 4 peaks, a pair for each 1-dimensional signal.

4.1.2 Spectral experiments

The upper part of Figure 4.15 depicts a typical application scheme of the Discrete Fourier Transform: the spectrum generated by the DFT is manipulated (HP) and then transformed back by an inverse DFT (DFT⁻¹). In Figure 4.15, the example manipulator is a high-pass (HP) filter which suppresses the low frequencies residing in the corners of the spectrum. Since the high frequencies are responsible for graylevel steps, these steps are emphasized in the resulting image.

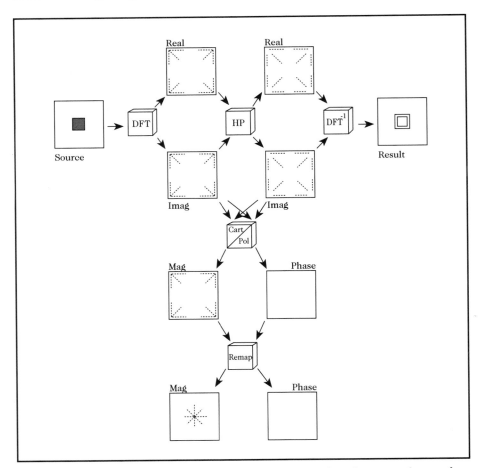

Figure 4.15 The upper part of this figure depicts a typical application scheme of the Discrete Fourier Transform: the spectrum generated by the DFT is manipulated (HP) and transformed backward by an inverse DFT (DFT⁻¹; Figure 4.28). Here, the manipulation is a high-pass (HP) filter operation which suppresses the low frequencies. The lower part depicts two procedures supporting the presentation of the spectrum to a human observer. The first procedure changes the Cartesian to a polar representation (Figure 4.3), while the second procedure swaps the positions of the low and high frequencies so that the low frequencies are in the middle of the frame. Note that the source image is supposed to consist of a real part only. The imaginary input vector for the the DFT is set to 0. In practice, images are always real.

The lower part of Figure 4.15 depicts two procedures making the presentation of the spectrum more useful for a human observer. The first procedure changes the Cartesian to a polar representation (Figure 4.3), while the second procedure replaces the positions of the low and high frequencies so that the low frequencies are now in the middle of the frame. This is the most commonly used representation of the spectrum.

Figure 4.16 shows the spectrum of a square image region. The five small grids arranged in Figure 4.17 illustrate the manipulation of this spectrum: the shaded squares indicate the frequencies to be set to 0. Below the grids, the result of the inverse transform of the manipulated spectrum is shown. Obviously, the graylevel steps are emphasized by these high-pass operations. That is, a high rate of higher harmonics indicates steep graylevel steps in the source image. The influence of a low-pass filter is complementary. Since higher harmonics are suppressed, graylevel transitions become flat, resulting in a blurred image.

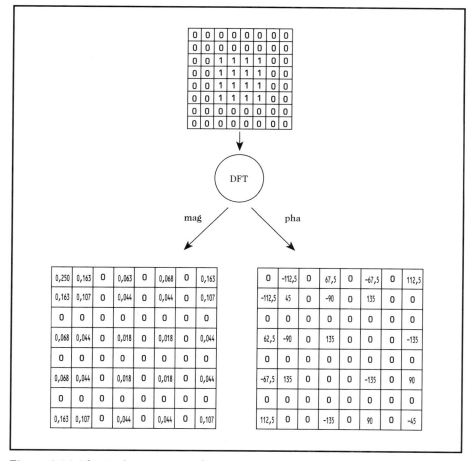

Figure 4.16 This is the spectrum of a square image region. It is the basis for high-pass and low-pass filter experiments according to the application scheme shown in Figure 4.15.

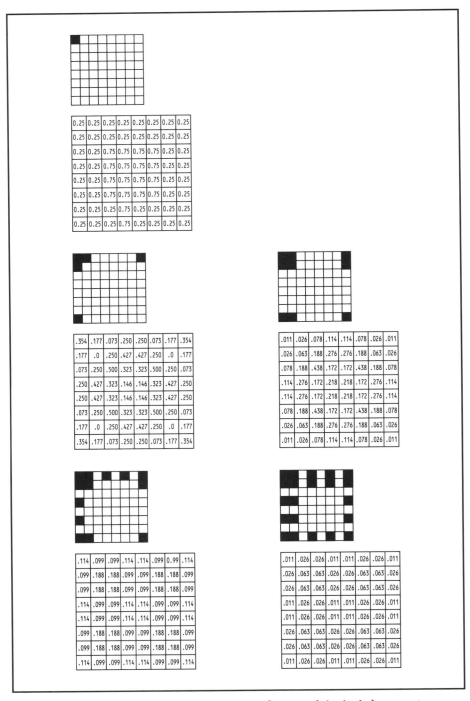

Figure 4.17 This example demonstrates the influence of the high frequencies.

While high-pass and low-pass filters influence the 'borders' of the spectrum, another interesting application is the suppression of specific frequencies which are known to be the result of global interference in the source image. Figure 4.18 shows a 2-dimensional cosinusoidal signal which is similar to that already depicted in Figure 4.14, except for interference. This interference leads to the 0.063 entries in the magnitude spectrum. It is possible to reconstruct the original 2-dimensional cosinusoidal signal exactly, since the frequencies in the spectrum which result from the interference and the frequencies representing the cosinusoidal signal, have no intersection.

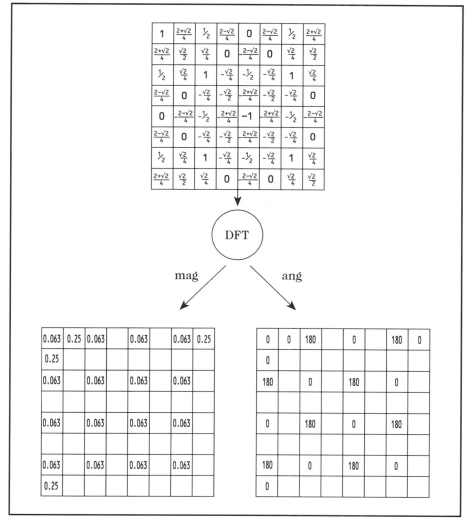

Figure 4.18 This is a 2-dimensional cosine signal which is similar (except for an interference) to that already depicted in Figure 4.14.

A completely different example stems from pattern recognition. Suppose the aim is to find a certain graylevel pattern in an image. The problem is that the position of the pattern is not known in advance. The solution is based on the property that the magnitude spectrum is invariant to shifts of the signal. That is, the magnitude spectrum of the graylevel pattern is independent of its position in the image. Therefore, the recognition process should be executed on the magnitude spectrum instead of on the original image. Figure 4.19 shows a simple string-like graylevel pattern and its spectral representation. In Figure 4.20 and Figure 4.21 the position of the pattern has changed. These changes are reflected in the phase spectra but not in the magnitude spectra.

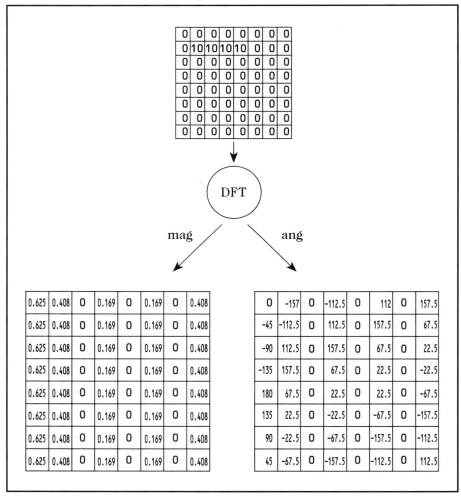

Figure 4.19 A simple string-like graylevel pattern and its spectrum. Figure 4.20 and Figure 4.21 demonstrate the effect of moving this pattern to different positions.

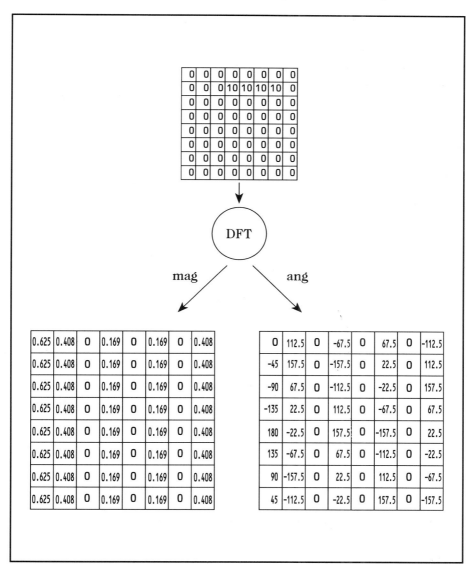

Figure 4.20 The shift of the graylevel pattern shown in Figure 4.19 has no effect on the magnitude spectrum.

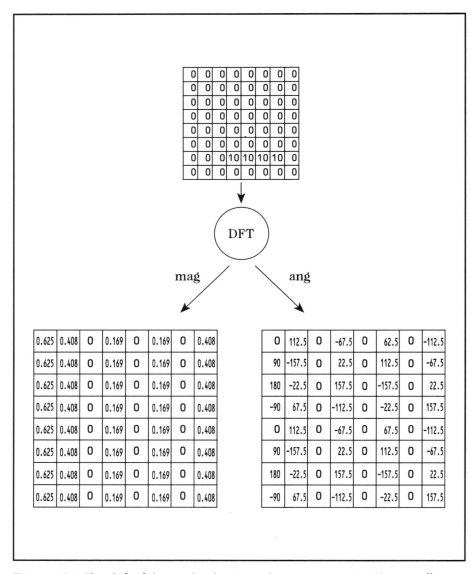

Figure 4.21 The shift of the graylevel pattern shown in Figure 4.19 has no effect on the magnitude spectrum.

4.2   Ad Oculos experiments

The aim of the first experiment is familiarization with the Fourier Transform function. As described in Section 1.5, realize the New Setup shown in Figure 4.22. The source image (BREMSRC.128; Figure 4.23) to be loaded into (1) shows a badge lying on the floor of a laboratory.

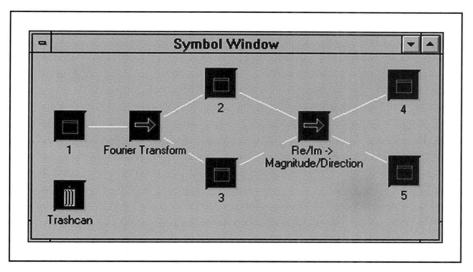

Figure 4.22 The aim of the first experiment is familiarization with the Fourier Transform function. This New Setup is realized according to the steps described in Section 1.5. The results are shown in Figure 4.23.

Image (2) and (3) show the real and the imaginary parts of the result of the Fourier transform. Changing the current Cartesian representation to a polar representation clarifies the spectrum. Images (4) and (5) show the magnitude and the phase of the spectrum. To become acquainted with the Fourier transform, trying source images from different scenes is highly recommended.

The second experiment explores the mechanism of spectrum manipulation. As described in Section 1.5, the New Setup shown in Figure 4.24 is used. The source image (BREMSRC.128, Figure 4.25) to be loaded into (1) is again the badge.

In a similar way to the first experiment, images (2) and (3) show the result of the Fourier transform. This Cartesian representation of the spectrum is to be manipulated by the High-Pass function which suppresses the low harmonics. The Window Size parameter of the High-Pass function defines the cut off radius as shown in (4) and (5). For the current experiment, this parameter is 80 pixels. It may be varied by clicking the right mouse button on the function symbol High-Pass.

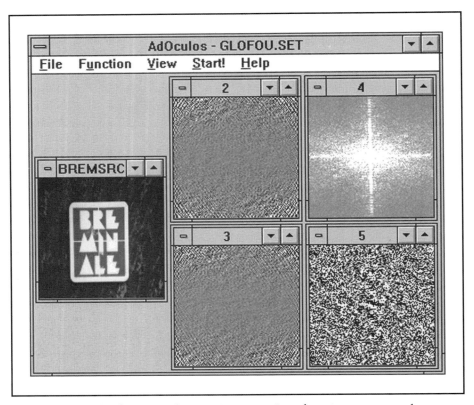

Figure 4.23 In the first step, the Fourier Transform function computes the spectrum of the input image (BREMSRC.128). Images (2) and (3) show the real and the imaginary part of the result. Changing the current Cartesian representation to a polar representation clarifies the spectrum. Images (4) and (5) show the magnitude and the phases of the spectrum.

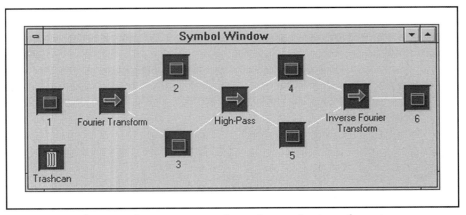

Figure 4.24 The second experiment explores the mechanism of spectrum manipulation. This New Setup is realized according to the steps described in Section 1.5. The results are shown in Figure 4.25.

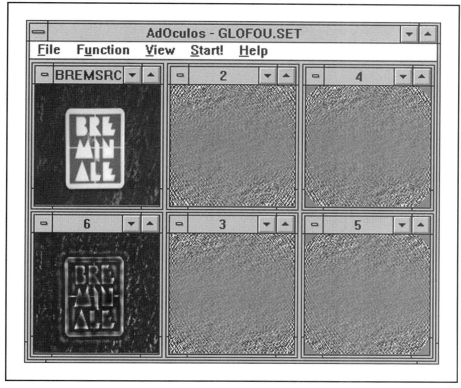

Figure 4.25 Similar to Figure 4.23, Images (2) and (3) show the result of the Fourier transform. This Cartesian representation of the spectrum is to be manipulated by the High-Pass function which suppresses the low harmonics. The Window Size parameter of the High-Pass function defines the cut off radius as shown in (4) and (5). For the current experiment, this parameter is 80 pixels. It may be varied by clicking the right mouse button on the function symbol High-Pass.

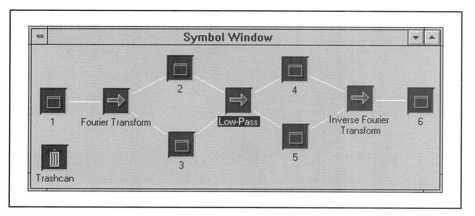

Figure 4.26 The third experiment replaces the High-Pass function by the Low-Pass function. This New Setup is realized according to the steps described in Section 1.5. The results are shown in Figure 4.27.

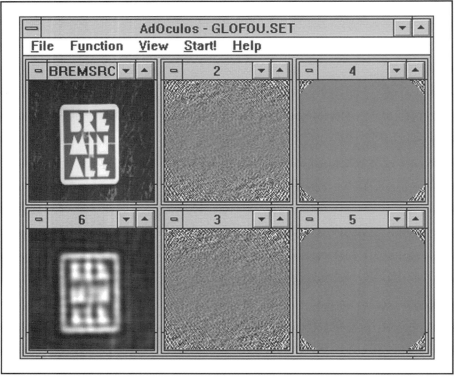

Figure 4.27 The results of the Low-Pass function are complementary to those of the High-Pass function shown in Figure 4.25.

Image (6) shows the result of the application of the Inverse Fourier Transform on the manipulated spectrum. As expected, the resulting image (6) shows the emphasized graylevel steps of the source image (BREMSRC.128).

Replacing the High-Pass function by the Low-Pass function yields the results shown in Figure 4.26 and Figure 4.27.

Note that the realization of the High-Pass and Low-Pass functions serves the purpose of demonstration only. These violate basic rules of filter design and should not be used in practical applications [4.5] [4.9].

4.3   Source code

Figure 4.28 shows a procedure which realizes the Fast Fourier Transform. Formal parameters are:

Forward: Boolean variable which controls forward or backward
           transformation
Size: vector size
VecRe: real part of vector
VecIm: imaginary part of vector

```
void fft (Forward, Size, VecRe, VecIm)
int    Forward, Size;
float * VecRe, * VecIm;
{
    int    LenHalf, Stage, But, ButHalf, i,j,k, ip, pot2;
    float  ArcRe,ArcIm, dArcRe,dArcIm, ReBuf,ImBuf, ArcBuf;
    double Arc;
    pot2 = 0;
    while (Size != (1 << pot2))  pot2++;
    LenHalf = Size >> 1 ;
    j = 1;
    for (i=1; i<Size; i++) {
        if (i<j) {
            ReBuf = VecRe[j-1];
            ImBuf = VecIm[j-1];
            VecRe[j-1] = VecRe[i-1];
            VecIm[j-1] = VecIm[i-1];
            VecRe[i-1] = ReBuf;
            VecIm[i-1] = ImBuf;
        }
        k = LenHalf;
        while (k<j) {
            j -= k;  k = k >> 1;
        }
        j += k;
    }
    for (Stage=1; Stage<=pot2; Stage++) {
        But = 1 << Stage;
        ButHalf = But >> 1;
        ArcRe = (float)1;
        ArcIm = (float)0;
        Arc = (double) (PI/ButHalf);
        dArcRe = (float) cos(Arc);
        dArcIm = (float) sin(Arc);
        if (Forward)  dArcIm = -dArcIm;
        for (j=1; j<=ButHalf; j++) {
            i = j;
            while (i<=Size) {
                ip = i + ButHalf;
                ReBuf = VecRe[ip-1] * ArcRe - VecIm[ip-1] * ArcIm;
                ImBuf = VecRe[ip-1] * ArcIm + VecIm[ip-1] * ArcRe;
                VecRe[ip-1] = VecRe[i-1] - ReBuf;
                VecIm[ip-1] = VecIm[i-1] - ImBuf;
                VecRe[i-1]  = VecRe[i-1] + ReBuf;
                VecIm[i-1]  = VecIm[i-1] + ImBuf;
                i += But ;
            }
            ArcBuf = ArcRe;
            ArcRe = ArcRe  * dArcRe - ArcIm * dArcIm;
            ArcIm = ArcBuf * dArcIm + ArcIm * dArcRe;
    } }
    if (Forward) {
        for (j=1; j<=Size; j++) {
            VecRe[j-1] /= Size;
            VecIm[j-1] /= Size;
} } }
```

Figure 4.28 C realization of the Fast Fourier Transform. If Forward is 0, the procedure performs the inverse transform.

Note that Size must be to the power of 2, and that the procedure only works on square images.

Since the FFT algorithm works 'in-place', a separation of input and output vector is not required. Details of the FFT algorithm are described by Burrus [4.2], Elliot et al. [4.3] and Ramirez [4.11].

Figure 4.29 shows a procedure which realizes the Fourier transform of an image. Formal parameters are:

Forward: Boolean variable which controls forward or backward
transformation
ImSize: image size
RealIm: real part of image
ImagIm: imaginary part of image (zero in the case of the source image)

```
void TransIm (Forward, ImSize, RealIm, ImagIm)
int Forward, ImSize;
float ** RealIm;
float ** ImagIm;
{
   int    r,c;
   float  *VecRe;
   float  *VecIm;

   VecRe = (float *) malloc (ImSize*sizeof(float));
   VecIm = (float *) malloc (ImSize*sizeof(float));

   for (r=0; r<ImSize; r++) {
      for (c=0; c<ImSize; c++) {
         VecRe[c] = RealIm[r][c];
         VecIm[c] = ImagIm[r][c];
      }
      fft (Forward, ImSize, VecRe, VecIm);
      for (c=0; c<ImSize; c++) {
         RealIm[r][c] = VecRe[c];
         ImagIm[r][c] = VecIm[c];
      }
   }

   for (c=0; c<ImSize; c++) {
      for (r=0; r<ImSize; r++) {
         VecRe[r] = RealIm[r][c];
         VecIm[r] = ImagIm[r][c];
      }
      fft (Forward, ImSize, VecRe, VecIm);
      for (r=0; r<ImSize; r++) {
         RealIm[r][c] = VecRe[r];
         ImagIm[r][c] = VecIm[r];
      }
   }
   free (VecRe);
   free (VecIm);
}
```

Figure 4.29 C realization of a two-dimensional, Discrete Fourier Transform. The procedure fft is defined in Figure 4.28.

The procedure starts by allocating memory for both the arrays VecRe and VecIm. They serve as row and column buffers. The transformation commences with the image rows. The index of the current row is r. In preparation, the buffers VecRe and VecIm must be filled with the graylevels of the current row. After calling fft, the transformation result is kept in the buffers since the FFT calculates in-place. In the last step, the transformation result is rewritten into the input image store. The column transformation proceeds in a similar way.

Typical manipulations of the spectrum are the suppression of high frequencies (low-pass filter) or low frequencies (high-pass filter). These operations may be performed using the procedures shown in Figure 4.30. The suppression of high spatial frequencies takes place for both the real and the imaginary part of the spectrum outside a circle around the origin: all spectral values in this area are set to 0. The suppression of low spatial frequencies is performed in a complementary way. Formal parameters of the procedures LowPass and HighPass are:

Rad: radius of the manipulation section
ImSize: image size
Image: array representing the part of the spectrum (usually real or
          imaginary part) which must be manipulated

```
void LowPass (Rad, ImSize, Image)
int   Rad, ImSize;
float ** Image;
{
   int   r,c, Bot,Up;
   long  rr,cc;

   Bot = ImSize/2 -1;
   Up  = ImSize/2 +1;
   for (r=-Bot; r<Up; r++)
      for (c=-Bot; c<Up; c++)
        if (Rad < (int) sqrt ((double) r*r+c*c))
           Image [r+Bot] [c+Bot] = (float)0;
}

void HighPass (Rad, ImSize, Image)
int   Rad, ImSize;
float ** Image;
{
   int   r,c, Bot,Up;
   long  rr,cc;

   Bot = ImSize/2 -1;
   Up  = ImSize/2 +1;
   for (r=-Bot; r<Up; r++)
      for (c=-Bot; c<Up; c++)
        if (Rad > (int) sqrt ((double) r*r+c*c))
           Image [r+Bot] [c+Bot] = (float)0;
}
```

Figure 4.30 C realization of two procedures which manipulate the spectrum of an image.

Both procedures are self-explanatory. Please note that the realizations shown in Figure 4.30 serve the purpose of demonstration only. They violate basic rules of filter design and should not be used in practical applications.

4.4 Supplement

In Section 4.1 a simplified form of the Discrete Fourier Transform (DFT; Figure 4.3) has been used to make the examples more illustrative. Now the original form of the DFT will be discussed.

Let x_m be a complex element of the samples serving as an input signal for the DFT

$$x_m \in \{x_0, x_1, \ldots x_{M-1}\}$$

With

$$k = 0 \ldots m-1$$
$$m = 0 \ldots m-1$$

the DFT yields the individual frequencies of the spectrum $\{X_0, X_1, \ldots X_{M-1}\}$ by computing

$$X_k = \frac{1}{M} \sum_{m=0}^{M-1} x_m e^{-j\frac{2\pi mk}{M}}$$

In order to execute this formula with a computer it is more convenient to have a Cartesian representation of the DFT. With

$$x_m = a_m + jb_m$$
$$e^{\pm j\alpha} = \cos\alpha \pm j\sin\alpha$$

the following is obtained:

$$X_k = \frac{1}{M} \sum_{m=0}^{M-1} (a_m + jb_m)(\cos\tfrac{2\pi mk}{M} - j\sin\tfrac{2\pi mk}{M})$$

Isolating the real A_k and the imaginary part B_k gives

$$X_k = A_k + jB_k$$

and

$$A_k = \tfrac{1}{M} \sum_{m=0}^{M-1} \left(a_m \cos \tfrac{2\pi mk}{M} + b_m \sin \tfrac{2\pi mk}{M} \right)$$

$$B_k = \tfrac{1}{M} \sum_{m=0}^{M-1} \left(b_m \cos \tfrac{2\pi mk}{M} - a_m \sin \tfrac{2\pi mk}{M} \right)$$

The inverse DFT is defined by the reciprocal

$$x_m = \tfrac{1}{M} \sum_{k=0}^{M-1} X_k \, e^{\, j \frac{2\pi mk}{M}}$$

In the Cartesian representation

$$x_m = a_m + jb_m$$

with

$$a_m = \sum_{k=0}^{M-1} A_k \cos \tfrac{2\pi mk}{M} + B_k \sin \tfrac{2\pi mk}{M}$$

$$b_m = \sum_{k=0}^{M-1} B_k \cos \tfrac{2\pi mk}{M} - A_k \sin \tfrac{2\pi mk}{M}$$

The only difference between the forward and backward transform is the factor $1/M$ scaling the sums. Furthermore, it does not matter whether this factor scales the sums of the forward or the backward transform.

The theoretical background of the DFT is discussed in all of the references given at the end of this chapter. Of special interest is the book by Ramirez [4.11] which gives a very illustrative and practice-oriented introduction.

The DFT is an important global operation in digital image processing. But, of course, it is not the only one. There are many orthogonal, linear or non-linear transformations in which each coefficient depends on every pixel of the input image. Some examples are the Walsh, the cosine and the sine transformation. A typical application of these in image processing is image coding. The non-linear rapid transforms can be applied in the context of pattern recognition. There are many other applications of global operators described in the relevant literature: for examples consult the reference list.

An important application of the Fourier transformation is in the area of image *treatment* (Chapter 1), which includes such topics as noise suppression and the enhancement of blurred images. A typical application in the area of image *analysis* is the representation of contours by the so-called Fourier descriptors. In the context of pattern recognition, the Fourier transform is used to achieve a shift invariance of the objects to be detected.

4.5   Exercises

4.1   Extract the simplified DFT shown in Figure 4.3 from the original DFT.

4.2   Apply the simple DFT (according to Figure 4.5) to the sinusoidal signal shown in Figure 4.31.

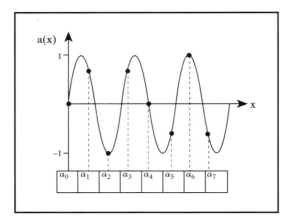

Figure 4.31
Exercise 4.2 demonstrates the analysis of the second harmonic.

4.3 Apply the simple DFT (according to Figure 4.5) to the cosinusoidal signal shown in Figure 4.32.

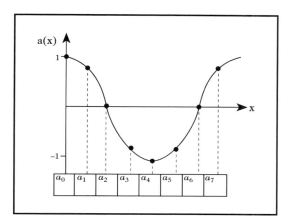

Figure 4.32
Exercise 4.3 returns to the fundamental frequency. It demonstrates the transformation of a cosinusoidal signal.

4.4 Apply the simple DFT (according to Figure 4.5) to the cosinusoidal signal shown in Figure 4.33.

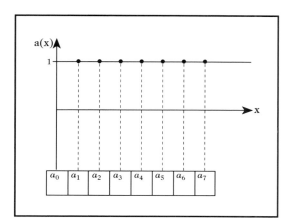

Figure 4.33
Exercise 4.4 demonstrates the simplest case, that is, the spectrum of a DC signal.

4.5   Apply the simple DFT (according to Figure 4.5) to the cosinusoidal signal shown in Figure 4.34.

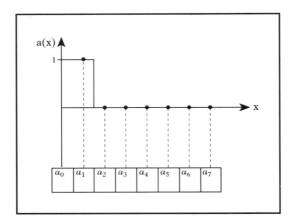

Figure 4.34
Exercise 4.5
demonstrates the
transformation of
a pulse.

4.6   Figure 4.35 shows horizontal and vertical sinusoidal signals. Super-impose them to obtain a 2D sinusoidal signal and apply the 2-dimensional DFT to it. It is best to use the DFT program discussed in Exercise 4.14.

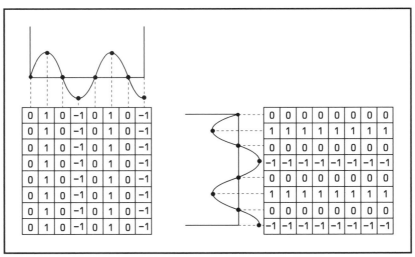

Figure 4.35 Exercise 4.6 demonstrates the analysis of the first 2-dimensional harmonic.

4.7   Superpose the sinusoidal signals shown in Figure 4.36 and apply the 2-dimensional DFT to it. It is best to use the DFT program discussed in Exercise 4.14.

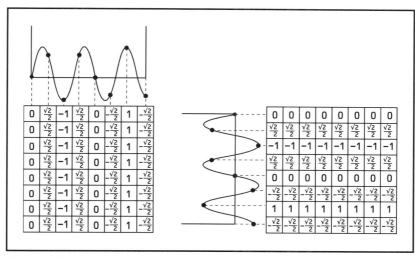

Figure 4.36 Exercise 4.7 demonstrates the analysis of the second 2-dimensional harmonic.

4.8   Superpose the sinusoidal signals shown in Figure 4.37 and apply the 2-dimensional DFT to it. It is best to use the DFT program discussed in Exercise 4.14.

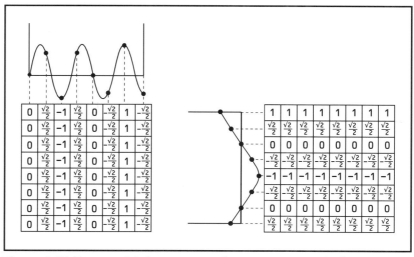

Figure 4.37 Exercise 4.8 demonstrates the superposition of a fundamental cosine and its second harmonic.

4.9   Superpose the sinusoidal signals shown in Figure 4.38 and apply the
       2-dimensional DFT to it. It is best to use the DFT program discussed
       in Exercise 4.14.

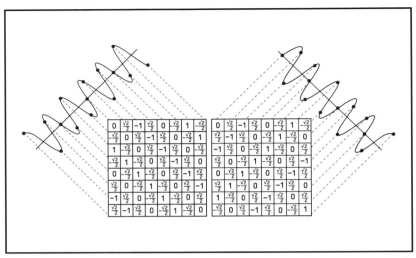

Figure 4.38 Exercise 4.9 demonstrates the superposition of two sinusoidal
signals.

4.10   Figure 4.39 shows four empty frames similar to those used in the
       experiment shown in Figure 4.16 and Figure 4.17. Fill them with the
       result of the inverse DFT applied to the spectrum shown in Figure
       4.16. The shaded squares in the small grids indicate the frequencies
       to be set to 0. It is best to use the DFT program discussed in Exercise
       4.14.

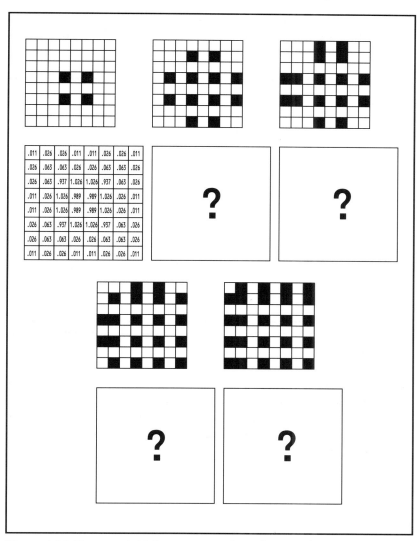

Figure 4.39 Exercise 4.10 demonstrates the influence of the low frequencies.

4.11   Is the magnitude spectrum invariant to the rotated graylevel pattern shown in Figure 4.40 (the original position is shown in Figure 4.19)? Find the answer by computing the spectra. It is best to use the DFT program discussed in Exercise 4.14

0	0	0	0	0	0	0	0
0	0	0	0	0	0	0	0
0	0	0	0	10	0	0	0
0	0	0	0	10	0	0	0
0	0	0	0	10	0	0	0
0	0	0	0	10	0	0	0
0	0	0	0	0	0	0	0
0	0	0	0	0	0	0	0

Figure 4.40
The rotation of the graylevel pattern shown in Figure 4.19 leads to a different magnitude spectrum.

4.12   Is the magnitude spectrum invariant to the rotated graylevel pattern shown in Figure 4.41 (the original position is shown in Figure 4.19)? Find the answer by computing the spectra. It is best to use the DFT program discussed in Exercise 4.14.

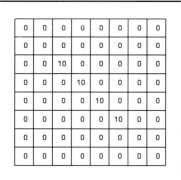

0	0	0	0	0	0	0	0
0	0	0	0	0	0	0	0
0	0	10	0	0	0	0	0
0	0	0	10	0	0	0	0
0	0	0	0	10	0	0	0
0	0	0	0	0	10	0	0
0	0	0	0	0	0	0	0
0	0	0	0	0	0	0	0

Figure 4.41
The rotation of the graylevel pattern shown in Figure 4.19 leads to a different magnitude spectrum.

4.13   Compute the Fourier transform of the following functions using the procedure shown in Figure 4.28. Plot the magnitude and phase spectra.

(a) $a(x) = \begin{cases} 0 & 0 \leq x \leq 127 \\ 1 & x = 128 \\ 0 & 129 \leq x \leq 255 \end{cases}$

What do the results tell you about the frequency content of an impulse function (refer to the magnitude spectrum)?

(b) $b(x) = \begin{cases} 0 & 0 \le x \le 120 \\ 1 & 121 \le x \le 136 \\ 0 & 137 \le x \le 255 \end{cases}$

Note that $b(x)$ is a box filter of width 16 (*see also* Section 3.1). Verify that the magnitude spectrum of $b(x)$ is a sinc function.

(c) $c(x) = \begin{cases} 0 & 0 \le x \le 112 \\ 1 & 113 \le x \le 144 \\ 0 & 145 \le x \le 255 \end{cases}$

Function $c(x)=b(x/2)$. How does scaling the spatial domain affect the frequency domain?

(d) $d(x) = 1$ $0 \le x \le 255$

What is the Fourier transform of a constant signal?

(e) $e(x) = b(x) + \cos(8\pi x / 256)$

How does the Fourier transform of $e(x)$ differ from that of $b(x)$? Comment on the effects of adding a cosine signal to $b(x)$.

(f) $g(x) = b(x - 16)$

What are the effects of shifting $b(x)$ to the right by 16 pixels? Refer to the magnitude and phase spectra.

4.14   Implement the 2-dimensional DFT as shown Figure 4.29.

4.15   Generate a 128*128 spectrum consisting of one harmonic only. Perform the inverse FFT and describe the resulting image. Try different harmonics.

4.16   The high-pass filter demonstrated in Figure 4.17 suppresses lower harmonics completely. Write a program which only decreases the lower harmonics with respect to their position in the spectrum. Try a complementary low-pass approach.

4.17   Become familiar with all the global operations offered by Ad Oculos (*see* Ad Oculos Help).

4.6   References

[4.1]   Ahmed, N. and Rao, K. R.: *Orthogonal Transforms for Digital Signal Processing*. Berlin, Heidelberg, New York: Springer-Verlag 1975

[4.2]   Burrus, C.S. and Parks, T.W.: *DFT/FFT and Convolution Algorithms.* New York: Wiley Sons 1985

[4.3]   Elliott, D.F. and Rao, K. R.: *Fast Transforms, Algorithms, Analysis, Applications*. New York, London: Academic Press 1982

[4.4]   Gonzalez, R.C.; Woods, R.E.: *Digital image processing*. Reading MA: Addison-Wesley 1992

[4.5]   Hall, E.L.: *Computer image processing and recognition*. New York: Academic Press 1979

[4.6]   Jähne, B.: *Digital Image Processing. Concepts, Algorithms, and Scientific Applications*. Berlin, Heidelberg, New York: Springer 1991

[4.7]   Jain, A.K.: *Fundamentals of digital image processing*. Englewood Cliffs: Prentice-Hall 1989

[4.8]   Netravali, A.N.; Haskell, B.G.: *Digital pictures*. New York, London: Plenum Press 1988

[4.9]   Oppenheim, A.V. and Willsky, A.S.: *Signals and Systems*. Englewood Cliffs: Prentice-Hall 1983

[4.10] Pratt, William K.: *Digital Image Processing*. New York: Wiley Sons 1978

[4.11] Ramirez, R.W.: *The FFT, Fundamentals and Concepts*. Englewood Cliffs: Prentice-Hall 1985

5

Region-oriented segmentation

5.1 Foundations

The requirements for understanding this chapter are:

- to be familiar with basic mathematics.
- to have read Chapter 1.

In the context of human perception, *segmentation* means extracting an object from its background. This procedure is not limited to visual perception. The 'acoustic world' of a railway station yields interesting examples. A typical 'object' in this confusing environment is the announcement of a delay. All the other sounds are interpreted as background noise.

The object 'announcement' has a special *meaning* for most people in the station. Meaning and segmentation are usually closely connected. The immediate recognition of a friend in a busy pedestrian precinct is another example of this. A flashy poster in the pedestrian precinct is another object (even if only for a short time for most of the people passing) which is easily separable from the background of moving pedestrians. However, there is an important difference from the object 'friend': although the contents of the poster may have a special meaning to some people, the poster itself is a separable object for all, due to the signal 'color'.

This 'meaningless' form of segmentation is typical for technical image analysis. Common segmentation procedures are based on graylevel differences. Since color image processing systems are becoming cheaper, the use of color differences may increase. An approach currently used in scientific image processing is the so-called *knowledge-based segmentation*, which tries to imitate the segmentation capability of humans. This approach is still a matter of laboratory experiments and is of little relevance for current practical applications (Section 1.2).

Figure 5.1 depicts an example of region-oriented segmentation. The procedure starts by generating and analysing the graylevel histogram of the source image (Section 2.1). Assume the source image consists roughly of two graylevels representing the background and the objects. In this case, the histogram is composed of two peaks. The valley between these peaks constitutes the threshold which is used to obtain a binary image (Section 1.4). Graylevels of the source image which are below this threshold are set to the *label* '0', while those above it are set to '1'.

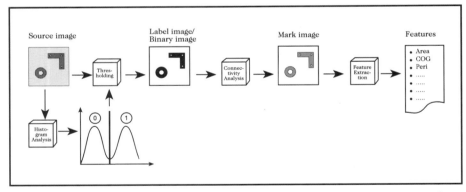

Figure 5.1 This is an example of region-oriented segmentation. Its aim is to isolate regions of similar graylevels and to describe these regions by features, such as their area, their center of gravity or their perimeter length. Such features are necessary to classify the image region as any known object or as an unknown object.

The connectivity analysis collects neighboring pixels of the same label, assigning *marks* to them. Thus, marks indicate connected pixels, while labels indicate graylevel ranges.

Connected pixels constitute image regions which are now ready for description by *features,* such as their area, their center of gravity or their perimeter length. Such features are necessary in order to classify the image region as a known object or as an unknown object (Chapter 10).

5.1.1 Thresholding

As mentioned in the introduction, common segmentation procedures are based on graylevel differences in the source image. A typical example is the image shown in Figure 5.2 (*left-hand side*). It consists of two distinguishable graylevel regions: the right area of the image is emphasized by high graylevels, similar to the poster in the pedestrian precinct which is emphasized by bright colors. Thus it should be easy to separate the two regions.

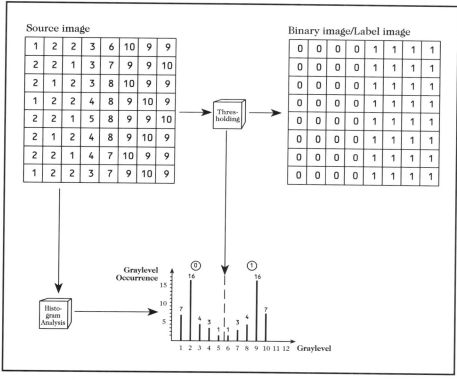

Figure 5.2 This is an example of the application of a histogram analysis for binarizing a graylevel image. The histogram displays the frequency of the graylevels in the source image. In this case, it reflects the two separate graylevel regions. Placing a threshold between the two maxima of the histogram and assigning the *label* '0' to the graylevels below the threshold and '1' to the graylevels above yields the binary image.

Usually, a graylevel histogram is used for this purpose (Figure 5.2). The histogram displays the frequency of the graylevels in the input image. The example shown in Figure 5.2 reflects the two separate graylevel regions. Placing a threshold into the valley between the two maxima of the histogram and assigning the *label* '0' to the graylevels below the threshold and '1' to the graylevels above yields the binary image shown in Figure 5.2 (*right-hand side*).

1	1	1	1	1	2	1	2	1	1	1	2	1	1	1	2
2	2	1	2	3	3	2	2	3	1	2	1	1	2	1	1
1	2	10	11	10	12	11	11	10	10	10	10	10	9	3	2
3	4	10	10	10	12	13	14	13	13	13	12	11	10	1	3
1	3	10	10	9	13	15	17	19	20	16	12	11	10	2	1
1	2	10	11	10	11	16	20	21	20	18	11	12	10	5	1
1	1	9	10	11	11	15	19	20	18	17	13	10	8	4	1
1	2	10	10	12	13	18	20	22	21	15	14	11	10	1	1
1	1	9	10	10	13	17	19	18	17	14	14	12	11	3	1
1	3	10	11	10	12	11	11	11	12	12	13	10	10	2	1
1	2	10	10	12	10	10	11	12	12	10	11	11	9	1	1
1	2	9	10	11	10	12	11	10	11	11	10	11	10	1	2
1	2	10	8	10	9	11	10	10	9	10	9	10	8	2	1
1	1	2	3	4	3	3	2	3	4	4	10	3	3	2	1
1	1	1	3	2	2	1	2	1	1	2	1	2	1	1	2
1	1	1	1	1	1	1	1	2	1	1	1	1	1	1	1

Figure 5.3 This is a new source image which is used to demonstrate the handling of more than one threshold.

At first glance, thresholding seems to be a simple job. Nevertheless, suppose for instance that the perimeter of workpieces has to be measured in the context of industrial quality control. The examples shown in Figure 5.1 suggest an ideal graylevel step between the image background and the regions representing the workpieces. However, in practice such a step is often more gradual than that of the source image shown in Figure 5.2. Consequently, the precision of the measurement depends strongly on the correct choice of threshold.

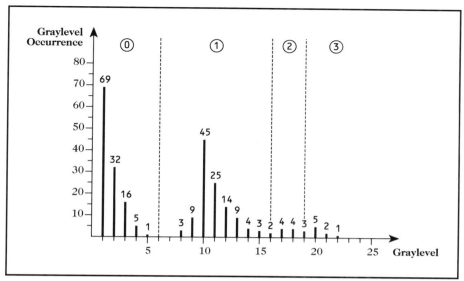

Figure 5.4 The histogram of the source image shown in Figure 5.3 has valleys at graylevels **6**, **16** and **19**. Thus, three thresholds have to be applied.

The rule of thumb for thresholding is: if measurement is the aim, ensure excellent (especially stable) illumination conditions (Section 1.3) and try to use fixed thresholds. If the aim is object recognition under variable conditions, an automatic method of choosing a threshold may be good enough, for instance with the aid of graylevel histograms.

Figure 5.3 shows a new source image. Its graylevel histogram is depicted in Figure 5.4. It has three local minima (valleys), and thus three thresholds (at graylevels **6**, **16** and **19**) have to be applied to the new source image. The resulting label image is shown in Figure 5.5.

The example reveals two typical problems of histogram analysis. The graylevel region (with graylevels of about **20**) positioned in the middle of the source image (Figure 5.3) is clearly separated from the surrounding graylevel region (graylevels of about **10**), but since the number of pixels with graylevels around **20** is small, their influence on the histogram almost vanishes. The solution of this problem, however, is the logarithmic scaling of the histogram entries.

The second problem is the significance of local minima. In the example, the minimum at graylevel **19** is a 'ghost valley'. It produces a superfluous threshold, splitting the region which consists of graylevels of around **20**. Averaging the histogram entries fills in the small valleys.

0	0	0	0	0	0	0	0	0	0	0	0	0	0	0	0
0	0	0	0	0	0	0	0	0	0	0	0	0	0	0	0
0	0	1	1	1	1	1	1	1	1	1	1	1	1	0	0
0	0	1	1	1	1	1	1	1	1	1	1	1	1	0	0
0	0	1	1	1	1	1	2	2	3	1	1	1	1	0	0
0	0	1	1	1	1	2	3	3	3	2	1	1	1	0	0
0	0	1	1	1	1	1	2	3	2	2	1	1	1	0	0
0	0	1	1	1	1	2	3	3	3	1	1	1	1	0	0
0	0	1	1	1	1	2	2	2	2	1	1	1	1	0	0
0	0	1	1	1	1	1	1	1	1	1	1	1	1	0	0
0	0	1	1	1	1	1	1	1	1	1	1	1	1	0	0
0	0	1	1	1	1	1	1	1	1	1	1	1	1	0	0
0	0	1	1	1	1	1	1	1	1	1	1	1	1	0	0
0	0	0	0	0	0	0	0	0	0	0	1	0	0	0	0
0	0	0	0	0	0	0	0	0	0	0	0	0	0	0	0
0	0	0	0	0	0	0	0	0	0	0	0	0	0	0	0

Figure 5.5 Applying the thresholds found in Figure 5.4 to the source image shown in Figure 5.3 leads to this image.

5.1.2 Connectivity analysis

The segmentation is not complete yet. From the point of view of a human observer, the label image shown in Figure 5.1 already consists of two distinct and *connected* regions. However, the computer 'sees' only an array of zeros and ones and it does not 'know' anything about their neighbors. Thus, a *connectivity analysis*, which in the case of region-oriented segmentation is known as *blob coloring*, *component labelling* or *component marking*, is required.

Figure 5.6 shows a source image which is segmented by two thresholds yielding a label image consisting of four regions, but only three labels. The pixels of the top left region (label '1') do not know that they belong together and not to the other label '1' region in the middle of the image. The connectivity analysis helps here. Suppose, the algorithm starts at the top left corner encountering label '1'. Now it gathers all neighboring pixels with label '1' and assigns mark 'a' to this collection. Next, the procedure encounters label '0', collects the corresponding pixels and assigns a '−' which defines this region as background. Further processing yields labels 'b' and 'c'.

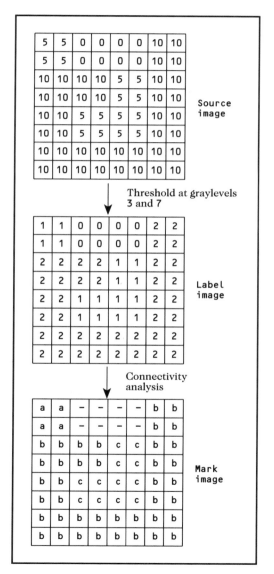

Figure 5.6
In this example, the label image consists of four regions, but only three labels. The connectivity analysis gathers neighboring pixels of the same label and assigns a mark to them. The region with label '0' is interpreted as background.

5.1.3   Feature extraction

In order to analyze the separated regions, information measurements about all their pixels could be used. However, in practice the realization of the analysis is based on a few typical features of these regions.

For a human observer it is evident that region 'a' shown in Figure 5.6 consist of four corners, that it is not tilted and that it is a square, while region 'c' is L-shaped. Unfortunately, a computer needs special algorithms to recognize such information. Typical features in the context of region-oriented segmentation are:

- area,

- perimeter,

- compactness = perimeter^2 / (4π × area),

- polar distance (also called *distance-versus-angle signature*) and

- center of gravity (to determine the position of the object).

In the case of a circle, the compactness is 1. It *increases* if the perimeter of a region becomes longer in comparison with its area. Please note that this definition does *not* correspond to the everyday meaning of 'compact'.

The polar distance indicates the distance between the center of gravity of the region and the border of the region. Again, the circle represents a special case: the polar distance is the same for any point on the border. All other shapes have distances which vary from border point to border point. The form of variation is characteristic of the shape. Figure 5.7 shows an equilateral triangle and a diagram which depicts the variation of the polar distance.

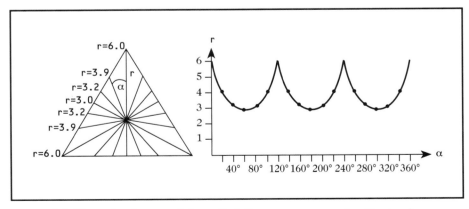

Figure 5.7 The polar distance (also called distance-versus-angle signature) indicates the distance between the center of gravity and the border of the region. The form of variation is characteristic of the region shape.

Most of the features depend on the position, rotation and scaling of regions. This may be desirable, but sometimes it is inconvenient. For instance, the center of gravity depends on the position of the region. This is useful, since the center of gravity determines the position of an object. The compactness is a ratio measurement and thus independent of position, rotation or scaling. The compactness is therefore especially useful as a simple shape feature.

5.2   Ad Oculos experiments

To become familiar with region-oriented segmentation, realize the New Setup shown in Figure 5.8 (*see also* Section 1.5). The example image which will be used in the following section depicts part of a tower block (Figure 5.10 (MZHSRC.128)). This picture is especially suitable due to its homogeneous regions of various graylevels.

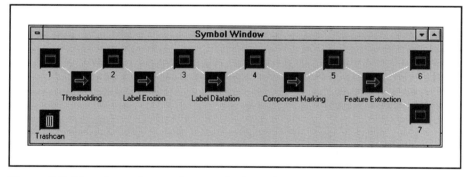

Figure 5.8 This chain of procedures is the basis for experiments concerning region oriented segmentation. The New Setup is realized according to the steps described in Section 1.5. The results are shown in Figure 5.10.

5.2.1   Thresholding

Starting the processing chain with Thresholding, we encounter the dialog box shown in Figure 5.9. The histogram clearly shows that the source image consists of three easily separable *graylevel* regions. Since these regions correspond to meaningful *picture* regions (the bright background represents the sky, the windows are dark and the remaining areas belong to the building), a segmentation by thresholding is practicable. The next step is to smooth the histogram and to start the automatic search for local minima.

The result of these operations is shown in Figure 5.10 (2). The local minima serve as thresholds: the graylevels of the source image which are between zero and the lowest threshold obtain label '0' (the black regions in (2)). Label '1' is assigned to the graylevels between the two thresholds (gray color in (2)). Finally, the remaining graylevels above the high threshold are labelled with '2' (represented by the white regions in (2)).

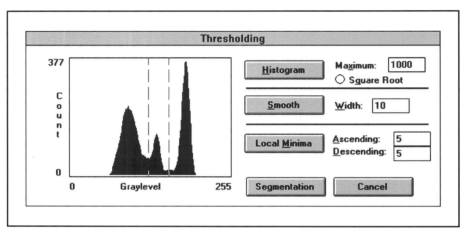

Figure 5.9 Starting the processing chain with Thresholding, we encounter this dialog box. The histogram shows clearly that the source image consists of three easily separable graylevel regions. Since these regions correspond to meaningful *picture* regions (the bright background represents the sky, the windows are dark and the remaining areas belong to the building), a segmentation by thresholding is practicable. The next step is to smooth the histogram and to start the automatic search for local minima.

Since the transitions between the picture regions are not ideal steps, the threshold procedure yields 'noise' at the borders of these regions. In order to clean them, morphological operators (erosion and dilation) are used (Chapter 8). For this purpose, the label image is converted into several binary images: each label in turn represents the object, while the other labels are interpreted as background. Now, the borders of the regions corresponding to the current label are cleaned with the aid of binary erosion, followed by a binary dilation with a structuring element of size 3*3 (Chapter 8). The result of the cleaning step is shown in (4).

5.2.2   Connectivity analysis

In Figure 5.10 (4), 16 separate regions have been found. The separation is due to different labels or the spatial distance between regions with identical labels. Label '0' (black in (4)) represents a large connected region. Label '1' (gray) is divided into 10 smallish regions. Label '2' (white) comprises one large and four small regions. The purpose of the connectivity analysis is to *mark* these 16 areas. The result is shown in (6). Successful marking is portrayed with the aid of a border. The region represented by label '0' is an exception. For the sake of clarity, it is interpreted as background.

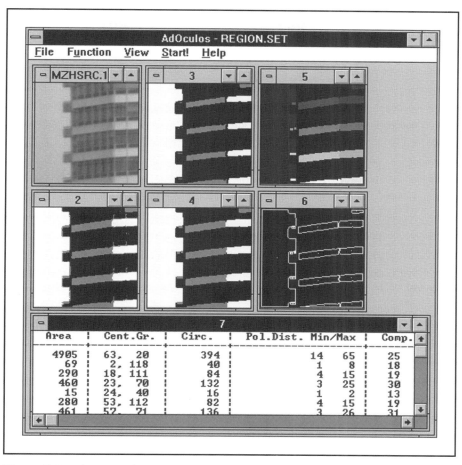

Figure 5.10 The example image (MZHSRC.128) depicts part of a tower block. This picture is especially suitable for the experiment, due to its homogeneous regions of different graylevels. (2) is the result of the Thresholding step (label image). This procedure obtains its parameters from the dialog box shown in Figure 5.9. (3) and (4) show the results of cleaning the label image (2). The operations are discussed in detail in Chapter 8. (5) is the result of the connectivity analysis, while (6) and (7) represent the results of feature extraction.

5.2.3   Feature extraction

Figure 5.10 (7) lists the features of the regions shown in (6). The list entries start with the top left region which, in the current case, is the large region to the left of (6). The next one is the small top right region, and so on.

5.3   Source code

5.3.1 Thresholding

Figure 5.11 shows a procedure which generates a graylevel histogram. Formal parameters are:

ImSize: image size

NofGV: highest graylevel to be processed (usually 255)

MaxAcc: maximum histogram entry; after the generation of the histogram, its entry must be normalized according to MaxAcc

Sqrt: if Sqrt is not zero, the original histogram entries must be replaced by their square root

Image: image from which the histogram has to be taken

Histo: array representing the histogram

```
void Histogram (ImSize, NofGV, MaxAcc, Sqrt, Image, Histo)
int  ImSize, NofGV, MaxAcc, Sqrt;
BYTE ** Image;
int  * Histo;
{
   int  r,c, gv, Max;

   for  (gv=0; gv<NofGV; gv++)  Histo[gv] = 0;

   Max=0;
   for (r=0; r<ImSize; r++) {
      for (c=0; c<ImSize; c++) {
         gv = Image[r][c];
         Histo[gv] ++;
         if (Histo[gv] > Max)  Max = Histo[gv];
   } }

   if (Sqrt) {
      for (gv=0; gv<NofGV; gv++)
         if (Histo[gv])
            Histo[gv] = (int) sqrt ((float)Histo[gv]);
      Max = (int) sqrt ((float)Max);
   }

   for (gv=0; gv<NofGV; gv++)
      Histo[gv] = (int) (((float)Histo[gv] * MaxAcc) / Max);
}
```

Figure 5.11 C realization of histogram generation.

The procedure starts by initializing the histogram array `Histo`, forcing each graylevel entry `gv` to zero. The generation of the histogram requires the graylevels of all the pixels comprising the image. The graylevel of the current pixel is `gv = Image[r][c]`. The corresponding histogram entry `Histo[gv]` must be incremented. Furthermore, it has to be tested whether `Histo[gv]` is the maximum value. `Max` is required by the final normalization step.

If the dynamic range of the histogram entries has to be compressed, the `Sqrt` flag must be set to one. Now, the lower entries are emphasized. Please note that `Max` is to be dealt with in the same way.

Even in the case of small images, rather high histogram entries may occur. This may cause problems in succeeding procedures, due to overflow events. Moreover, a fine resolution of entries is not necessary, since only obvious histogram valleys are of interest. Therefore, the user should determine the maximum entry with the aid of `MaxAcc`. The final step of the procedure normalizes the histogram according to `MaxAcc`.A robust segmentation via histogram analysis occurs when there are few, but distinct peaks and valleys in the histogram. Thus, smoothing the histogram to remove insignificant local maxima should precede the actual analysis procedure. Figure 5.12 shows an appropriate smoothing procedure. Formal parameters are:

`NofGV:`	highest graylevel to be processed
`Width:`	size of the neighborhood of entries whose average value is to be taken
`Histo:`	array of the original histogram
`Smooth:`	array of the smoothed histogram

```
void SmoothHistogram (NofGV, Width, Histo, Smooth)
int   NofGV, Width;
int   *Histo;
int   *Smooth;
{
    int   r,c, i,gv,Cen;
    long h;

    Cen = Width/2;
    for (gv=0; gv<NofGV; gv++)  Smooth[gv] = 0;

    for (gv=0; gv<=NofGV-Width; gv++) {
        h=0;
        for (i=gv; i<gv+Width; i++)
            h += (long)Histo[i];
        Smooth[gv+Cen] = (int) (h/Width);
} }
```

Figure 5.12 C realization of histogram smoothing.

The procedure starts by initializing the output array Smooth. The smoothing is realized by an averaging operation applied to a neighborhood of histogram entries of size Width. The resulting mean value is assigned to the middle entry Smooth[gv+Cen].

After smoothing, another routine is used to search for the histogram valleys. This search is realized by the procedure LocMin, which again is based on the procedures NofUp and NofDown. They detect rising and falling histogram entries, respectively. Formal parameters of NofUp are (Figure 5.13):

NofGV: highest graylevel to be processed
Start: graylevel (index of the histogram array), from which the procedure should begin
Histo: histogram array

At the beginning, the procedure checks whether a rise is present. This is the case if the histogram entry Histo[Start] is less than the entry of its neighbor to the right Histo[Start+1]. Otherwise, the procedure will be left returning zero.

```
int NofUp (NofGV, Start, Histo)
int NofGV, Start;
int * Histo;
{
    int  i,iStep;

    if (Histo[Start] >= Histo[Start+1])  return (0);
    iStep = Start;
    for (i=Start; i<NofGV-1; i++)
      if (Histo[i] < Histo[i+1])
        iStep = i;
      else
        if (Histo[i] > Histo[i+1]) break;
    return (iStep-Start);
}
```

Figure 5.13 C realization of the detector for rising histogram entries.

If we are able to proceed, we progress through the histogram (from left to right), as long as the left entry is less than its right neighbor (Histo[i] < Histo[i+1]). This means a rising histogram at position i which is 'remembered' by istep. If, on the other hand, the current entry is greater than its right neighbor (Histo[i] > Histo[i+1]), the histogram is descending and consequently the procedure stops. But what about the special case of equal histogram entries? We are now moving on a plateau where no special action is taking place. In particular, the 'marker' istep must not be increased, because it indicates the last *rising* position. However, the return value is equal to the number of entries between the Start position and the last rising position iStep.

```
int NofDown (NofGV, Start, Histo)
int NofGV, Start;
int * Histo;
{
   int  i,iStep;

   if (Histo[Start] <= Histo[Start+1])  return (0);
   iStep = Start;
   for (i=Start; i<NofGV-1; i++)
      if (Histo[i] > Histo[i+1])
         iStep = i;
      else
         if (Histo[i] < Histo[i+1]) break;
   return (iStep-Start);
}
```

Figure 5.14 C realization of the detector for falling histogram entries.

The procedure NofDown is similar to NofUp, except that it detects falling histogram entries (Figure 5.14). As already described, the above two procedures will be used in LocMin (Figure 5.15) whose formal parameters are:

ImSize: image size
NofGV: highest graylevel to be processed
MinDown: minimum number of falling histogram entries to be regarded as significant of a descending histogram
MinUp: minimum number of rising histogram entries to be regarded as significant of a rising histogram
Histo: histogram array
Thres: array which collects the indices of the histogram valleys

The procedure returns the number of valleys.

The first step of the procedure is allocating memory for the first element of the array Thres. This first element corresponds to the graylevel 0, which is defined as the lowest threshold. The succeeding procedure will profit from this arrangement. Index i counts the number of histogram valleys.

The example shown in Figure 5.16 illustrates the behavior of LocMin. Starting with the current value of index d, NofDown calculates the number of falling histogram entries Down. If this number is less than a user-defined minimum MinDown, d will be incremented and the search proceeds. Otherwise, NofUp calculates the number of rising histogram entries Up, beginning with d+Down. The search for rising entries stops if at least MinUp of such entries are found. Thus, we have 'walked' through a significant histogram valley. The indices of the peaks to the left and to the right of this valley are located at the current values of d and u+Up.

```
int LocMin (ImSize, NofGV, MinDown, MinUp, Histo, Thres)
int ImSize, NofGV, MinDown, MinUp;
int * Histo;
int * Thres;
{
    int  i, r,c, d,u, Down, Up;

    GetMem (Thres);
    Thres[0] = 0;
    i=1;
    for (d=0; d<NofGV; d++) {
        Down = NofDown (NofGV, d, Histo);
        if (Down>=MinDown) {
            for (u=d+Down; u<NofGV; u++) {
                Up = NofUp (NofGV, u, Histo);
                if (Up>=MinUp) {
                    GetMem (Thres);
                    Thres[i] = d+Down + (u-d-Down)/2;
                    i++;
                    d = u+Up;   /*<<<<<<<<< attention: loop counter */
                    break;
    } } } }
    GetMem (Thres);
    Thres[i] = NofGV-1;
    return (i);
}
```

Figure 5.15 C realization of the detection of local minima (valleys) in a histogram. Procedure GetMem is defined in Appendix B.

It seems reasonable to place the threshold exactly in the middle between the two peaks. However, if, for instance, the left peak slopes gently in the direction of the right peak, then this placement would be unfavorable. It seems better to place the threshold in the valley between the positions d+Down and u. Having found this new threshold, index d is forwarded to the right peak u+Up. Here, the search for a new valley starts. The search ends when the right edge NofGV-1 of the histogram is encountered. As the maximum graylevel, NofGV-1 is defined as being the last and highest threshold and is added to Thres. The procedure ends by returning the number of thresholds stored in Thres.

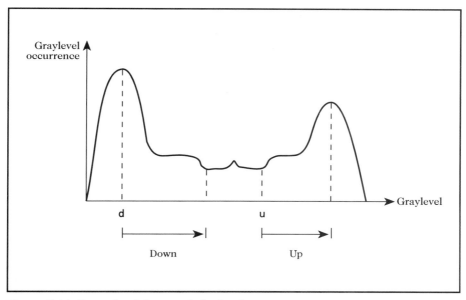

Figure 5.16 Example of the search for local minima.

In order to apply the thresholds to the source image, the procedure ThresIm is used (Figure 5.17). Formal parameters are:

ImSize:	image size
n:	number of thresholds
Thres:	array, which contains the thresholds
ThresIm:	image the thresholds are applied to. Since this is a pixel operation, input and output image are identical.

The threshold operation is fairly simple: for each pixel ThresIm[r][c] we must check, between which thresholds Thres[i] and Thres[i+1] its graylevel lies. The index of the lower threshold is taken as a new graylevel. In order to distinguish between the original graylevel and this new one, it is called a *label* (Section 5.1).

As described in Section 5.2, the 'raw' label images may be noisy at the borders between neighboring label regions. Typically, tiny 'islands' of 'foreign' labels between two desired 'principal' regions are found. Furthermore, the borders of desired regions may be frayed. Morphological image processing offers appropriate tools to remove these distortions. Chapter 8 is devoted to this subject. In the context of label images, a binary erosion and a binary dilation are needed. However, one detail must be added to the original procedures (shown in Figure 8.12): since there are usually more than background and one label in the label image (this would be a binary image), the morphological operations must be applied to each label separately. The variations of the original procedures are shown in Figure 5.18 and Figure 5.19.

```
void ThresIm (ImSize, n, Thres, ThresIm)
int  ImSize, n;
int  * Thres;
BYTE ** ThresIm;
{
   int  i,r,c, gv;

   for (r=0; r<ImSize; r++)
      for (c=0; c<ImSize; c++)
         for (i=0; i<n-1; i++) {
            gv = (int)ThresIm[r][c];
            if (Thres[i]<gv && gv<=Thres[i+1]) {
               ThresIm[r][c] = (BYTE)i;
               break;
}                                }  }
```

Figure 5.17 C realization of a threshold operation.

```
void EroThres (ImSize, Thres, StrEl, InIm, OutIm)
int      ImSize;
int      *Thres;
StrTypB  *StrEl;
BYTE     **InIm;
BYTE     **OutIm;
{
   int  r,c, y,x, i,j, dummy;
   int  NofThres=Thres[0]-1;

   for (r=0; r<ImSize; r++)
      for (c=0; c<ImSize; c++)  OutIm [r][c] = 0;

   for (j=1; j<NofThres; j++) {
      for (r=0; r<ImSize; r++) {
         for (c=0; c<ImSize; c++) {
            for (i=1; i<=StrEl[0].r; i++) {
               y = r + StrEl[i].r;
               x = c + StrEl[i].c;
               if (y>=0 && x>=0 && y<ImSize && x<ImSize)
                  if (InIm [y][x] != (BYTE)j)  goto Failed;
            }
            OutIm [r][c] = (BYTE)j;
Failed:     dummy = 0;
}  }  }  }
```

Figure 5.18 C realization of an erosion used to 'clean' a label image. Type
StrTypB is defined in Appendix B.

```
void DilThres (ImSize, Thres, StrEl, InIm, OutIm)
int      ImSize;
int      *Thres;
StrTypB *StrEl;
BYTE     **InIm;
BYTE     **OutIm;
{
    int   r,c, y,x, i,j, th, dummy;
    int   NofThres=Thres[0]-1;

    for (r=0; r<ImSize; r++)
        for (c=0; c<ImSize; c++)  OutIm [r][c] = 0;

    for (j=1; j<NofThres[0]; j++) {
        for (r=0; r<ImSize; r++) {
            for (c=0; c<ImSize; c++) {
                for (i=1; i<=StrEl[0].r; i++) {
                    y = r - StrEl[i].r;
                    x = c - StrEl[i].c;
                    if (y>=0 && x>=0 && y<ImSize && x<ImSize) {
                        if (InIm [y][x] == (BYTE)j) {
                            OutIm [r][c] = (BYTE)j;
                            break;
} } } } } } }
```

Figure 5.19 C realization of a dilation used to 'clean' a label image. Type StrTypB is defined in Appendix B.

5.3.2 Connectivity analysis

Figure 5.20 illustrates a simple procedure which realizes the connectivity analysis. It is known as 'blob coloring' [5.1]. The input to this procedure is the label image. The results are represented by a mark image. The operator is realized by two L-shaped masks which are shown in Figure 5.20a. We need one specimen for the label image and another for the mark image. Both masks work always on the same position in their respective 'host images'. The mask elements are named L (Left), U (Up) and C (Center, the current pixel). The asterisk indicates the corresponding elements in the mark image.

The structure of the procedure is shown in Figure 5.20b. After initializing the variable Mark, each pixel C of the label image is tested for being part of the background. This scanning routine starts at the top left corner of the label image and stops at the bottom right corner. If C does not belong to the background, the procedure has to decide on one of the following four cases (see also the example in Figure 5.20c and the C realization shown in Figure 5.23):

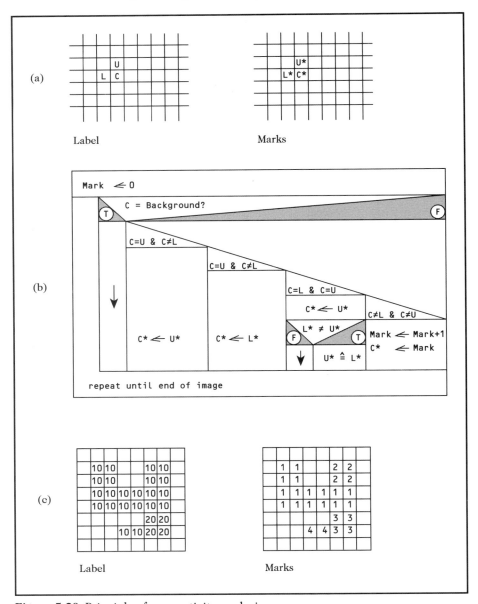

Figure 5.20 Principle of connectivity analysis.

- **C=U & C≠L**: the label of the current pixel C is identical to that of the pixel above. Thus, the corresponding mark U* is assigned to the current pixel C*.

- **C=L & C≠U**: the label of the current pixel C is identical to that of the left pixel. Consequently, the mark L* is assigned to the current pixel C*.

- **C=L & C=U**: if all of the three labels are identical, any of the two marks U^* and L^* may be assigned to the current pixel C^*. We use L^*. Although the *three* labels are identical, this may not apply to the marks U^* and L^*. An example of this is shown in Figure 5.20c. The solution of this problem requires an *equivalence list*, storing the information that the different marks U^* and L^* are actually identical.

- **C≠L & C≠U**: a current pixel C, which is not identical to any of its neighbors, indicates the appearance of a new region. Thus, the current pixel C^* receives a new mark. A new mark is obtained simply by incrementing the old value of `Mark`.

The handling of the equivalence list is a little tricky. Some important details must be taken into account. The data structure of the equivalence list is simple. It is an array whose index is realized by one of the equivalent marks. The other mark is the corresponding array entry (Figure 5.23). But what about marks which are free of any equivalence? Such a situation may result in undefined array entries. To avoid this, the equivalence list should be initialized in an appropriate way. Using a new mark as index *and* entry of the array is recommended here (`EquLst[Mark] = Mark` in Figure 5.23). Thus, during the later analysis of the equivalence list, a pair consisting of an identical index and entry indicates that the corresponding mark is free of any equivalence.

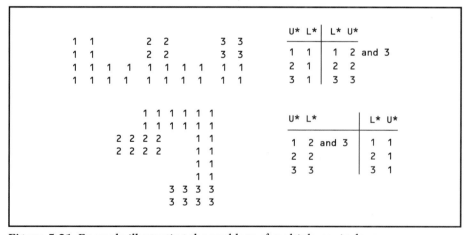

Figure 5.21 Example illustrating the problem of multiple equivalences.

Figure 5.21 shows two examples of the equivalence problem. Let us start with the top one: due to the W-shaped region, the blob coloring procedure extracts three different marks. On the right, two possible equivalence lists are shown. The first version (U^* is the array index) creates no difficulties. However, the other version (L^* represents the array index) leads to two entries in the case of mark '1'. Since the equivalence list is a simple one-dimensional array, it is only able to store one entry. Thus, the second entry ('3') eliminates the first one ('2'). Unfortunately, choosing the first version of the list does not solve the problem. The second example of blob coloring illustrates the problem of multiple equivalences the other way round. Thus, the realization of equivalence lists by simple arrays seems to be wrong. It is not: the short recursive procedure shown in Figure 5.22 solves the problem. Formal parameters are:

```
List:  equivalence list
i:     entry which has to be checked
```

```
int LastMark (List, i)
int *List;
int i;
{
   if (i==List[i])  return (i);
             else   return (LastMark (List, List[i]));
}
```

Figure 5.22 C realization which removes multiple equivalences.

The procedure returns the mark whose index and entry are identical. The idea of the procedure is based on the following considerations:

(a) If a mark a is equivalent to other marks $b, c, ...$, the marks $b, c, ...$ are also equivalent to each other. Thus, only one of the marks $b, c, ...$ is needed to describe the equivalence with a, provided (and this is essential) the equivalence between the remaining marks is expressed by the list.

(b) The above mentioned provision means that the list contains chains of equivalent marks. Realizing this idea in the context of the example shown in Figure 5.21, index '1' would have the entry '2', mark '3' would be assigned to index '2' and, finally, index '3' obtains mark '3', indicating the end of the chain.

(c) The entry of a new mark is to be put into the array element with an index which is identical to this new mark. According to (b), such an index is positioned at the end of an equivalence chain.

(d) The direct entry into the list of a pair of equivalent marks is not allowed. Before this can be done, the end of the chain within which each mark appears, has to be found. Instead of the original equivalent marks, these 'end of chain marks' serve as index and entry of the equivalence list.

```
int ConCom (ImSize, MaxMark, InIm, MarkIm, EquLst)
int   ImSize, MaxMark;
BYTE ** InIm;
int   ** MarkIm;
int   * EquLst;
{
    int   r,c, yu,xu,yc,xc,yl,xl, U,C,L, Mark, Um,Lm;

    for (r=0; r<ImSize; r++)
        for (c=0; c<ImSize; c++)  MarkIm[r][c] = 0;

    for (r=0; r<ImSize; r++) InIm[r][0] = 0;
    for (c=0; c<ImSize; c++) InIm[0][c] = 0;
    for (r=0; r<ImSize; r++) InIm[r][ImSize-1] = 0;
    for (c=0; c<ImSize; c++) InIm[ImSize-1][c] = 0;

    Mark = 0;
    GetMem (EquLst);
    EquLst[Mark] = Mark;
    for (r=1; r<ImSize-1; r++) {
        for (c=1; c<ImSize-1; c++) {
            yu = r-1;  xu = c;
            yc = r;    xc = c;
            yl = r;    xl = c-1;
            U = (int) InIm [yu][xu];
            C = (int) InIm [yc][xc];
            L = (int) InIm [yl][xl];
            if (C) {
                if (C==U && C!=L) {
                    MarkIm [yc][xc] = MarkIm [yu][xu];
                }else{
                    if (C==L && C!=U) {
                        MarkIm [yc][xc] = MarkIm [yl][xl];
                    }else{
                        if (C==L && C==U) {
                            Lm = MarkIm [yl][xl];
                            Um = MarkIm [yu][xu];
                            MarkIm [yc][xc] = Lm;
                            if (Lm!=Um) {
                                Lm = LastMark (EquLst, Lm);
                                Um = LastMark (EquLst, Um);
                                EquLst [Lm] = Um;
                            }
                        }else{ /*(!L && !U)*/
                            Mark++;
                            MarkIm [yc][xc] = Mark;
                            GetMem (EquLst);
                            EquLst[Mark] = Mark;
    } } } } } }
Leave:
    return (Mark);
}
```

Figure 5.23 C realization of connectivity analysis. Procedure `GetMem` is defined in Appendix B.

The search for these 'end of chain marks' is performed by the procedure LastMark. The application of this procedure in the context of blob coloring is shown in Figure 5.23. ConCom realizes the approach illustrated in Figure 5.20. Formal parameters are:

ImSize:	image size
MaxMark:	maximum number of marks
InIm:	label image on which the connectivity analysis is to be carried out
MarkIm:	mark image
EquLst:	equivalence list

The procedure starts by initializing the mark image MarkIm. Additionally, the blob coloring procedure requires a label image InIm with a border which is free of labels. The width of this border should be one pixel. The next step initializes the variable Mark with zero and allocates memory for the first element of the equivalence list EquLst.

The kernel of the procedure is as usual framed by two for loops. The coordinates of the L-shaped masks are yu, xu, yc, xc, yl and xl. They are indices which point to the labels U, C and L. Label zero is interpreted as background. If the current label C belongs to the background, no further processing is necessary. Otherwise, the connectivity analysis proceeds according to Figure 5.20b, considering the equivalence problems. The procedure returns the number of marks in MarkIm.

5.3.2.1 Enhancement of equivalence list

The equivalence list connects two marks. However, usually more than two marks are equivalent. This leads to an equivalence chain which has already been discussed in the context of the procedure ConCom. A typical example of the equivalence problem is shown in Figure 5.24. i is the index of the equivalence list, representing the marks from '1' to '14'. The equivalent marks are positioned on the right of the indices (EquLst). For instance, the marks '1' and '4' are equivalent. Mark '4' is again equivalent to mark '5', which itself is equivalent to '2'. Thus, equivalence applies to all of the marks '1', '2', '4' and '5'.

It is the purpose of the enhancement procedure to replace different, but equivalent marks by only one 'new' mark. Assume that '1' is the new mark in the example. Then the indices '1', '2', '4' and '5' of the new list NewLst, yield the entry '1'. The next index to work on is '3'. This mark is not equivalent to any other mark. Thus, only the 'old' mark '3' is replaced by the 'new' mark '2'. Index '6' is the next candidate. It is the first element of the following equivalence chain: '9', '8', '13'. Now a new situation arises: EquLst contains another mark '13' whose index is '10'. However, '10' is also a mark which appears in EquLst. The corresponding index is '7'.

If we return to the starting point i='13', the equivalences '11' and '12' are detected. To sum up: all the marks from '6' to '13' are equivalent and obtain the 'new' mark '3'. In the end, index '14' is left. It is replaced by the 'new' value '4'. The enhancement procedure has reduced the number of marks from 14 to 4. This example is not an extreme one, it is typical. The large number of different marks is due to the extremely local scope of the blob coloring procedure.

Although the enhancement operation seems to be rather complicated, it is realizable by a simple recursive procedure. First of all, the frame procedure of the enhancement operation is illustrated (Figure 5.26). Formal parameters are:

ImSize:	image size
n:	number of marks in MarkIm
EquLst:	list reflecting the equivalences in MarkIm
MarkIm:	mark image which has to be cleaned

The enhancement procedure already mentioned is FillEquiv. It replaces the different marks in an equivalence chain by the last mark of the chain. At the end of the filling procedure, the differences between the remaining marks in EquLst are usually greater than 1. However, according to the example shown in Figure 5.24, the marks should be represented by increments. This is realized by the procedure IncEquLst. Both procedures manipulate the original equivalence list EquLst without using a buffer list. Thus, in contrast to the example shown in Figure 5.24, the frame procedure CorrectMarks does not need a NewLst. CorrectMarks ends with the replacement of the old marks in MarkIm.

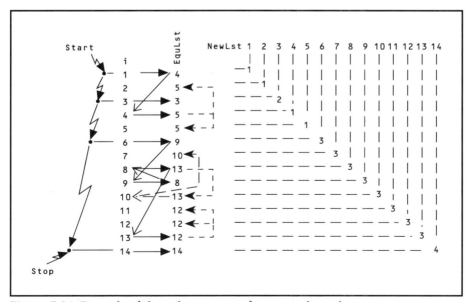

Figure 5.24 Example of the enhancement of an equivalence list.

The most important procedure of the whole enhancement process is FillEquiv (Figure 5.27). It is based on the principles of the procedure LastMark (Figure 5.22). Formal parameters are:

Lst: equivalence list
Mark: current mark

The procedure is calling itself until it encounters the end of the equivalence chain (Equ=Lst[Equ]), whose beginning is indicated by the value of Mark at the first calling. Since the recursive calling is connected with an assignment of the current return value to the current index (return (Lst[Equ] = FillEquiv (Lst, Equ))), the whole chain is filled with the return value of the last recursive calling (return (Equ)) during the backtracking process.

Mark	Equ	Lst[Equ]	
1	4	5	
4	5	5	← a
2	5	5	← b
3	3	3	← c
4	5	5	← d
5	5	5	← e
6	9	8	
9	8	13	
8	13	12	
13	12	12	← f
7	10	13	
10	13	12	
13	12	12	← g
8	12	12	← h
9	12	12	← i
10	12	12	← j
11	12	12	← k
12	12	12	← l
13	12	12	← m
14	14	14	← n

Index	Start	a	b	c	d	e	f	g	h	i	j	k	l	m	n
1	4	5													
2	5		5												
3	3			3											
4	5	5			5										
5	5					5									
6	9						12								
7	10							12							
8	13						12		12						
9	8						12			12					
10	13							12			12				
11	12											12			
12	12												12		
13	12						12	12						12	
14	14														14

Figure 5.25 Tracing the enhancement process shown in Figure 5.24.

Applying FillEquiv to the example shown in Figure 5.24, the result depicted in Figure 5.25 is obtained. The left table shows a trace of the variables during the recursive calls of FillEquiv. Starting point is mark '1'. It is equivalent to '4', which again is equivalent to '5'. This is the end of the chain. New chains start with the marks '2', '3', '5', and so on. The end of each chain is marked in the left table by small letters. The end of a chain starts the backtracking of the recursion. This process is illustrated with the aid of the right-hand table. The columns *Index* and *Start* represent the original equivalence list. For each recursion end from *a* to *n*, the new mark is noted. This new mark replaces the old mark of an equivalence chain during backtracking.

Finally, the marks '3', '5', '12' and '14' 'survive'. The desired incremental representation of these new marks is performed by the procedure IncEquLst (Figure 5.28). Formal parameters are:

n: number of marks
Lst: equivalence list

The new representatives of the marks are generated with the aid of the variable New. Initially, the values of New are negative and replace the old entries of the equivalence list. The negative sign serves as an indicator for entries which have already been replaced. At the end of IncEquLst, the negative signs are removed. Now, the enhanced equivalence list is available for further processing.

```
void CorrectMarks (ImSize, n, EquLst, MarkIm)
int ImSize, n;
int *EquLst;
int ** MarkIm;
{
    int  i,r,c;

    for (i=1; i<=n; i++)
       EquLst[i] = FillEquiv (EquLst, i);

    IncEquLst (n, EquLst);

    for (r=0; r<ImSize; r++)
       for (c=0; c<ImSize; c++)
          if (MarkIm[r][c])
             MarkIm[r][c] = EquLst [MarkIm[r][c]];
}
```

Figure 5.26 C realization of the recursive enhancement of equivalence lists: the frame procedure.

```
int FillEquiv (Lst, Mark)
int *Lst;
int Mark;
{
    int  Equ;
    Equ = Lst [Mark];
    if (Equ==Lst[Equ])  return (Equ);
                  else  return (Lst[Equ] = FillEquiv (Lst, Equ));
}
```

Figure 5.27 C realization of the recursive enhancement of equivalence lists: the filling procedure.

```
void IncEquLst (n, Lst)
int n;
int *Lst;
{
    int i,j, Old, New;

    New = -1;
    for (i=1; i<n; i++) {
        Old = Lst[i];
        if (Old >= 0) {
            for (j=i; j<n; j++)
                if (Lst[j]==Old)  Lst[j] = New;
            New--;
    }  }

    for (i=1; i<n; i++)  Lst[i] = abs (Lst[i]);
}
```

Figure 5.28 C realization of the recursive enhancement of equivalence lists: the cleaning procedure.

5.3.3 Feature Extraction

Figure 5.29 shows a procedure which extracts the features *area, center of gravity, perimeter, polar distance* and *compactness*. Formal parameters are:

```
ImSize:  image size
M:       number of marks in MarkIm
MarkIm:  mark image
RegIm:   image which stores the region under consideration
OutlIm:  image which stores the outline of the region under consideration
```

It is the purpose of this procedure to store that region in the image RegIm which corresponds to the current mark m in order to extract the features of this region. Except for compactness, each feature requires a special procedure. The filling of RegIm is performed with the aid of the procedure LoadRegIm (Figure 5.30). Formal parameters are:

```
m:       current mark
ImSize:  image size
MarkIm:  mark image
RegIm:   image which stores the region under consideration
```

```
void Features (ImSize, M, MarkIm, RegIm, OutlIm)
int  ImSize, M;
BYTE ** MarkIm;
BYTE ** RegIm;
BYTE ** OutlIm;
{
    int    r,c, m, Area, Peri;
    float  Com;
    CGTyp  CenGra;
    PolTyp Pol;

    for (m=1; m<=M; m++) {
        LoadRegIm (m, ImSize, MarkIm, RegIm);
        Area   = CountPixel (ImSize, RegIm);
        CenGra = CentOfGrav (Area, ImSize, RegIm);
        Peri   = GenOutLine (ImSize, RegIm, OutlIm);
        Pol    = PolarCheck (ImSize, CenGra, OutlIm);
        Com    = (float) (Peri*Peri) / (12.56*Area);
} }
```

Figure 5.29 C realization of feature extraction. Data types `CGTyp` and `PolTyp` are defined in Appendix B.

```
void LoadRegIm (m, ImSize, MarkIm, RegIm)
int  m,ImSize;
BYTE ** MarkIm;
BYTE ** RegIm;
{
    int  r,c;
    for (r=0; r<ImSize; r++)
        for (c=0; c<ImSize; c++)
            if ((int)MarkIm[r][c] == m)  RegIm [r][c] = 1;
                                   else  RegIm [r][c] = 0;
}
```

Figure 5.30 C realization of the determination of the current region.

The procedure is simple and self-explanatory. A typical region feature is *area*. In order to be independent of a particular scale, we use the number of pixels measured.

The procedure `CountPixel`, which is shown in Figure 5.31, calculates the number of pixels. Formal parameters are:

`ImSize:`   image size
`RegIm:`   image which stores the region under consideration

```
int CountPixel (ImSize, RegIm)
int  ImSize;
BYTE ** RegIm;
{
    int  r,c,n;
    n=0;
    for (r=0; r<ImSize; r++)
        for (c=0; c<ImSize; c++)
            if (RegIm[r][c])  n++;
    return(n);
}
```

Figure 5.31 C realization of the calculation of area.

The procedure returns the number of pixels of the region under consideration. Like the preceding one, the current procedure is simple and self-explanatory. The center of gravity of a region is important in localizing this region. The center coordinates are:

$$r_G = \tfrac{1}{N} \sum_{r=0}^{R-1} \sum_{c=0}^{C-1} r f (r,c)$$

$$c_G = \tfrac{1}{N} \sum_{r=0}^{R-1} \sum_{c=0}^{C-1} c f (r,c)$$

r and c are the coordinates of the image, while R and C indicate the number of rows and columns. N represents the number of pixels of the region. $f(r,c)$ is the image function. It yields 1 if the current pixel (r,c) belongs to the region. Otherwise we obtain 0. Figure 5.32 shows the procedure `CentOfGrav` which calculates the center of gravity. Formal parameters are:

n: number of pixels in the region
ImSize: image size
RegIm: image which stores the region under consideration

The procedure returns the coordinates of the center of gravity. It is self-explanatory. The shape of a region is determined by its outline. `GenOutLine` extracts this feature. (Figure 5.33). Formal parameters are:

ImSize: image size
RegIm: image which stores the region under consideration
OutlIm: image which stores the outline of the region under consideration

```
CGTyp CentOfGrav (n, ImSize, RegIm)
int n, ImSize;
BYTE ** RegIm;
{
  int r,c;
  CGTyp CenGra;
  long yc,xc;
  yc=0;
  xc=0;
  for (r=0; r<ImSize; r++)
   for (c=0; c<ImSize; c++)
     if (RegIm[r][c]) {
       yc += r;
       xc += c;
       }
  CenGra.r = (int) (yc/n);
  CenGra.c = (int) (xc/n);
  return (CenGra);
}
```

Figure 5.32 C realization of the calculation of center of gravity. Data type CGTyp is defined in Appendix B.

```
int GenOutLine (ImSize, RegIm, OutlIm)
int  ImSize;
BYTE ** RegIm;
BYTE ** OutlIm;
{
    int  r,c,n;

    for (r=0; r<ImSize; r++)
       for (c=0; c<ImSize; c++)  OutlIm [r][c] = 0;

    for (r=1; r<ImSize; r++)
       for (c=1; c<ImSize; c++)
          if (!RegIm [r][c-1] && RegIm [r][c])  OutlIm [r][c] = 1; else
          if (RegIm [r][c-1] && !RegIm [r][c])  OutlIm [r][c-1] = 1;

    for (r=1; r<ImSize; r++)
       for (c=1; c<ImSize; c++)
          if (!RegIm [r-1][c] && RegIm [r][c])  OutlIm [r][c] = 1; else
          if (RegIm [r-1][c] && !RegIm [r][c])  OutlIm [r-1][c] = 1;

    n=0;
    for (r=0; r<ImSize; r++)
       for (c=0; c<ImSize; c++)
          if (OutlIm[r][c])  n++;

    return(n);
}
```

Figure 5.33 C realization of the outline extraction.

The procedure returns the number of outline pixels. It starts by initializing OutlIm and ends by counting the outline pixels. The kernel of the procedure determines the vertical and horizontal shares of the outline. A pixel belongs to the region outline if one of two neighboring pixels (vertical or horizontal) belongs to the background, while the other is part of the region.

A simple method of describing the shape is offered by the minimum and maximum polar distances. These features are extracted by the procedure PolarCheck (Figure 5.34). Formal parameters are:

---

n: number of outline pixels
ImSize: image size
CenGra: center of gravity
OutlIm: image which stores the outline of the region under consideration

---

The procedure returns the minimum and maximum polar distances relative to the mean distance. The polar distance is calculated with the aid of the Euclidean distance d = (int) sqrt ((float)dy* dy + dx*dx).

```
PolTyp PolarCheck (n, ImSize, CenGra, OutlIm)
int   n, ImSize;
CGTyp CenGra;
BYTE  ** OutlIm;
{
    int    r,c, d,dy,dx, Min,Max;
    long   Mean;
    PolTyp Pol;

    Min = 2*ImSize;
    Max = 0;
    Mean = 0;
    for (r=0; r<ImSize; r++)
       for (c=0; c<ImSize; c++)
          if (OutlIm[r][c]) {
             dy = CenGra.r - r;
             dx = CenGra.c - c;
             d = (int) sqrt ((float)dy*dy + dx*dx);
             if (d<Min)
                Min = d;
             else if (d>Max)
                Max = d;
             Mean += d;
          }
    Mean /= n;
    Pol.Min = (float) Min/Mean;
    Pol.Max = (float) Max/Mean;
    return (Pol);
}
```

Figure 5.34 C realization of the calculation of polar distances. Data types CGTyp and PolTyp are defined in Appendix B.

5.4   Supplement

A fundamental problem of region-oriented segmentation procedures is their sensitivity to unusual region shapes. Difficulties are typically caused by regions containing holes, overlapping areas and spiral areas. In order to 'toughen' the basic procedures (described in the preceding section) against such cases, they must be adequately modified. The specific modification depends very much on the problem which has been encountered. Such special cases are not a subject of this book. Thus, the following sections offer only some general tips for further work.

5.4.1 Thresholding

The binarization of graylevel images with the aid of thresholds is the most popular method of segmentation. This applies especially to industrial image processing. A thorough survey of this subject is offered by Sahoo, Soltani and Wong [5.11]. Some interesting alternatives to thresholding (for example, region growing and split-and-merge approaches) are presented by Rosenfeld/ Kak [5.10], Horn [5.2], Young et al. [5.13].

In the following section, a few variations to the threshold approach are outlined. The idea of positioning the thresholds in the histogram valleys is derived from efforts to maximize the number of pixels with graylevels which lie between two thresholds. A more sophisticated approach from Kohler [5.6] includes the contrast information: the optimum threshold yields more contours of high contrast and fewer contours of low contrast than any other threshold. Kohler finds this optimum threshold with the aid of a special contrast histogram.

Otsu [5.7] uses normal graylevel histograms. Based on them, he obtains simple statistical measures from which the threshold can be extracted. An appropriate measurement is the entropy of the graylevel histogram. Many authors describe threshold procedures based on entropy (for example, [5.8] [5.9] [5.5] [5.4]). Tsai [5.12] interprets a graylevel image as an ideal binary image. Accordingly Tsai claims that a threshold should be found which yields a binary image, whose first three moments equal the moments of the graylevel image.

These variations of threshold procedures offer interesting approaches. However, regarding practical applications, the following points should be considered:

- A lot of procedures are designed for the optimum positioning of only one threshold. Usually, it is no problem to adapt them to a search for multiple thresholds.

- Threshold procedures do not 'know' anything about the contents of the image. Thus, they only work satisfactorily if it is guaranteed that meaningful regions are represented by similar graylevels, in which case, a region is represented in the histogram by a peak. Note that the image of a chessboard yields the same histogram as an image which contains one white and one black region of identical size.

5.4.2   Connectivity analysis

The procedures described in Section 5.3.2 represent only one possible realization of connectivity analysis. The variations of these procedures depend on the application being considered and also on constraints such as the necessity of a hardware realization. The following two points outline refinements of general interest:

- The first variation concerns the L-shaped masks shown in Figure 5.20. They find connected labels based on a 4-connected neighborhood (Section 6.1.2, Figure 6.11). This approach is simple and clearly arranged. However, Horn points out that problems with line-shaped label regions may arise [5.2]. To solve these problems, he proposes a mask which is based on a 6-connected neighborhood. In practice, such problems are not of importance, since line-shaped regions do not often appear. Users who want to be on the safe side should use the Horn approach.

- The representation of regions by the coordinates of the corresponding pixels is straightforward, but requires unnecessary memory. A more sophisticated approach is based on those image rows which belong to a region. When stepping (from left to right) along one of these rows, sooner or later the left border of the region is encountered, the region is crossed and finally the right border is found. The column indices of the left and right border represent the region completely and in a very memory-efficient way. Furthermore, this procedure allows an efficient solution of the equivalence problem. A detailed description of the entire approach can be found in [5.10].

5.4.3   Feature extraction

The region features described in Section 5.1.3 are only a few of the large spectrum of possible features whose choice depends on the application. Thus, the following points only mention a few generally applicable features:

- **Eccentricity** is the ratio of the maximum and the minimum polar distances.

- **Orientation** is the angle between the axis of the first moment of inertia and the coordinate system.

- **Bounding** rectangle is the rectangle with minimum area, which completely surrounds the region. It is easily calculated with the aid of orientation.

- **Symmetry** in different variations.

These and other features are described by many authors. Two examples are [5.1] and [5.3].

5.5 Exercises

5.1 Apply a threshold of 2.5 and 8.5 to the source image shown in Figure 5.2. Compare the results.

5.2 Apply an average operation over 3 entries to the histogram shown in Figure 5.4, take the thresholds from this manipulated histogram and apply them to the source image shown in Figure 5.3.

5.3 Segment the source image shown in Figure 5.35 using the thresholds 8, 13 and 17 and apply a connectivity analysis to the label image.

20	20	15	10	10	12	15	15
20	20	15	10	10	12	15	15
20	20	15	10	10	12	15	15
15	15	15	10	10	12	15	15
10	10	10	10	10	12	15	15
10	10	10	10	12	15	15	15
5	5	5	5	7	15	12	12
1	1	1	1	7	15	12	12

Figure 5.35
This is the source image used in Exercise 5.3.

5.4 Write a program which computes and applies thresholds locally.

5.5 Write a program which computes a contrast histogram as described in Section 5.4.1.

5.6 Acquire workpiece images and write a program which measures them. Implement calibration mechanisms.

5.7 Write a program which realizes a connectivity analysis that fills label regions with a mark and avoids the necessity of an equivalence list.

5.8   Write a program which determines the features eccentricity, orientation and bounding rectangle.

5.9   Acquire workpiece images and write a program which determines their position and orientation relative to the origin of the image.

5.10   Become familiar with every region operation offered by Ad Oculos (Ad Oculos Help).

5.6   References

[5.1]   Ballard, D.H.; Brown, C.M.: *Computer vision.* Englewood Cliffs: Prentice-Hall 1982

[5.2]   Horn, B.K.P.: *Robot vision.* Cambridge, London: MIT Press 1986

[5.3]   Jain, A.K.: *Fundamentals of digital image processing.* Englewood Cliffs: Prentice-Hall 1989

[5.4]   Johannsen, G.; Bille, J.: A threshold selection method using information measures. Proceedings, *6th Int. Conf. Pattern Recognition*, Munich, Germany, (1982) 140-143

[5.5]   Kapur, J.N.; Sahoo, P.K. and Wong A.K.C.: A new method for gray-level picture thresholding using the entropy of the histogram. *Computer Vision Graphics Image Processing 29*, (1985) 273-285

[5.6]   Kohler, R.: A segmentation system based on thresholding. *Computer Vision Graphics Image Processing 15*, (1981) 319-338

[5.7]   Otsu, N.: A threshold selection method from gray-level histograms. *IEEE Trans. Systems, Man Cybernet. SMC-8*, (1978) 62-66

[5.8]   Pun, T.: A new method for gray-level picture thresholding using the entropy of the histogram. *Signal Processing 2*, (1980) 223-237

[5.9]   Pun, T.: Entropic thresholding: A new approach. *Computer Vision Graphics Image Processing 16*, (1981) 210-239

[5.10] Rosenfeld, A. and Kak, A.C.: *Digital picture processing.* Orlando: Academic Press 1982

[5.11] Sahoo, P.K.; Soltani, S.; Wong, A.K.C.: A survey of thresholding techniques. *Computer Vision Graphics Image Processing 41*, (1988) 233-260

[5.12] Tsai, W.: Moment-preserving thresholding: A new approach. *Computer Vision Graphics Image Processing 29*, (1985) 377-393

[5.13] Young, T.Y.; Fu, K.S. (Eds.): *Handbook of pattern recognition and image processing.* New York: Academic Press 1986

6

Contour-oriented segmentation

6.1   Foundations

The requirements for understanding this chapter are:

- to be familiar with terms such as derivative, gradient and convolution,

- to have read Chapter 1 (Introduction), Section 3.1.2 (Emphasizing gray-level differences) and the beginning of Section 5.1 (Foundations; the discussion of the basics of segmentation).

As already discussed in Section 5.1, common segmentation procedures are based on graylevel differences within the source image. This is also valid for contour-oriented segmentation. Thus, this form of segmentation starts by emphasizing graylevel differences (Figure 6.1) and is typically performed by a gradient operation, as discussed in Section 3.1.2. Changing the Cartesian representation of the gradient operator into a polar representation yields the magnitude and direction of the maximum graylevel change. In order to obtain a more illustrative representation, the gradient direction is rotated by 90°, because the direction is then aligned with the direction of the contour. In this book the direction of a contour is defined so that the higher graylevels are at the right-hand side of the contour.

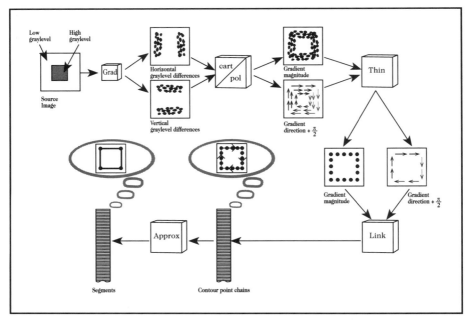

Figure 6.1 The aim of contour segmentation is to describe the borders of image regions by means of only a few segments. This means firstly a huge data reduction and secondly the possibility of a high-level description of the region borders.

The gradient operator 'smears' the contour due to its low-pass filter effect. To enhance the contour, a thinning procedure is applied which leaves a gradient image with lines which are only one pixel wide.

A linking procedure collects connected contour points forming a line (like the pearls of a necklace). Thus, linking contour points is the realization of the connectivity analysis in the context of contour-oriented segmentation, just as blob coloring is the realization in the context of region-oriented segmentation (Section 5.1.2). The linking procedure provides lists containing the coordinates of connected contour points.

In the last step, the contour represented by contour point chains is approximated by segments. Thus, the result of the whole process of contour segmentation is a list of segments represented by the coordinates of their terminating points. The advantages of contour segmentation are:

- Comparing the enormous number of pixels of the source image with the few coordinates of the segment list shows that a considerable data reduction has been achieved.

- A *structural description* of the contour of image regions is obtained. Thus, we are able to describe contours in abstract terms such as 'these segments are parallel'.

6.1.1   Detection of contour points

The first step towards the detection of contour points is the enhancement of graylevel differences in a source image. There are many methods available to achieve this end. In practice, however, the gradient operation is widely used, because it is simple and robust. A gradient operator yields the magnitude of graylevel differences as well as the direction of the highest graylevel difference (Figure 6.2). Although most authors emphasize the representation of the gradient magnitude, the gradient direction is in fact more important. This realization forms the focus of the following sections.

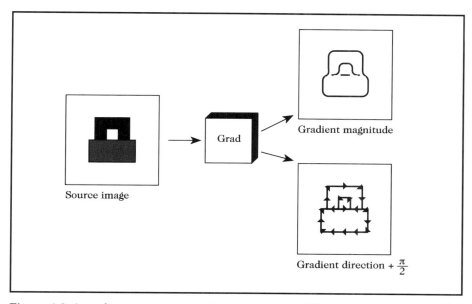

Figure 6.2 A gradient operation emphasizes graylevel differences since it yields, for every pixel, the magnitude and direction of the maximum graylevel change. To obtain a more illustrative representation, the gradient direction is rotated by 90°. Then the direction is now aligned with the direction of the contour. In this book, the direction of a contour is defined so that the higher graylevels are on the right-hand side of the contour.

The following examples of gradient operations are based on the source image shown in Figure 6.3. The simplest gradient operation is realized by subtracting the graylevels of two horizontally and two vertically neighboring pixels. This is equivalent to the convolution of the source image with the masks shown in Figure 6.4. The results of this convolution (Δx and Δy), as well as its polar representation (*Magnitude* and *Direction*), are also shown in Figure 6.4.

The disadvantage of this simple operator is its sensitivity to the 'digital nature' of the graylevel transition in the source image (Figure 6.3). If the transition is interpreted as a straight border of an image region, then the gradient magnitude and direction should be equal at every pixel of the source image. To obtain the desired result, the convolution mask must be enlarged to increase its smoothing effect (Section 3.1.1).

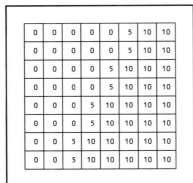

Figure 6.3
This source image is used as the basis for experiments with gradient operators.

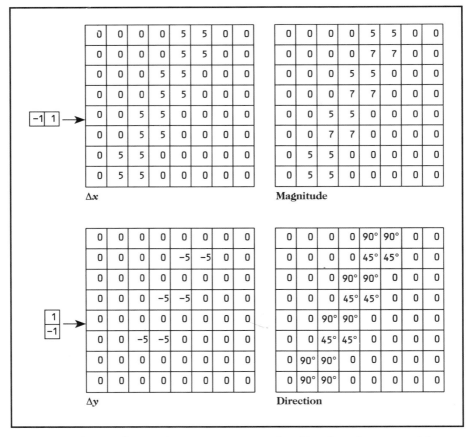

Figure 6.4 The simplest gradient operation is realized by the subtraction of the graylevels of two horizontally and two vertically neighboring pixels. Δx and Δy are the results of the convolution of the masks with the source image (Figure 6.3). *Magnitude* and *Direction* stand for the polar representation of the gradient.

Following the size of the gradient operator, the next most important parameter concerns the choice of the mask coefficients. The aim here is to approximate the ideal gradient operation as closely as possible. This objective is especially important for the gradient direction, because even small errors may have a detrimental impact on the results of successive processing steps. From this point of view, the 3*3 gradient operator should not be used. In practice, a 5*5 mask has proved to be a good compromise. Larger masks yield only marginally better results, while consuming far more computation time. If there are relatively large objects in an image, and if the image is noisy, the application of a 9*9 mask is to be recommended. The higher low-pass filter effect of this mask frequently improves the results.

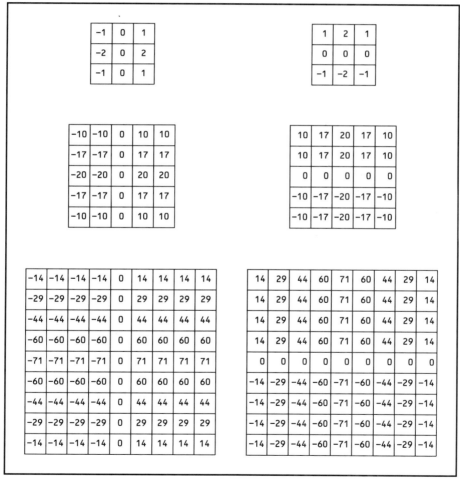

Figure 6.5 The 3*3 mask is known as the Sobel operator. The larger masks are 'inflated' Sobel masks. From a practical point of view, the 5*5 mask has proved to be a good compromise between simplicity, a good approximation of the ideal gradient operation and processing speed.

The mask coefficients are determined by some basic investigations (for example, [6.7]). Nevertheless, these approaches are based on constraints which are often not appropriate in an industrial environment. For industrial applications, the original idea of Sobel (namely, the decrease of the coefficients towards the border of the mask) is sufficient for most cases. For instance, an arched form like the positive part of a sine function proves suitable. The coefficients shown in Figure 6.5 have been chosen based on this model. The sum of the coefficients should be zero, in order to avoid shifting the local mean of the graylevels.

A lot of computation time can be saved if the coefficients are only +1 and −1, as in the examples above. However, the approximation error of the Sobel masks is smaller.

6.1.2 Contour enhancement

As a result of a gradient operation, the gradient magnitudes near a contour are often distributed in a way similar to an extended mountain ridge (Figure 6.6). The 'summit pixels' are those having *locally* the highest gradient magnitudes. These points are very likely to represent the actual location of the contour of a region. That is, the description of the contour by the 'summit pixels' should be sufficient. Sticking to the 'ridge' metaphor, this means: the slopes of the ridges on the left-hand and the right-hand side of the summit are superfluous and should be removed (non-maxima suppression). This 'thinning' of the chain of ridges eventually leaves a thin wall of width 1 pixel (Figure 6.7). In most cases, the height of this wall is irrelevant.

Figure 6.8 (*left*) shows a gradient image in polar representation. To find the local maximum magnitudes, the left-hand and the right-hand side neighbors of every gradient pixel have to be determined. However, what is considered to be left or right? The location of the neighbors is defined relative to the gradient direction of the current pixel. Therefore, four neighbor relations have to be dealt with. They are depicted in Figure 6.9. Figure 6.8 (*right*) shows the neighborhood relations and the local maxima of the current example.

In practice, non-maxima suppression should not only be based on the comparison of neighboring gradient magnitudes, but also on the comparison of the gradient directions. Since 'inside' the smeared contour, neighboring gradient directions are similar, this similarity should be checked, and irregular local maxima which are caused by noise should be removed.

Figure 6.10 shows the results of three different direction checks. Since the source image (Figure 6.8 (*left*)) represents the corner of a region, the variations of the gradient directions are comparatively high. Thus, the similarity check should permit a variation of up to ±30° to keep the contour closed.

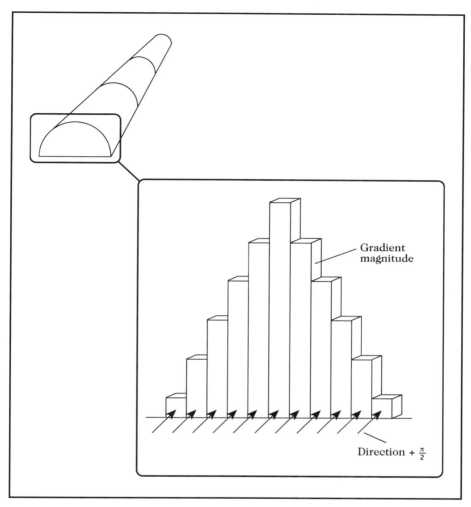

Figure 6.6 The gradient magnitudes are distributed like an extended mountain ridge. The 'summit pixels' are those having the highest local gradient magnitudes. These points are very likely to represent the actual location of a region's contour.

The thinning procedure yields contours which are indeed one pixel wide, but the contour points are 4-connected. Figure 6.11 (a) shows an example of such a chain of contour points. A 4-connected chain is only one pixel wide, if neighborhoods are only permitted in a horizontal or in a vertical orientation. However, if a diagonal neighborhood is permissible, too, the chain shown in Figure 6.11 (a) has redundant contour points which may even interfere with further processing steps such as linking (Section 6.1.3). Thus, the aim should be to obtain an 8-connected chain as shown in Figure 6.11 (b).

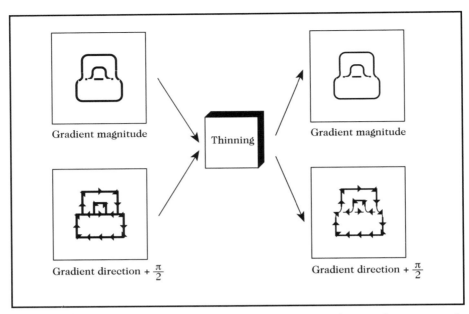

Figure 6.7 The aim of a thinning procedure is to enhance a 'smeared' contour such that lines which are only one pixel wide remain.

To transform a 4-connected chain into an 8-connected one, the masks shown in Figure 6.12 are used. The bold lines depict pixels which are part of a 4-connected chain. The current pixel of each mask corresponds to the superfluous contour point. The algorithm using these mask works directly on the pixels of the source image. Thus, this procedure constitutes an exception to the rule which requires separate images for input and output. If the algorithm (starting as usual in the top left corner of the image) encounters one of the four constellations, the current pixels of the magnitude image and of the direction image are set to 0, that is, they become part of the background. Figure 6.13 shows a simple example for the transformation of a 4-connected chain of contour points (*Start*) into an 8-connected chain (*Result*). Although the chain of contour points shown in Figure 6.14 (*Start*) is unusual, the gradient operator produces such chains under certain constraints. As the example indicates, the basic 4-to-8 transform fails in its attempt at processing these unusual chains. To be successful, the application of the 4 masks shown in Figure 6.12 has to be refined.

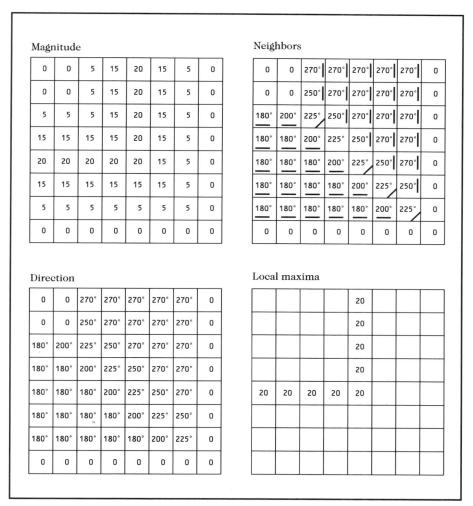

Figure 6.8 This is a simple example demonstrating the non-maxima suppression procedure.

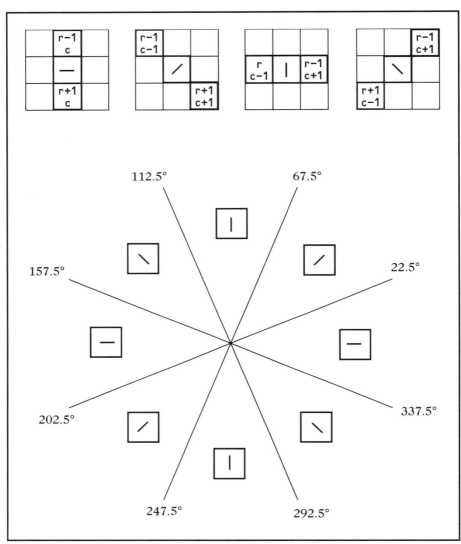

Figure 6.9 Determination of neighborhoods in the context of the non-maxima suppression. To give one example: if the gradient direction of the current pixel (r,c) is between 67.5° and 112.5° or 247.5° and 292.5°, the neighbor pixels are $(r,c-1)$ and $(r,c+1)$.

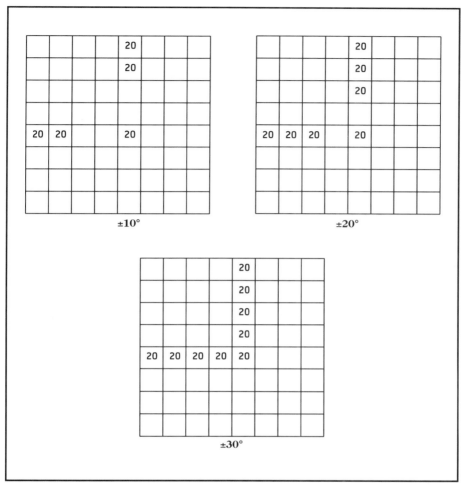

Figure 6.10 These are the results of 3 different direction checks. Since the source image shown in Figure 6.8 (*left*) represents the corner of a region, the variations of the gradient directions are comparatively high. Thus, the similarity check should permit a difference of up to ±30° to keep the contour closed.

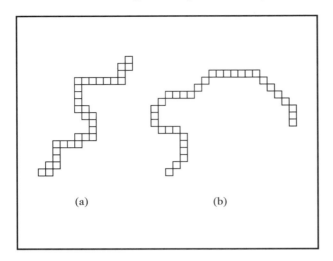

Figure 6.11
Both chains are only
one pixel wide, but the
connection of their
elements differs.
(a) shows a 4-connected
chain whose elements
permit only horizontal
or vertical orientations.
The 8-connected chain
(b) allows diagonal
neighborhoods, too.
A 4-connected chain
has redundant elements
which may disturb
further processing steps.

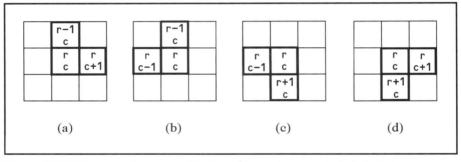

Figure 6.12 These masks are used to transform a 4-connected chain into an
8-connected one (Figure 6.11). The bold lines depict pixels which are part of a
4-connected chain. The current pixel of each mask corresponds to the superfluous
contour point.

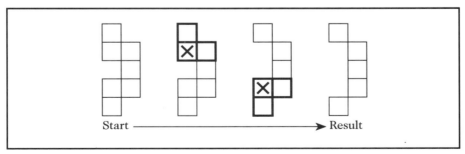

Figure 6.13 This is a simple example for the transformation of a 4-connected chain
of contour points (*Start*) into an 8-connected chain (*Result*).

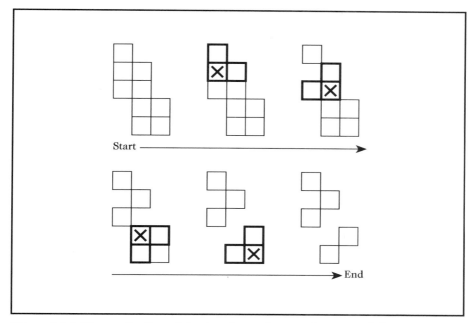

Start ⟶

⟶ End

Figure 6.14 The application of the 4-to-8 transform to the unusual (but not impossible) chain yields a broken chain.

Figure 6.15 shows the application of a mask on part of a chain. Firstly, not only the middle element of the masks has to be considered, but all three mask elements are equally and simultaneously under consideration. Secondly, two forms of neighbors have to be distinguished. A corner neighbor is an 8-connected chain element, while a border neighbor is 4-connected to the mask element currently under consideration. While border neighbors may be covered by other mask elements, corner neighbors must lay outside of the mask.

The above definitions are the basis for the new 4-to-8 algorithm, if the following conditions are met:

- the mask element under consideration has either one or two border neighbors and
- it has no corner neighbor.

Next, delete the chain element covered by the mask element under consideration.

Figure 6.16 demonstrates the application of the refined transformation to the unusual chain shown in Figure 6.14.

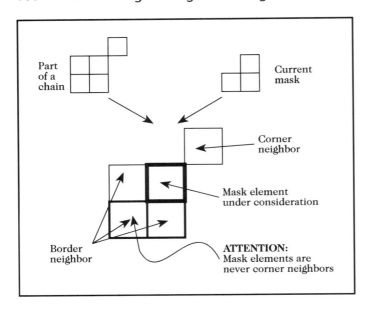

Figure 6.15
The refined application of the 4-to-8 masks is based on a more detailed consideration of the neighborhood and the connectivity of the chain and mask elements. Firstly, all the elements of the mask have to be given equal consideration. Secondly, corner neighbors and border neighbors have to be distinguished as shown in the example above.

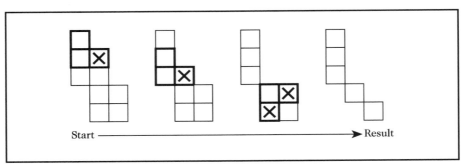

Figure 6.16 The application of the refined 4-to-8 transform to the unusual chain shown in Figure 6.14.

6.1.3   Linking contour points

Thinning the gradient images does not complete contour-oriented segmentation. If a human observer focuses on Figure 6.17, he or she will recognize three lines. In contrast, the computer only 'knows' about certain contour points. Hence, a *connectivity analysis* (Chapter 5) is required which collects connected contour points and provides lists containing their coordinates. In the case of contour segmentation, this procedure is known as contour linking.

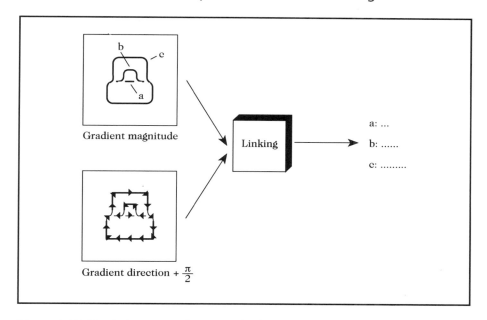

Figure 6.17 The linking procedure provides lists containing the coordinates of connected contour points.

Figure 6.18 demonstrates the search for neighboring contour points in a source image. Starting with the 'eastern' neighbor of the current contour point (marked by a cross), a search is made counterclockwise for another contour point. The first contour point which is encountered becomes the new current contour point, while the current one is kept in the current contour point list and deleted from the source image.

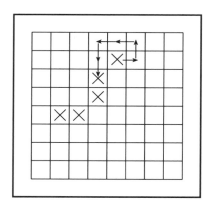

Figure 6.18
The search for neighboring contour points starts with the 'eastern' neighbor of the current contour point (marked by a cross), searching counterclockwise for another contour point. The first contour point which is encountered becomes the new current contour point, while the current one is kept in the current contour point list and deleted from the source image.

Figure 6.19 (*left-hand side*) shows two chains of contour points. The linking procedure yields two chains *a* and *b* (*right-hand side*). Note that the data structure used to represent the chains is a list. Thus, the right-hand side image is only used to illustrate the result.

Figure 6.17 suggests the utilization of the gradient direction for the linking procedure. This is indeed a way to avoid the fragmentation of chains as demonstrated in Exercise 6.5. *See* Section 6.4.3 (Linking contour points) *for further explanation.*

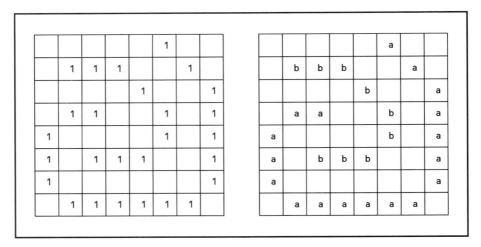

Figure 6.19 The application of the linking procedure to the source image (*left-hand side*) yields two chains *a* and *b* (*right-hand side*).

6.1.4 Contour approximation

In the case of region segmentation (Chapter 5), connectivity analysis is followed by feature extraction. These features (for example, compactness) are typically numerical. In contrast, features describing contours are often structural (for example, parallelism of segments). Thus, a description of contours by segments is required. These can be obtained by contour approximation. Figure 6.20 shows an example. The idea of a simple approximation procedure is illustrated in Figure 6.21. At the beginning, the chain of contour points is tentatively approximated by a single segment. If the greatest perpendicular distance between segment and contour chain exceeds a user defined tolerance value, the segment is split at the location of the greatest distance. This procedure is repeated until the greatest distance is within the user-defined tolerance.

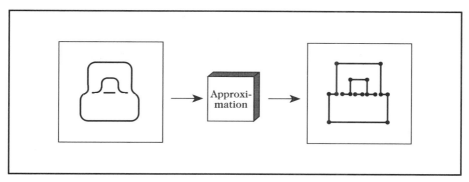

Figure 6.20 Features describing contours are often structural, for example, the parallelism of segments. Segments describing contours are achieved with the aid of an approximation algorithm.

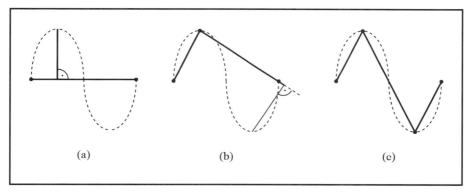

(a)   (b)   (c)

Figure 6.21 A simple approximation algorithm tentatively starts by approximating the chain of contour points by a single segment. If the greatest perpendicular distance between segment and contour chain exceeds the tolerance value defined by the user, the segment is split at the location of the greatest distance. This procedure is repeated until the greatest distance is below the user-defined tolerance value.

6.2   Ad Oculos experiments

To become familiar with contour-oriented segmentation, the New Setup shown in Figure 6.22 is invoked as described in Section 1.5. The example image which will be used in the current section depicts simple geometric objects cut out of cardboard (Figure 6.23 (KDVSRC.128)). A piece of black cardboard serves as a background, while the objects are gray or white. This image is suitable for demonstration purposes because of the simple contours of its objects.

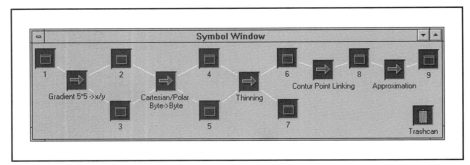

Figure 6.22 This chain of procedures is the basis for experiments concerning contour-oriented segmentation. The New Setup is realized according to the steps described in Section 1.5. The results are shown in Figure 6.23.

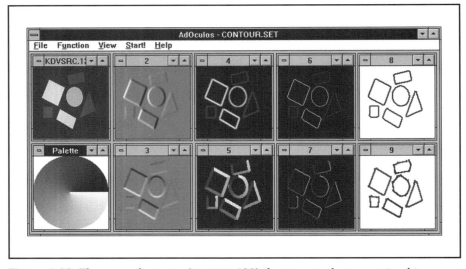

Figure 6.23 The example image (KDVSRC.128) depicts simple geometric objects cut out of cardboard. A piece of black cardboard serves as background, while the objects are gray or white. This image is suitable for demonstration purposes because of the simple contours of its objects. (2), (3), (4) and (5) are the results of the gradient operation. The interpretation of the gradient direction (5) is based on the palette. (6) and (7) represent the thinning result. The chains of contour points (8) are easy to interpret if the image is magnified and colored (View menu). The same holds for (9) which shows the segments computed by the approximation function.

6.2.1 Detection of contour points

Contour points are detected by a gradient operation using a 5*5 processing window. Figure 6.23 (2) and (3) show the graylevel differences in Cartesian representation. The gradient magnitudes of the contour points are shown in (4). The gradient direction is depicted in (5), where graylevels are used to represent the directions of gradients according to the palette.

The parameter used by `Cartesian/Polar...` was

```
Threshold:  10
```

This parameter may be varied by clicking the right mouse button on the function symbol. The threshold defines a value, below which the gradient magnitudes are set to zero.

6.2.2   Contour enhancement

The next step in the procedure of contour segmentation is thinning the gradient image. The results of this process are shown in Figure 6.23 (6) and (7). The parameter used by `Thinning` was:

```
Max. Angle: 30
```

This parameter may be varied by clicking the right mouse button on the function symbol. The parameter controls the direction check discussed in Section 6.1.2.

The use of simple 'artificial' objects emphasizes that the thinning procedure is not faultless:

- Vertices are deformed, rounded or even destroyed.

- Contours of objects which were originally straight, are often 'bent'. This observation demonstrates an unfortunate fact: a perfect placement of thin contours is not possible.

- Due to the small dimensions of the objects used here, the 'digital nature' of the processing becomes visible. For round shapes, this may cause severe distortion.

6.2.3   Linking contour points

The result of the linking operation is shown in Figure 6.23 (8). Magnification and coloring (`View` menu) of (8) supports the illustration of the result. Contour points which are linked together have the same color. It is obvious that the computer 'sees' different concatenations than humans: while a human observer can easily recognize the closed contours of the objects, the computer does not perform well. These problems are mainly caused by small gaps in the contour. This kind of fault typically occurs at vertices and is due to the low-pass filter effect of the preceding gradient operation.

The results of the linking procedure are visualized by means of a pixel matrix. Note that the actual data structure of a chain of contour points is a list or a one-dimensional array.

6.2.4   Contour approximation

The remarks made at the end of the preceding section (concerning the visualization of chains of contour points) are also valid in the case of contour approximation. The results of the approximation are segments which are eventually completely defined by their terminating points. These points are emphasized in Figure 6.23 (9). Again, magnification and coloring (**View** menu) should be used in support of this illustration.

The parameter used in **Approximation** was:

```
Max. Error: 3
```

This parameter may be varied by clicking of the right mouse button on the function symbol **Approximation**.

As a result of accepting this fairly high approximation error (in comparison with the size of the regions) the circle has lost its original shape. Alternatively, a smaller maximum error would have caused many short segments. The choice of an optimal tolerance must finally depend on the specific task at hand.

6.3   Source code

6.3.1   Detection of contour points

Figure 6.24 shows a procedure which realizes a 5*5 gradient operation. Formal parameters are:

MaxGV:	maximum graylevel permitted in the output images
ImSize:	image size
InImage:	input image on which the gradient operation has to be performed
DeltaX:	output image of column differences
DeltaY:	output image of row differences

The current procedure uses 5*5 masks for calculating the gradient (Figure 6.5). In the program these masks are represented by the static variables

Xmask and Ymask. The first step of the program serves to initialize the output
images DeltaX and DeltaY.

```
void GradOp5 (MaxGV, ImSize, InImage, DeltaX, DeltaY)
int MaxGV, ImSize;
BYTE ** InImage;
int ** DeltaX;
int ** DeltaY;
{
  long dXl, dYl;
  int  r,c, dX,dY, gv, y,x, MaxMag;
  static int Xmask [5][5] = { { -10, -10, 0, 10, 10},
                { -17, -17, 0, 17, 17},
                { -20, -20, 0, 20, 20},
                { -17, -17, 0, 17, 17},
                { -10, -10, 0, 10, 10} };
  static int Ymask [5][5] = { { 10, 17, 20, 17, 10},
                { 10, 17, 20, 17, 10},
                { 0,  0,  0,  0,  0},
                { -10, -17, -20, -17, -10},
                { -10, -17, -20, -17, -10} };
  for (r=0; r<ImSize; r++) {
   for (c=0; c<ImSize; c++) {
     DeltaX [r][c] = 0;
     DeltaY [r][c] = 0;
  } }
  MaxMag = 0;
  for (r=2; r<ImSize-2; r++) {
   for (c=2; c<ImSize-2; c++) {
     dXl = 0;
     dYl = 0;
     for (y=-2; y<=2; y++) {
      for (x=-2; x<=2; x++) {
        gv = InImage [r+y] [c+x];
        dXl += (gv*Xmask [y+2] [x+2]);
        dYl += (gv*Ymask [y+2] [x+2]);
     } }
     dX = (int) (dXl/25);
     dY = (int) (dYl/25);
     if (abs(dX) > MaxMag) MaxMag = abs(dX);
     if (abs(dY) > MaxMag) MaxMag = abs(dY);
     DeltaX [r][c] = dX;
     DeltaY [r][c] = dY;
  } }
  for (r=0; r<ImSize; r++) {
   for (c=0; c<ImSize; c++) {
     DeltaX [r][c] = (int) (((long) DeltaX [r][c]*MaxGV) / MaxMag);
     DeltaY [r][c] = (int) (((long) DeltaY [r][c]*MaxGV) / MaxMag);
} } }
```

Figure 6.24 C realization of the gradient operation.

The following part of the program realizes the gradient operation itself. r and c are the coordinates of the current pixel. The two inner for loops perform the local convolution of the input image InImage with both masks, Xmask and Ymask. The coordinates of the pixels in the window around the current pixel are r+y and c+x. The graylevel of each pixel in the window is gv. The corresponding coefficients in the two masks are addressed by x+2 and y+2.

Graylevels and coefficients are multiplied, and the 25 products summed up in the variables dXl and dYl. Because sums may exceed the range of an int variable, long variables are used. Division of the sums by 25 eliminates this danger. Thus, the final results of the local convolution are assigned to the int variables dX and dY. Before their results are assigned to the output images, they are checked to see if either of the variables exceeds the maximum value which has occurred so far.

Finally, the calculated data are normalized. This step ensures that the highest magnitude equals MaxGV. For the purpose of visualization, 255 is a reasonable value for MaxGV. However, it is important to keep in mind that the values of the output images DeltaX and DeltaY may be negative. Thus, we need the int type for DeltaX and DeltaY. Applying an abs operation to the output value and assigning the result to the BYTE arrays, guarantees perfect visualization. However, some of the following contour procedures need signed data.

A typical example of these procedures is the transformation from Cartesian to polar representation. The corresponding procedure is shown in Figure 6.25. Formal parameters are:

MaxGV:	highest gradient magnitude permitted
ImSize:	image size
MagThres:	threshold of the gradient magnitude: values below this threshold are set to zero and interpreted as background
DeltaX:	input image of the column differences (cartesian representation)
DeltaY:	input image of the row differences (cartesian representation)
GradMag:	output image of the gradient magnitude
GradAng:	output image of the gradient direction (plus 90°)

At the beginning of this procedure, the output images GradMag and GradAng are initialized. Determination of the highest gradient magnitude requires calculation of the expression $\sqrt{x^2 + y^2}$. A straightforward C realization would need a great deal of computing time. Since the precision required for the gradient magnitude is minimal, it is advantageous to use the approximation $|x|+|y|$ (abs(dX) + abs(dY)).

The last step of the procedure uses the highest gradient magnitude to normalize the magnitude values with respect to MaxGV. This parameter is user defined, but must not exceed 255, since the output image GradMag is of type BYTE. Calculation of the gradient *direction* is based on the procedure DiscAtan256 which is defined in Appendix B.4. According to this procedure, the complete circle is represented by the range of BYTE variables (that is, from 0 to 255). Since the gradient direction has to be rotated by 90° (Section 6.1.1), a value of 64 is added. ANDing the value of the direction with 255 is equivalent to a modulo-2^8 operation which forces the values of the gradient direction into the range of a BYTE variable.

```
void CarToPol (MaxGV, ImSize, MagThres, DeltaX, DeltaY, GradMag,
               GradAng)
int MaxGV, ImSize, MagThres;
int ** DeltaX;
int ** DeltaY;
BYTE ** GradMag;
BYTE ** GradAng;
{
  int r,c, dX,dY, Mag, MaxMag;
  for (r=0; r<ImSize; r++) {
   for (c=0; c<ImSize; c++) {
     GradMag [r][c] = 0;
     GradAng [r][c] = 0;
  } }
  MaxMag = 0;
  for (r=0; r<ImSize; r++) {
   for (c=0; c<ImSize; c++) {
     dX = DeltaX [r][c];
     dY = DeltaY [r][c];
     Mag = abs(dX) + abs(dY);
     if (Mag > MaxMag) MaxMag = Mag;
  } }
  for (r=0; r<ImSize; r++) {
   for (c=0; c<ImSize; c++) {
     dX = DeltaX [r][c];
     dY = DeltaY [r][c];
     Mag = abs(dX) + abs(dY);
     if (Mag > MagThres) {
       GradMag [r][c] = (BYTE) (((long)Mag*MaxGV) / MaxMag);
       GradAng [r][c] = (BYTE) ((DiscAtan256 (dY,dX)+64) & 255);
} } } }
f_KaPoCode
```

Figure 6.25 C realization of the transformation from Cartesian to polar gradient representation. Procedure DiscAtan is defined in Appendix B.4.

6.3.2   Contour enhancement

Figure 6.26 shows a procedure which realizes contour thinning. The formal parameters are:

ImSize: image size
DeltaDir: highest value permitted for the deviation between two adjacent gradient directions
GradMag: input image of the gradient magnitude
GradAng: input image of the gradient direction
ThinMag: output image of the thinned gradient magnitude
ThinAng: output image of the thinned gradient direction

The first step in this procedure initializes the output images ThinMag and ThinAng. The following thinning procedure is only activated if the gradient magnitude of the current pixel (r,c) is greater than 0. Otherwise, the pixel is considered to be a background pixel (Section 6.3.1).

The thinning procedure compares the magnitude and the direction of the current pixel with that of its neighbors on the left-hand and the right-hand sides. However, what is considered to be left or right? The location of the neighbors is defined relative to the gradient direction of the current pixel. Therefore, we have to deal with four neighbor relations. They are depicted in Figure 6.9. The current neighborhood is determined by four if expressions, which are decided according to the gradient direction C. The result is a pair of coordinates [N1r][N1c] and [N2r][N2c] which represent the two neighbors. Thus, the gradient directions are N1 = GradAng [N1r][N1c] and N2 = GradAng [N2r][N2c]. The next question concerns the deviations between the gradient direction of the current pixel (C) and the gradient directions of the neighbors (N1 and N2). The highest deviation permitted is user-specified by setting the variable DeltaDir. N1 and N2 are neither allowed to fall below Cmin nor to exceed Cmax. Care has to be taken when performing the necessary comparisons: if Cmin and Cmax are not in the range of gradient directions (that is, from 0 to 255), the result of any comparison may be incorrect. There are several ways to solve this problem. The one chosen for the thinning procedure is straightforward: the direction represented by C is rotated by 128 (corresponding to 180°). Provided that DeltaDir is smaller than 64 (corresponding to 90°), Cmin and Cmax remain in the range between 0 and 255. Naturally, for correct comparisons the directions represented by N1 and N2 have to be rotated accordingly.

If the comparison of the gradient directions of adjacent pixels yields a deviation exceeding DeltaDir, the procedure is aborted. Otherwise, the current pixel is likely to belong to a region of homogeneous gradient directions. Using the figurative description of Section 6.1.2, this corresponds to the gradient direction of the current pixel being aligned with the 'chain of mountains'. The remaining question is whether or not the current pixel is a 'summit pixel'. To answer this question, the gradient magnitudes are utilized:

if the magnitude of the current pixel is greater than or equal to the magnitude of both the neighbors, it is classified as a 'summit pixel'. In this case, the magnitude and direction of the current pixel are retained in the output images `ThinMag` and `ThinAng`, respectively.

```
void Thinning (ImSize, DeltaDir, GradMag, GradAng, ThinMag, ThinAng)
int ImSize, DeltaDir;
BYTE ** GradMag;
BYTE ** GradAng;
BYTE ** ThinMag;
BYTE ** ThinAng;
{
   int r,c, N1,N2, N1c,N1r, N2c,N2r, N1m,N2m, N1ok,N2ok;
   int C, Cm, Cmax,Cmin;
   for (r=0; r<ImSize; r++) {
    for (c=0; c<ImSize; c++) {
      ThinMag [r][c] = 0;
      ThinAng [r][c] = 0;
   } }
   for (r=1; r<ImSize-1; r++) {
    for (c=1; c<ImSize-1; c++) if (GradMag[r][c]) {
      C = (int) GradAng [r][c];
      if (0<=C && C<=15 || 240<=C && C<=255 || 112<=C && C<=143) {
          N1r = r-1; N1c = c;
          N2r = r+1; N2c = c;    /* west, east */
      }else if (16<=C && C<=47 || 144<=C && C<=175) {
          N1r = r-1; N1c = c-1;
          N2r = r+1; N2c = c+1;  /* north-east, south-west */
      }else if (48<=C && C<=79 || 176<=C && C<=207) {
          N1r = r;   N1c = c-1;
          N2r = r;   N2c = c+1;  /* north, south */
      }else if (80<=C && C<=111 || 208<=C && C<=239) {
          N1r = r-1; N1c = c+1;
          N2r = r+1; N2c = c-1;  /* north-west, south-east */
      }
      Cmin = C - DeltaDir;
      Cmax = C + DeltaDir;
      N1 = GradAng [N1r][N1c];
      N2 = GradAng [N2r][N2c];
      if (Cmin>=0 && Cmax<=255) {
          N1ok = (Cmin<=N1 && N1<=Cmax);
          N2ok = (Cmin<=N2 && N2<=Cmax);
      }else{
          C += 128; C &= 255;
          Cmin = C - DeltaDir;
          Cmax = C + DeltaDir;
          N1 += 128; N1 &= 255; N1ok = (Cmin<=N1 && N1<=Cmax);
          N2 += 128; N2 &= 255; N2ok = (Cmin<=N2 && N2<=Cmax);
      }
      if (N1ok && N2ok) {
          N1m = GradMag [N1r][N1c];
          N2m = GradMag [N2r][N2c];
          Cm = GradMag [r][c];
          if (N1m<=Cm && N2m<=Cm) {
              ThinMag [r][c] = GradMag [r][c];
              ThinAng [r][c] = GradAng [r][c];
} } } } }
```

Figure 6.26 C realization of the thinning operation.

The thinning procedure yields contours which are indeed one pixel wide, but the contour points are 4-connected. Figure 6.11 (a) shows an example of such a *chain of contour points*. Actually, a 4-connected chain is only one pixel wide, if neighborhoods are only permitted in a horizontal or vertical orientation. However, if a diagonal neighborhood is permissible, too, parts of a 4-connected chain become two pixels wide. This disadvantage disappears if contour points are 8-connected (Figure 6.11 (b)).

```
void FourToEight (ImSize, ThinMag, ThinAng)
int  ImSize;
BYTE ** ThinMag;
BYTE ** ThinAng;
{
    int   r,c, Cm, N1c,N1r, N2c,N2r, N1m,N2m;

    for (r=1; r<ImSize-1; r++) {
        for (c=1; c<ImSize-1; c++)  if (ThinMag[r][c]) {
            N1r = r-1;  N1c = c;
            N2r = r;    N2c = c+1;
            Cm  = ThinMag [r][c];
            N1m = ThinMag [N1r][N1c];
            N2m = ThinMag [N2r][N2c];
            if (Cm && N1m && N2m) {
                ThinMag [r][c] = 0;
                ThinAng [r][c] = 0;
            }else{
                N1r = r-1;  N1c = c;
                N2r = r;    N2c = c-1;
                Cm  = ThinMag [r][c];
                N1m = ThinMag [N1r][N1c];
                N2m = ThinMag [N2r][N2c];
                if (Cm && N1m && N2m) {
                    ThinMag [r][c] = 0;
                    ThinAng [r][c] = 0;
                }else{
                    N1r = r+1;  N1c = c;
                    N2r = r;    N2c = c-1;
                    Cm  = ThinMag [r][c];
                    N1m = ThinMag [N1r][N1c];
                    N2m = ThinMag [N2r][N2c];
                    if (Cm && N1m && N2m) {
                        ThinMag [r][c] = 0;
                        ThinAng [r][c] = 0;
                    }else{
                        N1r = r+1;  N1c = c;
                        N2r = r;    N2c = c+1;
                        Cm  = ThinMag [r][c];
                        N1m = ThinMag [N1r][N1c];
                        N2m = ThinMag [N2r][N2c];
                        if (Cm && N1m && N2m) {
                            ThinMag [r][c] = 0;
                            ThinAng [r][c] = 0;
} } } } } } }
```

Figure 6.27 C realization of the transformation of 4-connected neighborhoods into 8-connected neighborhoods.

Figure 6.27 shows a procedure, which realizes the transformation of 4-connected neighborhoods into 8-connected neighborhoods. The formal parameters are:

ImSize: image size

ThinMag: magnitude image in which the superfluous contour points have to be erased

ThinAng: direction image in which the superfluous contour points have to be erased

This procedure constitutes an exception to the rule which requires separate images for input and output. Thus, the usual initialization of the images is not necessary. Figure 6.12 shows four possible configurations for 4-connected neighborhoods. The bold lines depict pixels which are part of a 4-connected chain. The current pixel of each mask corresponds to the superfluous contour point. If the algorithm encounters one of the four configurations, then the current pixels of the magnitude image and of the direction image are set to 0, that is, they become part of the background.

6.3.3   Linking contour points

Figure 6.28 shows a procedure which realizes the linking of contour points. Formal parameters are:

ImSize: image size

ThinMag: input image, which represents the thinned gradient magnitude (8-connected neighborhood)

Chain: output vector, which contains all chains of contour points in ThinMag

The procedure returns the length of the vector Chain. The two vectors x and y, which are defined at the beginning of the procedure, support a simple addressing of each of the eight neighbors of the current pixel. The coordinates of the current pixel (whose gradient magnitude is greater than 0) are rf and the coordinates of the neighbor cc are rf+y[cc] and cf+x[cc]. For the 'eastern' neighbor cc is 0. cc is incremented counterclockwise, that is, cc is 7 for the 'south-eastern' neighbor (*see the definition part of the procedure in* Figure 6.28).

Continuation of the linking algorithm is controlled by two variables:

i: addresses the contour points in a chain beginning with i=1 for the first point. For the last point i corresponds with the number of contour points in the current chain.

l: counts the number of *all* contour points which are linked in any given chain.

```
int Linking (ImSize, ThinMag, Chain)
int      ImSize;
BYTE     ** ThinMag;
ChnTyp   *Chain;
{
   /* chain code (cc): O NO N NW W SW S SO   */
   static int y [8] = {0,-1,-1,-1, 0, 1, 1, 1};
   static int x [8] = {1, 1, 0,-1,-1,-1, 0, 1};
   int r,c, rf,cf, rs,cs, i,l, cc;
   l = 0;
   for (r=1; r<ImSize-1; r++) {
        for (c=1; c<ImSize-1; c++) if (ThinMag [r][c]) {
             rf = r;
             cf = c;
             i = 1;
             Chain[l].r = rf;
             Chain[l].c = cf;
             Chain[l].i = i;
             i++;
             l++;
             ThinMag [rf][cf] = 0;
             for (cc=0; cc<8; cc++) {
                  rs = rf + y[cc];
                  cs = cf + x[cc];
                  if (ThinMag [rs][cs]) {
                       rf = rs;
                       cf = cs;
                       GetMem (Chain);
                       Chain[l].r = rf;
                       Chain[l].c = cf;
                       Chain[l].i = i;
                       i++;
                       l++;
                       ThinMag [rf][cf] = 0;
                       cc=-1;  /* attention: reset of loop counter */
   } } } }
   l ;
   return (l);
}
```

Figure 6.28 C realization of contour point linking. The data type ChnTyp and the procedure GetMem are defined in Appendix B.

The frame of the linking algorithm is realized by two **for** loops which scan the whole of the input image **ThinMag** for contour points. The gradient magnitudes of these points are not used by this simple type of algorithm. They have to be greater than 0.

If a contour pixel is encountered, it is interpreted as the first element of a chain. Thus, i is set to 1 and the coordinates of this point must be retained in Chain. Since i is also part of Chain, the beginning of a new chain can be identified without problems. This is important for succeeding procedures which use Chain. Before searching for further contour points in the neighborhood, it is necessary to mark the current pixel as 'found'. This is simply done by ThinMag[rf][cf]=0, which means, however, that the input image is destroyed at the end of the procedure.

The inner for loop scans (by variation of x and y) the neighborhood around the current pixel, searching for further contour points. The coordinates of the neighbors are rs and cs. If this search fails for all of the eight neighbors, the current pixel is the last point in the chain. The control is then returned to the outer two for loops in order to search for the beginning of a new chain.

Consider the case of a successful search for a neighboring contour point. In this case, first of all Chain has to be reallocated in order to provide memory for the new contour point. After assigning rf, cf and i to Chain, the control variables i and l are incremented and the neighbor is marked as 'found'.

The termination of this procedure is in violation of an important rule of good programming: never manipulate a loop counter. However, pragmatic programmers appreciate such exceptions which confirm the rules. In our case, the 'reset' of the loop counter is a simpler and clearer realization than any practical alternative.

The procedure Linking is the simplest realization of a linking algorithm. In practice, this procedure should be elaborated in order to realize the function described in Section 6.1.3. For further information, *see* Section 6.4.3.

6.3.4   Contour approximation

Figure 6.30 shows the procedure Approx which realizes the contour approximation. Formal parameters are:

ChnLen:	length of the vector Chain
MaxErr:	maximum approximation error (in pixels) permitted
Chain:	input vector, which contains the chains of contour points
Segs:	output vector, which contains the segments

The procedure Approx merely serves as a frame for the original approximation algorithm. It works on the vector Chain, beginning at the end, picking up the successive chains and starting the procedure Polygon with the current chain which is determined by the index TopOfCurve, which points to the end of the chain, and the parameter CurveLen represented by the length of the chain. The procedure Polygon approximates the current chain by segments and retains the coordinates of the segment termination points in the vector Segs.

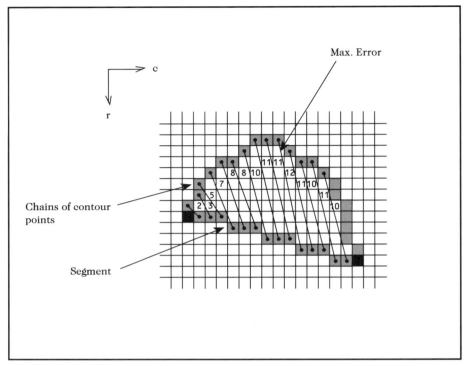

Figure 6.29 The realization of the split algorithm, whose original idea is illustrated in Figure 6.21. The method differs a little from the ideal approach: the approximation error is expressed by the city block distance between the pixels of the chain and the pixels of the segment. This offers the advantage of a fast and simple realization.

```
void Approx (ChnLen, MaxErr, Chain, Segs)
int    ChnLen, MaxErr;
ChnTyp *Chain;
SegTyp *Segs;
{
  int NofSegs, CurveLen, TopOfCurve;
  NofSegs = 0;
  TopOfCurve = ChnLen;
  while (TopOfCurve >= 0) {
     CurveLen = Chain[TopOfCurve].i;
     Polygon (TopOfCurve, CurveLen, MaxErr, &NofSegs, Chain, Segs);
     TopOfCurve -= CurveLen;
} }
```

Figure 6.30 C realization of contour approximation (frame). The data types ChnTyp and SegTyp are defined in Appendix B.

Figure 6.31 shows the procedure Polygon which realizes the actual approximation algorithm. Formal parameters are:

TopOfCurve: index which points to the last contour point of the
current chain
CurveLen: length of the current chain
MaxErr: highest approximation error permitted
NofSegs: return parameter representing the number of segments
Chain: vector containing the chains
Segs: output vector containing the segments

```
void Polygon (TopOfCurve, CurveLen, MaxErr, NofSegs, Chain, Segs)
int    TopOfCurve, CurveLen, MaxErr, *NofSegs;
ChnTyp *Chain;
SegTyp *Segs;
{
   int    r0,c0,r1,c1, m,n, LineLen, Difference, MaxErrPos, MaxDiff;
   LinTyp *Line;
   r1 = Chain[TopOfCurve].r;
   c1 = Chain[TopOfCurve].c;
   r0 = Chain[TopOfCurve-CurveLen+1].r;
   c0 = Chain[TopOfCurve-CurveLen+1].c;
   LineLen = GenLine (r0,c0,r1,c1, Line);
   MaxErrPos = 0;
   MaxDiff  = 0;
   for (m=1, n=TopOfCurve-CurveLen+1; m<=LineLen; m++, n++) {
       Difference = abs (Line[m].c - Chain[n].c) +
                        abs (Line[m].r - Chain[n].r);
       if (Difference > MaxDiff) {
           MaxErrPos = m;
           MaxDiff  = Difference;
   } }
   if (MaxDiff > MaxErr) {
       Polygon (TopOfCurve, CurveLen-MaxErrPos+1, MaxErr, NofSegs, Chain,
               Segs);
       Polygon (TopOfCurve-CurveLen+MaxErrPos, MaxErrPos, MaxErr,
               NofSegs, Chain, Segs);
   }else{
       GetMem (Segs);
       Segs[*NofSegs].r0 = Line[0].r;
       Segs[*NofSegs].c0 = Line[0].c;
       Segs[*NofSegs].r1 = Line[LineLen-1].r;
       Segs[*NofSegs].c1 = Line[LineLen-1].c;
       ++*NofSegs;
} }
```

Figure 6.31 C realization of contour approximation (split algorithm). The data types ChnTyp, SegTyp and LinTyp and the procedures GenLine and GetMem are defined in Appendix B.

The approximation of contours is based on the split algorithm which is described in Section 6.1.4. Figure 6.29 shows the basic realization of the algorithm. In order to compute the approximation error, the segment is represented by a list of pixels. The error is expressed by the city block distance between the pixels of the chain and the pixels of the segment. This does not exactly correspond to the original principle (Figure 6.21), but offers the advantage of a fast and simple realization.

The pixels representing the segment are computed by the procedure GenLine (Figure 6.31). The coordinates of these pixels are contained in the vector Line. The procedure GenLine returns the length LineLen of this vector. The following for loop computes the city block distances Difference between the pixels of the chain Chain and the segment Line (Figure 6.29).

The index of the maximum error MaxDiff is MaxErrPos. If MaxDiff does not exceed the user-defined parameter MaxErr, the current segment is to be retained in Segs. Previously, Segs must have been reallocated in order to provide more memory. This is realized with the aid of the procedure GetMem. Now, the termination points of the segment Line are assigned to the vector Segs. If the approximation error is unacceptable (that is, (MaxDiff > MaxErr)), then two recursive calls of the procedure Polygon are processed in order to approximate the two parts of the chain which arose from the splitting process.

Bear in mind that the procedure Polygon is a very simple realization of the split algorithm. In order to keep the procedure easily understandable, mechanisms, which are necessary to cope with 'inconvenient' contours, have not been implemented. This applies especially to the case of closed contours.

6.4   Supplement

6.4.1   Detection of contour points

Figure 6.32 visualizes two basic approaches to contour detection: both the maximum of the first derivative and the zero-crossing of the second derivative detect the highest local graylevel difference. A graylevel image may be interpreted as a function $f(x,y)$ of two coordinates x and y of a two-dimensional coordinate system having the unit vectors $\mathbf{i}$ and $\mathbf{j}$. The first derivative of this function realizes the gradient:

$$\nabla f(x,y) = \frac{\partial f}{\partial x}\mathbf{i} + \frac{\partial f}{\partial y}\mathbf{j}$$

The magnitude of the gradient is:

$$|\nabla f(x,y)| = \sqrt{\left(\frac{\partial f}{\partial x}\right)^2 + \left(\frac{\partial f}{\partial y}\right)^2}$$

and the direction:

$$\Theta(\nabla f(x,y)) = \arctan\left(\frac{\partial f}{\partial x}\ \middle/\ \frac{\partial f}{\partial y}\right)$$

The second derivative realizes the Laplace operator:

$$\nabla^2 f(x,y) = \frac{\partial^2 f}{\partial x^2}\mathbf{i} + \frac{\partial^2 f}{\partial y^2}\mathbf{j}$$

which is rotation invariant. Thus, the Laplace operator yields no information about the direction of the contour.

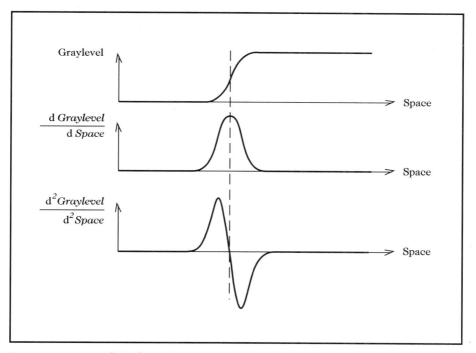

Figure 6.32 Use of the first and the second spatial derivatives of the graylevel permits the detection of contour points.

Realizations of these two approaches are based on local convolutions (Section 3.1) of a graylevel image with coefficient masks, which approximate the gradient or the Laplace operator. In this context, the size of the mask and the choice of its coefficients are important parameters. For determination of these parameters, three requirements have to be taken into account [6.7]:

- Contour points must be safely detected.
- The positioning of contour points must be accurate.

- The contour represented by the contour points should be thin and unique.

Based on these requirements, the academic community has developed several operators (for example, [6.7] [6.8]). Compared to the rather expensive realization of these operators, their practical benefits are poor. The reasons for this limitation are:

- Each of these 'edge detectors' only yields graylevel differences. However, the correspondence of these differences to the edges of the objects within the image is generally not guaranteed. There is no exact correspondence. In fact, no operator 'knows' anything about the objects. The operator merely processes (two-dimensional, discrete, spatial) signals which are meaningless to it.
- The design of the operators has been optimized for certain ideal types of graylevel differences (typically for ideal step edges). These types are rarely found in practice, except in the case of images which have been obtained under ideal illumination conditions. Such 'clean' images, however, do not need sophisticated operators.
- In order to find the best performance for a certain purpose, the various tools on offer must be evaluated. However, in the case of edge detectors, there is no performance measure which is widely accepted.

Consistently, for practical application one should remember the 'good old' operators, such as the gradient operator, which has already been described in the preceding sections.

A good realization of the zero-crossing operator is the classic approach introduced by Marr and Hildreth [6.12] [6.13]. However, the invariance of the Marr/Hildreth operator to rotation is a decisive drawback: one abandons the important direction information. When considering this aspect, it seems advisable to give preference to the gradient operator.

Finally, it should be emphasized that sophisticated modern operators are not simply academic 'toys'. On the contrary, these operators are most important for a deep understanding and for further development of image processing procedures. Please bear in mind that the operators which have now become classic operators were originally developed in the academic 'playground', too.

6.4.2   Contour enhancement

The aim of contour enhancement is the removal of superfluous contour points as well as the closing of broken contours. This task can never be quite satisfactorily performed, because the enhancement procedures have no knowledge of the objects in the image. The decision as to whether a contour point is superfluous or not can only be taken on the strength of the local configuration of the *signal* 'image'. Similar problems arise for the task of closing gaps. The danger of making decisive errors is inseparable from this operation: certain gaps in a contour may be meaningful, and in this case must not be closed.

A typical tool which removes superfluous contour points is the thinning procedure described in the preceding sections. This procedure is well-known as *non-maxima suppression*. It is simple and effective. However, if the information concerning the gradient magnitude has to be preserved, the representation of the contour by its 'summit pixels' (Section 6.1.2) is not sufficient. In this case, the width and the form of the 'gradient ridge' must be taken into account for the thinning process. A method of achieving this is the so-called *non-maxima absorption* method. Pictorially speaking, the 'summit' absorbs parts of the mountain slope on its right-hand and left-hand sides and in the process becomes higher.

Enhancement procedures which are able to fill gaps in contours are much more complex. A well-known tool that is not confined to image processing is the so-called *relaxation procedure*. It checks adjacent objects (of whatever kind) for certain homogeneity criteria. Objects which do not fit into a homogeneous neighborhood are forced to assimilate. Application of this principle to the enhancement of contours means:

- Strong contour elements which occur in a neighborhood of weak elements should be suppressed, since they are likely to be caused by noise.

- Weak contour elements which are part of a distinct contour should be strengthened.

- A contour element which is not aligned with a distinct contour should be adapted to the contour.

The basic principles of the classic relaxation procedures were described in [6.11]. An interesting alternative is discussed in [6.3]. It synergetically combines a non-maxima suppression, a non-maxima absorption and a relaxation procedure.

Most of the relaxation procedures suffer from a common drawback: they require a lot of computing power, often without returning an adequate performance. To make relaxation an appropriate tool for closing gaps in contours, a considerable amount of research work still needs to be done. Thus, in practice one should first try to solve current enhancement problems by using the simple non-maxima suppression procedure.

6.4.3   Linking contour points

The linking procedure which was presented in Section 6.1.3 is simple and fast. However, it has two disadvantages. They are illustrated in Figure 6.33. Consider a thin contour image which represents a bright semicircular object on a dark background (Figure 6.33 (a)). The corresponding direction of the contour (gradient direction plus 90°) is symbolized by arrows. At the lower vertices the contour is broken.

The linking algorithm starts its search for contour points at the top left-hand corner of the image and proceeds row by row. Thus, it encounters the first contour point at the top of the semicircle. From there it starts tracking adjacent contour points until it finds one of the terminating points. The contour points found between start and termination establish the first chain. The other half of the semicircle is *not* part of this chain. It requires another chain. Thus, we end up with three chains (Figure 6.33 (b)), where two chains would have been sufficient.

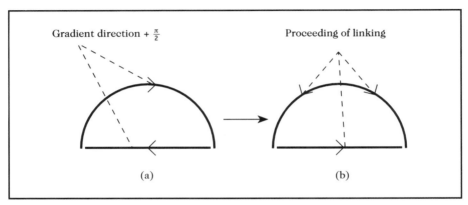

Gradient direction + $\frac{\pi}{2}$ Proceeding of linking

(a)   (b)

Figure 6.33 The disadvantage of the simple linking procedure which leads to fragmented chains can be overcome by the using the gradient direction.

The second problem concerns the direction of the linking procedure. For two of the three chains depicted in Figure 6.33 (b) it does not correspond with the original direction of the contour. This fault is not crucial, but may be inconvenient for some applications.

Both problems can be easily solved:

1. Recall the linking approach described in Section 6.1.3: in preparation, the procedure searches for any of the two terminating points and only starts the tracking from there.

2. Proceed according to 1, but make the preparatory search against the gradient direction of the contour points.

In spite of these improvements, the linking algorithm is only capable of linking adjacent contour points: for this reason it is called *local*. *Global* linking strategies use context information in order to perform well. This information may range from the progress of the entire chain which has been linked so far, to information concerning the objects which are supposed to be part of the image. Such algorithms are very time-consuming. Moreover, they are not yet well enough developed or understood for practical use.

Nevertheless, one of these procedures, the so-called Hough transform, has made its way into practical application. Since it is an interesting method even beyond the scope of contour point linking, a special section has been devoted to the Hough transform (Chapter 7).

6.4.4   Contour approximation

The aim of contour approximation is the representation of contour point chains by a minimum number of segments under the constraint of a maximum approximation error. These conditions are met by Dunham's optimal algorithm [6.9].

This algorithm has a serious drawback: it consumes an enormous amount of computing time. On the other hand, it is an excellent reference for comparison with other algorithms. Dunham himself conducted such comparisons and concluded that the simple split strategy (Section 6.3.4 and [6.15]) performs acceptably well. In view of the simple realization and the low consumption of computing time, it is a good practical choice.

6.4.5   Other contour procedures

The procedure of contour segmentation introduced in the preceding sections is classic, but certainly not the only one possible. There are a few interesting alternatives, two of which are introduced in the following section.

One of these alternatives is derived from the work of Prager [6.14]. The basis of his idea is a special form of contour representation as depicted in Figure 6.34. Prager calls his approach the *interpixel model*. Other authors speak of 'crack edges' [6.1]. Contour elements are positioned between any two vertically or horizontally neighboring pixels. The magnitude of such a contour element is determined by the difference of the two graylevels. To avoid negative magnitudes, the absolute value of the differences is utilized. The direction of the contour elements is determined by their positions between adjacent pixels. That is to say, there are only two directions, namely 'horizontal' and 'vertical'. The simple relationship between neighborhoods strongly influences the succeeding procedures. For example, based on the interpixel model, Prager introduces a relaxation algorithm which is simple, fast and robust.

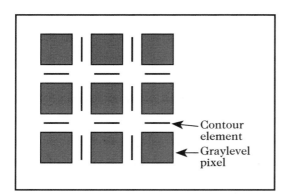

Figure 6.34
The interpixel model proposed by Prager is based on contour elements which are positioned between any two vertically or horizontally neighboring pixels. The magnitude of such a contour element is determined by the absolute difference of the two graylevels.

Another alternative is described by Burns *et al.* [6.6]. The procedure starts in the usual way: a simple gradient operation is executed in order to detect contour points. Inspecting the gradient directions in the examples of Section 6.3, it becomes obvious that there are large regions of similar gradient direction. These homogeneous regions are the basis for further processing. Burns *et al.* approximate the curve of the *gradient magnitude* in these regions by planes. From the positions of these planes, segments are determined which approximate the contour. Therefore, neither a thinning nor a linking procedure is required. However, this does not mean that the approach of Burns *et al.* would necessarily save computing resources. On the contrary: the amount of memory and time required is clearly larger than the classic procedure. Nevertheless, it is a very interesting approach which provides a deeper insight into the problems of contour segmentation.

6.5   Exercises

6.1   Apply the masks shown in Figure 6.35 to the source image shown in Figure 6.3.

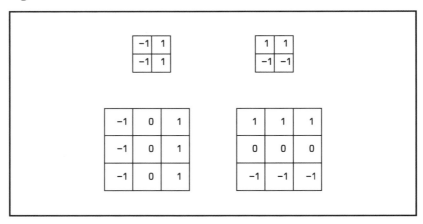

Figure 6.35 Like the simple operator shown in Figure 6.4, these masks realize the gradient operation. However, due to their size they have a smoothing effect which decreases their sensitivity to very local graylevel changes.

6.2   Apply the non-maxima suppression procedure to the gradient image shown in Figure 6.36. Performing the similarity check, allow differences of ±5°, ±10° and ±15°.

Magnitude

0	0	18	22	16	20	15	0
0	19	67	101	92	104	89	41
0	41	127	186	173	192	192	135
0	70	175	231	197	208	243	224
20	112	210	228	156	136	197	234
45	152	229	204	100	42	95	155
81	188	234	176	66	0	16	54
125	217	223	134	31	0	0	0

Direction

0	0	38°	25°	0	325°	329°	0
0	45°	44°	31°	7°	342°	326°	323°
0	58°	53°	39°	13°	346°	333°	329°
0	65°	65°	52°	23°	346°	335°	335°
45°	68°	70°	66°	38°	343°	332°	335°
56°	70°	75°	73°	59°	336°	325°	329°
62°	72°	73°	70°	59°	0	318°	321°
68°	73°	73°	69°	52°	0	0	0

Figure 6.36
This is the part of a gradient image produced by a 5*5 Sobel operator (Figure 6.5).

6.3   Apply the 4-to-8 transform to the chain shown in Figure 6.13, starting at the bottom right.

6.4   Apply the refined 4-to-8 transform to the chain shown in Figure 6.37.

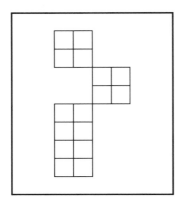

Figure 6.37
This chain of contour points is another unusual result of the non-maxima suppression.

6.5   Apply the linking procedure to the chain shown in Figure 6.38.

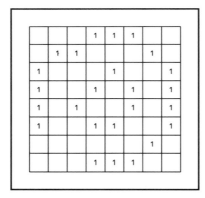

Figure 6.38
This image is used as source image for Exercise 6.5.

6.6   Write a program which evaluates the precision of the direction calculated by various gradient operators. Note that the precision of the direction depends on the direction itself.

6.7   Write a program which realizes the refined 4-to-8 transform as discussed in Section 6.1.2.

6.8   Write a program which realizes the improved link procedure as discussed in Section 6.4.3.

6.9   Figure 6.29 illustrates a realization of the split procedure which is fast and simple, but tends to inconvenient split errors in certain situations. Write a program which realizes the split procedure according to its original principle.

6.10   Write a program which is able to detect parallel segments. Assume that the segments are described by their terminating points.

6.11   Write a program which finds graylevel steps based on the zero-crossing approach.

6.12   Write a program which finds graylevel steps based on the interpixel approach.

6.13   Apply the 5*5 gradient operator to the cardboard shapes image (Figure 6.23 (**KDVSRC.128**)). Also, apply a 5*5 smoothing operator followed by a simple differentiation. Compare the results obtained.

6.14   Become familiar with every contour operation offered by Ad Oculos (Ad Oculos Help).

6.6   References

[6.1]   Ballard, D.H.; Brown, Ch.M.: *Computer vision.* Englewood Cliffs, New Jersey: Prentice-Hall 1982

[6.2]   Bässmann, H.; Besslich, Ph.W.: *Konturorientierte Verfahren in der digitalen Bildverarbeitung.* Berlin, Heidelberg, New York, London, Paris, Tokyo: Springer 1989

[6.3]   Besslich, Ph.W.; Bässmann, H.: Curve enhancement using rule-based relaxation. *Int. Cong. on Optical Science and Engineering, Hamburg,* 19–23 Sept. 1988, (P.J.S. Hutzler and A.J. Oosterlinck, Eds.), *Image Processing II, SPIE Proc. No. 1027 (1989),* 154–160

[6.4]   Besslich, Ph.W.; Bässmann, H.: A tool for extraction of line-drawings in the context of perceptual organization: *Proceedings of the International Conference on Computer Analysis of Images and Patterns,* Leipzig, 8–10 Sept., (K. Voss, D. Chetverikov and G. Sommer, Eds.), (1989) 54–56

[6.5]   Besslich, Ph.W.; Bässmann, H.: Gestalt-based approach to robot vision. In: B.J. Torby and T. Jordanides (Eds.): *Expert systems and robotics.* Berlin, Heidelberg, New York, London, Paris, Tokyo: Springer, (1991) 1–34

[6.6]   Burns, J.B.; Hanson, A.R. and Riseman, E.M.: Extracting straight lines. *IEEE Trans. PAMI-8,* (1986) 425–455

[6.7]   Canny, J.: A computational approach to edge detection. *IEEE Trans. PAMI-8,* (1986) 679–698

[6.8]   Deriche, R.: Using Canny's criteria to derive a recursively implemented optimal edge detector. *Int. Journal on Computer Vision 1 (1987)* 167–187

[6.9]   Dunham, J.G.: Optimum uniform piecewise linear approximation of planar curves. *IEEE Trans. PAMI-8 (1986)* 67–75

[6.10] Grimson W.E.L.: *Object recognition by Computers.* Cambridge, Massachusetts: The MIT Press 1990

[6.11] Kittler, J.; Illingworth, J.: Relaxation labeling algorithms – a review. *Image and Vision Computing 1, (1985)* 206–216

[6.12] Marr D., Hildreth E.: Theory of edge detection. *Proc. R. Soc. Lond. B 207 (1980)* 187–217

[6.13] Marr D.: *Vision.* San Francisco: Freeman 1982

[6.14] Prager, J.M.: Extracting and labeling boundary segments in natural scenes. *IEEE Trans. PAMI-2, (1980)* 16–27

[6.15] Ramer, U.: An iterative procedure for the polygonal approximation of plane curves. *Computer Vision and Image Processing 1 (1972)* 244–256

Hough transform

7.1 Foundations

The requirements for understanding this chapter are:

- to be familiar with geometry,

- to have read Chapter 1 (Introduction) Section 6.1.1 (Detection of contour points), and Section 6.1.2 (Contour enhancement).

The idea of the Hough transform was introduced by P.V.C. Hough in 1962. Duda and Hart [7.5] exploited this idea to detect collinear points (points which lie on a straight line). Although the Hough transform refers to contour-oriented segmentation (Chapter 6), a chapter of its own has been devoted to this application. One reason for this was to achieve greater clarity in Chapter 6. The other reason was that the special qualities of the Hough transform justify dedicating a separate chapter to it.

The basic idea of the Hough transform is illustrated in Figure 7.1: on the left, a straight line in the Cartesian coordinate system is shown. Usually, we determine such a straight line by its slope and its intersection with the *y*-axis. Another description uses the perpendicular distance *r* to the origin and the angle θ between *r* and the *x*-axis (Figure 7.1 (a)). Both descriptions are connected by the so-called *normal representation* of a line

$$r = x \cos\theta + y \sin\theta$$

θ lies in the interval [0,π). *r* may have positive and negative values.

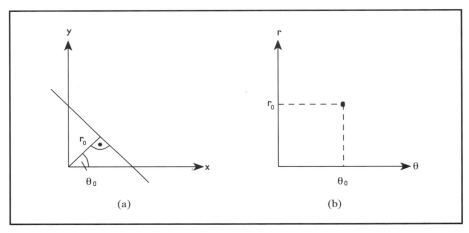

(a)   (b)

Figure 7.1 Usually, a straight line is determined by its slope and its intersection with the *y*-axis (a). Alternatively a straight line is described by the perpendicular distance r to the origin and the angle θ between r and the x-axis. Using r and θ to construct a two-dimensional coordinate system the straight line becomes a point (b). This line-to-point transform is realized by r = x cosθ + y sinθ.

In a coordinate system which is determined by *r* and θ (Figure 7.1 (b)), the original straight line is a point. Clearly, this line-to-point transform is not a tool which evaluates data. However, it serves for the enhancement of these data and therefore *simplifies* the following data analysis.

Figure 7.2 illustrates an example of using the Hough transform for contour segmentation. On the left, a section of a thinned gradient image (Section 6.1.2) is shown. The five arrows represent contour points which lie on a straight line (note that a contour point consists of a magnitude and a direction). A human observer notices this at first sight. However, the computer only 'sees' the single contour points. Their collinearity is revealed with the aid of the Hough transform.

From the gradient direction of the contour points (*x*, *y*) we obtain θ=45°. Thus, the thinned gradient image yields all the data required to carry out the operation *r* = *x* cosθ + *y* sinθ. With the current data for each contour point, the result is *r*=23.

In practice, the (r,θ) domain (the so-called accumulator, Figure 7.2) is quantized as a digital image. All the accumulator cells (these are the 'pixels' of the accumulator) are initially set to zero. Carrying out the Hough transform turns out to be simple: for each contour point of the gradient image, the Hough transform determines a coordinate pair (r,θ) and increments the contents of the corresponding accumulator cell. In the current example, each of the five contour points yields the coordinate pair $(r=23, \theta=45)$.

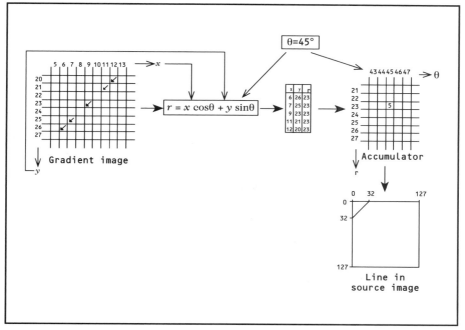

Figure 7.2 This is an example of using the Hough transform for contour segmentation. On the left, a section of a thinned gradient image is shown. The five arrows represent contour points which lie on a straight line. The Hough transform reveals the collinearity of these contour points.

Now, the actual Hough transform is finished and its result is to be found in the accumulator. The next step is to analyze the accumulator. The starting point of this analysis is obvious: all of the accumulator cells (r,θ) whose entries are greater than 1, represent at least 2 contour points lying on a straight line. This straight line is completely determined by r and θ. In order to illustrate this in the context of the example shown in Figure 7.2, the straight line determined by $(r=23, \theta=45)$ is entered into a 128*128 image (*bottom right*).

For further processing, knowledge of the intersections between the straight line and the image border is advantageous. These are easy to obtain with the aid of $r = x \cos\theta + y \sin\theta$, since r and θ are known and one of the intersection coordinates x and y is given by the image border. Applying the data of the current example to this procedure, the intersections (0,32) and (32,0) are obtained (Figure 7.2). Note that the straight lines obtained by the Hough transform (like any straight line) have no terminating points.

The straight lines obtained so far only indicate the collinearity of contour points. Thus, the use of the Hough transform to detect contours of objects requires further processing steps which are dependent on the actual application. The improvement of contour point linking procedures is obviously desirable. While popular linking procedures only make use of local contour information (Section 6.1.3), the use of the Hough transform allows the inclusion of global information such as the collinearity of contour points [7.3]). Here, another interesting use of the Hough transform will be discussed: the straight lines obtained by the Hough transform serve as 'signposts' indicating those regions of the *source image* which have the best chance of representing meaningful contours. Focussing the attention on these *regions of interest* avoids wasting computing time with redundant regions. Besides this signpost function, the Hough transform yields important information concerning the geometry of straight lines. We have already become acquainted with *collinearity*. In addition, the accumulator directly reflects parallelism: all straight lines represented by the entries of *one* accumulator *column* are parallel [7.4].

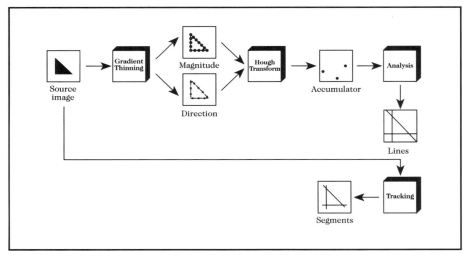

Figure 7.3 This is a survey of a chain of procedures, based on the Hough transform, for extracting segments. A gradient operation followed by a thinning step extracts the contour points of the source image. For each of the contour points, the Hough transform calculates the coordinates of the corresponding accumulator cell and increments its entry. The analysis of the accumulator yields straight lines representing collinear contour points. The tracking procedure 'scans' along these lines through the source image, searching for object contours.

Figure 7.3 shows a survey of the complete procedure. A gradient operation, followed by a thinning step, extracts the contour points of the source image. The resulting thinned gradient image is binary: the gradient magnitude of any contour point is 1, while background pixels are represented by 0. For each of the contour points, the Hough transform calculates the coordinates of the corresponding accumulator cell and increments its entry. The analysis of the accumulator yields straight lines representing some collinear contour points. The tracking procedure 'scans' along these lines through the source image, searching for object contours. Indicators for such contours are significant graylevel differences between the left-hand side and the right-hand side of the straight lines. The scanning procedure detects the first and last points of each encounter (or 'contact') with such differences. These 'contacts' are the termination points of a straight line segment representing a part of an object contour.

Figure 7.4 illustrates a simple realization of tracking. The scanning routine is based on a 'glider' which moves along the straight lines. The glider compares the graylevels on its left-hand side and on its right-hand side. If the graylevel difference is significant (the significance is defined by the user), the glider is likely to be moving along the contour of an object.

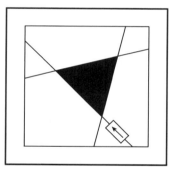

Figure 7.4
In order to find object contours, a glider moves along the straight lines. The glider compares the graylevels on its left and on ist right-hand side. If the graylevel difference is significant, the glider is likely to be moving along an object contour.

The principle illustrated in Figure 7.3 covers some basic problems of applying the Hough transform. These are discussed in Section 7.4.

7.2 Ad Oculos experiments

To become familiar with the Hough transform, realize the `New Setup` shown in Figure 7.5 according to the steps described in Section 1.5. The example image which will be used in the current section contains two wooden building blocks on a dark background (Figure 7.6 (`BLOCKSRC.128`)). The image is blurred and of low contrast. Such problems should be overcome by robust image processing procedures.

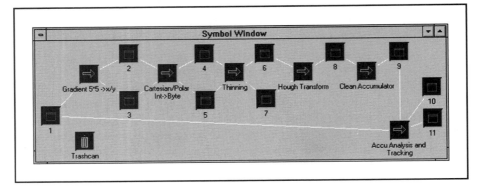

Figure 7.5 This chain of procedures is the basis for experiments concerning Hough transformation. The New Setup is realized according to the steps described in Section 1.5. The results are shown in Figure 7.6.

According to the summary shown in Figure 7.3, the first step is a gradient operation, which is then followed by a thinning procedure. The gradient operation is realized by a 5*5 Sobel mask, while the thinning is carried out by a non-maxima suppression. Both procedures are described in detail in Chapter 6. Figure 7.6 (6) and (7) show their results.

The parameters used by Cartesian/Polar... and Thinning were:

```
Threshold:   10
Max. Angle: 30.
```

These parameters may be varied by clicking the right mouse button on the function symbols.

Now, we have the starting point for the Hough transform whose result is an accumulator with mainly high entries. (8) shows that high entries are rather rare, even though the low entries are emphasized. If the actual accumulator is depicted, then there are only a few light clusters. These clusters consist of several accumulator cells with high entries which represent straight lines determined by very similar parameters r and θ. The next step is to replace such bundles of straight lines by a single 'superior' line. A simple realization of this idea is a two-dimensional non-maxima suppression in which only the highest entry of a cluster 'survives'. Such a procedure is described in Section 7.3 (Figure 7.8), and in the current setup it is realized by the function Clean Accumulator. The result of this cleaning step is shown in (9).

(10) depicts the straight lines represented by the highest entries of the cleaned accumulator. The brightness of a line corresponds to the height of the entry in question. The glider moves along these lines, detecting the segments shown in (11). The parameters used by Accu Analysis... were:

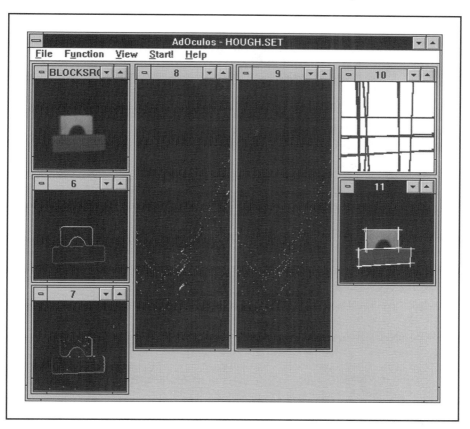

Figure 7.6 The example image (BLOCKSRC.128) contains two wooden building blocks on a dark background. The image is blurred and of low contrast. (6) and (7) show the results of the gradient and thinning procedures. The parameters were Threshold: 10 and Max. Angle: 30. These parameters may be varied by clicking the right mouse button on the function symbols. (8) is the content of the accumulator, (9) is the result of the cleaning step. (10) depicts the straight lines represented by the highest entries of the cleaned accumulator. The parameters used by Accu Analysis... were Glider Length: 10, Min. Significant Graylevel Difference: 10 No. of Significant Graylevel Differences on the Glider: 7 Threshold for Accumulator Points: 50. These parameters may be varied by clicking the right mouse button on the function symbol Accu Analysis...

Glider Length:	10
Min. Significant Graylevel Difference:	10
No. of Significant Graylevel Differences on the Glider:	7
Threshold for Accumulator Points:	50

These parameters may be varied by clicking the right mouse button on the function symbol Accu Analysis...

By now it will be obvious that the procedure is only able to find straight contours. Moreover, the segment representing the top contour of the lower building block is too short to be recognized. Comparing the course of this segment with the course of the block contour from right to left, a slight but clear deviation is obvious. Thus, at the left end of the segment the glider (Figure 7.4) was not able to detect significant graylevel differences and as a result had to stop the tracking prematurely. The original cause of this error was due to the misalignment of the straight line which is the result of the cleaning step applied to the accumulator. Thus, the (at first sight) good idea of replacing clusters in the accumulator by a single point involves a certain risk. Section 7.4 offers a detailed discussion of this problem.

7.3   Source code

Figure 7.7 shows a procedure for carrying out the Hough transform. Formal parameters are:

`ImSize:`	image size
`AccuRows:`	number of accumulator rows
`AccuCols:`	number of accumulator columns
`MaxGV:`	maximum accumulator entry; after the generation of the accumulator its entries must be normalized according to `MaxGV` (`MaxGV` must not exceed 255)
`ThinMag:`	input image representing the gradient magnitude
`ThinAng:`	input image representing the gradient direction
`IntAccu:`	accumulator of type `int`
`Accu:`	accumulator of type `BYTE`.

The gradient image (represented by `ThinMag` and `ThinAng`) should be thinned (Section 6.1.2). The use of the original gradient image does not cause poor results, but the transform requires more computing time than is necessary (Section 7.1).

The procedure starts by initializing the accumulator arrays `IntAccu` and `Accu` by setting each entry to zero. The Hough transform has to be carried out for each pixel in the gradient magnitude `ThinMag[r][c]` which has a non-zero value. The transformation starts by changing the gradient direction `Alpha` into the accumulator coordinate `Theta` as shown in Section 7.1. `Dtheta` is the radius representation of `Theta`. According to the normal representation of a line, the missing accumulator coordinate `Rad` is obtained with the aid of `Dtheta` and the coordinates r and c of the current pixel (Section 7.1). Since `Rad` may be negative, the origin of this coordinate should correspond to the mean accumulator row (`[Rad+(AccuRows>>1)]`). The last transformation step increments the entry of the current accumulator cell.

```
void HoughTrans (ImSize, AccuRows, AccuCols, MaxGV,
                 ThinMag, ThinAng, IntAccu, Accu)
int  ImSize, AccuRows, AccuCols, MaxGV;
BYTE ** ThinMag;
BYTE ** ThinAng;
int  ** IntAccu;
BYTE ** Accu;
{
   int    r,c, Alpha, Theta, Rad, Mag, MaxMag;
   double Dtheta;

   for (r=0; r<AccuRows; r++) {
      for (c=0; c<AccuCols; c++) {
         IntAccu [r][c] = 0;
         Accu [r][c] = 0;
   } }

   for (r=0; r<ImSize; r++) {
      for (c=0; c<ImSize; c++) {
         if (ThinMag [r][c]) {
            Alpha = (int) ThinAng [r][c];
            if (Alpha >= 128)  Alpha -= 128;
            if (Alpha <=  64)  Theta = 64 - Alpha;
                        else   Theta = 192 - Alpha;
            Dtheta = (Theta*PI)/128;
            Rad = (int) (c*cos(Dtheta) + r*sin(Dtheta));
            IntAccu [Rad+(AccuRows>>1)] [Theta] ++;
   } } }

   MaxMag = 0;
   for (r=0; r<AccuRows; r++) {
      for (c=0; c<AccuCols; c++) {
         Mag = IntAccu [r][c];
         if (Mag>MaxMag)  MaxMag = Mag;
   } }

   for (r=0; r<AccuRows; r++) {
      for (c=0; c<AccuCols; c++) {
         Mag = IntAccu [r][c];
         Accu [r][c] = (BYTE) (((long)Mag * MaxGV) / MaxMag);
} } }
```

Figure 7.7 C realization of the Hough transform.

In the case of `IntAccu`, the entry of an accumulator cell ranges from 0 to
32,767. This is sufficient, since even larger thinned gradient images are
unlikely to contain 32,767 contour points of identical `Theta` and `Rad` values.
Further procedures do not require such a range. Therefore, the last two steps
of the procedure compress the original range of an `int` variable into the
range of a `BYTE` variable.

Cleaning the accumulator is a typical additional procedure. It is realized by CleanAccu (Figure 7.8). Formal parameters are:

ImSize:	image size
AccuRows:	number of accumulator rows
AccuCols:	number of accumulator columns
WinSize:	size of the operator mask
InAccu:	accumulator to be cleaned
OutAccu	cleaned accumulator

```
void CleanAccu (ImSize, AccuRows, AccuCols, WinSize, InAccu, OutAccu)
int  ImSize, AccuRows, AccuCols, WinSize;
BYTE ** InAccu;
BYTE ** OutAccu;
{
    BYTE Inc, Max;
    int  r,c, yw,xw, ya,xa, h;

    for (r=0; r<AccuRows; r++)
       for (c=0; c<AccuCols; c++)  OutAccu [r][c] = 0;

    h = WinSize>>1;

    for (r=0; r<AccuRows; r++) {
       for (c=0; c<AccuCols; c++) {
          Inc = InAccu[r][c];
          if (Inc) {
             Max = 0;
             for (yw=r-h; yw<=r+h; yw++) {
                for (xw=c-h; xw<=c+h; xw++) {
                   if (xw<0) {
                      xa = xw+AccuCols;
                      ya = AccuRows-yw;
                   }else if (xw>=AccuCols) {
                      xa = xw-AccuCols;
                      ya = AccuRows-yw;
                   }else{
                      xa = xw;
                      ya = yw;
                   }
                   if (InAccu[ya][xa] > Max)  Max = InAccu[ya][xa];
             } }
             if (Inc==Max)  OutAccu[r][c] = Inc;
} } } }
```

Figure 7.8 C realization which cleans the accumulator.

At the beginning of the procedure, the output accumulator OutAccu is initialized. The size of the quadratic operator mask WinSize should be odd.

Typical values of WinSize are 3 and 5. The origin of the mask is its central pixel, the and variable h represents the maximum index magnitude of the mask.

The cleaning is carried out for each accumulator cell whose entry Inc is greater than 0. If the current entry holds the maximum value of all the entries covered by the operator mask, it is transferred into the output accumulator OutAccu (Section 7.1). Thus, only the local maxima of the clusters appearing in the accumulator 'survive'. As long as the operator mask completely covers the accumulator (the coordinates ya and xa do not exceed the accumulator border), the determination of the maximum entry is no problem. But on encountering the border, the typical problems already discussed in Section 3.1 arise. In the case of the accumulator *rows*, the solution is simple: the accumulator contains 'spare' rows at the 'top' and 'bottom', so that the operator mask never touches the horizontal border. The solution for the accumulator *columns* is more complicated, since the columns represent an angle (that is, q). As an angle is cyclical, the 'far left' and 'far right' columns are direct neighbors. Furthermore, the neighborhood is determined by the polarity of the row index.

The example shown in Figure 7.9 illustrates the connections. It depicts a small accumulator in order to keep the example simple. The column index xa ranges from 0 to 7 (representing a semicircle) while the row index ya ranges from 0 to 15. Thus, AccuCols is 8 and AccuRows is 16. Please note that r (as shown in Figure 7.9) may be positive or negative (the definition of the normal representation of a line in Section 7.1).

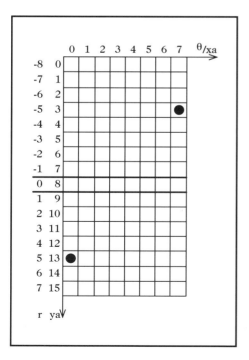

Figure 7.9
Example of the relations between neighboring accumulator cells. The two corresponding straight lines are shown in Figure 7.10.

The model accumulator consists of two entries. The corresponding straight lines are shown in Figure 7.10: they are close neighbors, although their positions in the accumulator suggest a considerable separation. As discussed in Section 7.2, θ requires a fine quantization in order to avoid misplacements. Thus, apart from the current example, θ ranges from 0 to 127. Using this range in the context of the current example, the two straight lines would almost merge.

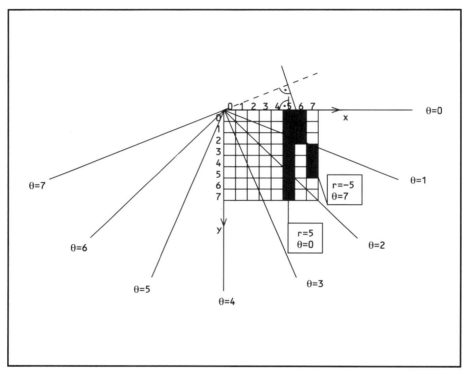

Figure 7.10 Two neighboring straight lines, whose parameters r and q differ considerably. The corresponding accumulator entries are shown in Figure 7.9.

Obviously the solution of the border problem must differ from the usual one (Section 3.1). In procedure CleanAccu, the solution starts with the test if (xw<0) (Figure 7.8). If the index xw reaches the bottom left (*top*) border of the accumulator, the resulting accumulator indices xa and ya are at the top right (*bottom*) border of the accumulator. The solution of the reverse case (xw>=AccuCols) is similar.

Before discussing the analysis of the accumulator, it should be remembered that there are fundamental problems concerning the displacement of straight lines caused by the cleaning procedure (Section 7.2 and Section 7.4).

```
int AnalyzeAccu (ImSize, AccuRows, AccuCols, Thres, Accu, Lines)
int     ImSize, AccuRows, AccuCols, Thres;
BYTE    ** Accu;
LinTypH *Lines;
{
    #define  XCONV(y)   (int) ((Rad - y*sin(Dtheta)) / cos(Dtheta))
    #define  YCONV(x)   (int) ((Rad - x*cos(Dtheta)) / sin(Dtheta))

    int    r,c, v,u, i, NofLines, Theta, Rad, Cy[2], Cx[2];
    double Dtheta;

    NofLines = 0;
    Cy[0]=0;  Cx[0]=0;  Cy[1]=0;  Cx[1]=0;

    for (r=0; r<AccuRows; r++) {
        for (c=0; c<AccuCols; c++) {
            if ((int)Accu[r][c] > Thres) {
                Rad = r - (AccuRows>>1);
                Theta = c;
                Dtheta = (Theta*PI)/128;
                if (Theta==0) {
                    Cy[0]=0;  Cx[0]=Rad;  Cy[1]=ImSize-1;  Cx[1]=Rad;
                }else{
                    if (Theta==64) {
                        Cy[0]=Rad;  Cx[0]=0;  Cy[1]=Rad;  Cx[1]=ImSize-1;
                    }else{
                        i = 0;
                        v = 0;
                        u = XCONV(v);
                        if (0<=u && u<ImSize)  {Cy[i] = 0;  Cx[i] = u;  i++;}
                        v = ImSize-1;
                        u = XCONV(v);
                        if (0<=u && u<ImSize)  {Cy[i] = ImSize-1;
                                                Cx[i] = u;  i++;}
                        if (i<2) {
                            u = 0;
                            v = YCONV(u);
                            if (0<=v && v<ImSize)  {Cy[i] = v;
                                                    Cx[i] = 0;  i++;}
                            if (i<2) {
                                u = ImSize-1;
                                v = YCONV(u);
                                if (0<=v && v<ImSize)  {Cy[i] = v;
                                                        Cx[i] = ImSize-1; i++;}
            } } } }
                GetMem (Lines);
                Lines[NofLines].r0 = Cy[0];
                Lines[NofLines].c0 = Cx[0];
                Lines[NofLines].r1 = Cy[1];
                Lines[NofLines].c1 = Cx[1];
                Lines[NofLines].Inc = Accu[r][c];
                Lines[NofLines].Dir = (BYTE) Theta;
                NofLines++;
    } } }
    return (NofLines);
}
```

Fig 7.11 C realization of the accumulator analysis. Type LinTypH and procedure GetMem are defined in Appendix B.

A simple analysis is carried out by the procedure AnalyzeAccu (Figure 7.11). Formal parameters are:

ImSize:	image size
AccuRows:	number of accumulator rows
AccuCols:	number of accumulator columns
Thres:	minimum value of an accumulator entry the coordinates of which determine a straight line
Accu:	accumulator
Lines:	list of straight lines which are detected by AnalyzeAccu

The procedure returns the number of straight lines detected in the accumulator.

The principle of the analysis procedure is simple: the coordinates Rad and Theta of those accumulator cells whose entries exceed the threshold Thres, represent a straight line marking significant graylevel differences from the source image.

For the efficient handling of these straight lines, the parameters Rad and Theta are often inconvenient. Usually, it is easier to determine the straight line by its intersections with the image border. These intersections are simply obtained with the aid of the normal representation of a line. (Section 7.1). The corresponding formulas are realized by the macros XCONV(y) and YCONV(x) in AnalyzeAccu. The coordinates of the intersections are: Cy[0] and Cx[0]; and Cy[1] and Cx[1].

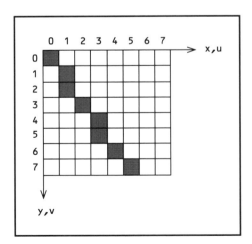

Figure 7.12
Example of an ambiguous intersection.

For the special cases (Theta==0) and (Theta==64), the intersecting coordinates are obvious. All other cases require testing of the four sections of the image border with regard to an intersection. Unfortunately, the image corners cause ambiguity. The straight line shown in Figure 7.12 intersects the left and the top part of the border at only one point. Which of these two possibilities is finally chosen does not matter, however. The important point is that the algorithm extracting the intersections should detect the ambiguity and randomly choose one intersection.

In order to store the intersection parameters, the list Lines has to be extended in preparation for a new element (GetMem (Lines)). This new element retains the intersection coordinates (Cy[0], Cx[0], Cy[1], Cx[1]), the entry of the corresponding accumulator cell (Accu[r][c]) and the direction of the straight line (Theta).

After the straight lines are determined, they are used to 'track along' the significant graylevel differences of the lines (Section 7.1). For this purpose, the Tracking procedure was developed (Figure 7.13). Formal parameters are:

ImSize:	image size
GlidLen:	length of the glider
MinDif:	minimum graylevel which is considered to be significant
NofHit:	minimum number of significant graylevel differences detected by the glider
NofLines:	number of straight lines extracted by the Hough transform
Lines:	list of straight lines
Image:	source image to be analyzed
Segs:	list of segments detected by the glider

```
int Tracking (ImSize, GlidLen, MinDif, NofHit, NofLines, Lines,
              Image, Segs)
int     ImSize, GlidLen, MinDif, NofHit, NofLines;
LinTypH *Lines;
BYTE    **Image;
SegTyp  *Segs;
{
    BYTE   Inc, Dir;
    int    i,j,n, r,c, r0,c0,r1,c1, NofSegs, LineLen;
    LinTyp *Line;

    NofSegs = 0;
    Line = (LinTyp *) malloc ((ImSize+ImSize)*sizeof(LinTyp));

    for (i=0; i<NofLines; i++) {
       r0  = Lines[i].r0;
       c0  = Lines[i].c0;
       r1  = Lines[i].r1;
       c1  = Lines[i].c1;
       Dir = Lines[i].Dir;
       LineLen = GenLine (r0,c0,r1,c1, Line);
       ScanLine (ImSize, Dir, GlidLen, MinDif, NofHit, LineLen,
                 &NofSegs, Line, Image, Segs);
    }
    free (Line);
    return (NofSegs);
}
```

Figure 7.13 C realization of the tracking (frame procedure). Data types LinTyp, LinTypH and SegTyp as well as procedure GenLine are defined in Appendix B.

The procedure returns the number of segments detected by the glider.

In order to realize the tracking, the straight line which determines the track should be represented by a chain of pixels. The generation of such a chain is carried out by the procedure GenLine which is defined in Appendix B.5. The current chain is stored in the array Line. Before the start of the tracking, the parameter Line requires the allocation of sufficient memory space.

The actual tracking is carried out by the procedure ScanLine (Figure 7.14). Formal parameters are:

ImSize: image size
Dir: direction of the straight line
GlidLen: length of the glider
MinDif: minimum graylevel which is considered to be significant
NofHit: minimum number of significant graylevel differences detected by the glider
LineLen: length of the pixel chain
NofSegs: number of segments detected along the pixel chain Line
Line: pixel chain
Image: source image to be analyzed
Segs: list of segments detected by the glider

```
void ScanLine (ImSize, Dir, GlidLen, MinDif, NofHit, LineLen,
               NofSegs, Line, Image, Segs)
int     ImSize, Dir, GlidLen, MinDif, NofHit, LineLen, *NofSegs;
LinTyp  *Line;
BYTE    **Image;
SegTyp  *Segs;
{
    int  i,j, r,c, rc,cc, r0,c0,r1,c1, n, Start, Stop;

    Start = -1;
    for (i=0; i<LineLen-GlidLen; i++) {
      n = 0;
      for (j=0; j<GlidLen; j++) {
        r = Line[i+j].r;
        c = Line[i+j].c;
        NeighInds (ImSize, Dir, r,c, &r0,&c0,&r1,&c1);
        if (abs (Image [r0][c0] - Image [r1][c1]) > MinDif)  n++;
      }
      if (n>=NofHit) {
        if (Start<0)  Start = i;
      }else{
        if (Start>=0) {
          Stop = i+GlidLen-1;
          Segs[*NofSegs].r0  = Line[Start].r;
          Segs[*NofSegs].c0  = Line[Start].c;
          Segs[*NofSegs].r1  = Line[Stop].r;
          Segs[*NofSegs].c1  = Line[Stop].c;
          ++*NofSegs;
          Start = -1;
} } } }
```

Figure 7.14 C realization of the tracking (core procedure). Data types LinTyp and SegTyp are defined in Appendix B.

The whole procedure is embedded in a `for` loop, which scans the pixel chain `Line` with the aid of the index `i`. This index, so to speak, 'pushes' the glider (with length `GlidLen`). Those pixels in the chain which are covered by the glider are addressed by index `j`. The image coordinates of these pixels are `r` and `c`. The procedure `NeighInds` (*see below*) determines the coordinates of the right and left neighbor pixels of the glider (Figure 7.15). For each of these pairs of neighboring pixels, the absolute magnitude of the graylevel difference is computed (`abs (Image [r0][c0] - Image [r1][c1])`). If this difference is greater than the threshold `MinDif` (which is defined by the user), then the counter `n` is incremented.

This counter serves as an indicator for a significant graylevel difference along the *entire* length of the glider: if `n` exceeds the threshold chosen by the user (`NofHit`), then the glider is very likely to 'sit' at the edge of an object. In order to determine this edge by a segment, we only need the first and last encounters of the glider. The corresponding indices of the pixel chain are `Start` and `Stop`.

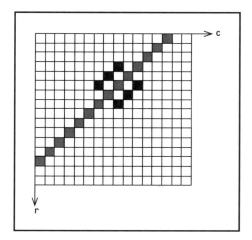

Figure 7.15
Principle of the glider realization.

Finally, consider the procedure `NeighInds` which has already been mentioned (Figure 7.16). Formal parameters are:

`ImSize:`	image size
`Dir:`	direction of the straight line the glider is 'moving' along
`r,c:`	coordinates of the current pixel of the straight line
`r0,c0:`	coordinates of the right (left) neighbor
`r1,c1:`	coordinates of the left (right) neighbor

This procedure is self-explanatory.

```
void NeighInds (ImSize, Dir, r,c, r0,c0,r1,c1)
int ImSize, Dir, r,c, *r0,*c0,*r1,*c1;
{
    if (80<=Dir && Dir<112) {
        *r0 = r-1;   *c0 = c+1;   /* NO-SW */
        *r1 = r+1;   *c1 = c-1;
    }else if (48<=Dir && Dir<80) {
        *r0 = r-1;   *c0 = c;     /* N-S */
        *r1 = r+1;   *c1 = c;
    }else if (16<=Dir && Dir<48) {
        *r0 = r-1;   *c0 = c-1;   /* NW-SO */
        *r1 = r+1;   *c1 = c+1;
    }else{
        *r0 = r;     *c0 = c+1;   /* O-W */
        *r1 = r;     *c1 = c-1;
    }
    if (*r0>=ImSize)  *r0 = ImSize-1;   if (*r0<0)  *r0 = 0;
    if (*c0>=ImSize)  *c0 = ImSize-1;   if (*c0<0)  *c0 = 0;
    if (*r1>=ImSize)  *r1 = ImSize-1;   if (*r1<0)  *r1 = 0;
    if (*c1>=ImSize)  *c1 = ImSize-1;   if (*c1<0)  *c1 = 0;
}
```

Figure 7.16 C realization of the determination of the glider's pixel positions.

7.4   Supplement

In Section 7.1, the basic principle of the Hough transform and its application were discussed. In practice, one has to deal with the following problems:

- The proposed procedure is restricted to straight contours. In principle, the expansion of the transformation to include other contour shapes is not difficult, since a 'shape-to-point transform' exists for any particular curve [7.1] [7.2]. A typical example of expansion is the *circle*-to-point transform proposed by Wallace [7.6], which analyzes workpieces with circular and straight contours.

- The tracking mechanism requires a comparatively large amount of computing time. Consequently, the procedure is only useful in the case of a few straight lines or object contours.

- The accumulator array requires a lot of memory, since the quantization of the accumulator coordinates r and θ corresponds to the image resolution. For a gradient image of size 512*512, the maximum distance to the origin is $r = \pm 512 \sqrt{2}$. The gradient direction of a contour point is represented by 1 byte. Thus, the gradient direction ranges from 0 to 255, while the scale of the angle of inclination θ is 0 to 127. Therefore, the memory requirement for the entire accumulator array is 360k bytes. This is an enormous amount of memory, especially in view of the limited number of straight lines yielded by the accumulator. An image representing simple objects is unlikely to comprise more than 100 of such straight lines. Their specification requires at most 400 bytes.

- Usually, the accumulator increments the entries of its cells. Thus, a 'long' straight contour causes a high entry independently of the graylevel difference along this contour. This is desirable, since due to its length the contour is very likely to be significant. On the other hand, short contours which separate regions with significantly different graylevels, would also be expected to yield a high accumulator entry. Due to their shortness, however, they only cause a low entry. The simple solution to this problem is the accumulation of the gradient magnitudes. But in this case, the weighting of long (and thus significant) contours with low gradient magnitudes may be too low.

- At first sight, it seems useful to carry out the accumulator analysis with the aid of standard clustering algorithms. But these procedures are too expensive and (more importantly in the context of our application) cause unacceptable errors: ultimately they lead to a coarser quantization of the accumulator which may have serious consequences. Figure 7.17 illustrates the fundamental problem of quantization. For a straight line $r = x \cos\theta + y \sin\theta = 0$ running through the origin, we obtain $y = -x\cot\theta$. With $\theta = 90°$, the straight line equals the x-axis. Considering a deviation of one degree (for example, $\theta = 91°$), then at $x = 511$, the corresponding straight line is 9 pixels away from the x-axis. This is a worst-case example, but it illustrates the vulnerability of the procedure to false (or too coarsely quantisized) accumulator coordinates. Such errors cause serious problems for the tracking mechanism.

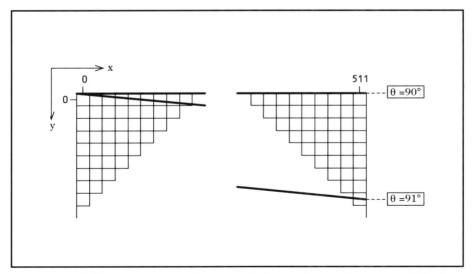

Figure 7.17 Different positions of two straight lines whose inclinations q differ by only 1 degree.

Unfortunately, the solution of one problem increases another problem. For instance, a finer quantization of θ and r is only feasible at the expense of memory. In practice, the application of the Hough transform is restricted by the following rules (though doubtless none of these rules is without an exception):

- The contour to be detected must be of simple shapes such as straight lines or circles.
- The number of such contours must be low.
- The quantization of θ and r must avoid misplacements.

Thus, the enormous memory requirements of the accumulator seem at first glance to be unavoidable. In some cases, however, the following strategy can be used: if only point or local operations (Chapter 2 and Chapter 3) are applied to the accumulator, its realization by a two-dimensional array is unnecessary. Since the cleaning of the accumulator involves a certain danger, it is sometimes best avoided. In this case, the accumulator may be realized by a *one-dimensional* array representing the *rows* of the original accumulator. Thus, we are only able to vary the column index r. This restriction requires a sorting of the contour points according to their inclination θ. Since a thinned gradient image usually consists of only a few contour points, the sorting procedure does not consume much computing time.

Starting with $\theta = 0$, the Hough transform computes the parameter r for each contour point which holds $\theta = 0$ and increments the entry of the corresponding accumulator cell. The final step is similar to the analyzing procedure in the case of a two-dimensional accumulator: a threshold extracts those accumulator entries whose coordinates determine straight lines.

The remaining question concerns the decision on incremental accumulation vs. accumulation of the gradient magnitudes. This decision depends on the application in question. The most interesting alternative is the combination of the two approaches. Clearly, while such a combination requires more computing resources, the resulting procedure may be much more robust than either incremental accumulation or accumulation of gradient magnitudes alone.

7.5   Exercises

7.1   Why is it very simple to identify parallel lines with the aid of the Hough transform?

7.2   Figure 7.18 shows a thinned gradient image consisting of 16 contour points with gradient directions 0°, 90°, 180° and 270°. The gradient directions of the four remaining contour points are 45°, 135°, 225°

and 315°. Apply the Hough transform to the source image shown in Figure 7.18. Create an accumulator with θ-quantization of 45° and r-quantization of 1.

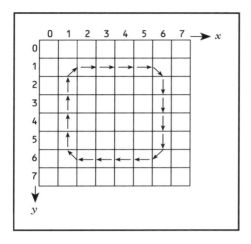

Figure 7.18
This is a thinned gradient image which is used as the source image for Exercise 7.2.

7.3   Analyze the accumulator obtained from the solution of Exercise 7.2 (Figure 7.19), using every entry which is greater than 0 (note that such a low threshold makes no sense in practice, but is only used here for demonstration purposes). Enter the straight lines extracted from the accumulator into an 8*8 image using the intersections with the image border.

7.4   If the result of Exercise 7.3 is not completely satisfying, the reason is likely to be the displacement of the diagonal straight lines. This is due to the quantization effects of calculating r and the intersection points at the image border. Re-calculate the intersection points at the image border using the non-quantized values of r. Enter the straight lines into a Cartesian coordinate system.

7.5   Given the parametric equation for a circle:

$$x = a + r \cos\theta$$
$$y = b + r \sin\theta$$

Define the Hough transform for detecting circles. How can the transform be optimized if the approximate radius of a circle is known?

7.6   Write a program which realizes the 1-dimensional Hough transform described in Section 7.4.

7.7   Write a program which realizes the circle-to-point transform as described in Section 7.4.

7.8   Become familiar with every Hough operation offered by Ad Oculos (Ad Oculos Help).

7.6   References

[7.1]   Ballard, D.H.: Generalizing the Hough transform to detect arbitrary shapes. *Pattern Recognition 13* (1981) 111–122

[7.2]   Ballard, D.H.; Brown, Ch.M.: *Computer vision.* Englewood Cliffs, New Jersey: Prentice-Hall 1982

[7.3]   Bässmann, H.; Besslich, Ph.W.: *Konturorientierte Verfahren in der digitalen Bildverarbeitung.* Berlin, Heidelberg, New York, London, Paris, Tokyo: Springer 1989

[7.4]   Besslich, Ph.W.; Bässmann, H.: A tool for extraction of line-drawings in the context of perceptual organization: *Proceedings of the International Conference on Computer Analysis of Images and Patterns*, Leipzig, 8–10 Sept., (K. Voss, D. Chetverikov and G. Sommer, Eds.), (1989) 54-56

[7.5]   Duda, R.O.; Hart, P.E.: Use of the Hough transformation to detect lines and curves in pictures. *Comm. ACM 15* (1972) 204–208

[7.6]   Wallace, A.M.: Greyscale image processing for industrial applications. *Image and Vision Computing 1* (1983) 178–188

Morphological image processing

8.1 Foundations

The requirements for understanding this chapter are:

- to be familiar with basic mathematics,

- to have read Chapter 1 (Introduction) and Section 3.1 (Foundations of local operations).

8.1.1 Binary morphological procedures

As the example of the median operator has already shown, there are interesting alternatives to classic linear convolution (Section 3.1). Yet another alternative is morphological image processing (morphology = science of shapes) which should not be confused with *morphing*, a technique used to manipulate the shape of regions of an image for esthetic purposes [8.3]. The basic idea of morphological image processing is to exploit prior knowledge of the shape of image distortions in order to support the removal of these distortions. In the context of binary images, such distortions are *regions* of 0 or 1, which are clearly distinguishable from 'useful image regions' due to their predictable shapes. Note that 'distortion' is not limited to noise, it also describes an image background which is to be suppressed.

A simple example illustrating the application of morphological image processing descends from the analysis of chromosomes. Figure 8.1 shows so-called metaphases. These are blobs formed by chromosomes belonging to one nucleus. Thus, the blobs are the 'useful image region', while the fine (1 or 2 pixel broad) vertical strokes are due to noise. The shapes of the 'useful image region' and the distortion are obviously different. Moreover, the variation of the two basic forms is slight. This information can simplify the morphological procedure considerably, but is not a prerequisite.

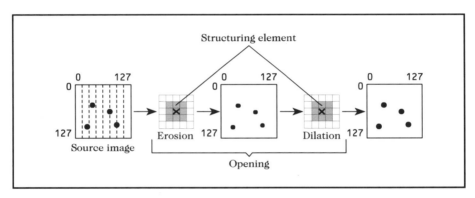

Figure 8.1 This example illustrates the application of morphological image processing to chromosome analysis. The source image shows the so-called metaphases. These blobs are formed by chromosomes belonging to one nucleus. Thus, the blobs are the 'useful image region', while the (1 or 2 pixel broad) vertical strokes are due to noise. The shapes of the 'useful image region' and the distortion are obviously different. (X marks the current pixel).

In the context of morphological image processing, the so-called *structuring element* and the basic operators *erosion* and *dilation* are the focus of attention (Figure 8.1). As the name suggests, *erosion* removes pixels from region borders. In contrast, *dilation* adds pixels to a border. The removal or addition is determined by a structuring element which is an operator mask of a given shape. It is handled like the local operators described in Chapter 3. The crosses in the structuring elements (Figure 8.1) mark the current pixel. The operations using the structuring element are based on the following rules:

- **Erosion**
  If the *whole* structuring element lies inside a region in the source image, then set the current pixel in the output image to 1.

- **Dilation**
  If at least *one* pixel of the structuring element lies inside a region in the source image, then set the current pixel in the output image to 1.

Applied to the source image shown in Figure 8.1, a simple erosion with a 3*3 structuring element completely removes the noisy background: the structuring element does not 'fit' any of the fine vertical degrading strokes. However, it is evident that the blobs are smaller. It is possible to compensate for this 'side effect' with the aid of a dilation, but it is not possible to reverse the shrinking process, since morphological operators are *non-linear*.

Imagining erosion and dilation as the 'atoms' of morphological image processing, simple combinations of erosion and dilation are, so to speak, 'molecules'. These combinations bear their own names:

- **Opening**
  An erosion followed by a dilation. The opening is used for removing the borders of frayed regions borders and for eliminating tiny regions.

- **Closing**
  A dilation followed by an erosion. As the name suggests, the closing procedure fills the gaps between 'fringes'.

Figure 8.2 shows two simple examples. A more complex example is depicted in Figure 8.3. This example demonstrates the detection of a region whose shape is known. Consider the small rectangle in the middle of the source image to be the desired region. The first step of the extraction procedure uses a structuring element, which completely removes this rectangle with the aid of an opening (erosion, dilation). Obviously smaller regions that are not part of the desired region are also eliminated. Thus, the image resulting from the opening contains only the larger regions (whose borders have been smoothed) of the source image. Therefore, this image only approximately represents the background of the image. Hence, the first step of the procedure, as well as the resulting image, are referred to as *background estimation*.

The second step compares source image and background estimation with the aid of an XOR function. The resulting image contains:

- the desired region,
- the borders of the large regions,
- all of the smaller regions.

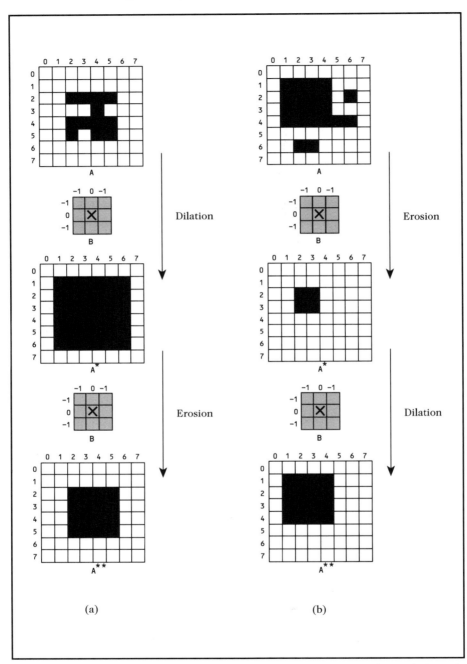

Figure 8.2 Erosion and dilation may be considered as the 'atoms' of morphological image processing. The 'molecules' are *closing* (dilation, erosion), which fills the gaps between the 'fringes', and *opening* (erosion, dilation), which is used to remove frayed region borders and to eliminate tiny regions.

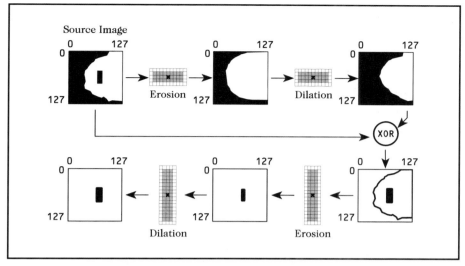

Figure 8.3 This example demonstrates the detection of a region whose shape is known (in the case of binary images). Consider the small rectangle in the middle of the source image to be the desired region. The initial opening (erosion, dilation) realizes a so-called background estimation. The second step compares the source image and background estimation with the aid of a XOR function. A second opening eliminates the undesired regions.

A second opening eliminates the undesired regions. For this purpose, the structuring element is shaped so that the erosion leaves a small part of the desired region behind. The subsequent dilation expands the desired region to approximately its original size.

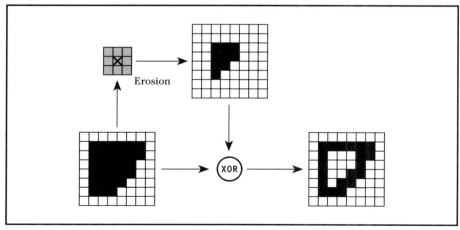

Figure 8.4 This example demonstrates the extraction of contours with the aid of an erosion and an XOR operation. Note that, in contrast to the gradient operation discussed in Chapter 6, the current operation yields no information concerning the contour direction.

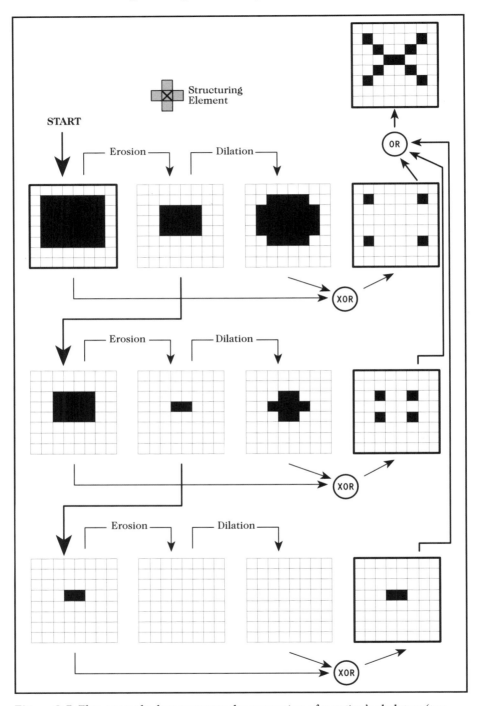

Figure 8.5 This example demonstrates the extraction of a region's skeleton (*top right*).

The applications shown so far are typical, but the influence of morphological image processing is much broader. The example shown in Figure 8.4 demonstrates the extraction of contours, a subject which has already been discussed in Chapter 6.

Figure 8.5 shows the extraction of the *skeleton* of a region. Like the outline, a skeleton yields structural features of a region. Typical application areas of skeletonizing are character recognition and the thinning of gradient images (discussed in Section 6.1.2).

Apart from its broad range of applications, the attraction of morphological image processing is due to three essential advantages:

- Even complex image processing problems can be reduced to simple elementary operations.

- These elementary operations are based on Boolean algebra.

- It is easy to realize morphological image processing on parallel machines.

These features make morphological image processing suitable for hardware realizations.

8.1.2   Morphological processing of graylevel images

In the case of morphological processing of binary images, the steps from graylevel 0 to graylevel 1 determine the shape of the desired regions in an image. Thus, this is a two-dimensional problem. The morphological processing of graylevel images requires a third dimension which represents the graylevels. A good way of visualizing this is the idea of graylevel *mountains*. In this context, an erosion clears the top layer of the mountains away, while a dilation covers the mountains with a new layer. An opening is used to remove peaks, a closing fills valleys. The shape of such peaks or valleys determines the shape of the three-dimensional structuring element. Figure 8.6 illustrates the procedures with the aid of a non-digitized image. The structuring elements are balls. In the case of the closing, the ball is rolled along the ridge of the mountains, and the valleys below the ball are filled. In order to apply the opening, the ball is rolled along the inner contour of the ridge of the mountains, and any peak which the ball does not make contact with is removed.

Figure 8.7 shows a detailed example of a dilation. On the left, a cross-section of a graylevel mountain is depicted. The origin of the structuring element (*middle of* Figure 8.7) is marked by a cross which corresponds to the current pixel during processing. The structuring element is applied upside down to the graylevel mountain: coming from the top, it moves downward until at least one of its pixels and at least one pixel of the top mountain layer overlap. For the last step, the position of the origin of the structuring element is decisive. Its spatial coordinates determine the position of the current pixel in the resulting image, while its coordinate on the graylevel axis determines the graylevel of this current pixel. Doing this for each pixel of the source image, the result shown in Figure 8.7 (*right*) is obtained.

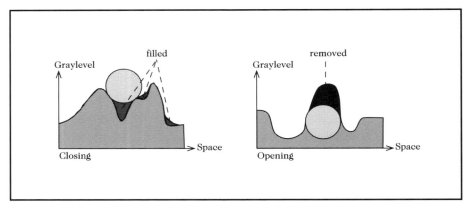

Figure 8.6 Illustration of closing and opening in the case of graylevel images: the figure shows cross-sections of two graylevel mountains and ball-shaped structuring elements.

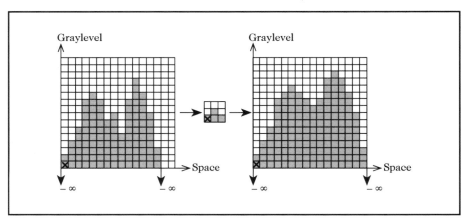

Figure 8.7 Carrying out the dilation of graylevel images.

The border problem, which is typical for local operations (Section 3.1), is simply, but effectively solved with the aid of the following definitions:

- Everywhere outside the image, the graylevel is 0.
- All pixels with graylevel 0 (including the pixels in the image) are handled as if their graylevel were $-\infty$.
- Thus, a structuring element never collides with the 'floor'.
- If the position of the current pixel is out of the image, its graylevel 'drops' to $-\infty$.

Figure 8.8 shows the procedure in the case of an erosion with the structuring element scanning the graylevel mountains from below: it moves upward until it encounters the highest position where all its pixels are inside the mountains. The remaining steps are similar to those of dilation.

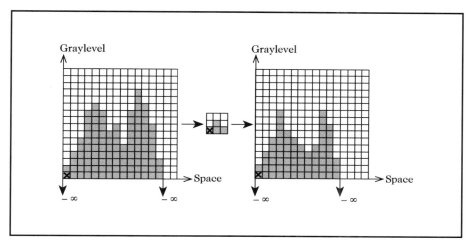

Figure 8.8 Carrying out the erosion of graylevel images.

Figure 8.3 shows an example of the detection of binary image regions (representing an object) which has a known shape. The corresponding problem for graylevel images is depicted in Figure 8.9. The aim is to extract the top corner of the mug's handle from the source image. A practical application for such an example is hard to imagine, but it illustrates the use of asymmetrical structuring elements.

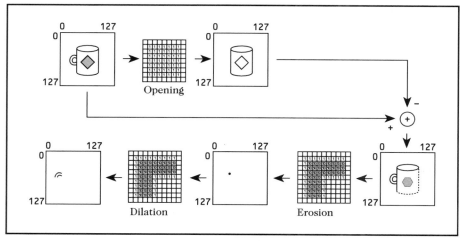

Figure 8.9 Example of detection of an image region, whose shape is known (in the case of graylevel images). The basic procedure is similar to that used in the case of binary images shown in Figure 8.3.

The basic structure of the procedure is similar to that used for binary images: it starts with an estimation of the background, followed by its subtraction from the source image, and finishes by enhancing the difference image. The background estimation is carried out by an opening with a structuring element which removes the handle. The design of such a structuring element is straightforward: it must be just big enough not to fit inside the handle. The subtraction of the images yields absolute magnitudes. Signs are of no interest. Obviously, the difference image contains the desired region, but also several degraded regions, too, none of which is similar to the desired region. Thus, an erosion with a structuring element adapted to the graylevel mountains of the handle corner removes the degraded regions. Now, the position of the handle has been detected. If the desired region is to be emphasized, a dilation with the same structuring element is required.

8.2   Ad Oculos experiments

8.2.1   Binary morphological procedures

To become familiar with morphological image processing, we realize the **New Setup** shown in Figure 8.10 as described in Section 1.5. For the current experiment, the structuring element **3X3.SEB** was selected. A structuring element has to be loaded by clicking the right mouse button on the function symbol of a morphological operator. Ad Oculos offers several structuring elements which can be found in the **STRELEM** subdirectory. A structuring element is represented by a text file which may be manipulated with any text editor in order to change its elements.

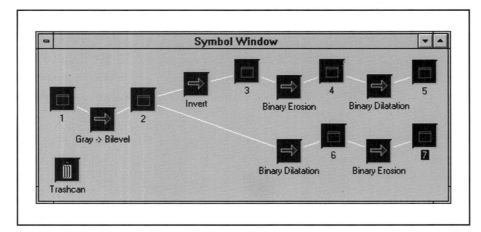

Figure 8.10 This chain of procedures is the basis of experiments with morphological image processing. The **New Setup** is realized according to the steps described in Section 1.5. The results are shown in Figure 8.11.

In Section 8.1, the extraction of metaphases from a source image was used as an introductory example. Figure 8.11 (METASRC) shows the original image. The picture has low contrast and is degraded by interference bands. The purpose of the subsequent process is therefore to isolate the metaphases from the noisy background.

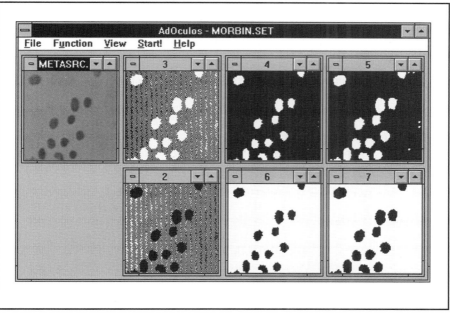

Figure 8.11 The example image (METASRC.128) is the original metaphases image as discussed in Section 8.1. The picture has low contrast and is degraded by interference bands. The task here is to isolate the metaphases from the noisy background. (2) is the result of thresholding the source image at graylevel 143, while (3) is the inverted version of (2). (4) and (5) are the erosion and dilation results of the inverted binary image, while the complementary dilation and erosion of the original binary image is demonstrated with (6) and (7).

The mean graylevel of the metaphasis is clearly lower than that of the background. Thus, the first step should be a binarization using a threshold. Figure 8.11 (2) shows the binarization result. The threshold was 143. Usually, the pixels with a graylevel of 0 (black in Figure 8.11) are defined as background. In order to keep to this convention, the binary image must be inverted (3).

At first glance, the background disturbance seems to be really bad. However, on closer inspection the disturbance turns out to consist of tiny regions which seem to have acquired their value ('0' or '1') by chance. In contrast to this, the metaphases are represented by comparatively large regions. Therefore, an opening with a 3*3 structuring element removes the disturbances without any difficulty. The result of the erosion is image (4). The subsequent dilation yields the resulting image (5).

The inversion of the source image would not be very expensive, and is in any case unnecessary. So, consider the original binarization result (2) as the starting point. In order to remove the disturbances (now represented by '0' pixels), the first step should be a dilation. The result is image (6). Consistently, the second step is an erosion yielding the final result image (7).

8.2.2   Morphological processing of graylevel images

A detailed example of the morphological processing of graylevel images is illustrated in Appendix A.1 (Industrial image processing).

8.3   Source code

8.3.1   Binary morphological procedures

Figure 8.12 shows a procedure which realizes a binary erosion and dilation. Formal parameters are:

ImSize:	image size
InIm:	input image
OutIm:	output image
StrEl:	list of the structuring element coordinates which relate to the origin of the structuring element (Figure 8.2)
Black:	code representing binary 0 (background)
White:	code representing binary 1 (desired region)

The procedure starts by initializing the output image. The subsequent part of the procedure carries out the erosion. It is embedded in two for loops, which 'guide' the current pixel (represented by the coordinates r and c) through the *whole* image, ignoring the border problem. The inner for loop tests the erosion condition for each element of the structuring element (Section 8.1.1): in order to obtain an entry in the output image, the desired region (in the input image) has to enclose the structuring element completely. y and x are those row and column coordinates of the input image which are covered by the structuring element positioned at the current pixel (r, c). Before testing for the erosion condition, the coordinates y and x have to be checked to see if they cross the image border. The actual test is simple: if pixel (y, x) belongs to the background (InIm [y][x] == Black), the inner for loop is stopped. This break-off takes place unless every pixel (y, x) belongs to the desired region. In this event, a 1 is entered into the output image OutIm.

```
void EroBin (ImSize, InIm, OutIm, StrEl, Black, White)
int    ImSize;
BYTE   **InIm;
BYTE   **OutIm;
StrTypB *StrEl;
BYTE   Black, White;
{
   int r,c,y,x,i;
   for (r=0; r<ImSize; r++)
       for (c=0; c<ImSize; c++) OutIm [r][c] = Black;
   for (r=0; r<ImSize; r++) {
       for (c=0; c<ImSize; c++) {
           for (i=1; i<=StrEl[0].r; i++) {
               y = r + StrEl[i].r;
               x = c + StrEl[i].c;
               if (y>=0 && x>=0 && y<ImSize && x<ImSize)
                   if (InIm [y][x] == Black) goto Failed;
           }
       OutIm [r][c] = White;
Failed: ;
} } }


void DilBin (ImSize, InIm, OutIm, StrEl, Black, White)
int    ImSize;
BYTE   **InIm;
BYTE   **OutIm;
StrTypB *StrEl;
BYTE   Black, White;
{
   int r,c,y,x,i;
   for (r=0; r<ImSize; r++)
       for (c=0; c<ImSize; c++) OutIm [r][c] = Black;
   for (r=0; r<ImSize; r++) {
       for (c=0; c<ImSize; c++) {
           for (i=1; i<=StrEl[0].r; i++) {
               y = r - StrEl[i].r;
               x = c - StrEl[i].c;
               if (y>=0 && x>=0 && y<ImSize && x<ImSize)
                  if (InIm [y][x] == White) {
                      OutIm [r][c] = White;
                      goto Leave;
           }    }
Leave:  ;
} } }
```

Figure 8.12 C realization of binary erosion and dilation. Data type StrTypB is defined in Appendix B.

The realization of dilation is very similar to that of erosion. Only the inner for loops differ (Figure 8.12). This loop realizes the dilation condition: if at least one pixel of the desired region and one pixel of the structuring element overlap, then a 1 is entered into the output image. Note that the structuring element has to be applied upside down.

8.3.2 Morphological processing of graylevel images

Figure 8.13 shows a procedure which realizes erosion and dilation of gray-level images. Formal parameters are:

ImSize: image size
InIm: input image
OutIm: output image
StrEl: list of the structuring element coordinates which relate to the origin of the structuring element (Figure 8.2)

```
void EroGray (ImSize, InIm, OutIm, StrEl)
int   ImSize;
int   **InIm;
int   **OutIm;
StrTypG *StrEl;
{
  int  r,c,y,x,i,gv,min;
  for (r=0; r<ImSize; r++)
      for (c=0; c<ImSize; c++) OutIm [r][c] = 0;
  for (r=0; r<ImSize; r++) {
      for (c=0; c<ImSize; c++) {
          min = 32767;
          for (i=1; i<=StrEl[0].r; i++) {
              y = r + StrEl[i].r;
              x = c + StrEl[i].c;
              if (y>=0 && x>=0 && y<ImSize && x<ImSize) {
                  gv = InIm[y][x] - StrEl[i].g;
                  if (gv < min) min = gv;
          }    }
      OutIm [r][c] = min;
} } }

void DilGray (ImSize, InIm, OutIm, StrEl)
int   ImSize;
int   **InIm;
int   **OutIm;
StrTypG *StrEl;
{
  int r,c,y,x,i,gv,max;
  for (r=0; r<ImSize; r++)
      for (c=0; c<ImSize; c++) OutIm [r][c] = 0;
  for (r=0; r<ImSize; r++) {
      for (c=0; c<ImSize; c++) {
          max = -32768;
          for (i=1; i<=StrEl[0].r; i++) {
              y = r - StrEl[i].r;
              x = c - StrEl[i].c;
              if (y>=0 && x>=0 && y<ImSize && x<ImSize) {
                  gv = InIm[y][x] + StrEl[i].g;
                  if (gv > max) max = gv;
          }    }
      OutIm [r][c] = max;
} } }
```

Figure 8.13 C realization of graylevel erosion and dilation. Data type StrTypB is defined in Appendix B.

The procedure starts by initializing the output image. The frame of the following erosion algorithm is similar to the binary case. Obviously, though, the kernel of the algorithm does not correspond to the idea of graylevel erosion proposed in Section 8.1.2: the graylevels of the structuring element StrEl[i].g are subtracted from the graylevels of the input image InIm[y][x] and the minimum min of these values is entered into the output image OutIm[y][x]. Thus, the graylevels of the structuring element realize the third dimension of the structuring element (Section 8.1.2).

The algorithm realizing dilation differs from that of erosion in the following respects:

- Since the structuring element has to be applied 'upside down' (Section 8.1.2), the coordinates y and x are obtained by subtracting the coordinates of the structuring element from r and c.

- The graylevels of the structuring element have to be added to the corresponding graylevels of the input image.

- The result of the dilation is the maximum sum.

8.4   Supplement

Morphological image processing is based on mathematical morphology which has been mainly developed by Serra [8.5] [8.6]. The following Sections 8.1.1 and 8.1.2 offer a short introduction to these more or less theoretical aspects of morphological image processing. Readers more interested in applications will find information for further work in the papers or books of Giardina and Dougherty [8.1], Schalkoff [8.4] and Sternberg [8.7].

8.4.1   Binary morphological procedures

The theoretical base of morphological image processing as well as that of mathematical morphology is set theory. Against this background a binary image is a function $f(r,c)$ (discrete in space and value), which depends on the row coordinate r and the column coordinate c. The function yields the values 0 (background) or 1 (desired region). In the case of only one desired region, it is simply represented by the set of all pixels (r,c) for which $f(r,c)=1$. The background is the complement of this set.

Now, consider that a desired region is represented by set A and the structuring element by set B. The coordinate origin of the structuring element corresponds to the current pixel $p=(r,c)$. Then, the set B_p is the structuring element at place p. A dilation requires a structuring element B_p^* which is upside down. Now, the definitions of erosion and dilation are:

Erosion: $A \ominus B = \{p: B_p \subseteq A\}$
Dilation: $A \oplus B = \{p: B_p^* \cap A \neq \varnothing\}$

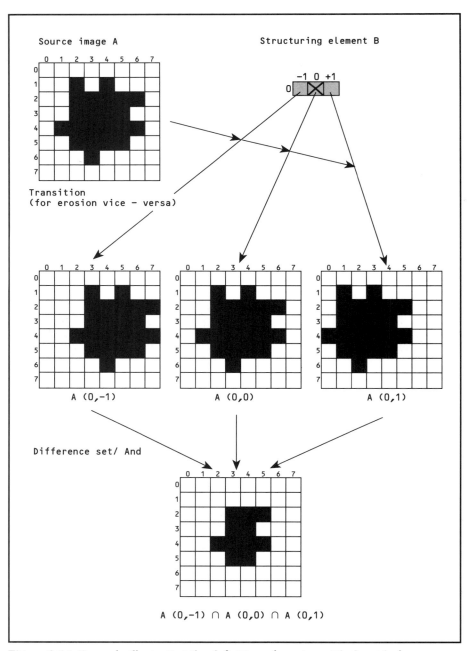

Figure 8.14 Example illustrating the definition of erosion with the aid of a transition and a set difference operation.

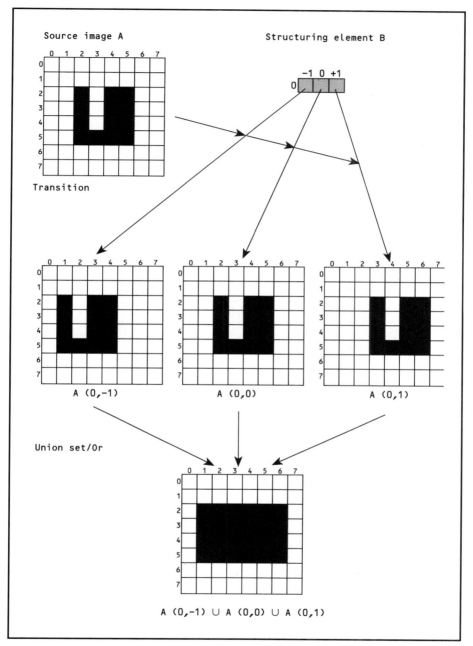

Figure 8.15 Example illustrating the definition of dilation with the aid of a transition and a set union operation.

Another definition of the basic morphological operations is illustrated by the example shown in Figure 8.14 and Figure 8.15. The individual elements (pixels) of the structuring element determine a transition in the source image. For instance, the element with the coordinates $(0,-1)$ causes a transition of one column to the left in the case of a dilation and one column to the right in the case of an erosion. Since each of the structuring elements shown in Figure 8.14 and Figure 8.15 consists of three single elements, three variations on the source image are generated. They are represented by the sets $A_{(0,-1)}$, $A_{(0,0)}$ and $A_{(0,1)}$. With these sets the basic morphological operations are:

Erosion: $A \ominus B = A_{(0,-1)} \cap A_{(0,0)} \cap A_{(0,1)}$

Dilation: $A \oplus B = A_{(0,-1)} \cup A_{(0,0)} \cup A_{(0,1)}$

or more generally:

Erosion: $A \ominus B = \bigcap\limits_{(r,c)\in B} A_{(r,c)}$

Dilation: $A \oplus B = \bigcup\limits_{(r,c)\in B} A_{(r,c)}$

Furthermore, it is possible to replace the set operations $\cap$ and $\cup$ by the Boolean operators and and or.

8.4.2 Morphological processing of graylevel images

Similar to the binary morphological procedures, the starting point is an image, which is defined by a function $f(r,c)$ (discrete in space and value). This function yields values ranging from 0 to 255. Such an image may be illustrated by a tower block landscape (Figure 8.16). The number of floors of the towerblock on 'grid square' (r,c) corresponds to the graylevel of the pixel with coordinates (r,c).

In order to transfer the morphological operations from the binary domain to the graylevel domain, the graylevel *function* has to be described by a set. For this purpose, Sternberg [8.7] developed the operations 'umbra' and 'top surface'.

Suppose the 'tower blocks' (Figure 8.16) are illuminated by an infinitely distant light source which is positioned exactly above the blocks, so that the blocks cast a downwardly-directed shadow continuing to infinity. Thus, the blocks produce a basement consisting of an infinite number of subterranean floors. Now, 'umbra' is the set consisting of all (underground and overground) floors, or alternatively an operation which generates this set with the aid of the top floors (black in Figure 8.16) causing the shadow. Then 'top surface' is the set consisting of all these floors, or, alternatively, an operation which extracts the set of top floors from the 'umbra' set.

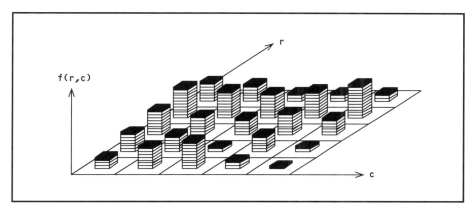

Figure 8.16 Illustration of the morphological processing of graylevel functions.

The *set* of floors which causes shadows corresponds to the graylevel *function* $f(r,c)$. Thus, the 'umbra' operation may be defined as a function $U[f]$ of the graylevel function. The 'top surface' operation acts in reverse: $f=T[U[f]]$. Now, the desired link between functions and sets is created. The brackets are to indicate that we have a function of a function.

Among others, two equivalences between set operations and function operations of two graylevel functions $f(r,c)$ and $g(r,c)$ are:

$$T[U[f] \cap U[g]] = \min \{f(r,c), g(r,c)\}$$
$$T[U[f] \cup U[g]] = \max \{f(r,c), g(r,c)\}$$

In this context the definitions of erosion and dilation are:

Erosion: $f \ominus g = T[U[f] \cap U[g]]$
Dilation: $f \oplus g = T[U[f] \cup U[g]]$

The linking of the sets $U[f]$ and $U[g]$ is a binary erosion, while the linking of the functions f and g represents the desired graylevel erosion. A corresponding process applies to dilation. Let $f(r,c)$ be the graylevel function of the image. Then $g(r,c)$ is the graylevel structuring element (also known as the *structuring function*).

8.5   Exercises

8.1   Perform erosion and dilation using the structuring element shown in Figure 8.17. Comment on the result.

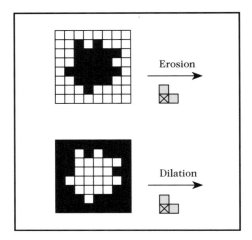

Figure 8.17
Exercise 8.1 demonstrates the relation between erosion and dilation.

8.2   Design a morphological procedure which removes the angular fragments in the top corners of the source image shown in Figure 8.18.

Figure 8.18
Exercise 8.2 demonstrates the removal of the angular fragments in the top corners of this image.

8.3   Extract the contours of the image shown in Figure 8.19 with the aid of a morphological procedure. Compare the results of applying the two structuring elements one after the other.

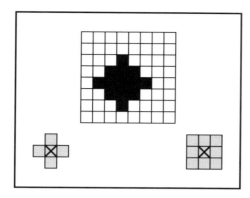

Figure 8.19
Exercise 8.3 demonstrates
the extraction of contours.

8.4   Extract the skeleton of the two images shown in Figure 8.5.
        Comment on the result.

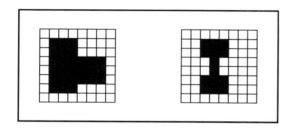

Figure 8.20
Exercise 8.4
demonstrates the
extraction of
skeletons.

8.5   Become familiar with every morphological operation offered by Ad
        Oculos (*see* Ad Oculos Help).

8.6   As discussed in Section 8.1.1, Figure 8.3 demonstrates the extraction
        of a small rectangle. This example originates from the Ad Oculos
        example image **BOLTSRC.128** showing a pin welded onto a piece of
        bodywork. Construct an Ad Oculos setup which realizes the example
        shown in Figure 8.3 using binary morphological operations. The first
        step would be the binarization of **BOLTSRC.128**.

8.7   As discussed in Section 8.1.2, Figure 8.9 demonstrates the extraction
        of part of a cup. This example originates from the Ad Oculos sample
        image **CUPSRC.128**. Construct an Ad Oculos setup which realizes the
        example shown in Figure 8.9 using morphological operations for
        graylevel images.

8.8   Experiment with morphological operations to manipulate images
        from an esthetic point of view.

8.6   References

[8.1]   Giardina, C.R.; Dougherty, E.R.: *Morphological methods in image and signal processing.* Englewood Cliffs: Prentice-Hall 1988

[8.2]   Haralick, R.M.; Shapiro, L.G.: *Computer and Robot Vision, Vol. 1 & 2.* Reading MA: Addison-Wesley 1992

[8.3]   Morrision, M.: *The magic of image processing.* Carmel: Sams Publishing 1993

[8.4]   Schalkoff, R.J.: *Digital image processing and computer vision.* New York, Chichester, Brisbane, Toronto, Singapore: Wiley 1989

[8.5]   Serra, J.: *Image analysis and mathematical morphology.* Orlando, San Diego, San Francisco, New York, London, Toronto, Montreal, Sydney, Tokyo: Academic Press 1982

[8.6]   Serra, J.: *Image analysis and mathematical morphology, Volume 2: Theoretical advances.* Orlando, San Diego, San Francisco, New York, London, Toronto, Montreal, Sydney, Tokyo: Academic Press 1982

[8.7]   Sternberg, S.R.: Grayscale morphology. *Computer Vision Graphics and Image Processing 29* (1985) 377–393

Texture analysis

9.1   Foundations

The requirements for understanding this chapter are:

- to be familiar with basic mathematics,
- to be familiar with local operations (Section 3.1),
- to have read Chapter 1.

Compared to other subjects of image processing, texture analysis is an unpopular topic. The problem begins with the attempt to define 'texture'. Two typical examples of texture are shown in Figure 9.1. A pullover's cuff is easily distinguishable from its sleeve due to different textures (Figure 9.1(a)). Figure 9.1 (b) depicts an example arising from a completely different context: the image suggests a path which is paved with round tiles or a riverbed which has been cracked because of a drought. Furthermore, the image gives a strong impression of space. A third example occurs in the context of satellite pictures: certain regions such as urban or forest areas are separable from their surroundings, due to their texture.

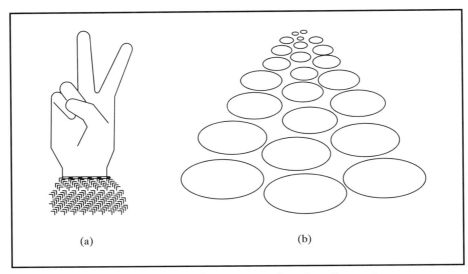

(a)   (b)

Figure 9.1 Two typical examples of texture: a pullover's cuff is easily distinguishable from its sleeve due to different textures. Figure 9.1 depicts an example arising from a completely different context, the image suggests a path which is paved with round tiles or a riverbed which has been cracked because of a drought. Furthermore, the image gives a strong impression of space.

The attempt to find an exact and generally accepted definition of 'texture' has failed up to now and may be impossible anyway. Therefore, this section will simply not make the attempt.

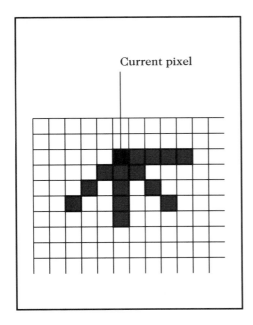

Current pixel

Figure 9.2
The purpose of the co-occurrence matrix is to describe the relationships between the current pixel and the graylevels of the neighboring pixels. However, in contrast to local operators, the co-occurrence matrix only needs certain 'graylevel samples' from the neighborhood. In this drawing, typical sample pixels have been shaded.

Let us start with a source image which is *completely* filled with a single uniform texture. Our aim is to find characteristic features of this texture. Very simple features are the mean and variance of the graylevels in a small operation mask (local mean, local variance). A spectral analysis offers further possibilities of describing a texture. However, a more common tool for texture analysis is the so-called *co-occurrence matrix*, which is also known as a spatial graylevel dependence matrix (SGLD).

The purpose of the co-occurrence matrix is to describe the relationships between the current pixel and the graylevels of the neighboring pixels. However, in contrast to local operators, the co-occurrence matrix only needs certain 'graylevel samples' from the neighborhood. In Figure 9.2, typical sample pixels have been shaded.

The realization of a co-occurrence matrix is best described with the aid of an example. Figure 9.3 shows a simple source image and four co-occurrence matrices originating from four different sample pixels *a* and *b*. The number of rows and columns of the co-occurrence matrix equals the number of graylevel variations in the source image. The current example uses only four different graylevels and the co-occurrence matrices are rather small. The entry of the co-occurrence matrix at position (*a,b*) corresponds to the frequency of the graylevel combination (*a,b*) in the source image. Take the neighborhood '*b* east of *a*' as an example. For this neighborhood, we find the graylevel combinations (0,0); (1,1); (2,2); (3,3) 12 times, the graylevel combination (2,1) four times and the graylevel combination (0,3) four times in the source image.

The basic operations used to realize a co-occurrence matrix are addressing pixels in the source image, addressing 'cells' of the co-occurrence matrix and counting. This is advantageous with regard to computing time. However, the memory requirement in the case of a typical image with 256 graylevels is enormous: the size of each of the co-occurrence matrices is 256*256. Fortunately, such a fine graylevel quantization is usually unnecessary for the purpose of texture analysis. Normally, 16 graylevels are sufficient, in which case the memory requirements decrease drastically.

The generation of co-occurrence matrices resembles the Fourier transform (Section 4.1) in the following way: both procedures transform the source image into another representation. In the case of the co-occurrence matrix, this procedure is not reversible (in contrast to the Fourier transform). For both approaches, the desired texture features must be extracted in a second step. Since the generation of a co-occurrence matrix is much faster than the computation of a Fourier transform, we tend to concentrate on the features extracted from co-occurrence matrices.

Typical features derived from co-occurrence matrices are *Energy*, *Contrast*, *Entropy* and *Homogeneity*. They are defined as follows (*f* is the co-occurrence matrix):

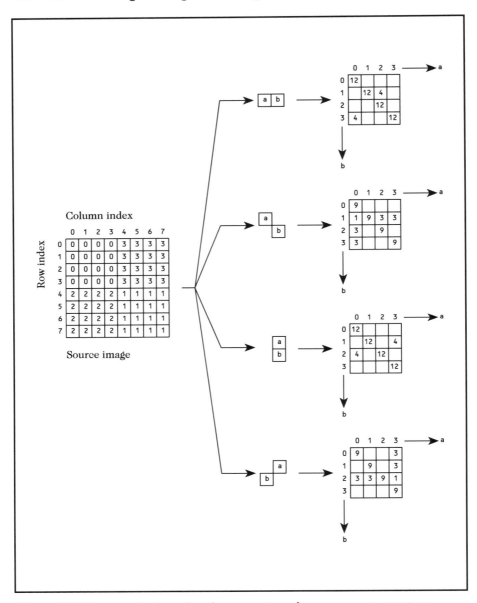

Figure 9.3 This example describes the generation of co-occurrence matrices (shown on the right-hand side). The number of rows and columns of the co-occurrence matrix equals the number of graylevel variations in the source image. The current example uses only four different graylevels and the co-occurrence matrices are rather small. The entry of the co-occurrence matrix at position (a,b) corresponds to the frequency of the graylevel combination (a,b) in the source image.

$$\text{Energy:} \quad M_1 = \sum_{r=0}^{R-1} \sum_{c=0}^{C-1} f(r,c)^2$$

$$\text{Contrast:} \quad M_2 = \sum_{r=0}^{R-1} \sum_{c=0}^{C-1} (r-c)^2 * f(r,c)$$

$$\text{Entropy:} \quad M_3 = \sum_{r=0}^{R-1} \sum_{c=0}^{C-1} f(r,c) * \log(f(r,c))$$

$$\text{Homogeneity:} \quad M_2 = \sum_{r=0}^{R-1} \sum_{c=0}^{C-1} \frac{f(r,c)}{1 + |r-c|}$$

As one might have guessed from the experience of image processing so far, the definition of these parameters is partly an improvisation, and different authors propose different definitions.

The parameters described above are appropriate for describing only one particular texture. The realization of a texture segmentation algorithm is much more difficult, but it uses essentially the same ideas as region-oriented and contour-oriented *segmentation* (Chapter 5 and Chapter 6). Recalling the previous example of the pullover's cuff and sleeve, it can be said that the aim of texture segmentation is to extract the cuff and the sleeve as independent regions from the source image, or to determine the dividing line between cuff and sleeve (Figure 9.1).

To carry out texture segmentation, the well-known texture analysis methods have to be applied in the form of local operations. Typical sizes of such operators range from 9*9 to 15*15. The application of larger masks usually causes low-pass effects which are not acceptable: the borders between the texture regions become too blurred. Alternatively, smaller operators process only a few pixels and the resulting extraction of texture features is not robust. Partly due to this contradiction, the results of simple texture segmentation methods are often unsatisfactory. Good strategies for solving these problems are based on pattern recognition methods (Chapter 10).

9.2 Ad Oculos experiments

To become familiar with co-occurrence matrices, realize the `New Setup` shown in Figure 9.4 as described in Section 1.5. This setup is used to compare the co-occurrence matrices of four sample images derived from the 'textile trade'. The parameters used by `Co-Occurrence Matrix` were:

```
... x direction:              0
... y direction:              1
Size of Co-Occurrence Matrix: 128
```

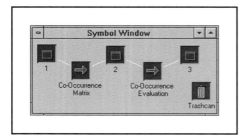

Figure 9.4
This chain of procedures is the basis for experiments with co-occurrence matrices. The `New Setup` is realized according to the steps described in Section 1.5. The results are shown in Figure 9.5.

Thus, the neighborhood consists of the current pixel and its southern neighbor. These parameters may be varied by clicking the right mouse button on the function symbol `Co-Occurrence Matrix`.

The first source image (`FURSRC.128`; Figure 9.5) to be loaded into (1) shows part of a glove lining. The material is synthetic fur. The transitions from light to dark are mainly smooth. The highest entries of the corresponding co-occurrence matrix (2) are concentrated on the main diagonal. These entries yield the texture features depicted in (3).

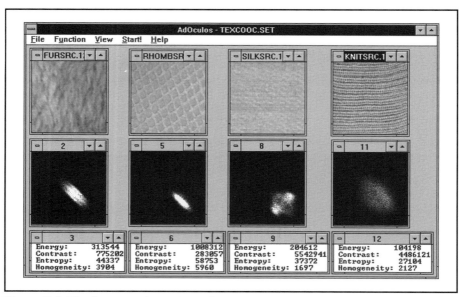

Figure 9.5 The four sample images, whose co-occurrence matrices are compared here, are derived from the 'textile trade'. (`FURSRC.128`) shows part of a glove lining. (`RHOMBSRC.128`) shows a sponge-like cloth with a rhombic patterned napped surface. (`SILKSRC.128`) shows part of a silk scarf. (`KNITSRC.128`) shows part of a pullover. The parameters used by `Co-Occurrence Matrix` were ... `x direction: 0`, ... `y direction: 1`, `Size of Co-Occurrence Matrix: 7`. These parameters may be varied by clicking the right mouse button on the function symbol `Co-Occurrence Matrix`.

The second sample image comes from the kitchen. `RHOMBSRC.128` shows a sponge-like cloth with a rhombic patterned napped surface. The image is characterized by a lot of regions of almost homogeneous graylevels. Thus, the high entries in the co-occurrence matrix (5) are concentrated in a small region on the main diagonal. The corresponding texture features are depicted in (6).

SILKSRC.128 shows part of a silk scarf. Due to its fine structure, light and dark pixels are in close proximity. Therefore, the high entries of the co-occurrence matrix accumulate in two regions next to the main diagonal (8). This pattern leads to the texture features listed in (9).

The last example is KNITSRC.128. This section of a pullover is characterized by different forms of graylevel transition. This variety causes a comparatively large 'cloud' of entries (11). Concentrations of high entries do not exist. The texture features are depicted in (12).

The contrast of the co-occurrence images (2), (5), (8) and (11) is low. Thus, the Image Attributes have been changed (by clicking the *right* mouse button on the image) as follows:

```
Min Graylevel: 0
Max Graylevel: 20
```

9.3 Source code

Figure 9.6 shows a procedure for calculating the mean and the variance of the graylevels in an operator mask. Formal parameters are:

ImSize: image size
WinSize: size of the operator mask
InIm: input image
MeanIm: output image of mean
VarIm: output image of variance

The procedure starts by initializing the output images VarIm and MeanIm, as well as the parameters Cen and WinArea. Cen serves to determine the coordinates of the current pixel, WinArea serves as a normalization factor.

The following step of the procedure calculates the mean of the graylevels in the operator mask. r and c are the coordinates of the top left corner of the operator mask. Its central coordinates are r+Cen and c+Cen. The actual mean calculation is realized by adding the graylevels together and normalizing the sum by the number of pixels in the mask.

The frame of the following variance calculation is similar to that of the mean calculation. The variance is obtained as the sum of the squares of the deviations between the current graylevel InIm[y][x] and the mean graylevel in the current operator mask Mean. The normalization factor is the number of mask pixels minus 1. This Bessel correction of the sample variance only affects results obtained with small masks.

```
void Variance (ImSize, WinSize, InIm, MeanIm, VarIm)
int ImSize, WinSize;
BYTE ** InIm;
BYTE ** MeanIm;
int  ** VarIm;
{
  int  r,c, y,x, Cen, WinArea, Mean;
  long Sum, Diff;
  Cen = WinSize/2;
  WinArea = WinSize*WinSize;
  for (r=0; r<ImSize; r++) {
      for (c=0; c<ImSize; c++) {
            MeanIm [r][c] = 0;
            VarIm [r][c] = 0;
  }   }
  for (r=0; r<ImSize-WinSize; r++) {
      for (c=0; c<ImSize-WinSize; c++) {
            Sum = 0;
            for (y=r; y<r+WinSize; y++)
                for (x=c; x<c+WinSize; x++)  Sum += (long) InIm [y][x];
            Sum /= WinArea;
            MeanIm [r+Cen][c+Cen] = (BYTE) Sum;
  }   }
  for (r=0; r<ImSize-WinSize; r++) {
      for (c=0; c<ImSize-WinSize; c++) {
            Mean = MeanIm [r+Cen] [c+Cen];
            Sum = 0;
            for (y=r; y<r+WinSize; y++) {
                for (x=c; x<c+WinSize; x++) {
                      Diff = (long) Mean - InIm [y][x];
                      Sum += Diff*Diff;
            }   }
            Sum /= WinArea-1;
            VarIm [r+Cen][c+Cen] = (int) Sum;
} }     }
```

Figure 9.6 C realization for calculating local mean and variance.

Figure 9.7 shows the procedures Cooccurrence and EvalCooc which generate and analyze the co-occurrence matrix. Formal parameters of Cooccurrence are:

ImSize:	image size
CoSize:	size of the co-occurrence matrix
Dy:	column distance between the current pixel and the neighbor pixel under consideration
Dx:	row distance between the current pixel and the neighbor pixel under consideration
InIm:	input image
CoMa:	co-occurrence matrix

The procedure starts by initializing the co-occurrence matrix `CoMa`. Then the factor `Resol` is calculated, to determine the resolution of the co-occurrence matrix. The maximum graylevel of the source image is 255. Thus, the co-occurrence matrix would be of size 256*256. If this size is too large, the graylevels have to be quantized more coarsely by using `Resol`.

The following step of the procedure generates the co-occurrence matrix. For each current pixel `[r][c]`, the graylevel `a` as well as the graylevel `b` of the neighbor pixel `[r+Dy][c+Dx]` are determined. Then `a` and `b` are the coordinates of the current element of the co-occurrence matrix. The last step of the procedure increments the entry of this element. The solution of the border problem is straightforward: the two differences `Dx` and `Dy` determine the width of the image border which is not to be processed.

The analysis of the co-occurrence matrix is carried out by the procedure `EvalCooc` (Figure 9.7). Formal parameters are:

`ImSize:`	image size
`CoSize:`	size of the co-occurrence matrix
`CoMa:`	co-occurrence matrix which is to be analyzed

`EvalCooc` returns the features `Energy`, `Contrast`, `Entropy` and `Homogeneity` extracted from the co-occurrence matrix. The computation of these features is based on the formulas described in Section 9.1.

In order to perform the texture segmentation, each pixel of the source image requires the texture features. Thus, the co-occurrence technique needs to be realized as a local operator. This is carried out by the procedure `LocalCooc` (Figure 9.8). Formal parameters are:

`ImSize:`	image size
`CoSize:`	size of the co-occurrence matrix
`WinSize:`	size of the operator mask
`Dy:`	column distance between the current pixel and the neighbor pixel under consideration
`Dx:`	row distance between the current pixel and the neighbor pixel under consideration
`InIm:`	input image
`CoMa:`	co-occurrence matrix which is to be analyzed
`EnerMa:`	output image of the feature *Energy*
`ContMa:`	output image of the feature *Contrast*
`EntrMa:`	output image of the feature *Entropy*
`HomoMa:`	output image of the feature *Homogeneity*

The procedure starts by initializing the co-occurrence matrix `CoMa`, as well as the output images `EnerMa`, `ContMa`, `EntrMa` and `HomoMa`. The parameters o, `Cen` and `Resol` have already been described in the context of the procedures `Variance` and `Cooccurrence`.

The subsequent step of the procedure is also similar to the procedures which generate the co-occurrence matrix and extract the texture features from this matrix. The only difference is the performance of these procedures in an operator mask of size `WinSize`. This mask is stepped through the source image `InIm` pixel by pixel under the control of the two outer `for` loops.

Note the basic problems of texture segmentation described in Section 9.1. These also apply to procedure `LocalCooc`.

```
void Cooccurrence (ImSize, CoSize, Dy,Dx, InIm, CoMa)
int ImSize, CoSize, Dy,Dx;
BYTE ** InIm;
int ** CoMa;
{
  int r,c, a,b, o, Resol;
  Resol = 256 / CoSize;
  for (r=0; r<ImSize; r++)
     for (c=0; c<ImSize; c++) CoMa [r][c] = 0;
  o = MaxAbs (Dx,Dy);
  for (r=o; r<ImSize-o; r++) {
     for (c=o; c<ImSize-o; c++) {
        a = InIm [r][c] / Resol;
        b = InIm [r+Dy][c+Dx] / Resol
        CoMa [a][b] ++;
} } }

EvalTyp EvalCooc (ImSize, CoSize, CoMa)
int ImSize, CoSize;
int ** CoMa;
{
  int   r,c;
  EvalTyp Eval;
  Eval.Energy = Eval.Contrast = Eval.Entropy = Eval.Homogen = (float)0;
  for (r=0; r<CoSize; r++)
     for (c=0; c<CoSize; c++)
        Eval.Energy += (float) CoMa[r][c]*CoMa[r][c];
  for (r=0; r<CoSize; r++)
     for (c=0; c<CoSize; c++)
        Eval.Contrast += (float) (r-c)*(r-c)*CoMa[r][c];
  for (r=0; r<CoSize; r++)
     for (c=0; c<CoSize; c++)
        if (CoMa[r][c])
           Eval.Entropy += (float) CoMa[r][c]*log((double)CoMa[r][c]);
  for (r=0; r<CoSize; r++)
     for (c=0; c<CoSize; c++)
        if (CoMa[r][c])
           Eval.Homogen += (float) CoMa[r][c] / (1 + abs(r-c));
  return (Eval);
}
```

Figure 9.7 C realization for generating and analyzing the co-occurrence matrix. Data type `EvalTyp` and procedure `MaxAbs` are defined in Appendix B.

```
void LocalCooc (ImSize, CoSize, WinSize, Dy,Dx, InIm, CoMa,
                EnerMa, ContMa, EntrMa, HomoMa)
int  ImSize, CoSize, WinSize, Dy,Dx;
BYTE ** InIm;
int  ** CoMa;
float ** EnerMa;
float ** ContMa;
float ** EntrMa;
float ** HomoMa;
{
   int  j,i, y,x, r,c, a,b, o, Resol, Cen;
   long l;
   o   = MaxAbs (Dx,Dy);
   Cen = WinSize / 2;
   Resol = 256 / CoSize;
   for (r=0; r<CoSize; r++)
      for (c=0; c<CoSize; c++) CoMa [r][c] = 0;
   for (r=0; r<ImSize; r++) {
      for (c=0; c<ImSize; c++) {
         EnerMa [r][c] = (float)0;
         ContMa [r][c] = (float)0;
         EntrMa [r][c] = (float)0;
         HomoMa [r][c] = (float)0;
   } }
   for (r=o; r<ImSize-WinSize-o; r++) {
      for (c=o; c<ImSize-WinSize-o; c++) {

         for (j=0; j<CoSize; j++)
            for (i=0; i<CoSize; i++) CoMa [j][i] = 0;
         for (y=r; y<r+WinSize; y++) {
            for (x=c; x<c+WinSize; x++) {
               a = InIm [y][x] / Resol;
               b = InIm [y+Dy][x+Dx] / Resol;
               CoMa [a][b] ++;
      } }
      /* - - - - - - - - - - - Gen Features */
      for (j=0; j<CoSize; j++)
         for (i=0; i<CoSize; i++)
            EnerMa [r+Cen][c+Cen] += (float) CoMa[j][i]*CoMa[j][i];
      for (j=0; j<CoSize; j++)
         for (i=0; i<CoSize; i++)
            ContMa [r+Cen][c+Cen] += (float) (j-i)*(j-i)*CoMa[j][i];
      for (j=0; j<CoSize; j++)
       for (i=0; i<CoSize; i++)
          if (CoMa[j][i])
             EntrMa [r+Cen][c+Cen] += (float) CoMa[j][i]*
                                       log((double)CoMa[j][i]);
      for (j=0; j<CoSize; j++)
         for (i=0; i<CoSize; i++)
            if (CoMa[j][i])
               HomoMa [r+Cen][c+Cen] += (float) CoMa[j][i] /
                                         (1 + abs(j-i));
} } }
```

Figure 9.8 C realization which applies the co-occurrence technique locally.
Procedure MaxAbs is defined in Appendix B.

9.4   Supplement

Certainly, the co-occurrence approach introduced in the preceding sections is the most popular tool of texture analysis. However, many other methods exist, which may be more or less successful depending on the actual application. The following four examples represent a small selection of alternative methods:

- **Fourier Analysis**
  Obviously, texture characteristics influence the spatial frequency domain representation of an image. An image consisting of large homogeneous regions corresponds to a spectrum predominantly consisting of low frequencies. In contrast, 'busy' images yield more harmonics (Chapter 4).

- **Morphology**
  If it is possible to describe the structure of a texture with the aid of structuring elements, morphological image processing is likely to be an appropriate tool to analyze this texture (Chapter 8).

- **Orientation**
  If the texture under consideration is characterized by regions of homogeneous orientation (for example, fibrous material), the image may be preprocessed by gradient operations. The gradient *direction* is likely to represent the texture orientation. The gradient *magnitude* is useful for describing the 'strength' of the transitions from light to dark caused by the texture (Chapter 6).

- **Pattern Recognition**
  The purpose of pattern recognition is the classification of objects (of whatever kind) based on features representing these objects (Chapter 10). In the case of texture analysis, the objects are texture regions to be detected and separated. The features are derived from the local graylevel variations caused by the texture. The best method for describing such graylevel changes is dependent on the actual application. The advantage of pattern recognition methods is their ability to 'adapt themselves' to different textures. Thus, these methods are an appropriate tool for solving the texture segmentation problems (Section 9.1). However, it is important to understand that the success of a pattern recognition approach mainly depends on the appropriate selection of features. The choice of the actual classification procedure is of secondary importance.

In view of the problems involved in defining 'texture', further work should be based on several different references. Surveys of texture analysis are presented by Ballard and Brown [9.1], Haralick [9.2], Jain [9.3] and Schalkoff [9.4].

9.5   Exercises

9.1   Compute the global graylevel mean and variance of each of the two images shown in Figure 9.9. For the sake of simplicity, normalize the variance with n instead of $n-1$.

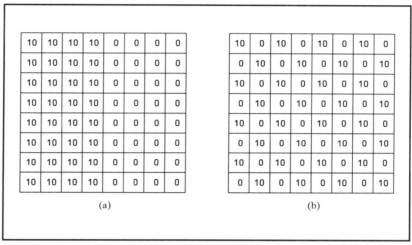

(a)   (b)

Figure 9.9 Exercise 9.1 and Exercise 9.2 demonstrate the use of graylevel mean and variance to describe different textures.

9.2   Compute the local graylevel mean and variance of each of the two images shown in Figure 9.9. Use a 3*3 mask.

9.3   Compute the co-occurrence matrices of the three images shown in Figure 9.10 according to the example illustrated in Figure 9.3.

9.4   Take the sample images used in Section 9.2 and apply a Fourier transform to them (*see* Chapter 4). Compare the results with texture analysis using the co-occurrence matrix approach.

9.5   Become familiar with every texture operation offered by Ad Oculos (*see* Ad Oculos Help).

9.6   Acquire different texture images and compare the performance of the mean/variance, the co-occurrence and the Fourier approach.

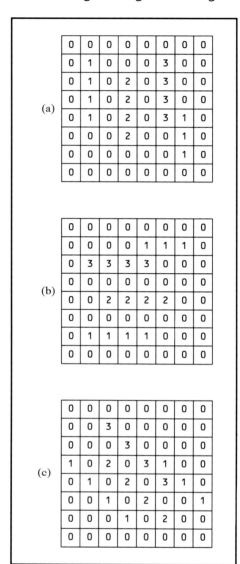

Figure 9.10
Exercise 9.3 demonstrates application of the co-occurrence matrix.

9.6   References

[9.1]   Ballard, D.H.; Brown, C.M.: *Computer vision.* Englewood Cliffs: Prentice-Hall 1982

[9.2]   Haralick, R.M.: Statistical image texture analysis. In: Young, T.Y.; Fu, K.-S.(Eds.): *Handbook of pattern recognition and image processing.* Orlando, San Diego, New York, Austin, London, Montreal, Sydney, Tokyo, Toronto: Academic Press 1986

[9.3]   Jain, A.K.: *Fundamentals of digital image processing.* Englewood Cliffs: Prentice-Hall 1989

[9.4]   Schalkoff, R.J.: *Digital image processing and computer vision.* New York, Chichester, Brisbane, Toronto, Singapore: Wiley 1989

10

Pattern recognition

10.1 Foundations

The requirements for understanding this chapter are:

- to be familiar with basic mathematics,
- to be familiar with probability theory (in order to understand the supplement section),
- to have read Chapter 1.

The purpose of pattern recognition is to place objects in a given world into categories. The interface between the world and the pattern recognition system is provided by sensors. The first step of the procedure extracts features from the input data which characterize the objects represented by these data. Based on these features, the final step identifies the objects and sorts them into certain classes.

Figure 10.1 illustrates the basic method with the aid of a simple example. The 'world' consists of various types of fruit. The sensor is a camera. Appropriate features to describe fruit are 'color' and 'shape' (Section 5.1.3).

If the fruit is to be sorted, the pattern recognition system needs information concerning the typical features of apples, bananas, oranges and so on. Figuratively speaking, the system needs a label for each type of fruit (note that the meaning of 'label' as used here is not to be confused with the meaning of 'label' used in Chapter 5).

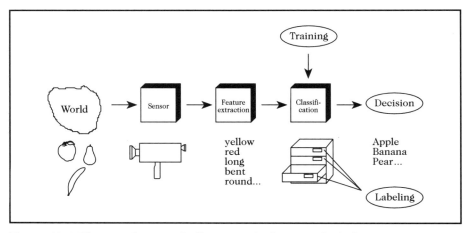

Figure 10.1 This simple example illustrates the basic method of pattern recognition. The 'world' consists of types of fruit. The sensor is a camera. Appropriate features for describing fruit are 'color' and 'shape'. If the fruit is to be sorted, the pattern recognition system needs information concerning the typical features of apples, bananas, oranges and so on. Figuratively speaking, the system needs a label for each type of fruit (note that the meaning of 'label' as used here is not to be confused with the meaning of 'label' used in Chapter 5).

Certain pattern recognition systems are able to generate these labels themselves, assigning them to objects with similar features which could belong to the same class. Note that these *un-supervised* classifiers do not yield information about the kind of object they 'recognize' (for example, 'Banana'). In contrast, the *supervised* classifiers are 'taught' such information as 'This is a banana'. These classifiers work in two stages. The first step (training step) needs a teacher who gives the classifier the typical representations of a class. The second step (classification step) compares the features of an actual object with the typical features which have been taught. Then the object is assigned to the class which fits it best.

Suppose somebody smuggled a pocket calculator into the world of fruit. Surely a class exists in which this calculator 'fits better' than in any other. Clearly, such a classification should be avoided, for instance by introducing a rejection level which tests the limits of similarity.

In the following section, the single components of a pattern recognition system are described in more detail. The features extracted from the input data span a so-called *feature space*. Figure 10.2 depicts a two-dimensional feature space for a small fruit world comprising the classes 'Apple', 'Banana', 'Orange' and 'Plum'. The feature 'Compactness' represents the ratio of surface area to volume of the fruit. In this sense, the compactness of a ball is low, while that of a pyramid is high (Section 5.1.3). The ovals shown in Figure 10.2 form the boundaries of the possible feature combinations constituting the single classes. For instance, bananas are more or less tubular (high compactness), and their color ranges from green to yellow. Oranges have colors from yellow to red and minimum compactness since they are spherical.

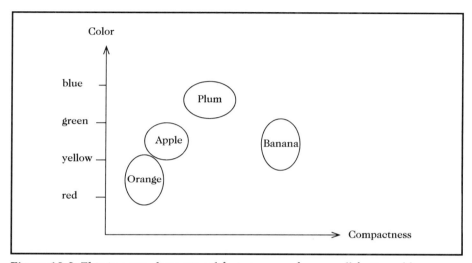

Figure 10.2 This is a two-dimensional feature space for a small fruit world comprising the classes 'Apple', 'Banana', 'Orange' and 'Plum'. The feature 'Compactness' represents the ratio of surface to volume of the fruit. In this sense, the compactness of a ball is low, while that of a pyramid is high (Section 5.1.3). The ovals form the boundaries of the possible feature combinations constituting the single classes. For instance, bananas are more or less tubular (high compactness) and their color ranges from green to yellow. Oranges have colors from yellow to red and low compactness since they are spherical.

The color variations of the 'model apples' used in the example shown in Figure 10.2 are rather limited. In reality, the colors of apples range from green to red. Admittedly, this range would cause an overlapping of the classes 'Apple' and 'Orange'. This leads us to a typical problem of pattern recognition: too few or unsuitable features result in classes which are not separable. Thus, the classification is not completely faultless. If an appropriate choice of features is not possible or is too expensive, the aim should obviously be to use features leading to a minimum classification error. To avoid these errors, it may be possible to 'reduce' the world, for instance by limiting the color range of apples as in the current example. However, if red apples are indispensable, a third feature must be introduced (for example, surface quality).

In order to describe classification procedures, let us consider the more abstract feature space shown in Figure 10.3. In a computer, any feature space must be realized by an array. Thus, the features are discrete. Our feature space contains 11 entries a to k which are named *feature vectors*. To simplify matters, the current example allows a feature vector to occur only once.

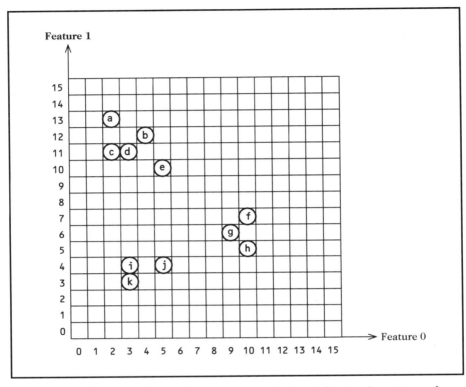

Figure 10.3 This more abstract feature space is the basis for the description of classification procedures. In a computer, any feature space must be realized by an array. Thus, the features are discrete. This example feature space contains 11 entries a to k which are named *feature vectors*.

Two simple and straightforward classification methods will be described: the non-supervised and the supervised *minimum distance classifier*. Figure 10.4 traces the non-supervised classification in the case of the feature space shown in Figure 10.3. The left column lists the distances between pairs of feature vectors. To calculate these distances, the city block distance (this is the sum of the vertical and horizontal distances) is used. Let the rejection level be 6.

Since classes are not trained, non-supervised classifiers build classes during processing. The search for classes usually starts in the top left corner of the feature space and proceeds row by row. The search algorithm first encounters the feature vector a, which is used as the center of the first class k_0. The next feature vector is b. The distance between a and b is 3. Thus, it does not exceed the rejection level, and b is therefore a member of the class k_0. The search continues, encountering the feature vectors c, d, e and f. The distance between f and the center of k_0 exceeds the rejection level, and thus it is the center of a new class k_1.

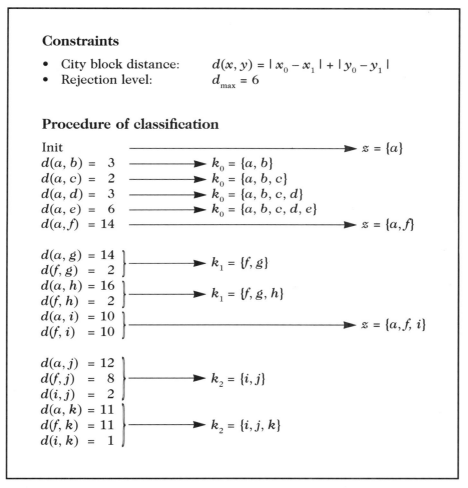

Constraints

- City block distance: $d(x, y) = |\, x_0 - x_1 \,| + |\, y_0 - y_1 \,|$
- Rejection level: $d_{max} = 6$

Procedure of classification

Init $z = \{a\}$

$d(a, b) = 3$ $k_0 = \{a, b\}$

$d(a, c) = 2$ $k_0 = \{a, b, c\}$

$d(a, d) = 3$ $k_0 = \{a, b, c, d\}$

$d(a, e) = 6$ $k_0 = \{a, b, c, d, e\}$

$d(a, f) = 14$ $z = \{a, f\}$

$\left. \begin{array}{l} d(a, g) = 14 \\ d(f, g) = 2 \end{array} \right\}$ $k_1 = \{f, g\}$

$\left. \begin{array}{l} d(a, h) = 16 \\ d(f, h) = 2 \end{array} \right\}$ $k_1 = \{f, g, h\}$

$\left. \begin{array}{l} d(a, i) = 10 \\ d(f, i) = 10 \end{array} \right\}$ $z = \{a, f, i\}$

$\left. \begin{array}{l} d(a, j) = 12 \\ d(f, j) = 8 \\ d(i, j) = 2 \end{array} \right\}$ $k_2 = \{i, j\}$

$\left. \begin{array}{l} d(a, k) = 11 \\ d(f, k) = 11 \\ d(i, k) = 1 \end{array} \right\}$ $k_2 = \{i, j, k\}$

Figure 10.4 This is the trace of the non-supervised classification applied to the feature space shown in Figure 10.3.

Since two classes exist, the distances between the next feature vector g and the centers of both the classes k_0 and k_1 have to be determined. The distance between g and f is less than the distance between g and a. Thus, g belongs to class k_1. Each of the remaining feature vectors is treated similarly until every feature vector is assigned to a class.

The advantage of non-supervised classification is the avoidance of the training step. Such a classification is thus able to process data without having any previous information. Obviously, a prerequisite for a successful classification is a feature space in which classes do not overlap. Often this condition is unrealizable.

If it is possible, beforehand, to take samples from the world to be classified, supervised classification may be used. Suppose a teacher has access to the different types of fruit in the fruit world. The teacher takes *sample classes* of fruit based on *his* or *her* knowledge about this world. For instance, the teacher assigns everything which he or she thinks of as being an apple to the sample class 'Apple'. The sample classes composed in this way serve as a basis for enabling the teacher to train the classifier.

		Mean 0	Mean 1		Variance 0	Variance 1
K_0	a	2	13		$(2–3.2)^2$	$(13–11.4)^2$
	b	4	12		$(4–3.2)^2$	$(12–11.4)^2$
	c	2	11		$(2–3.2)^2$	$(11–11.4)^2$
	d	3	11		$(3–3.2)^2$	$(11–11.4)^2$
	e	5	10		$(5–3.2)^2$	$(10–11.4)^2$
		16	57		6.8	5.2
	÷5	3.2	11.4	÷4	1.7	1.3
K_1	f	10	7		$(10–9.7)^2$	$(7–6)^2$
	g	9	6		$(9–9.7)^2$	$(6–6)^2$
	h	10	5		$(10–9.7)^2$	$(5–6)^2$
		29	18		0.67	2
	÷3	9.7	6	÷2	0.335	1
K_2	i	3	4		$(3–3.7)^2$	$(4–3.7)^2$
	j	5	4		$(5–3.7)^2$	$(4–3.7)^2$
	k	3	3		$(3–3.7)^2$	$(3–3.7)^2$
		11	11		2.67	0.67
	÷3	3.7	3.7	÷2	1.335	0.335

Figure 10.5   This is the training result of the supervised classification applied to the feature space shown in Figure 10.3. The center of sample class k_0 is (3.2; 11.4). The radius of the border of k_0 is 1.7, since usually the greater value of the variances is taken. The parameters of the classes k_1 and k_2 are obtained in a similar way.

With the aid of the example shown in Figure 10.5, the procedure is simple to illustrate. Now, the feature vectors from a to k represent the samples taken by the teacher. Suppose, this teacher composes the sample classes k_0 = {a,b,c,d,e}, k_1 = {f,g,h} and k_2 = {i,j,k}. During the *training step*, the *classifier* computes mean and variance of the features of the sample classes.

The mean values represent the centers of the sample classes, while the variances constitute the borders. Figure 10.5 depicts the training result of the current example. The center of sample class k_0 is (3.2; 11.4). The radius of the border of k_0 is 1.7, since usually the higher value of the variances is taken. The parameters of the classes k_1 and k_2 are obtained in a similar way.

The classification of a new feature vector comprises three steps:

- Determination of the distances between the new feature vector and the center of every sample class.

- Provisional assignment of the new feature vector to the sample class with the shortest distance.

- Final assignment if the distance is within the rejection level of the sample class.

10.2   Ad Oculos experiments

To become familiar with non-supervised classification, realize the New Setup shown in Figure 10.6 as described in Section 1.5. The examples used in this section originate from remote sensing. Figure 10.7 (CHOSRC.128), (CH1SRC.128) and (CH2SRC.128) show three LANDSAT pictures of Cologne, Germany. These are loaded into the input images (1), (2) and (3) (Figure 10.6). They represent the spectral channels ranging from 0.45–0.52 μm (Blue), 0.76–0.90 μm (Infrared) and 2.08–2.35 μm (Infrared). The aim of classification is to assign each pixel to a class such as 'Water', 'Coniferous Forest' or 'Urban Region'. The three graylevels of a pixel yielded by the three spectral channels are the features on which the classification of this pixel is based. Thus, the feature space is three-dimensional. The scaling of the features corresponds to the range of the 'spectral graylevels' (in our case 0 to 255). Take a 'water pixel' as an example. In each of the three channels, the graylevel of such a pixel is low. The typical 'water pixel' would thus be placed near the origin of the feature space.

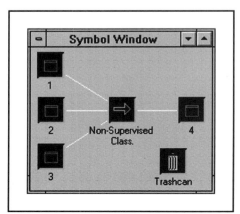

Figure 10.6
The aim of the first experiment is to become familiar with the Non–Supervised Class. function. This New Setup is realized according to the steps described in Section 1.5. The results are shown in Figure 10.7.

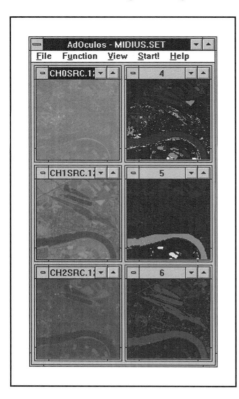

Figure 10.7
The examples originate from remote sensing: (CH0SRC.128), (CH1SRC.128) and (CH2SRC.128) show three LANDSAT pictures of Cologne, Germany which are loaded into the input images (1), (2) and (3) (Figure 10.6). They represent the spectral channels ranging from 0.45-0.52 μm (Blue), 0.76-0.90 μm (Infrared) and 2.08-2.35 μm (Infrared). The aim of classification is to assign each pixel to a class such as 'Water', 'Coniferous Forest' or 'Urban Region'. (4), (5) and (6) show the result of non-supervised minimum distance classification with rejection levels of 20, 30 and 40. As mentioned above, the scaling ranges from 0 to 255.

Note that a serious classification of satellite pictures requires considerably larger images. The examples used in this section only serve to demonstrate the classification procedures.

The non-supervised minimum distance classification starts with the top left pixel in the three source images. The three graylevels determine the center of the first class in the feature space. The classification proceeds by scanning the subsequent pixels row by row and checking whether their distance from the center of the first class is sufficiently small. The maximum distance (rejection level) must be determined by the user. If the current distance does not exceed the rejection level, the current pixel is assigned to the first class. Otherwise, it is used as the center of the second class. Each of the following pixels must be checked to determine whether it is closer to the center of the first or the second class: it can then be classified accordingly. However, if both distances exceed the rejection level, a third class must be established. The classification proceeds in this way until the end of the image is reached. Figure 10.7 (4), (5) and (6) show the result of non-supervised minimum distance classification with rejection levels of 20, 30 and 40. As mentioned above, the scaling ranges from 0 to 255.

A rejection level of **20** yields 26 classes. Obviously, the threshold is too 'strict': too many small fragmented regions appear. On the other hand, a threshold of **40** is too lax. 10 classes result from this classification. This is acceptable, but parts of the industrial areas (especially the extensive railway installation) are assigned to the same class as water. Using a threshold of **30** results in 20 classes. Now, the classification is satisfactory. Nevertheless, a supervised minimum distance classification (Figure 10.8) yields better results.

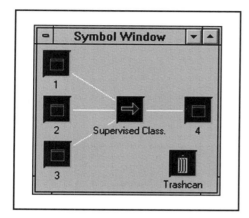

Figure 10.8
The aim of the second experiment is to become familiar with the **Supervised Class.** function. This **New Setup** is realized according to the steps described in Section 1.5. The results are shown in Figure 10.10.

In this case, a teacher is needed, who marks the regions of the image which belong to one class, for instance 'Water'. The three mean values of the graylevels of these training areas determine the center of the class (the 'typical water pixel'). The graylevel variance establishes the rejection level of the class. This threshold is usually manipulated by the user. In some cases, the variance yields a rejection level which is too strict, so that the user has to increase it.

In our example, the minimum distance classifier is trained to detect 'Water'. After the start of **Supervised Class.**, the dialog box shown in Figure 10.9 appears. The user has to enter training regions by pressing the Ctrl key and clicking the left mouse button in the top left corner of the training region. Holding the mouse button down and dragging the mouse changes the size of the region.

Figure 10.10 (4) and (5) show the classification results using the original variance and twice the variance as rejection levels. Obviously, in this case the original variance yields a better result.

The outcome of the simple classification method depicted in Figure 10.10 is quite satisfactory. Nevertheless, the 'water pixels' are fairly easy to classify due to their homogeneity. Even for a 'human classifier', the other classes are not that obvious.

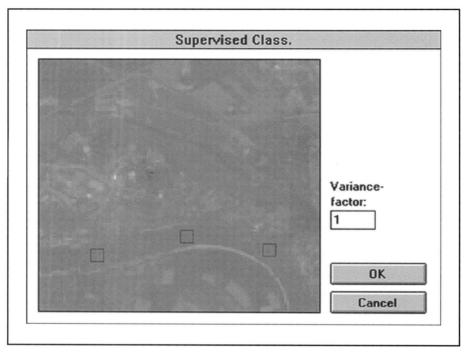

Figure 10.9 This window appears at the start of Supervised Class. (Figure 10.8). The example shows the choice of three training regions for the class 'Water'. Training regions are entered by pressing the [Ctrl] key and clicking the left mouse button at the top left-hand corner of the training region. Holding the mouse button down and dragging the mouse changes the size of the region. The graylevel variance establishes the rejection level of the class. This threshold may be manipulated by the user entering a Variance Factor. In the current case, the graylevel variance will not be changed since the multiplying factor is 1.

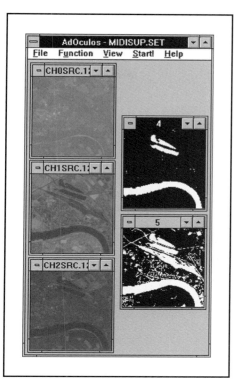

Figure 10.10
The source images shown here are identical to those used in Figure 10.7. (4) and (5) show the results of the supervised classification (Figure 10.8) based on the training of 'Water' and on the application of the original variance (4) and twice the variance (5) as the rejection level (Figure 10.9). Obviously, in this case the original variance yields a better result.

10.3   Source code

The procedures described in this section are designed for the classification of satellite images as illustrated in Section 10.2.

Figure 10.11 shows a procedure which realizes the supervised minimum distance classification. Formal parameters are:

ImSize:	image size
MaxDist:	rejection level
MaxCen:	maximum number of classes (must not exceed 255)
Ch0,Ch1,Ch2:	first, second and third input image
ClasIm:	output image representing the extracted classes

The procedure returns the number of classes found in the image. The first step of MinDist are certain initializations:

```
int MinDist (ImSize, MaxDist, MaxCen, Ch0, Ch1, Ch2, ClasIm)
int ImSize, MaxDist, MaxCen;
BYTE ** Ch0;
BYTE ** Ch1;
BYTE ** Ch2;
BYTE ** ClasIm;
{
  int  r,c, i, NofCen, FitCent;
  int  *Cent0, far *Cent1, far *Cent2;
  float Dist, MinDist, D0,D1,D2;
  NofCen = 1;
  for (r=0; r<ImSize; r++)
     for (c=0; c<ImSize; c++) ClasIm [r][c] = 0;
  Cent0 = malloc (MaxCen*sizeof(int));
  Cent1 = malloc (MaxCen*sizeof(int));
  Cent2 = malloc (MaxCen*sizeof(int));
  Cent0 [0] = Ch0 [0][0];
  Cent1 [0] = Ch1 [0][0];
  Cent2 [0] = Ch2 [0][0];
  for (r=0; r<ImSize; r++) {
     for (c=0; c<ImSize; c++) {
        MinDist = (float)1.0e37;
        FitCent = 0;
        for (i=0; i<NofCen; i++) {
           D0 = (float) Ch0[r][c] - Cent0[i];  D0 *= D0;
           D1 = (float) Ch1[r][c] - Cent1[i];  D1 *= D1;
           D2 = (float) Ch2[r][c] - Cent2[i];  D2 *= D2;
           Dist = (float) sqrt ((double) D0 + D1 + D2);
           if (Dist < MinDist) {
             MinDist = Dist;
             FitCent = i;
        } }
        ClasIm [r][c] = (BYTE) FitCent+1;
        if ((int)MinDist > MaxDist) {
          Cent0 [NofCen] = Ch0 [r][c];
          Cent1 [NofCen] = Ch1 [r][c];
          Cent2 [NofCen] = Ch2 [r][c];
          NofCen++;
          if (NofCen >= MaxCen) {
            NofCen = -1;
            goto Leave;
          }
          ClasIm [r][c] = (BYTE) NofCen;
     } } }
Leave:
  return (NofCen);
}
```

Figure 10.11 C realization of a non-supervised minimum distance classifier.

- The variable counting the number of classes found, `NofCen`, is set to a start value of 1.

- Every pixel of the output image `ClasIm` receives the value 0. This value means 'pixel not classified'.

- The three coordinates of the class centers `NofCen` are stored in the vector elements `Cent0[NofCen] Cent1[NofCen] Cent2[NofCen]`. In preparation, sufficient memory must be allocated for the vectors.

- The center of the first class (`Cent0[0]`, `Cent1[0]`, `Cent2[0]`) is assigned as the graylevels (spectral values) of the coordinate origin of the input images.

The classification of the current pixel `[r][c]` is carried out in two steps. The first step compares the Euclidean distances between the class centers (`Cent0[i]`, `Cent1[i]`, `Cent2[i]`) and the spectral values (`Ch0[r][c]`, `Ch1[r][c]`, `Ch2[r][c]`) of the current pixel. The minimum distance is assigned to `MinDist`. The index (`FitCent`) of the corresponding class center is stored in the output image `ClasIm`. Since a zero in `ClasIm` indicates an unclassified pixel, `FitCent` must be incremented.

The second step checks the result of the first step. If `MinDist` exceeds the user-defined threshold `MaxDist`, the values (`Ch0[r][c]`, `Ch1[r][c]`, `Ch2[r][c]`) of the current pixel do not match those of any existing class. Consequently, a new class has to be established. To simplify matters, the values of the current pixel are used as the center of this new class. Thus, the former assignment of `FitCent+1` to the output image `ClasIm` has to be corrected.

Since the data type of the output image `ClasIm` is BYTE and the value zero means 'not classified', the number of classes must not exceed 255. Nevertheless, in practice, a considerably lower maximum value is useful. The user may determine this value with the assistance of parameter `MaxCen`. If `MaxCen` is exceeded, the procedure stops and returns the value −1.

The realization of supervised classifiers requires more effort. In preparation, some 'auxiliary procedures' are needed. Figure 10.12 shows a procedure which computes the local mean. Formal parameters are:

`WinSize:`	size of the window to be processed
`r0,c0:`	row and column coordinates which determine the top left corner of this window
`Ch0,Ch1,Ch2:`	first, second and third input image
`m0,m1,m2:`	mean of the values in the window for each of the three images

```
void ChanMean (WinSize, r0,c0, Ch0,Ch1,Ch2, m0,m1,m2)
int  WinSize, r0,c0;
BYTE ** Ch0;
BYTE ** Ch1;
BYTE ** Ch2;
float *m0,*m1,*m2;
{
   int r,c,N;
   N = WinSize*WinSize;
   *m0 = *m1 = *m2 = (float)0;
   for (r=r0; r<r0+WinSize; r++) {
      for (c=c0; c<c0+WinSize; c++) {
         *m0 += (float)Ch0 [r][c];
         *m1 += (float)Ch1 [r][c];
         *m2 += (float)Ch2 [r][c];
   }  }
   *m0 /= N;
   *m1 /= N;
   *m2 /= N;
}
```

Figure 10.12 C realization for determining the local mean.

Figure 10.13 shows a procedure which determines the local variance. Formal parameters are:

WinSize:	size of the window to be processed
r0,c0:	row and column coordinates which determine the top left corner of this window
Ch0,Ch1,Ch2:	first, second and third input image
m0,m1,m2:	local mean values
v0,v1,v2:	corresponding variances

Both procedures are used by a supervised minimum distance classifier whose realization is depicted in Figure 10.14. Formal parameters are:

ImSize:	image size
VarFac:	parameter which is used to manipulate the rejection level computed by the procedure
Ch0,Ch1,Ch2:	first, second and third input image
ClasIm:	output image which illustrates the extracted classes
TrainFile:	name of the file containing position and size of the training areas for one class (for example, 'water')

```
void ChanVar (WinSize, r0,c0, Ch0,Ch1,Ch2, m0,m1,m2, v0,v1,v2)
int  WinSize, r0,c0;
BYTE ** Ch0;
BYTE ** Ch1;
BYTE ** Ch2;
float m0,m1,m2;
float *v0,*v1,*v2;
{
  int  r,c,N;
  float d0,d1,d2;
  N = WinSize*WinSize;
  *v0 = *v1 = *v2 = (float)0;
  for (r=r0; r<r0+WinSize; r++) {
    for (c=c0; c<c0+WinSize; c++) {
        d0 = Ch0 [r][c] - (float)m0;  *v0 += d0*d0;
        d1 = Ch1 [r][c] - (float)m1;  *v1 += d1*d1;
        d2 = Ch2 [r][c] - (float)m2;  *v2 += d2*d2;
  } }
  *v0 /= N-1;
  *v1 /= N-1;
  *v2 /= N-1;
}
```

Figure 10.13 C realization for determining the local variance.

The procedure starts by reading the parameters NofTrn (number of samples) and WinSize (window size of the samples) from the file TrainFile. This file also contains the coordinates [r0] and [c0] of the top left corner of the sample windows. Based on the data of these windows, the following for loop computes the mean values (M0, M1, M2) and variances (V0, V1, V2) of each window, as well as the total mean values (M0tot, M1tot, M2tot) and variances (V0tot, V1tot, V2tot). The total mean values establish the center of the class (for example, 'water') represented by the samples. The largest of the three total variances determines the rejection level Border of the class. The rejection level may be varied by the user with the assistance of parameter VarFac.

After these preparations, the actual classification is carried out. For each pixel, the distance Dist between the center (M0tot, M1tot, M2tot) of the trained class and the three values of the current pixel are determined. If the distance does not exceed the rejection level Border, the current pixel of the output image ClasIm[r][c] is given the (arbitrary) value 255. Otherwise, the current pixel does not belong to the trained class and therefore obtains the value zero.

```
void SupMD (ImSize, VarFac, Ch0,Ch1,Ch2, ClasIm, TrainFile)
int  ImSize;
float VarFac;
BYTE ** Ch0;
BYTE ** Ch1;
BYTE ** Ch2;
BYTE ** ClasIm;
char TrainFile[];
{
   int  r,c, r0,c0, i,NofTrn, WinSize;
   float M0,M1,M2, D0,D1,D2, V0,V1,V2;
   float M0tot,M1tot,M2tot, V0tot,V1tot,V2tot;
   float Dist, Border;
   FILE  *Stream;
   Stream = fopen (TrainFile, 'r');
   fscanf (Stream, '%d%d', &NofTrn, &WinSize);
   M0tot = M1tot = M2tot = (float)0;
   V0tot = V1tot = V2tot = (float)0;
   for (i=0; i<NofTrn; i++) {
       fscanf (Stream, '%d%d', &r0,&c0);
       ChanMean (WinSize, r0,c0, Ch0,Ch1,Ch2, &M0,&M1,&M2);
       ChanVar (WinSize, r0,c0, Ch0,Ch1,Ch2,
                        M0,M1,M2, &V0,&V1,&V2);
       M0tot += M0;  V0tot += V0;
       M1tot += M1;  V1tot += V1;
       M2tot += M2;  V1tot += V2;
   }
   fclose (Stream);
   M0tot /= NofTrn; V0tot /= NofTrn;
   M1tot /= NofTrn; V1tot /= NofTrn;
   M2tot /= NofTrn; V2tot /= NofTrn;
   Border = max (V0tot, max(V1tot,V2tot));
   Border *= (float)VarFac;
   for (r=0; r<ImSize; r++) {
       for (c=0; c<ImSize; c++) {
           D0 = M0tot - Ch0[r][c]; D0 *= D0;
           D1 = M1tot - Ch1[r][c]; D1 *= D1;
           D2 = M2tot - Ch2[r][c]; D2 *= D2;
           Dist = (float) sqrt ((double) D0 + D1 + D2);
           if (Dist <= Border) ClasIm [r][c] = 255;
                        else ClasIm [r][c] = 0;
} } }
```

Figure 10.14 C realization of a supervised minimum distance classifier.

10.4 Supplement

Section 10.1 describes supervised and non-supervised minimum distance classifiers. These are so-called *geometrical* classifiers.

An alternative to this approach is numerical classification. As an example, this section describes the *maximum likelihood* approach. Let us start with a simple example: the classification problem is to assign a piece of music either to category C 'Classical' or P 'Punk'. The decision is based on only one feature, namely the volume (v). Let the decision rule of the classifier be: assign a piece of music whose volume is below a threshold V to 'Classical'. Otherwise, it is 'Punk'.

The obvious question concerns the calculation of V. To obtain this value, a teacher who is able to identify classical or punk music is needed. A lot of pieces of music have to be analyzed in order to determine the frequency of appearance of classical $h_C(v)$ and punk music $h_P(v)$, depending on the volume in question v. This produces a histogram similar to the example shown in Figure 10.15 (a). After this training period, the classifier proceeds according to the decision rule: if $h_C(v) > h_P(v)$ is valid for the current piece of music with volume v, it is classical music, otherwise it is punk.

Unfortunately, if the teacher does not like punk music, then he or she will mainly listen to classically oriented radio stations or recordings, and therefore the histogram has to be corrected by dividing the absolute frequencies $h_C(v)$ and $h_P(v)$ by the respective number of samples listened to, in order to obtain the relative frequencies $H_C(v)$ and $H_P(v)$. Now, the histogram may be similar to the example shown in Figure 10.15 (b).

This more or less general form of classifying music may be varied to allow a more detailed procedure. A useful variation is to include the 'sources' of the music. For instance, it is clear from the start (*a priori*) that Radio Bremen 2 (*RB2*, a station devoted to 'people of culture') rarely (if ever) presents punk music, while Radio Bremen 4 (*RB4*, a station for the 'young') avoids classical music. Mathematically expressed: the *a priori* probabilities $p(P|RB2)$ (probability of punk, given that the music is broadcasted by Radio Bremen 2) and $p(C|RB4)$ are low, while the *a priori* probabilities $p(C|RB2)$ and $p(P|RB4)$ are high. Accordingly modified histograms are shown in Figure 10.15 (c) and Figure 10.15 (d). Now, the decision rule for Radio Bremen 2 is: if the volume of a piece of music is v and if

$$p(C|RB2)\, H_C(v) < p(P|RB2)\, H_P(v)$$

then it is classical music, otherwise it is punk. If this rule is considered separately from the music example, it represents the basic maximum likelihood decision rule.

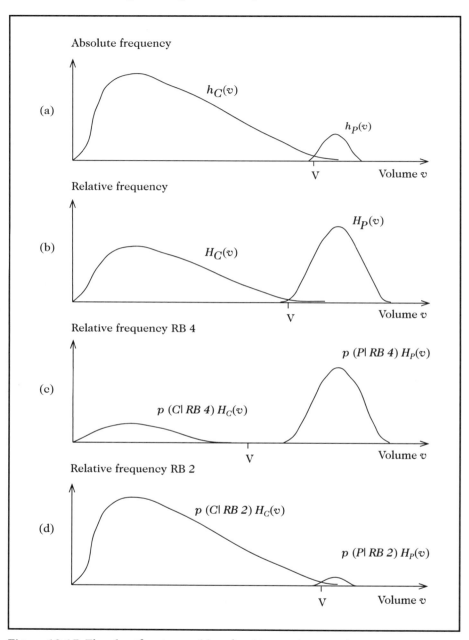

Figure 10.15 The classification problem for this simple example is to assign a piece of music either to category 'Classical' (C) or to 'Punk' (P). The decision is based on only one feature, namely the volume (v). Let the decision rule of the classifier be: assign a piece of music whose volume is below a threshold V to 'Classical', otherwise it is 'Punk'.

A more detailed description requires the following definitions:

(a) Starting point is a sample of n classes k_0, k_1 to k_{n-1}. For instance, k_0 may represent 'Classical', k_1 'Punk' and k_2 'Jazz'.

(b) The data obtained by any sensor are represented by a feature vector g consisting of m elements. Possible musical features are 'Volume', 'Rhythm' or 'Harmonic Structure'.

(c) Furthermore, the *a priori* probability $p(k_i)$ of the appearance of class k_i is available. This probability is assessable by experiment.

(d) $p(g|k_i)$ is the probability of the appearance of the feature vector g, provided that class k_i exists. In other words: $p(g|k_i)$ determines the probability distribution that a class k_i yields measurement g. This distribution is assessable on the basis of a histogram similar to the examples shown in Figure 10.15.

(e) $p(k_i|g)$ is the probability of the appearance of class k_i provided that the feature vector g exists. The decision process is based on this value.

(f) The normalization parameter $p(g)$ is defined as follows:

$$p(g) = \sum_{i=0}^{n-1} p(g|k_i)$$

Based on these definitions, the so-called Bayes decision rule is: a feature vector g is to be assigned to that class k_i for which $p(k_i|g)$ is a maximum.

This rule is intuitive, but the merit of Bayes is to have backed it up theoretically. The starting point of the idea is the minimization of classification error. Unfortunately, several kinds of errors may occur which are 'bad' in different ways. To simplify matters, consider all the errors to be identical.

The decisive question is how to obtain $p(k_i|g)$. Again, the answer originates from Bayes. He found that:

$$p(k_i|g) = \frac{p(g|k_i)\,p(k_i)}{p(g)}$$

Thus, Bayes' decision rule is:

$$\frac{p(g|k_i)\,p(k_i)}{p(g)} \rightarrow \max$$

Since this is a maximization problem the rule may be expressed more briefly:

$$d_i(g) = p(g|k_i)p(k_i) \rightarrow \text{max}$$

Against the background of Bayes' decision rule, the pattern recognition procedure is realized by the following steps:

(1) **Training**
   (a) Define the desired classes k_i ($i=0,1,...,n-1$) (for example, 'Classical' and 'Punk').
   (b) Define features and structure of the feature vector $g=\{g0, g1, ..., g_{m-1}\}$ (for example, 'Volume').
   (c) Take samples (for example, measure volume of *known* pieces of music).
   (d) Produce a histogram for the m-dimensional feature space and normalize this histogram. In the context of the example shown in Figure 10.15 this would be, for instance, $H_C(v)$. In a general sense this is $p(g|ki)$.
   (e) Determine the *a priori* probabilities $p(k_i)$ for each class and weight the histogram accordingly (Figure 10.15).

(2) **Classification**
   (a) Ensure that the feature vector g to be classified exists.
   (b) Interpret the values of the features as coordinates of the histogram and thus address the 'location' of these features.
   (c) Determine the histogram entries (corresponding to $d_i(g)$) for each class i at these locations.
   (d) Apply Bayes' decision rule: assign the current feature vector g to the class associated with the maximum $d_i(g)$.

The advantages of this approach are obvious:

- The classification is fast, since only addressing and comparing operations have to be carried out.
- Assuming a sufficient training, the classification is very exact.

Unfortunately, these advantages are confronted with the following striking disadvantage:

- Our approach causes a 'data explosion'.

The following two examples illustrate the problem: Let the number of classes n be 4 and the number of features m be 2. The features are quantized into 16 steps. Hence, the feature space comprises $16^2 = 256$ entries. Suppose the frequencies to be entered in the histogram do not exceed **256** (represented by a byte). Therefore, the amount of data required by the histogram is 256 bytes *4 classes. For this example, the training and classification procedures as discussed above are obviously useful.

The case of the classification of satellite pictures as presented in Section 10.2 requires $n = 16$ classes, $m = 3$ features and 256 quantization steps. Now, the feature space comprises $256^3 = 16$ Mbyte entries. Further consideration is unnecessary: this amount of data is only manageable at tremendous expense.

The so-called *parametric classifiers* offer a solution to this problem. This approach approximates the histogram entries by a known function (Figure 10.15). Usually, this function is a multi-dimensional Gaussian distribution. Now, $p(g|k_i)$ is no longer determined by the frequencies retained in the histogram (like $H_C(v)$), but by (Appendix G):

$$d_i(g) = p(k_i) \; \frac{1}{(2\pi)^{m/2} \sqrt{\det C_i}} \; \exp - \tfrac{1}{2}(g - z_i)^T C_i^{-1} (g - z_i)$$

In most cases it is sufficient to use the exponent

$$(g - z_i)^T C_i (g - z_i)$$

instead of the whole Gaussian function. This expression is known as the Mahalanobis distance and, consequently, one talks about a Mahalanobis classifier.

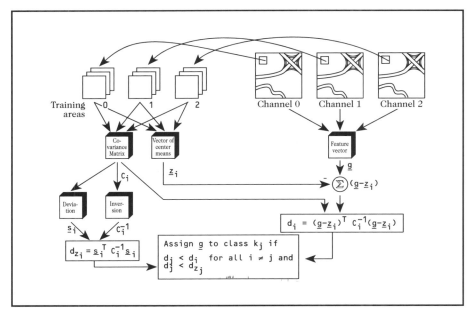

Figure 10.16 Supervised Mahalanobis classification used in an example of satellite pictures.

The classification of satellite pictures as described in Section 10.2 proceeds as follows (Figure 10.16):

(1) **Training**

(a) Define the desired classes k_i (i = 0,1,...,n–1). In the context of satellite pictures, a pixel has to be assigned to a class, such as 'Water'.

(b) Define features and the structure of the feature vector g = {$g0, g1,$ ..., g_{m-1}}. In the case of the satellite pictures, three features are available for each pixel. These are the graylevels of the spectral channels.

(c) Take samples. For the current example, this means choosing training areas which typically represent the classes.

(d) Determine the mean values of the features in the samples and put them together to form a vector $\underline{z}_i$. In the current case, these are the mean values $m0$, $m1$ and $m2$ of the graylevels of all 'Water' samples. Thus:

$$\underline{z}_i = \begin{pmatrix} m_0 \\ m_1 \\ m_2 \end{pmatrix}$$

(e) Generate the covariance matrix $\underline{C}_i$. In the current case, the training areas are based on three spectral channels. This leads to the 3*3 covariance matrix:

$$\underline{C}_i = \begin{pmatrix} v_{00} & v_{01} & v_{02} \\ v_{10} & v_{11} & v_{12} \\ v_{20} & v_{21} & v_{22} \end{pmatrix}$$

(f) Invert the covariance matrix $\underline{C}_i^{-1}$.

(g) Determine a deviation vector $\underline{s}_i$. The covariance matrix yields this vector:

$$\underline{s}_i = \begin{pmatrix} \sqrt{v_{00}} \\ \sqrt{v_{12}} \\ \sqrt{v_{22}} \end{pmatrix}$$

(h) Compute the rejection level $d_{\underline{s}_i}$ based on the Mahalanobis distance:

$$d_{z_i} = \underline{s}_i^T \, \underline{C}_i^{-1} \, \underline{s}_i$$

(2) Classification

(a) Ensure that the feature vector $\underline{g}$ to be classified exists. In the current case, the feature vector consists of the three 'spectral graylevels' of a pixel.

(b) Compute the deviations from the mean values $(\underline{g} - \underline{z}_i)$.

(c) Determine the Mahalanobis distance d_i:

$$d_i = (\underline{g} - \underline{z}_i)^T \underline{C}_i^{-1} (\underline{g} - \underline{z}_i)$$

(d) For all values of i, search for the minimum Mahalanobis distance d_i. If this distance is less than the rejection level $(d_i < d_{z_i})$, k_i is the class to which the pixel should be assigned.

Finally, the procedure of Mahalanobis classification is demonstrated with the assistance of the example shown in Figure 10.3: suppose the entries of the feature space a to e are the samples for class k_0. Now, the training yields:

$$\underline{z}_0 = \begin{pmatrix} 3.20 \\ 11.40 \end{pmatrix}$$

$$\underline{C}_0 = \begin{pmatrix} 1.70 & -0.85 \\ -0.85 & 1.30 \end{pmatrix}$$

$$\underline{C}_0^{-1} = \begin{pmatrix} 0.87 & 0.57 \\ 0.57 & 1.14 \end{pmatrix}$$

$$\underline{s}_0 = \begin{pmatrix} \sqrt{1.70} \\ \sqrt{1.30} \end{pmatrix}$$

$$d_{z_0} = 4.64$$

The Mahalanobis distance d_0 between the mean vector $\underline{z}_0$ and the entry e (coordinate pair (5, 10)) is 2.2. The distance between $\underline{z}_0$ and coordinate pair (6, 9) is 5.7 and thus already exceeds the rejection level $d_{z_0} = 4.64$. The 'strictness' of the Mahalanobis distance may be illustrated with the assistance of entry i (coordinate pair (3, 4)): now d_0 is 64.

Exceptionally, the section 'Supplement' uses a procedure in order to promote the understanding of the Mahalanobis classifier. In preparation, this procedure needs some 'auxiliary procedures'. Figure 10.17 shows such a procedure which calculates the covariance matrix. Formal parameters are:

WinSize:	size of the window to be processed
r0,c0:	row and column coordinates determining the top left corner of this window
Ch0,Ch1,Ch2:	first, second and third input image
m0,m1,m2:	mean of the values in the window for each of the three images
CoVar:	resulting covariance matrix

```
void ChanCoVar (WinSize, r0,c0, Ch0,Ch1,Ch2, m0,m1,m2, CoVar)
int   WinSize, r0,c0;
BYTE ** Ch0;
BYTE ** Ch1;
BYTE ** Ch2;
float m0,m1,m2;
float CoVar[3][3];
{
   int   r,c,N;
   float cv01,cv02,cv12;
   N = WinSize*WinSize;
   ChanVar (WinSize, r0,c0, Ch0,Ch1,Ch2, m0,m1,m2,
            &CoVar[0][0], &CoVar[1][1], &CoVar[2][2]);
   cv01 = cv02 = cv12 = (float)0;
   for (r=r0; r<r0+WinSize; r++) {
      for (c=c0; c<c0+WinSize; c++) {
            cv01 += ((float)Ch0[r][c] -
                    (float)m0)*((float)Ch1[r][c] -
                             (float)m1);
            cv02 += ((float)Ch0[r][c] -
                    (float)m0)*((float)Ch2[r][c] -
                             (float)m2);
            cv12 += ((float)Ch1[r][c] -
                    (float)m1)*((float)Ch2[r][c] -
                             (float)m2);
   } }
   CoVar[0][1] = CoVar[1][0] = cv01/(N-1);
   CoVar[0][2] = CoVar[2][0] = cv02/(N-1);
   CoVar[1][2] = CoVar[2][1] = cv12/(N-1);
}
```

Figure 10.17 C realization for computing the covariance matrix.

Figure 10.18 shows a procedure which inverts the covariance matrix. Formal parameters are:

CoVar: covariance matrix
CoInv: inverted covariance matrix

```
void InvCoVar (CoVar,CoInv)
float CoVar[3][3];
float CoInv[3][3];
{
  float D;
  D = CoVar[0][0]*CoVar[1][1]*CoVar[2][2] +
      CoVar[0][1]*CoVar[1][2]*CoVar[2][0] +
      CoVar[0][2]*CoVar[1][0]*CoVar[2][1] -
      CoVar[0][2]*CoVar[1][1]*CoVar[2][0] -
      CoVar[0][0]*CoVar[1][2]*CoVar[2][1] -
      CoVar[0][1]*CoVar[1][0]*CoVar[2][2];
  CoInv[0][0] = (CoVar[1][1]*CoVar[2][2] -
                 CoVar[1][2]*CoVar[2][1]) / D;
  CoInv[1][0] = (CoVar[1][2]*CoVar[2][0] -
                 CoVar[1][0]*CoVar[2][2]) / D;
  CoInv[2][0] = (CoVar[1][0]*CoVar[2][1] -
                 CoVar[1][1]*CoVar[2][0]) / D;
  CoInv[0][1] = (CoVar[0][2]*CoVar[2][1] -
                 CoVar[0][1]*CoVar[2][2]) / D;
  CoInv[1][1] = (CoVar[0][0]*CoVar[2][2] -
                 CoVar[0][2]*CoVar[2][0]) / D;
  CoInv[2][1] = (CoVar[0][1]*CoVar[2][0] -
                 CoVar[0][0]*CoVar[2][1]) / D;
  CoInv[0][2] = (CoVar[0][1]*CoVar[1][2] -
                 CoVar[0][2]*CoVar[1][1]) / D;
  CoInv[1][2] = (CoVar[0][2]*CoVar[1][0] -
                 CoVar[0][0]*CoVar[1][2]) / D;
  CoInv[2][2] = (CoVar[0][0]*CoVar[1][1] -
                 CoVar[0][1]*CoVar[1][0]) / D;
}
```

Figure 10.18 C realization for inverting the covariance matrix.

A procedure which determines the Mahalanobis distance is depicted in Figure 10.19. Formal parameters are:

d0,d1,d2:	deviations from the mean values of the three channels
CoInv:	inverted covariance matrix

```
float MahaDist (d0,d1,d2,CoInv)
float d0,d1,d2;
float CoInv[3][3];
{
  return(
   (float)d0*(CoInv[0][0]*(float)d0 + CoInv[1][0]*(float)d1 +
                                       CoInv[2][0]*(float)d2) +
   (float)d1*(CoInv[0][1]*(float)d0 + CoInv[1][1]*(float)d1 +
                                       CoInv[2][1]*(float)d2) +
   (float)d2*(CoInv[0][2]*(float)d0 + CoInv[1][2]*(float)d1 +
                                       CoInv[2][2]*(float)d2)
  );
}
```

Figure 10.19 C realization for computing the Mahalanobis distance.

The 'auxiliary procedures' ChanCoVar, InvCoVar and MahaDist are used by the procedure realizing the supervised maximum likelihood classifier (Figure 10.20). Formal parameters are:

ImSize:	image size
BorderFac:	parameter which is used to manipulate the rejection level computed by the procedure
Ch0,Ch1,Ch2:	first, second and third input image
ClasIm:	output image which illustrates the extracted classes
TrainFile:	name of the file containing position and size of the training areas *for one class* (for example, 'Water')

The procedure starts by reading the parameters NofTrn (number of samples) and WinSize (window size of the samples) from the file TrainFile. Furthermore, this file contains the coordinates [r0] and [c0] of the top left corner of the sample windows.

After initializing the total mean values M0tot, M1tot and M2tot as well as the covariance matrix CoVarTot and the inverted covariance matrix CoInvTot these parameters are determined with the aid of the procedures ChanMean (Figure 10.12), ChanCoVar and InvCoVar. The results are used by procedure MahaDist which computes the Mahalanobis distance MahaSample of the samples. Thus, MahaSample is the rejection level.

```
void MaxLike (ImSize, BorderFac, Ch0,Ch1,Ch2, ClasIm, TrainFile)
int  ImSize;
float BorderFac;
BYTE ** Ch0;
BYTE ** Ch1;
BYTE ** Ch2;
BYTE ** ClasIm;
char TrainFile[];
{
   int  r,c, y,x, r0,c0, i,NofTrn, WinSize;
   float M0,M1,M2, CoVar[3][3], CoInv[3][3];
   float M0tot,M1tot,M2tot, CoVarTot[3][3], CoInvTot[3][3];
   float MahaSample, Maha;
   FILE  *Stream;
   Stream = fopen (TrainFile, 'r');
   fscanf (Stream, '%d%d', &NofTrn, &WinSize);
   M0tot = M1tot = M2tot = (float)0;
   for (y=0; y<3; y++)
      for (x=0; x<3; x++) CoVarTot[y][x] = CoInvTot[y][x] = (float)0;
   for (i=0; i<NofTrn; i++) {
      fscanf (Stream, '%d%d', &r0,&c0);
      ChanMean (WinSize, r0,c0, Ch0,Ch1,Ch2, &M0,&M1,&M2);
      ChanCoVar (WinSize, r0,c0, Ch0,Ch1,Ch2, M0,M1,M2, CoVar);
      InvCoVar (CoVar,CoInv);
      M0tot += M0;
      M1tot += M1;
      M2tot += M2;
      for (y=0; y<3; y++) {
         for (x=0; x<3; x++) {
            CoVarTot[y][x] += CoVar[y][x];
            CoInvTot[y][x] += CoInv[y][x];
   } } }
   M0tot /= NofTrn;
   M1tot /= NofTrn;
   M2tot /= NofTrn;
   for (y=0; y<3; y++) {
      for (x=0; x<3; x++) {
         CoVarTot[y][x] /= NofTrn;
         CoInvTot[y][x] /= NofTrn;
   } }
   MahaSample = MahaDist (BorderFac*sqrt(CoVarTot[0][0]),
                          BorderFac*sqrt(CoVarTot[1][1]),
                          BorderFac*sqrt(CoVarTot[2][2]),
                          CoInvTot);
   for (r=0; r<ImSize; r++) {
      for (c=0; c<ImSize; c++) {
         Maha = MahaDist (Ch0[r][c] - M0tot,
                          Ch1[r][c] - M1tot,
                          Ch2[r][c] - M2tot,
                          CoInvTot);
      if (Maha < MahaSample) ClasIm[r][c] = 255;
                        else ClasIm[r][c] = 0;
} } }
```

Figure 10.20 C realization of a maximum likelihood classifier.

The actual classification is very simple: the first step determines the Mahalanobis distance Maha between the class center (M0tot, M1tot, M2tot) and the graylevels of the current pixels. If Maha is less than the rejection level MahaSample, the current pixel of the output image ClasIm[r][c] is assigned the (arbitrary) value 255. Otherwise, this value is 0.

Numerous books and papers are devoted to the subject of 'pattern recognition'. Horn [10.1], Niemann [10.3], Pao [10.5], Schalkoff [10.4], Shirai [10.6], as well as Young and Fu [10.7] offer various surveys and application notes. Nagy [10.2] gives some remarkable hints concerning the practical implementation of pattern recognition. Of course, pattern recognition applications are not confined to digital image processing. The above reference list contains example in domains such as speech recognition, medical data analysis, and so on.

10.5 Exercises

10.1   Apply a non-supervised minimum distance classification according to the example shown in Figure 10.4 to the feature space shown in Figure 10.21, representing a collection of coins. Use rejection levels 2, 3, 4, 5 and 6.

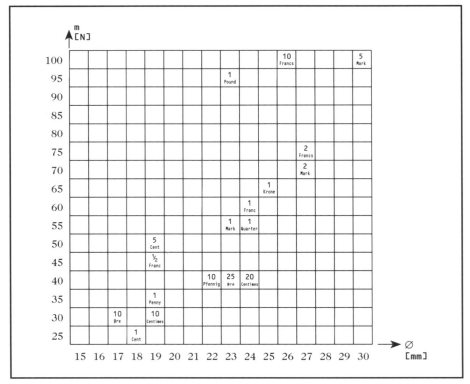

Figure 10.21 This feature space represents a collection of coins in terms of their weight (m) and their diameter (d).

10.2   Suppose, an experimental world consists of 37 objects of type 'a' and 33 objects of type 'b'. Figure 10.22 illustrates this world in terms of two features x and y. Train a supervised minimum distance classifier to distinguish between 'a' and 'b'.

(a)   Use as samples for 'a' ($x=3, y=10$), ($x=4, y=13$) and ($x=3, y=10$), for 'b' ($x=9, y=3$), ($x=12, y=6$) and ($x=14, y=3$). Compute the center and the border of the sample classes.

(b)   Find examples for good and bad samples.

(c)   Compare the sample results (center and border) with center and border of the whole population of 'a' and 'b'.

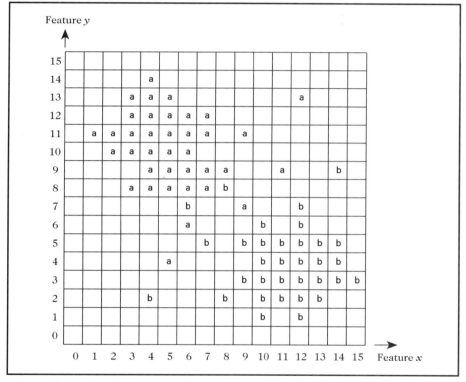

Figure 10.22 This feature space depicts an experimental world consisting of 37 objects of type 'a' and 33 objects of type 'b'. Exercise 10.2 demonstrates the choice of sample classes for training a supervised minimum distance classifier.

10.3   Become familiar with every aspect of pattern recognition offered by Ad Oculos (*see* Ad Oculos Help).

10.4   Find and discuss everyday examples of pattern recognition.

10.5   The programs described in Section 10.3 and delivered with Ad Oculos are devoted to the analysis of satellite pictures. Write a program which realizes a more general form of supervised minimum distance classifier and a supervised Mahalanobis classifier.

10.6 References

[10.1] Horn, B.K.P.: *Robot vision.* Cambridge, London: MIT Press 1986

[10.2] Nagy, G.: Candide's practical principles of experimental pattern recognition. *IEEE Trans. PAMI-1* (1983) 199–200

[10.3] Niemann, H.: *Pattern analysis.* Berlin, Heidelberg, New York, Tokyo: Springer 1981

[10.4] Schalkoff, R.J.: *Digital image processing and computer vision.* New York, Chichester, Brisbane, Toronto, Singapore: Wiley 1989

[10.5] Pao, Y.-H.: *Adaptive pattern recognition and Neural Networks.* Reading MA, London: Addison-Wesley 1987

[10.6] Shirai, Y.: *Three-dimensional computer vision.* Berlin, Heidelberg, New York, London, Paris, Tokyo: Springer 1987

[10.7] Young, T.Y.; Fu, K.S. (Eds.): *Handbook of pattern recognition and image processing.* New York: Academic Press 1986

11

Image sequence analysis

11.1 Foundations

The requirements for understanding this chapter are:

- to be familiar with terms such as derivative, gradient, convolution and correlation,

- to be familiar with basic calculus of variations (in order to understand the supplement section; *see also* Appendix C)

- to have read Chapter 1.

Analysis of image sequences is one of the most exciting areas of digital image processing, but it is also one of the most difficult. The enormous amount of data mentioned in Section 1.4 has already hinted at this fact.

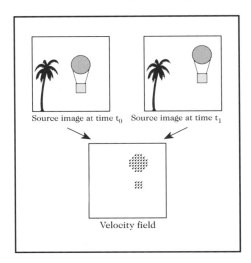

Source image at time t_0 Source image at time t_1

Velocity field

Figure 11.1
This is an example of a velocity field.
The velocity vectors (needles)
describe the direction and the
velocity of displacement of each pixel
in the source image pair.

The main topic of this chapter is the extraction of velocity fields. Figure 11.1 depicts an example: the velocity vectors describe the direction and the speed of displacement of each pixel in the source image pair. When trying to calculate these vectors correctly, two fundamental problems are encountered (Figure 11.2):

- **The correspondence problem**
  How does a pixel under consideration at time t_1 'know', to which pixel it corresponded at time t_0? At first glance, the answer seems to be easy: consider a neighborhood of sufficient size around the pixel in one image and search for the best fitting neighborhood in the other image. This procedure creates another problem: how to choose the size of this neighborhood? The neighborhood shown in Figure 11.2 (visualized by the zoomed circles) is certainly too small. It is not at all clear whether the vertical edge of the basket is positioned near the top or near the bottom. On the other hand, there is no such problem at a corner of the basket. In this case, the size of the neighborhood shown in Figure 11.2 is sufficient to find the corresponding corner.

- **The aperture problem**
  The search for corresponding image parts is a local operation (Chapter 3). The search algorithm 'looks' through a (more or less) small aperture (zoomed in Figure 11.2) at the image pair. An inconvenient consequence of this approach is shown by the example depicted in Figure 11.2: it is not possible to determine the vertical component of the movement. The basket seems to move only horizontally from left to right. Again, the problem does not occur at the corners of the basket. Thus, the aperture problem is eased by avoiding small apertures.

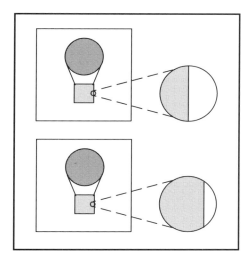

Figure 11.2
This is an example of the correspondence problem and the aperture problem. The question 'How does a pixel under consideration at time t_1 'know', to which pixel it corresponded at time t_0?' reflects the correspondence problem. The search for corresponding image parts is a local operation. The search algorithm 'looks' through a (more or less) small aperture (zoomed part of the figure) at the image pair. As a consequence, the basket only seems to have moved horizontally from left to right.

On the other hand, the computing time rises rapidly if the size of the neighborhoods is increased. Therefore, incorrect velocity vectors are unavoidable in practice and the errors have to be corrected by a subsequent correction procedure.

To summarize, procedures which extract velocity fields basically need two steps:

- A local displacement detector determines the initial vector field.

- A correction procedure corrects the errors in the initial vector field.

An obvious procedure for the local detection of velocity vectors is a correlation algorithm. An example of such a procedure is depicted in Figure 11.3. Consider a small neighborhood (matching window) around the current pixel (r_0, c_0) in the left image. The right image is then scanned with a window of the same size in order to find the best match. However, scanning the whole image would be extremely time-consuming. Therefore, the search is limited to a window around the current pixel (r_0, c_0). For each pixel in this search window, the graylevels of the small matching windows have to be compared. The comparison which yields the least square error, provides the displacement data, that is, direction and velocity.

At this point, another fundamental problem which has not been mentioned so far is encountered: the determination of the spatial parameter velocity vector is based on the comparison of graylevels. Therefore, the illumination has to remain constant, otherwise the relationship between graylevel variations and movement is no longer predictable. Imagine a source of light whose intensity increases. Exactly the same effect occurs if a source of light of constant intensity moves towards the observer.

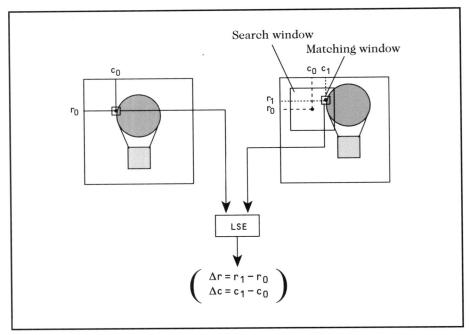

Figure 11.3 An obvious procedure for local detection of velocity vectors is a correlation algorithm as shown here. Consider a small neighborhood (matching window) around the current pixel (r_0, c_0) in the image on the left. The image on the right is then scanned with a window of the same size in order to find the best match. However, scanning the whole image would be extremely time-consuming. Therefore, the search is limited to a search window around the current pixel (r_0, c_0). For each pixel in this search window, the graylevels of the small matching windows have to be compared. The comparison which yields the least square error, provides the displacement data, that is, direction and velocity.

Correlation procedures must be followed by a procedure which corrects the correspondence and aperture errors. Such correction procedures are not discussed in this book. Instead, an alternative will be described which merges the initial detection of velocity vectors with the correction procedure: the classic algorithm introduced by Horn and Schunk [11.3] [11.4]. To explain their idea, some mathematical derivation is needed. Therefore, this section only outlines the procedure (Figure 11.4), while Section 11.4 is devoted to its mathematical derivation.

In the first step, the partial derivatives with respect to space and time are taken from the source images $E^{(t_0)}$ and $E^{(t_1)}$:

$$E_x = \frac{\partial E}{\partial x} \quad E_y = \frac{\partial E}{\partial y} \quad E_t = \frac{\partial E}{\partial t}$$

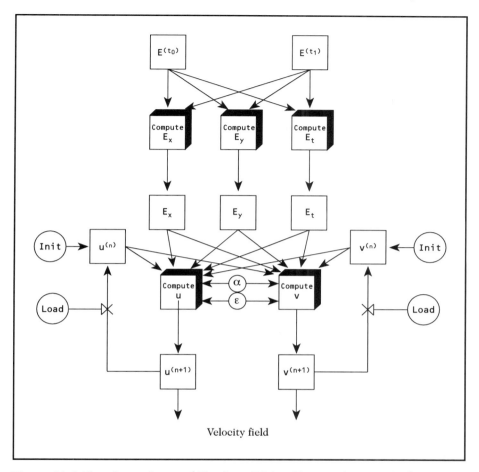

Figure 11.4 Flowchart scheme of Horn's and Schunk's procedure: in the first step, the components of the velocity vector, u and v, are calculated based on the partial derivatives of space (E_x, E_y) and time (E_t) which are taken from the source images $E^{(t_0)}$ and $E^{(t_1)}$. The second step is an iterative procedure which corrects these components. The iteration ends if a criterion for stopping (ε) is met. At the end of this process, the velocity field is obtained.

The components of the velocity vector, u and v, are defined as follows:

$$u = \frac{dx}{dt} \qquad v = \frac{dy}{dt}$$

The second step is an iterative procedure which corrects these components. The iteration ends if a criterion for stopping (ε in Figure 11.4) is met. At the end of this process, the velocity field is obtained. As will be shown in Section 11.4, the correction procedure is based on the minimization of a global error which represents two single errors. A parameter α determines the influence of these single errors on the global error.

The new values $u^{(n+1)}$ and $v^{(n+1)}$ are obtained following the $(n+1)$-th iteration from the local mean values $\bar{u}^{(n)}$ and $\bar{v}^{(n)}$ and the results of the preceding iteration ($u^{(n)}$ and $v^{(n)}$), using the following formulas (for derivation see Section 11.4):

$$u^{(n+1)} = \bar{u}^{(n)} - \frac{E_x \left(E_x \bar{u}^{(n)} + E_y \bar{v}^{(n)} + E_t \right)}{\alpha^2 + E_x^2 + E_y^2}$$

$$v^{(n+1)} = \bar{v}^{(n)} - \frac{E_y \left(E_x \bar{u}^{(n)} + E_y \bar{v}^{(n)} + E_t \right)}{\alpha^2 + E_x^2 + E_y^2}$$

11.2 Ad Oculos experiments

To become familiar with Horn's and Schunk's procedure, realize the New Setup shown in Figure 11.5 as described in Section 1.5. The example uses two images of an apple (Figure 11.6 (ASRC0-32.IV) and (ASRC1-32.IV)). (ASRC1-32.IV) is slightly reduced in size with the aid of camera zoom. The format of the source images was chosen to be only 32*32, due to the time-consuming iterative procedure. Moreover, the representation of the needle diagram (Figure 11.7) is more satisfactory if the resolution of the image is low.

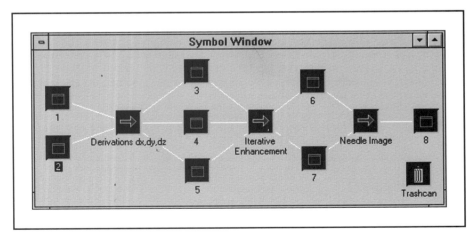

Figure 11.5 This chain of procedures is the basis for experiments concerning the Horn and Schunk algorithm. The New Setup is realized according to the steps described in Section 1.5. The results are shown in Figure 11.6.

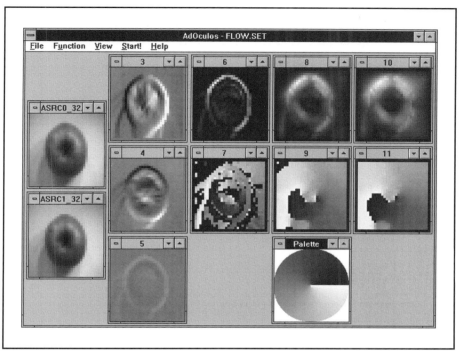

Figure 11.6 This example uses two images of an apple (ASRC0-32.IV) and (ASRC1-32.IV)). The second image has been slightly reduced in size with the aid of the camera zoom. The format of the source images was chosen to be only 32*32, due to the time-consuming iterative procedure. (3), (4) and (5) show the partial derivatives E_x, E_y and E_t of the source images. Dark areas represent negative values, the light parts represent positive values, and values which are approximately zero are represented by a medium gray color. (6) and (7) are the result of the first iteration of the enhancement procedure. Satisfactory results are obtained after 10 ((8) and (9)) and 50 ((10) and (11)) iterations. The needle image is shown in Figure 11.7. The parameters used by Iterative Enhancement were No. of Iterations: 1, 10 and 50 and for Alpha Value: 50. This parameter may be varied by clicking the right mouse button on the function symbol.

In preparation for the iterative part of the procedure, the partial derivatives E_x, E_y and E_t of the source images are needed. The results for the apple example are shown in Figure 11.6 (3), (4) and (5). In these figures, the dark areas represent negative values, the light parts represent positive values and values which are approximately zero are represented by a medium gray color.

The results of the first step of the iteration procedure are (6) and (7). The direction of movement (7) is indicated by the colors, in accordance with the palette. The necessity for a correction is obvious, considering the irregularities (especially of the direction). Already after 10 iterations, a nearly faultless result is obtained ((8) and (9)).

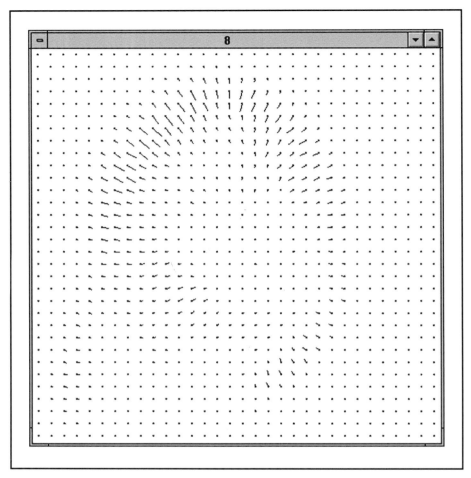

Figure 11.7 This needle image combines the velocity and direction images (10) and (11) shown in Figure 11.6.

After 50 iterations, no further improvement is discernible ((10) and (11)).

The movement direction of all pixels points to the center of the apple. The remaining inhomogeneities of the velocity field are mainly due to the small graylevel variations in the lower parts of the source images. Figure 11.7 combines the velocity and direction images (10) and (11) to form a needle diagram.

The parameters used by Iterative Enhancement were:

```
No. of Iterations: 1, 10 and 50
Alpha Value:        50
```

This parameter may be varied by clicking the right mouse button on the function symbol.

11.3 Source code

Figure 11.9 shows a procedure which computes the partial derivates E_x, E_y and E_t. Formal parameters are:

ImSize:	image size
In0,In1:	first and second input image
Ex,Ey,Et:	output image of the partial derivatives E_x, E_y and E_t

The procedure starts with initialization of the output images E_x, E_y and E_t. The following part realizes the computation of the three derivatives, which has to be carried out for each pixel. r and c are the coordinates of the current pixel.

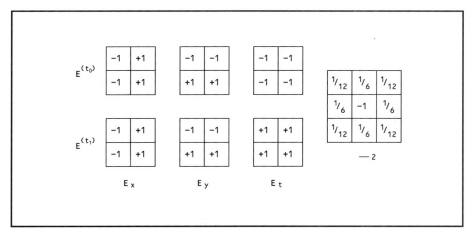

Figure 11.8 Masks to approximate partial derivatives and the Laplace operator.

The problem of approximating partial derivatives has already been discussed in Chapter 6. For the current case, the time-consuming procedures described in Chapter 6 are unnecessary. For the present case, the two spatial derivatives E_x and E_y are computed with the aid of the graylevel differences in a 2*2 neighborhood (Figure 11.8). Since there are two source images, the differences are computed for each of these images separately. The mean of the two resulting differences is utilized as the spatial derivative. The temporal derivative E_t is obtained by the difference between the source images.

```
void GenDerivates (ImSize, In0,In1, Ex,Ey,Et)
int ImSize;
BYTE ** In0;
BYTE ** In1;
int ** Ex;
int ** Ey;
int ** Et;
{
  int r,c;
  for (r=0; r<ImSize; r++) {
    for (c=0; c<ImSize; c++) {
      Ex[r][c] = 0;
      Ey[r][c] = 0;
      Et[r][c] = 0;
  } }
  for (r=0; r<ImSize-1; r++) {
    for (c=0; c<ImSize-1; c++) {
      Ex[r][c] = (int) In0[r][c+1] - In0[r][c] + In0[r+1][c+1] -
                       In0[r+1][c] + In1[r][c+1] - In1[r][c] +
                       In1[r+1][c+1] - In1[r+1][c];
      Ey[r][c] = (int) In0[r+1][c] - In0[r][c] + In0[r+1][c+1] -
                       In0[r][c+1] + In1[r+1][c] - In1[r][c] +
                       In1[r+1][c+1] - In1[r][c+1];
      Et[r][c] = (int) In1[r][c]  - In0[r][c]  + In1[r+1][c] -
                       In0[r+1][c] + In1[r][c+1] - In0[r][c+1] +
                       In1[r+1][c+1] - In0[r+1][c+1];
      Ex[r][c] /= 4;
      Ey[r][c] /= 4;
      Et[r][c] /= 4;
} } }
```

Figure 11.9 C realization for computing E_x, E_y and E_t.

The procedure shown in Figure 11.10 realizes the algorithm by Horn and Schunk. Formal parameters are:

ImSize:	image size
Alpha:	parameter which determines the ratio of errors (Section 11.1 and Section 11.4
Ex, Ey, Et:	input image containing the partial derivatives E_x, E_y and E_t
Un1,Vn1:	$(n+1)$-th iteration of the output images representing the horizontal and vertical components of movement
Un,Vn:	n-th iteration of the output images representing the horizontal and vertical components of movement

```
void GenFlow (ImSize, Alpha, ExIm,EyIm,EtIm, Un1,Vn1, Un,Vn)
int ImSize, Alpha;
int ** ExIm;
int ** EyIm;
int ** EtIm;
float ** Un1;
float ** Vn1;
float ** Un;
float ** Vn;
{
   int  r,c, Ex,Ey,Et, Alpha2;
   float u,v, um,vm, a,b;
   for (r=0; r<ImSize; r++) {
      for (c=0; c<ImSize; c++) {
         Un[r][c] = Un1[r][c];
         Vn[r][c] = Vn1[r][c];
   } }
   Alpha2 = Alpha*Alpha;
   for (r=1; r<ImSize-1; r++) {
      for (c=1; c<ImSize-1; c++) {
         um = (Un[r-1][c] + Un[r][c+1] + Un[r+1][c] + Un[r][c-1]) /6 +
              (Un[r-1][c-1]+ Un[r-1][c+1]+ Un[r+1][c+1]+ Un[r+1][c-1]) /12;
         vm = (Vn[r-1][c] + Vn[r][c+1] + Vn[r+1][c] + Vn[r][c-1]) /6 +
              (Vn[r-1][c-1]+ Vn[r-1][c+1]+ Vn[r+1][c+1]+ Vn[r+1][c-1]) /12;
         Ex = ExIm[r][c];
         Ey = EyIm[r][c];
         Et = EtIm[r][c];
         a = Ex*um + Ey*vm + Et;
         b = (float)Alpha2 + Ex*Ex + Ey*Ey;
         u = um - (Ex*a)/b;
         v = vm - (Ey*a)/b;
         Un1[r][c] = u;
         Vn1[r][c] = v;
} } }
```

Figure 11.10 C realization of the Horn and Schunk algorithm.

The procedure starts by moving the results of the preceding $(n+1)$-th iteration (Figure 11.4) into the data array Un and Vn which retains the n-th iteration. Furthermore, in order to save computing time, the product Alpha2 = Alpha*Alpha is computed in advance.

The procedure which determines the new iteration of the movement components is embedded in the following two for loops. At the beginning of this procedure, the mean values um (for $\bar{u}$) and vm (for $\bar{v}$) are computed. They are used to realize an approximation of the Laplace operator according to the formula $\nabla^2 u \approx (\bar{u} - u)$. Here, $\bar{u}$ represents a weighted mean. The weights for a 3*3 mask are shown in Figure 11.8. Note that the central pixel is not included. This pixel is represented by the parameter u.

The variables E_x, E_y and E_t serve merely for better readability. Now, all the parameters are present for running the iteration formulas:

$$u^{(n+1)} = \bar{u}^{(n)} - \frac{E_x\left(E_x\bar{u}^{(n)} + E_y\bar{v}^{(n)} + E_t\right)}{\alpha^2 + E_x^2 + E_y^2}$$

$$v^{(n+1)} = \bar{v}^{(n)} - \frac{E_y\left(E_x\bar{u}^{(n)} + E_y\bar{v}^{(n)} + E_t\right)}{\alpha^2 + E_x^2 + E_y^2}$$

Obviously, large parts of these formulas are identical, and are therefore represented by new variables a and b. Then the iteration formulas reduce to u = um - (Ex*a)/b; and v = vm - (Ey*a)/b;

To keep this section short the software implementation of the iteration control based on the stopping criterion ε (Figure 11.4) is not described.

The original representation of the movement components is Cartesian. A polar representation (that is, velocity and direction of movement) can be obtained using the algorithm introduced in Section 6.1.1. Algorithms for plotting needle diagrams are not part of image sequence analysis, they depend on the graphics environment being used and are therefore not discussed in this book.

11.4 Supplement

The main topic of the following section is a derivation of the algorithm by Horn and Schunk which was introduced in Section 11.1. The notation used is similar to that of the original work [11.3]. The algorithm basically aims to interpret graylevel changes as movement. The fundamental problems of this approach have already been described in Section 11.1.

The idea behind Horn's and Schunk's algorithm originates from a moving graylevel pattern. The scene must obey three constraints:

- The illumination is constant. Therefore, all temporal changes of graylevels are caused by the movement of graylevel patterns.

- The changes are smooth. Hence, the graylevel function is differentiable.

- The moving objects must not overlap.

Let the graylevel of a pixel whose coordinates are (x,y) at time t be $E(x,y,t)$. Relating the position of this pixel to the origin of the image function, it will be seen that its graylevel will have changed in the event of pixel movement. However, if the position of the pixel is related to a pattern which has moved (the pixel under consideration is part of this pattern), then its graylevel does not change. The graylevel is described by:

$$E(x,y,t) = E(x + \delta x, y + \delta y, t + \delta t)$$

δx, δy and δt represent the spatial and temporal displacement of the pattern. A Taylor expansion of the right term around the point (x,y,t) yields (Appendix E):

$$E(x,y,t) = E(x,y,t) + \delta x \frac{\partial E}{\partial x} + \delta y \frac{\partial E}{\partial y} + \delta t \frac{\partial E}{\partial t} + R$$

Thus:

$$\delta x \frac{\partial E}{\partial x} + \delta y \frac{\partial E}{\partial y} + \delta t \frac{\partial E}{\partial t} + R = 0$$

Disregarding the remaining part R and dividing by δt it follows:

$$\frac{\delta x}{\delta t} \frac{\partial E}{\partial x} + \frac{\delta y}{\delta t} \frac{\partial E}{\partial y} + \frac{\partial E}{\partial t} = 0$$

If δt becomes infinitesimally small, the equation which describes the spatial and temporal changes of graylevels is obtained:

$$\frac{\partial E}{\partial x} \frac{dx}{dt} + \frac{\partial E}{\partial y} \frac{dy}{dt} + \frac{\partial E}{\partial t} = 0$$

or, in short form:

$$E_x u + E_y v + E_t = 0$$

The partial derivatives of the graylevel (E_x, E_y and E_t) can be obtained without problems. However, for the determination of the two unknown parameters u and v, more than one differential equation is needed. The second equation is based on the so-called *smoothness constraint*. The idea which leads to this constraint is that single points in the image do not move irregularly. Adjacent pixels are very likely to move similarly. In order to describe this idea, Horn and Schunk use the spatial change of the movement components:

$$\left(\frac{\partial u}{\partial x}\right)^2 + \left(\frac{\partial u}{\partial y}\right)^2 \quad \text{and} \quad \left(\frac{\partial v}{\partial x}\right)^2 + \left(\frac{\partial v}{\partial y}\right)^2$$

Now, the smoothness constraint has to be joined with the differential equation. For this purpose, two errors are defined as follows:

$$\varepsilon_b = E_x u + E_y v + E_t$$

$$\varepsilon_c^2 = \left(\frac{\partial u}{\partial x}\right)^2 + \left(\frac{\partial u}{\partial y}\right)^2 + \left(\frac{\partial v}{\partial x}\right)^2 + \left(\frac{\partial v}{\partial y}\right)^2$$

These errors are computed for each pixel of the source images, and the overall error

$$\varepsilon^2 = \iint (\varepsilon_b^2 + \alpha^2 \varepsilon_c^2) \, dxdy$$

is to be minimized. α controls the ratio of the influence of the single errors on the overall error.

11.4.1 Minimizing the overall error

The classic tool used to solve minimization problems such as this one is the calculus of variations (Appendix C). The function to be integrated is structured as follows:

$$\iint F(x, y, u, v, u_x, u_y, v_x, v_y) \, dxdy$$

Hence we have the following two Euler equations:

$$\frac{\partial F}{\partial u} - \frac{\partial}{\partial x}\left(\frac{\partial F}{\partial u_x}\right) - \frac{\partial}{\partial y}\left(\frac{\partial F}{\partial u_y}\right) = 0$$

$$\frac{\partial F}{\partial v} - \frac{\partial}{\partial x}\left(\frac{\partial F}{\partial v_x}\right) - \frac{\partial}{\partial y}\left(\frac{\partial F}{\partial v_y}\right) = 0$$

With

$$F = (E_x u + E_y v + E_t)^2 + \alpha^2 (u_x^2 + u_y^2 + v_x^2 + v_y^2)$$

the partial derivatives of the first Euler equation are:

$$\frac{\partial F}{\partial u} = 2(E_x^2 u + E_x E_y v + E_x E_t)$$

$$\frac{\partial F}{\partial u_x} = 2\alpha^2 u_x$$

$$\frac{\partial F}{\partial u_y} = 2\alpha^2 u_y$$

$$\frac{\partial}{\partial x}\left(\frac{\partial F}{\partial v_x}\right) = 2\alpha^2 u_{xx}$$

$$\frac{\partial}{\partial y}\left(\frac{\partial F}{\partial v_y}\right) = 2\alpha^2 u_{yy}$$

The derivatives of the second Euler equation are determined in the same manner. Substituting the partial derivatives in the Euler equations, we obtain:

$$2(E_x^2 u + E_x E_y v + E_x E_t) - 2\alpha^2 u_{xx} - 2\alpha^2 u_{yy} = 0$$

$$2(E_y^2 v + E_x E_y u + E_y E_t) - 2\alpha^2 v_{xx} - 2\alpha^2 v_{yy} = 0$$

or, with $\nabla^2 u = u_{xx} + u_{yy}$:

$$E_x^2 u + E_x E_y v + E_x E_t - \alpha^2 \nabla^2 u = 0$$

$$E_y^2 v + E_x E_y u + E_y E_t - \alpha^2 \nabla^2 v = 0$$

Using the approximation $\nabla^2 u \approx \bar{u} - u$, the equation system becomes:

$$(\alpha^2 + E_x^2) u + E_x E_y v = \alpha^2 \bar{u} - E_x E_t$$

$$E_x E_y u + (\alpha^2 + E_x^2) v = \alpha^2 \bar{v} - E_y E_t$$

Isolation of u and v makes it possible to apply the Gauss-Seidel iteration, and thereby solving the equations (Appendix F):

$$u^{(n+1)} = \frac{\alpha^2 \bar{u}^{(n)} - E_x E_t - E_x E_y v^{(n)}}{\alpha^2 + E_x^2}$$

$$v^{(n+1)} = \frac{\alpha^2 \bar{v}^{(n)} - E_y E_t - E_x E_y u^{(n)}}{\alpha^2 + E_y^2}$$

In their original work, Horn and Schunk isolate u and v, ending up with the well-known formulas (Section 11.1):

$$u^{(n+1)} = \bar{u}^{(n)} - \frac{E_x \left(E_x \bar{u}^{(n)} + E_y \bar{v}^{(n)} + E_t \right)}{\alpha^2 + E_x^2 + E_y^2}$$

$$v^{(n+1)} = \bar{v}^{(n)} - \frac{E_y \left(E_x \bar{u}^{(n)} + E_y \bar{v}^{(n)} + E_t \right)}{\alpha^2 + E_x^2 + E_y^2}$$

These expressions allow the computing time to be reduced, since large parts of the formulas are identical.

Besides this classic algorithm by Horn and Schunk, there are several alternative approaches. Unfortunately, little work surveying *image sequence analysis* has been published. Jähne [11.5], however, provides a detailed consideration of this topic. Early survey work has been largely due to Nagel

[11.7] [11.8]. Schalkoff [11.9] also describes image sequence analysis fairly intensively.

11.5 Exercises

11.1   Figure 11.11 and Figure 11.12 show a sequence of two images representing a moving block. Apply a 3*3 matching window according to the example shown in Figure 11.3. Omit a search window. Determine for every moving pixel in Figure 11.11 the corresponding pixel in Figure 11.11. Sketch a needle image based on these results.

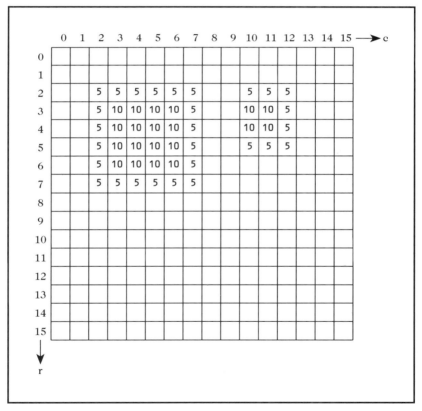

Figure 11.11 Exercise 11.1 demonstrates the application of the correlation procedure for analyzing image sequences. The second image is shown in Figure 11.12.

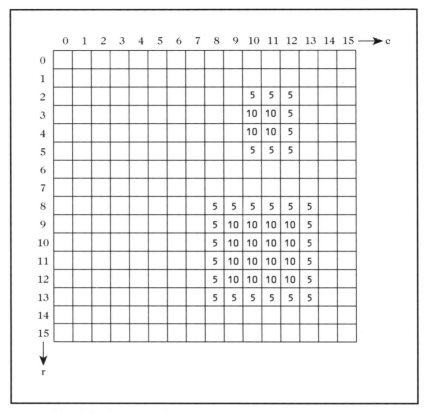

Figure 11.12 *See* Figure 11.11.

11.2   Acquire image sequences whose graylevels vary due to illumination changes. Analyze the 'pseudo motion' with the procedures demonstrated in Section 11.2.

11.3   Write a program which realizes the correlation procedure demonstrated in Figure 11.3.

11.4   Write a program which is able to track small moving objects. Acquire sequences of several images (for instance showing a moving light) to test your program. Alternatively, generate artificial sequences.

11.5   Become familiar with every aspect of image sequence analysis offered by Ad Oculos (*see* Ad Oculos Help).

11.6 References

[11.1] Aggarwal, E. and Nadhakumar, R.: On the computation o motion from sequences of images – a review. *Proc. IEEE, Vol. 76*, pp. 917–935, 1988

[11.2] Haralick, R.M.; Shapiro, L.G.: *Computer and Robot Vision, Vol. 2.* Reading MA: Addison-Wesley 1992

[11.3] Horn, B.K.P.; Schunck, B.G.: Determining optical flow. *Artificial Intelligence 17* (1981) 185–203

[11.4] Horn, B.K.P.; Schunck, B.G.: *Robot vision.* Cambridge, London: MIT Press 1986

[11.5] Jähne, B.: *Digital Image Processing. Concepts, Algorithms, and Scientific Applications.* Berlin, Heidelberg, New York, London, Paris, Tokyo: Springer 1991

[11.6] Murray, D.W. and Buxton, B.F.: *Experiments in the machine interpretation of visual motion.* Cambridge MA: MIT Press 1990

[11.7] Nagel, H.H.: Image sequence analysis: what can we learn from applications? In: Huang, T.S. (ed.): *Image sequence analysis.* Berlin, Heidelberg, New York: Springer 1981

[11.8] Nagel, H.H.: Image sequences — ten (octal) years — from phenomenology towards a theoretical foundation. *Proc 8th Int. Conf. Pattern Recognition* (1986) 1174–1185

[11.9] Schalkoff, R.J.: *Digital image processing and computer vision.* New York, Chichester, Brisbane, Toronto, Singapore: Wiley 1989

[11.10] Sonka, M.; Hlavac, V. and Boyle R.: *Image processing, analysis and machine vision.* London: Chapman and Hall 1993

[11.11] Weng, J.; Huang, T.S. and Ahuja, N.: *Motion and structure from image sequences.* Berlin, Heidelberg, New York: Springer 1992

Appendix A: Examples of industrial image processing

The following examples of industrial image processing are intended to demonstrate practical applications. Although the examples highlight the image processing part of the applications, they give an impression of the other parts, which often predominate (Chapter 1).

The examples originate from actual industrial image processing. The equipment described in this section has been developed and produced by companies joined in the *Bremer Arbeitskreis Bildverarbeitung* (working group for image processing in Bremen). One aim of this association is the support of practice-oriented teaching in engineering.

In each of the following sections, the problem and its constraints are described first. Then, the image processing part of the solution is outlined. An exact description of the solution would require an in-depth knowledge of many system details which are not relevant to this book.

A.1   Inspection of vehicle bodywork manufacturing processes

The following example from motor car production has been kindly placed at our disposal by Atlas Elektronik GmbH, Bremen, Germany.

A.1.1   Posing the problem

Welding bolts are small, but important parts of the bodywork. They serve in the fixing of several devices. The number of welding bolts used in one body shell can be as many as 200. The actual number and position of the bolts differ from car to car, depending on what equipment the customer orders. Hence, the variation of the bolt configurations is fairly high, and a visual inspection by human beings is hardly possible. The following example illustrates a solution using an image processing system.

A.1.2   Constraints

It is guaranteed that the bolts are reflective. Thus, illumination and camera should be positioned in a way that the reflection lights of the bolts (highlights) are visible to the camera (Section 1.3 and Figure 1.5). In contrast, the surface of the bodywork around the bolt (that is, the background of the bolt) may be quite different:

- Overall, the bodywork consists of different materials (for example, sheet-steel or galvanized sheet-metal).

- Locally, the background may be degraded for example, the metal may be discolored due to the welding process.

- The background reflections may be different due to inhomogeneous illumination.

A.1.3   Solving the problem

Since the graylevels of the background differ considerably, segmentation by simple thresholding (Section 5.1.1) is not feasible without preparation. Thus, what we need is a strategy for suppressing irrelevant parts of the image step by step. Such a strategy, illustrated in the following sections, is based on morphological image processing (Section 8.1). It works according to the flowchart shown in Figure A.1. The basic idea of this strategy is described in Section 8.1 and Figure 8.3.

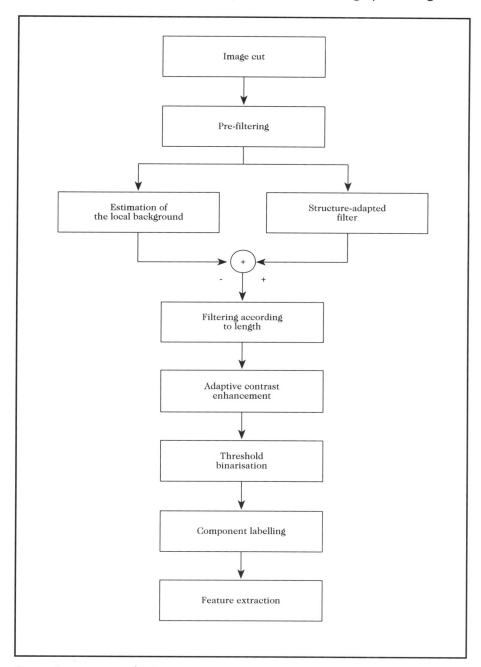

Figure A.1 Strategy of bolt detection.

Figure A.2 is the source image. We want to extract the vertical bolt in the middle of the image.

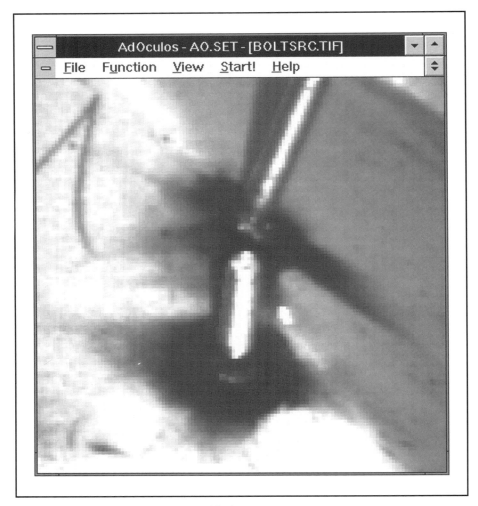

Figure A.2 Image showing a vertical bolt.

Pre-filtering

Light regions, which are small compared with the bolt highlight, may degrade successive operations, so they should be eliminated. In Figure A.2 (source image), such regions are at the bottom of the bolt. The result of the elimination shown in Figure A.3 is free of these degradations. The elimination is achieved by two openings. The structuring element of the first one is 1 pixel high and 3 pixels wide. Thus, it is formed like a small horizontal bar. The second structuring element is shaped like a vertical bar. It is 1 pixel wide and 7 pixels high.

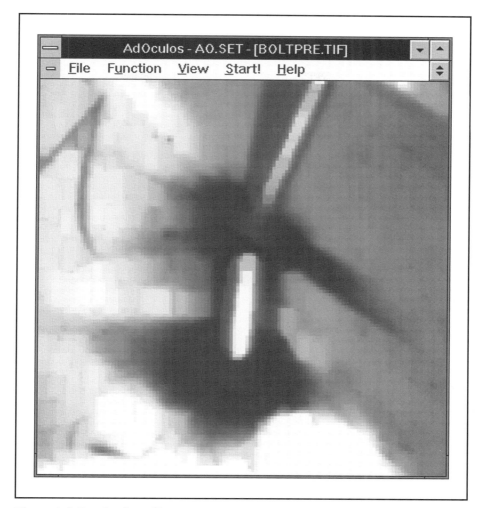

Figure A.3 Result of pre-filtering.

Background estimation

The overall aim of the procedure is the suppression of every part of the image which does not belong to the bolt. In order to find these parts, we first suppress the bolt highlight itself. The result is shown in Figure A.4. The highlight was removed by an opening with a horizontal structuring element formed like a bar. This structuring element must be slightly wider than the highlight. In this example, the structuring element was 11 pixels wide and 1 pixel high.

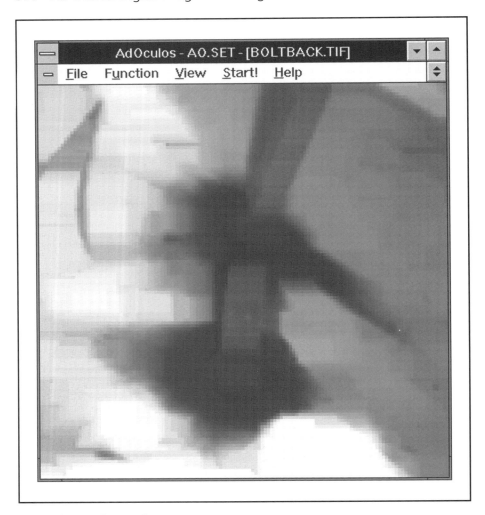

Figure A.4 Background estimation.

Structure-adapted filter

In principle, subtraction of the background (Figure A.4) from the smoothed source image (Figure A.3) would yield the bolt. This was done for the example shown in Figure 8.3. This simple approach results in some 'noise', whose effects are not serious, but 'inconvenient'. Avoiding them would result in a more robust system. These degradations appear because of the difference between the original background shown in Figure A.3 and the background estimation shown in Figure A.4. This effect is due to the non-linear character of morphological operators.

Application of another opening to the smoothed source, similar to the opening that yielded the background estimation, but *without* removing the highlight, will diminish the problem of different backgrounds. This is achieved by using a structuring element formed like a sinus arc with an amplitude of 64 graylevels instead of the 'flat' structuring element used for the background estimation. The result of this opening is shown in Figure A.5.

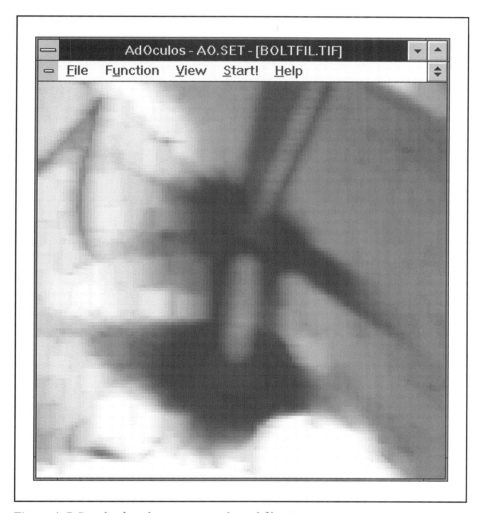

Figure A.5 Result after the structure-adapted filtering.

Computing the difference

After this careful preparation, it is a simple matter of subtracting the background estimation. The difference is shown in Figure A.6. The remaining degradations have to be erased in the next step.

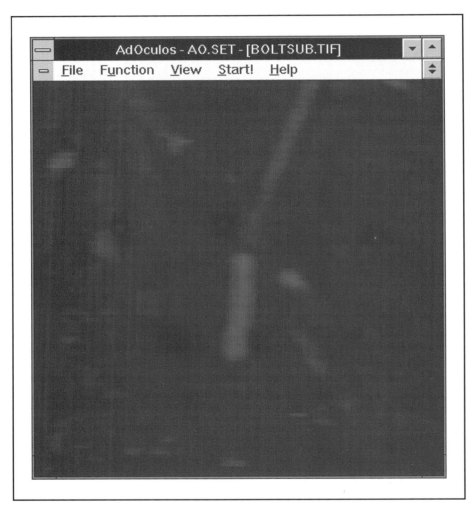

Figure A.6 Difference between the result of the structure-adapted filtering and the background estimation.

Filtering according to a length criterion

The degradations shown in Figure A.6 are significantly less than, or differently shaped from, the bolt highlight. Thus, it is easy to remove them with an opening and a structuring element formed like the bolt. Figure A.7 depicts the result of this filtering.

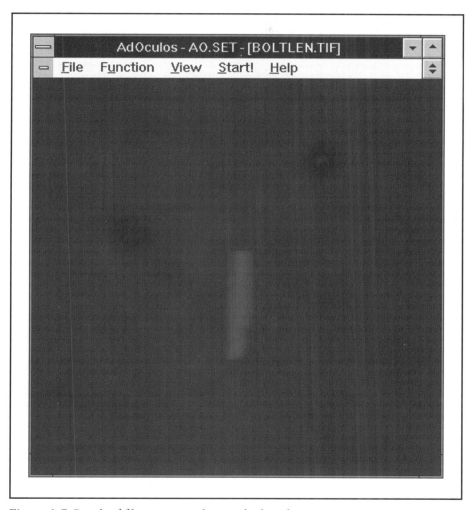

Figure A.7 Result of filtering according to the length criterion.

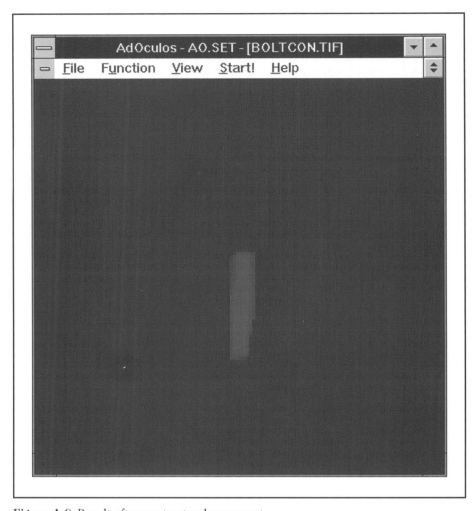

Figure A.8 Result after contrast enhancement.

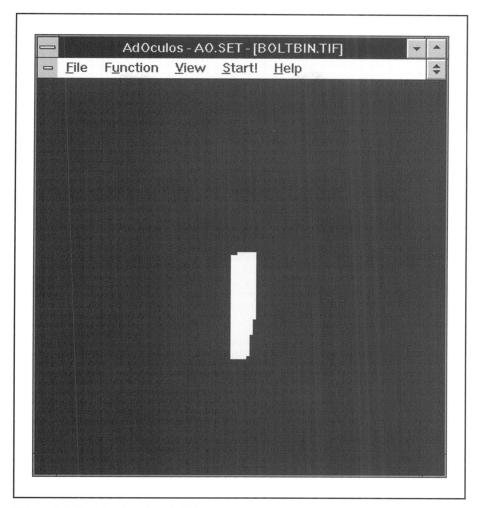

Figure A.9 Result after thresholding.

Adaptive contrast enhancement

During the preceding steps, the vertices of the bolt highlight have become rounded. That is, the graylevels are high in the middle of the bolt and are low at its borders. There is thus a risk that a robust thresholding (*see also* Section A.2.3 *and* Figure A.19) will not take place in the next step. A contrast enhancement procedure will solve the problem.

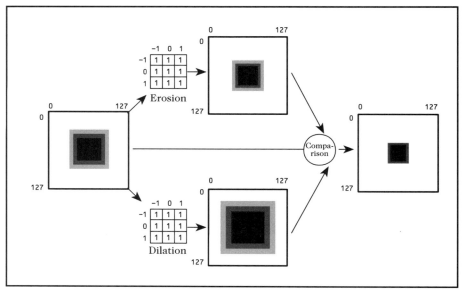

Figure A.10 Contrast enhancement based on morphological operations.

Figure A.10 shows such a procedure based on morphological operations. The enhanced image results from a comparison between the source image, its eroded and its dilated versions. Figure A.11 illustrates this comparison with the aid of an 'artificial' example, a ramp edge. The dilation expands the object (dotted line), while the erosion diminishes it (dashed line). The comparison is based on the graylevel differences between the source image and the dilated image |S-D|, and between the source image and the eroded image |S-E|. Now, we have to deal with the following three cases:

|S-D| > |S-E|:   The resulting graylevels (Figure A.11) are taken from the eroded image.

|S-D| < |S-E|:   The resulting graylevels are taken from the dilated image.

|S-D| = |S-E|:   The resulting graylevels are taken from the source image.

An important advantage of morphological contrast enhancement is its flexibility due to the structuring elements. For instance, in the case of the bolt highlight, it is sufficient only to sharpen the vertical edges of the highlight. Thus, the structuring element should be a small horizontal bar. The result shown in Figure A.8 was obtained by a structuring element 3 pixels wide and 1 pixel high.

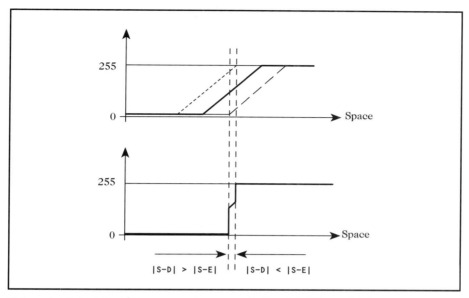

Figure A.11 Details of the comparison step depicted in Figure A.10.

Segmentation and feature extraction

Figure A.8 shows that the bolt highlight and the background are clearly indicated by different graylevels. We are now able to apply a region segmentation procedure as described in Section 5.1. The result of thresholding is shown in Figure A.9.

Feature extraction yields area, center of gravity, polar moment of inertion and the angle between the axis of moment, as well as the coordinate system and the strength of the highlight. These features guarantee a robust identification of the welding bolt.

A.2   Inspection of fiber positioning and splicing

The following example of an optical fiber splicing inspection system has been kindly placed at our disposal by DST Deutsche System-Technik GmbH, Bremen, Germany.

A.2.1   Posing the problem

In modern communication techniques, optical fibers are becoming increasingly important. In this context, the traditional soldering-iron is no longer an adequate tool. Optical fibers have to be spliced with the aid of an electrical arc.

In this example, 10 fibers are joined together to form a band. Figure A.12 shows two sledges on which the ends of the fiber bands are fixed. These sledges are used to determine the position of the fiber bands which are to be spliced together.

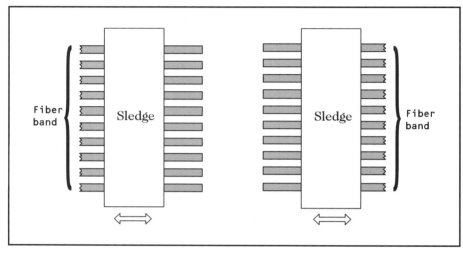

Figure A.12 Two sledges determine the position of the fibers to be spliced.

Control of the splicing process and inspection of the spliced seam is best performed by an image processing system. Some typical tasks for such a system are:

- controlling the fiber position (Figure A.13),
- checking the number of fibers (Figure A.14),
- controlling the horizontal and vertical distances between fibers (Figure A.15),
- checking whether all fibers are correctly joined after splicing (Figure A.16),
- checking the attenuation of the spliced seam.

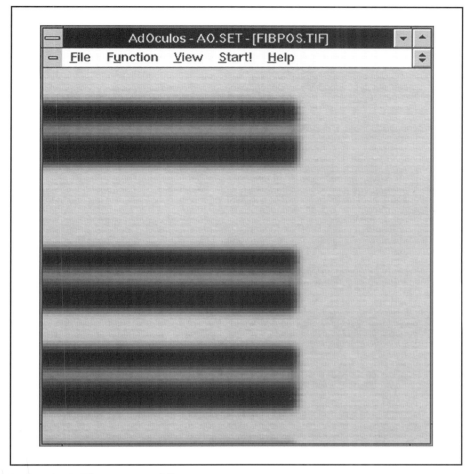

Figure A.13 The position of fibers is incorrect.

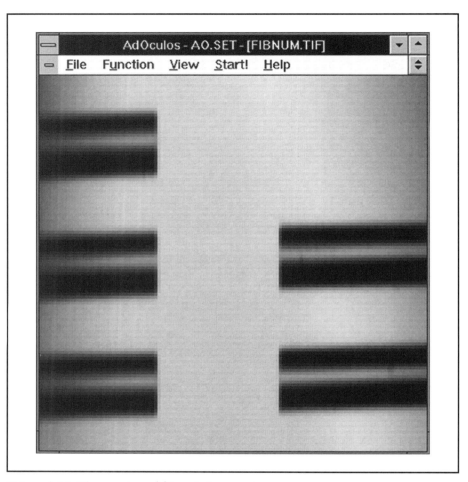

Figure A.14 The number of fibers is incorrect.

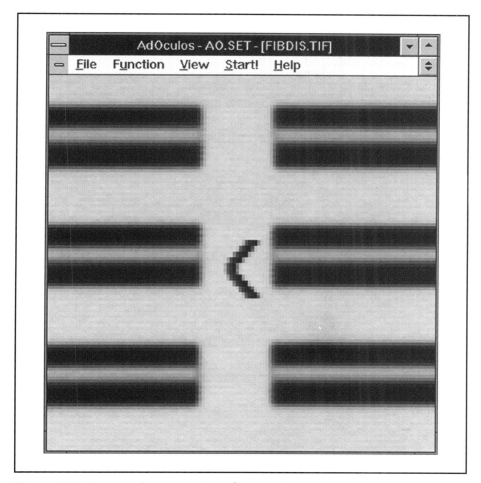

Figure A.15 Distances between various fibers are incorrect.

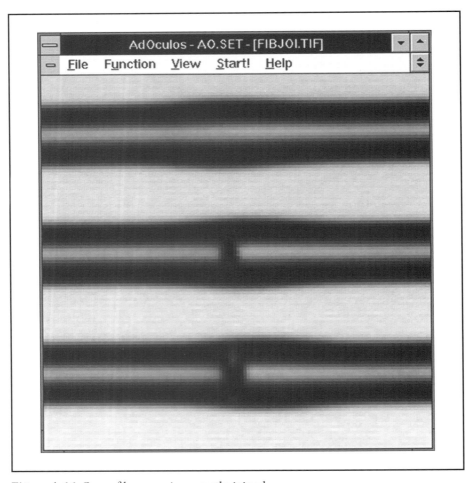

Figure A.16 Some fibers are incorrectly joined.

A.2.2 Constraints

The splicing device must:

- work in the open air (0 to 50° C, 32 to 120° F),
- be light, compact and portable,
- work in a dusty environment.

A.2.3 Solving the problem

The first task of any image processing system must be the optimization of the illumination conditions (Section 1.3), in order to obtain a fast and robust separation of the object(s) from the background ('segmentation', Chapter 5 and Chapter 6).

Fortunately, in this case it is easy to obtain the requisite binary image. Figure A.17 shows the intensity profile obtained after irradiating a fiber side on. The histogram shown in Figure A.18 also illustrates the binary character of the fiber images. It should be easy to obtain a binary image by thresholding (Chapter 5).

However, we have to be aware of a typical binarization problem (Figure A.19): the value of the threshold may influence the measurements of the objects. To avoid such errors, the following should be considered:

- The edges of the objects must be determined by a dark to light (or light to dark) step which is as steep as possible.
- The threshold should be the arithmetical mean of both the values associated with the maximum histogram values.
- Different thresholds may be applied and the objects in the corresponding binary images may be measured. The mean of these measurements is usually closer to reality than the measurements taken from only one image.

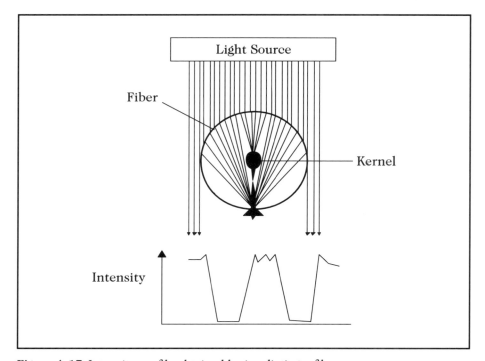

Figure A.17 Intensity profile obtained by irradiating a fiber.

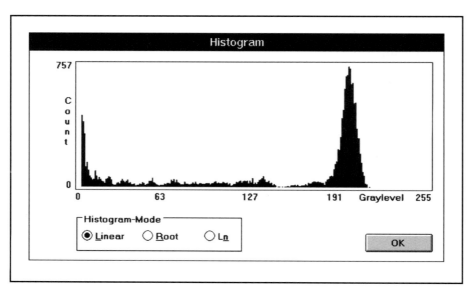

Figure A.18 Histogram of the image shown in Figure A.13.

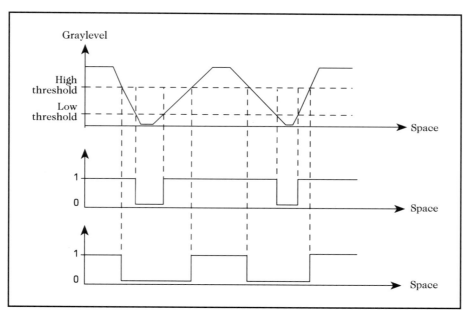

Figure A.19 Illustration of the problems which arise from using different threshold values.

After successful binarization, two basic inspection tasks have to be carried out. The first one concerns the determination of the fiber position before splicing. The second task is to evaluate the result of the splicing process. Figure A.20 shows the upper left part of a binary fiber image and a processing mask which is 2 pixels high and 8 pixels wide. This mask serves for the accomplishment of both tasks.

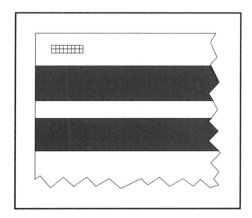

Figure A.20
Processing mask.

Determination of position

To find the horizontal position of the fiber, the mask shown in Figure A.20 is moved from the top down the vertical border of the image in order to detect the white to black and the black to white steps. The outer border line of a fiber is determined by a white to black step and then a successive black to white step. The position of the fiber is computed as the center line between its outer borders.

Splicing evaluation

An important measure of the splicing quality is the shape of the seam. It is evaluated using a mask (Figure A.20) similar to the one used for determining the positions of the fibers.

The attenuation of the seam is another important measure. The number of black pixels in the core of the fiber (which should be white) is an indicator for the value of its attenuation. This number is again easily obtainable using the mask shown in Figure A.20.

A.3   Adjustment of ink jet printers

The following example of an adjustment system based on image processing has been kindly placed at our disposal by Innovationstechnik Gesellschaft für Automation m.b.H., Bremen, Germany.

A.3.1 Posing the problem

For an ink jet printer, a good type quality requires the ink droplets to hit the paper under specific conditions. The corresponding parameters must be measured and, if necessary, corrected during the production process of the print heads. In order to optimize both quality and speed of production, the measurement and correction procedures should be automated.

In order to realize the automation of this production process, special test equipment has to be developed. With the aid of this equipment, two basic aims are to be pursued:

- Analysis of the trajectory of the droplets. Typical questions are:
  - Is the number of flying droplets correct?
  - Is the plane of flying droplets aligned?
- Analysis of the inkblots on the paper. Relevant questions here are:
  - Is the shape of the individual inkblots correct?
  - Have the inkblots been correctly placed?

A.3.2 Constraints

Conditions for image processing are almost ideal because the illumination can be accurately controlled. However, a problem arises from the high velocity of the flying droplets, especially if the aim is to use only a standard video camera.

A.3.3 Solving the problem

The aim of using a standard video camera is achieved by 'freezing' the movement of the flying droplets with the aid of a strobe light synchronized with the print head and a camera control system. Figure A.21 shows the industrial image processing computer VIP 2a which performs the synchronization task and the analysis of the trajectories of the ink droplets. The evaluation of the inkblots on the paper is also carried out by the VIP 2a system (Figure A.22).

Examples of trajectory analysis

An important factor concerning the quality of a print head is the correct functioning of every ink nozzle. For this to be tested, the spray velocity is maximized. Figure A.23 shows a typical image, taken by the system shown in Figure A.21. The most obvious method of analyzing this image starts by separating the ink jets from the background with the aid of binarization. Figure A.24 shows the result of binarization with a user-defined threshold. In practice, however, this approach proved to be a failure.

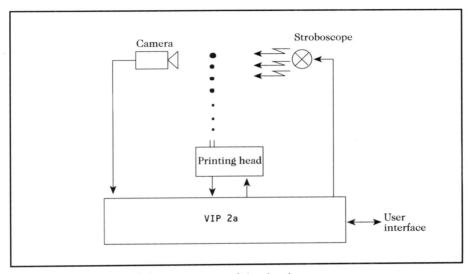

Figure A.21 Analysis of the trajectories of the droplets.

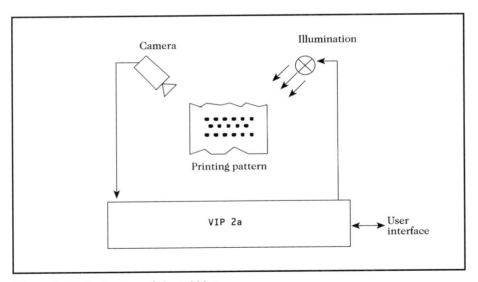

Figure A.22 Evaluation of the inkblots on paper.

A more sophisticated procedure is based on the following prior knowledge:

- The black area at the bottom of the image is the edge of the print head.
- The ink jets are vertically aligned.
- The distance between the jets is known.

Because of the vertical orientation of the jets, we can detect the absence of a jet by summing up the graylevels of each column. Figure A.25 shows another test image plus the overlay of the columnwise graylevel sums which look like an oscillation. An insufficiently low oscillation point indicates a missing or poor ink jet. The position of a low point corresponds to a column which is aligned with the middle of a jet. Tracing this column from top to bottom, we will encounter the leading droplet from the jet. In Figure A.26, each of these droplets is accentuated by the fade-in of a cross.

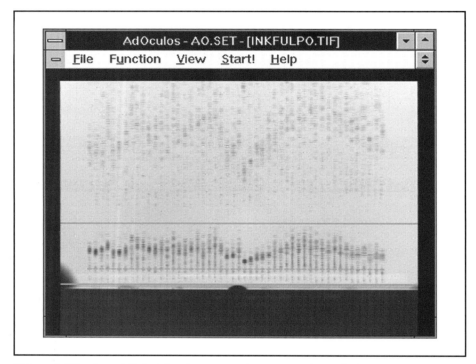

Figure A.23   Jets of flying droplets at maximum spraying velocity.

The positions of the leading droplets constitute another quality measure. If the cross is above the upper broken line, the droplet velocity is too high. If the droplet does not reach the solid line below, its velocity is too low. The lower broken line indicates the position of the droplet of lowest velocity. Thus, in this case all velocities of the leading droplets are within the permissible limits.

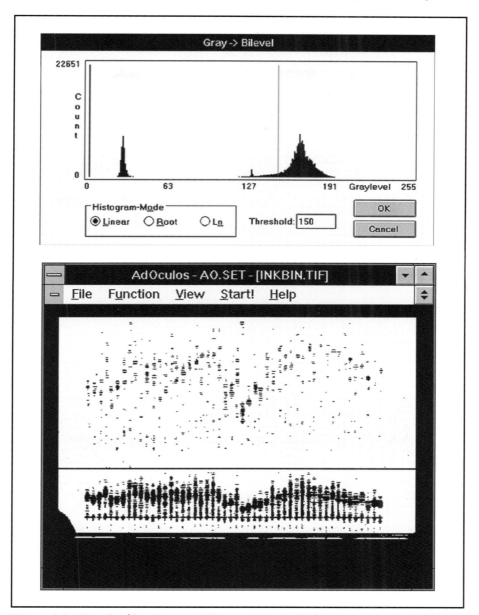

Figure A.24 Result of binarization. The input image is shown in Figure A.23.

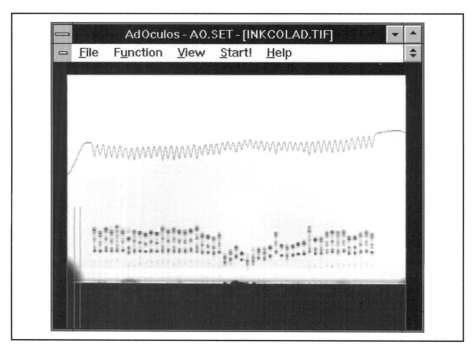

Figure A.25 Analysis of the jets by summing up the graylevels columnwise.

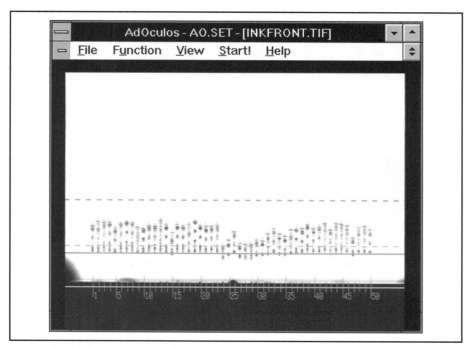

Figure A.26 Measurement of the positions of the leading droplets.

Examples of inkblot analysis

Figure A.27 shows a typical test pattern of inkblots for determining the quality of a print head. This image was taken with the set-up shown in Figure A.22. The analysis of the dot pattern is based on the classic binarization approach (Chapter 5). Figure A.28 shows the result of a binarization with a user-defined threshold. Since the contrast may change from sample to sample, the VIP 2a system uses an adaptive thresholding procedure. The demands for such a procedure have already been discussed in Section A.2.3 (Figure A.19).

After segmenting the image according to these demands, the dots are ready to be analyzed. A typical quality parameter is the position of the ink blots. The white circles shown in Figure A.29 represent the correct positions, while the actual positions are indicated by white crosses marking the centers of gravity of the inkblots.

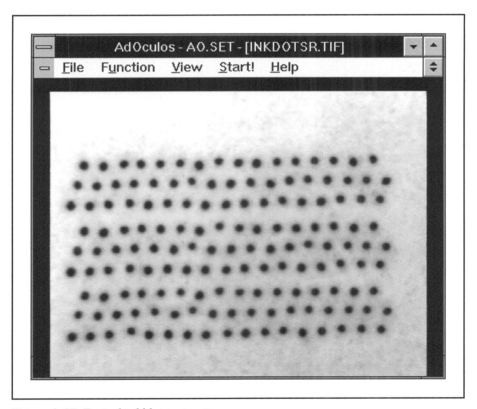

Figure A.27 Typical inkblot test pattern.

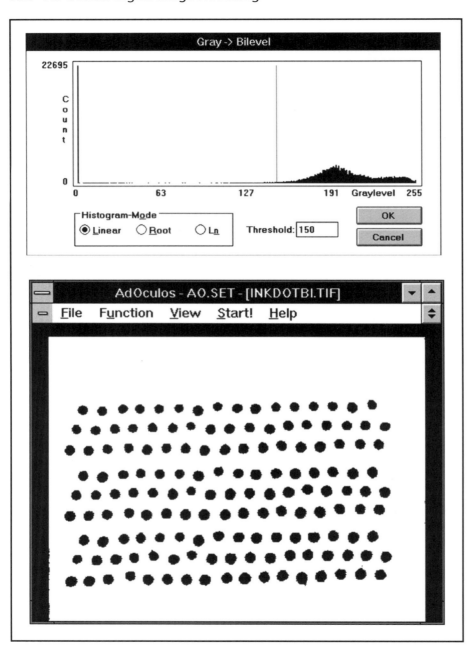

Figure A.28 Result of binarization. The input image is shown in Figure A.27.

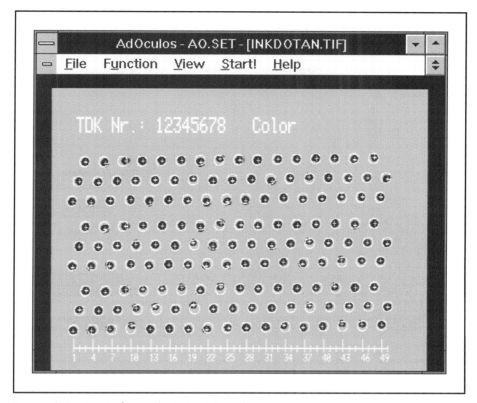

Figure A.29 Image for analyzing print quality.

A.4   Inspection of multilayer printed circuit boards

The following example, taken from the production of printed circuit boards, has been kindly placed at our disposal by O.S.T. Optische Systemtechnik GmbH & Co. KG, Bremen, Germany.

A.4.1   Posing the problem

A multilayer printed circuit board (PCB) consists of more than one insulating layer separating thin layers of copper foil. These copper layers are etched, leaving conductive tracks for connecting the terminals of electronic devices (Figure A.30). These component legs are then soldered into through-plated holes in the PCB. When a conductor in any given layer makes contact with a hole, the conductor must be formed with a concentric eyelet around that hole. During PCB production, the eyelets must be accurately etched.

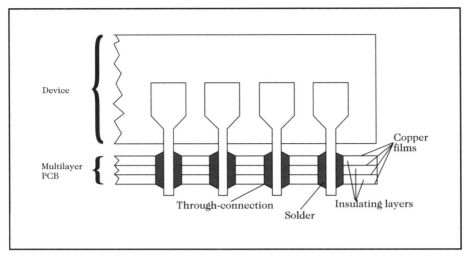

Figure A.30 Construction of a multilayer PCB.

Figure A.31 shows three eyelets which have not been positioned exactly one upon the other. In practice, of course, a slight displacement of the eyelets is unavoidable: for instance, the layers may be shifted, rotated or contracted.

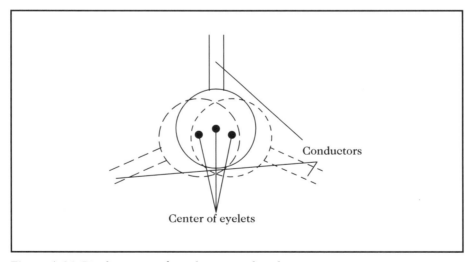

Figure A.31 Displacement of conductors and eyelets.

The aim of an inspection procedure is the evaluation of the displacements. In the case of an acceptable error the drilling machine must be positioned so that the hole is located in the center of the overlapping eyelets (Figure A.31). If the error is too great and the eyelets do not sufficiently overlap, the PCB has to be removed from the assembly line.

A.4.2 Constraints

The traditional evaluation process was based on random sampling. The selected PCBs were cut open and inspected with the aid of a microscope. This procedure is certainly unsatisfactory. A better procedure would inspect every PCB during the production process without, of course, destroying them. Such an inspection can be carried out by X-raying the PCBs.

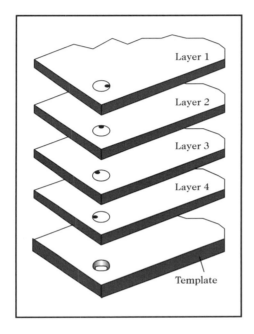

Figure A.32
Test patterns (dots) positioned at the four corners of a PCB.

To support the X-ray inspection, test patterns (dots) are positioned at the corners of the PCBs (Figure A.32). Figure A.33 depicts an example of such a pattern for eight layers. Here, the dot measurements are theoretical values which serve as references. The PCB is fixed to a template on the drilling machine which serves as a positioning jig.

Figure A.34 shows the X-ray image of a test pattern. X-ray images are typically very noisy, and this example is by no means a worst case. The system has to comply with this primary constraint.

The graylevel image shown in Figure A.34 was captured using a simple PC frame grabber. Therefore, the contrast of this image and of all the others which will be shown is not as good as it could be. Furthermore, due to the pixel geometry, the originally circular dots are represented as ellipses (Section 1.4). Note that the original inspection system OPS IV (Figure A.35) is a high-performance system which avoids these limitations. Nevertheless, the noise problem remains.

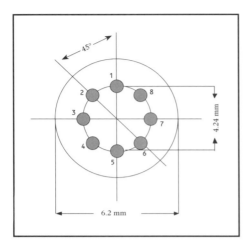

Figure A.33
Reference measurements of the dots used for evaluation.

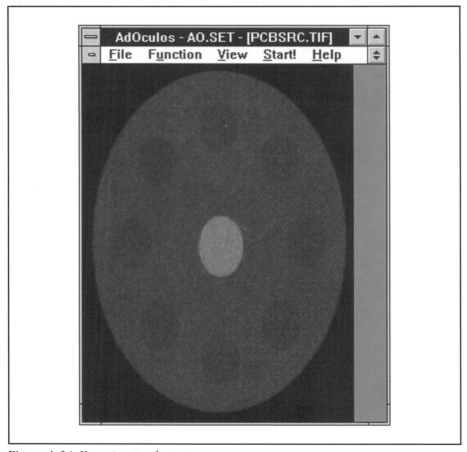

Figure A.34 X-ray image of a test pattern.

A.4.3   Solving the problem

The principle of the inspection system is shown in Figure A.35. This system is a typical representative of an industrial image processing system as discussed in Chapter 1 (Figure 1.4). We will concentrate on the discussion of its preprocessing components, whose tasks are:

- preprocessing to enhance contrast and to remove the noise,

- segmentation to separate the dots,

- evaluation to obtain the positions and dimensions of the dots.

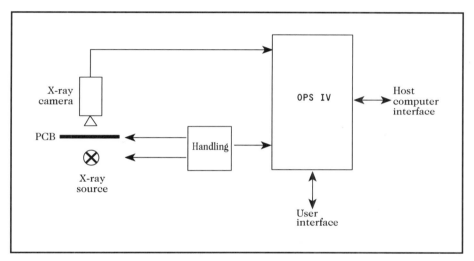

Figure A.35 Principle of the inspection system.

Preprocessing

First of all, it is advisable to obtain information about the graylevel distribution. Figure A.37 shows the histogram of the example image of Figure A.36. The histogram contains two peaks. The right-hand one is due to the higher graylevels representing the hole in the middle of the image. The left-hand peak comprises the graylevels of the background and the graylevels representing the dots. Thus, the hole could be easily segmented by thresholding. However, we are mainly interested in the dots.

In trying to segment these objects we encounter two problems:

- The mean graylevels of the background pixels and the dot pixels are rather similar.

- Compared to this small difference of mean values, the graylevel variances are high due to noise.

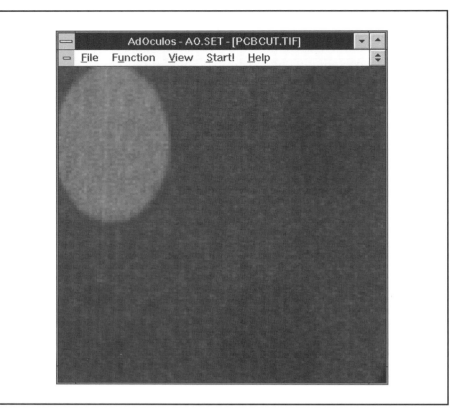

Figure A.36 Section of the image shown in Figure A.34.

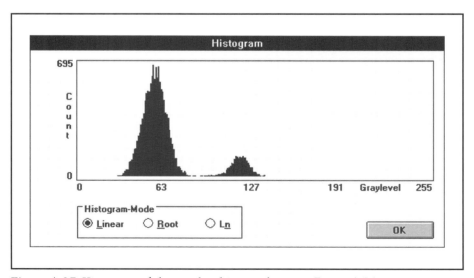

Figure A.37 Histogram of the graylevel image shown in Figure A.36.

An equalization (Chapter 2) of the original image increases the difference between the means (Figure A.38 and Figure A.39). A classical 'remedy' against noise is the median operator (Chapter 3). Figure A.40 shows that this 'classical' approach does not work well in every case.

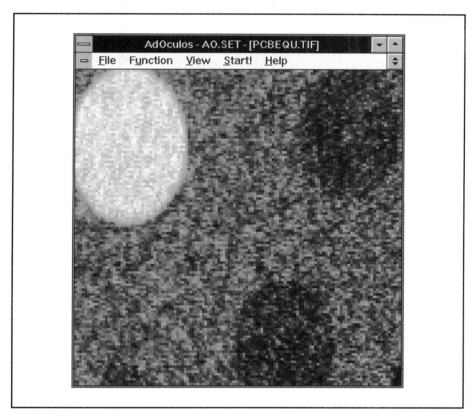

Figure A.38 Result after equalizing the original image shown in Figure A.36.

More sophisticated tools, namely morphological operators (Chapter 8), yield an image (shown by Figure A.41) as the result of a simple erosion. The structuring element was formed analogously to the degrading spots. The result is better than the one obtained by the median operator. Nevertheless, it is still unacceptable for further processing. More elaborate morphological procedures may yield better results as far as noise removal is concerned. However, we have to be careful not to destroy the original shape of the dots because that is what we want to measure.

Fortunately, in this case the simplest procedure of noise removal can be used. Since the noise pattern changes randomly from image frame to image frame while the objects do not move, averaging over several image frames reduces the noise effectively. The OPS IV system shown in Figure A.35 is equipped with hardware for realizing this summing and normalizing in real time. The average of 64 images is shown in Figure A.42.

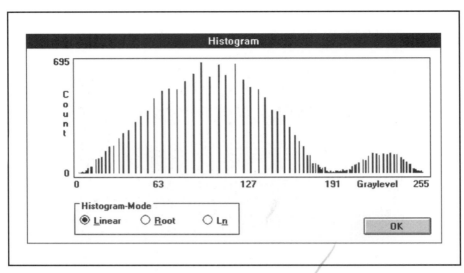

Figure A.39 Histogram of the equalized image shown in Figure A.38.

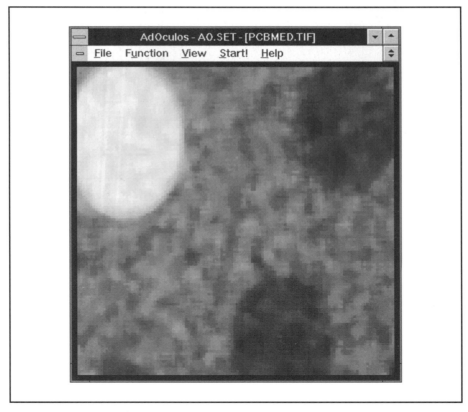

Figure A.40 Result of the median operation (5*5 mask) applied to the image shown in Figure A.38.

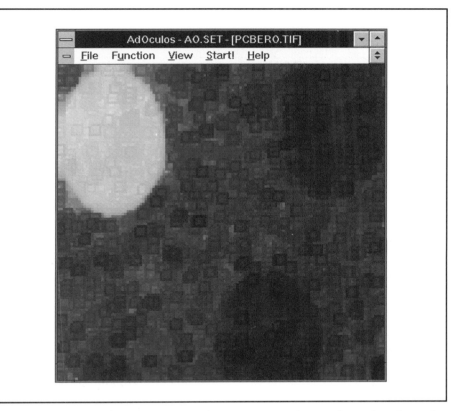

Figure A.41 Result after an erosion with a structuring element formed analogously to the degrading spots.

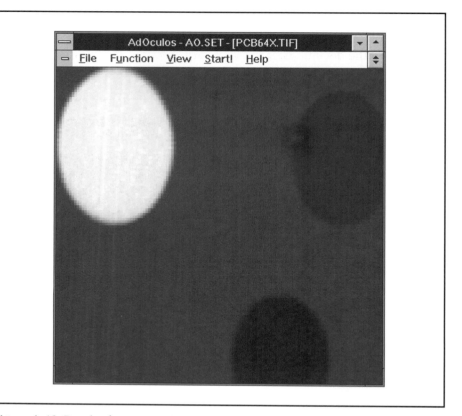

Figure A.42 Result of averaging 64 images.

Segmentation

Chapter 5 and Chapter 6 describe two different strategies for segmentation. In this case, however, contour extraction is the preferable one, because this approach is more robust when faced with shading (for example, due to inhomogeneous X-ray sources). Figure A.43 shows a thinned gradient image. The contour extraction procedure utilized in the OPS IV system works similarly. However, it is optimized for this particular problem.

Evaluation

The evaluation procedure consists of four steps:

- Determine the center of the template hole. This center serves as a reference for further measurements.

- Determine the centers of the dots.

- Compute the deviation between the model (Figure A.33) and the actual measurements.

- Compare the deviations of the four corners of the PCB to determine the type of error.

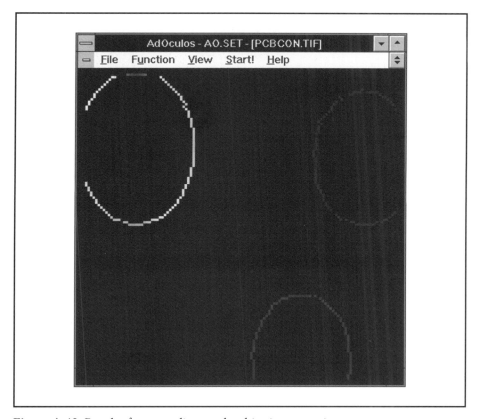

Figure A.43 Result after a gradient and a thinning operation.

Appendix B:
General purpose procedures

B.1   Definitions

Figure B.1 shows a list of data types used in the context of the *Realization* sections of this book.

Since the 'classic' graylevel image is based on an unsigned 8 bit data type, the definition of a corresponding type BYTE is useful.

The handling of region features (Section 5.3.3) requires some special data structures: CGStruc combines the coordinates of centers of gravity, while PolStruc is used during the evaluation of polar distances.

To represent a chain of contour points (Section 6.3.3), we need a data type which combines the coordinates of a contour point and its index for indicating its position in the chain. This is the purpose of the structure ChnStruc. The approximation of such chains by segments (Section 6.3.4) yields the coordinates of the segment terminating points. The points of one segment are determined with the aid of the structure SegStruc. The representation of a segment on a discrete grid is a basic problem of computer

345

graphics. A well-known algorithm for solving this problem is described in Appendix B.5. The handling of the pixels representing such a segment requires a data type which combines the coordinates of these pixels. The structure LinStruc serves this purpose.

```
#define 3.1415
#define BYTE unsigned char
struct CGStruc {
  int r;
  int c;
};
struct PolStruc {
  float Min;
  float Max;
};
struct ChnStruc {
  int r;
  int c;
  int i;
};
struct SegStruc {
  int r0;
  int c0;
  int r1;
  int c1;
};
struct LinStruc {
  int r;
  int c;
};
struct StrucStrucBin {
  int r;
  int c;
};
struct StrucStrucGrey {
  int r;
  int c;
  int g;
};
struct EvalStruc {
  float Energy;
  float Contrast;
  float Entropy;
  float Homogen;
};
typedef struct CGStruc         CGTyp;
typedef struct PolStruc        PolTyp;
typedef struct LinStruc        LinTyp;
typedef struct ChnStruc        ChnTyp;
typedef struct SegStruc        SegTyp;
typedef struct StrucStrucBin   StrTypB;
typedef struct StrucStrucGrey  StrTypG;
typedef struct EvalStruc       EvalTyp;
```

Figure B.1 Definition of non-standard data types.

The heart of morphological image processing (Section 8.3) is the structuring element. The shape of a structuring element is represented by coordinates relating to the origin of this structuring element. In the case of the morphological processing of graylevel images, the coefficients ('graylevel' of the structuring element) are added. The handling of the structuring elements is based on the data structures StrucStrucBin and StrucStrucGrey.

The evaluation of various textures (Section 9.1) with the aid of a co-occurrence matrix yields different texture features. The structure EvalStruc combines four features which are used in Section 9.3.

B.2   Memory management

A basic problem underlying the procedures described in this book is memory management. Since the realization of memory management functions depends on the operating system, only the purpose of the functions used in the *Realization* sections is described:

ImAlloc: serves to allocate memory for an image. The data type of a pixel (usually BYTE) and the image size must be defined before the allocation is carried out.
ImFree: frees the memory previously allocated with the aid of ImAlloc
GetMem: extends a list by an element of any data type

B.3   The procedures MaxAbs and MinAbs

Figure B.2 shows two functions returning the minimum (or maximum) absolute value of the two input values x and y. They are mainly used to support a fast transformation from Cartesian to polar representation (*for an instance see* Section 6.3.1). Both functions are self-explanatory.

```
int MinAbs (x,y)
int x,y;
{
  int ax,ay;
  ax = (x<0) ? -x : x;
  ay = (y<0) ? -y : y;
  return ((ax<ay) ? ax : ay);
}
int MaxAbs (x,y)
int x,y;
{
  int ax,ay;
  ax = (x<0) ? -x : x;
  ay = (y<0) ? -y : y;
  return ((ax<ay) ? ay : ax);
}
```

Figure B.2 C realization of procedures for calculating absolute values.

B.4 The discrete inverse tangent

The standard implementation of trigonometrical functions usually requires a lot of computing time. Image processing algorithms rarely depend on high-accuracy trigonometry. For instance, the gradient direction is mainly quantized only by 3 (0 to 7 'degree'), 4 (0 to 15 'degree'), or 8 (0 to 255 'degree') bits. The 4-bit quantization is illustrated in Figure B.3, where 16 partitions divide the circle into segments of 22.5°. The partition borders are 11.25°, 33.75°, ..., 348.75°. The corresponding values of the inverse tangent are depicted in the boxes. A typical application for such an inverse tangent is the fast transformation from Cartesian to polar representation (Section 6.3.1).

Figure B.4 shows a procedure which derives the polar direction (quantized in 16 steps) from the Cartesian coordinates **dy** and **dx**. The calculation of the inverse tangent is required for only one quadrant. Therefore, the procedure starts by calculating the absolute values of **dy** and **dx**. Using these values, the special cases of horizontal and vertical lines are checked and, if necessary, a corresponding value is returned.

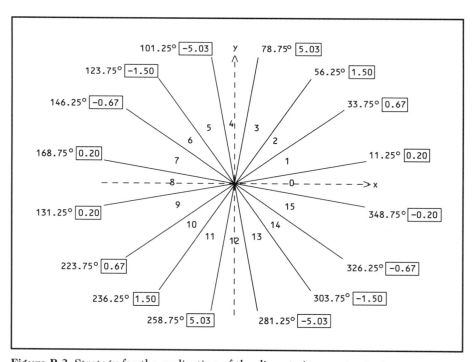

Figure B.3 Strategy for the realization of the discrete inverse tangent.

However, if none of the coordinates is zero, we need the quotient **Ady/Adx**. To avoid floating-point arithmetic in further steps, the quotient is multiplied by 100. This value derives from the following pragmatic approach:

the accuracy of the quotient quo is sufficient, while the range of Ady is large enough in the context of the current application. Please note that Ady is a long variable.

The actual calculation of the inverse tangent is based on a comparison of the quotient quo and the partition borders (obviously also multiplied by 100) shown in Figure B.3. This comparison yields angle values ranging from 0 to 4 for the first quadrant (Figure B.4). The actual quadrant is determined by the signs of the coordinates dy and dx. Consequently, the basic angle value must be corrected (by a type of shifting operation; see last return statement in Figure B.4) according to the actual quadrant.

```
int DiscAtan16 (dy,dx)
int dy,dx;
{
    int  phi;
    long quo, Adx, Ady;
    Adx = (long) abs (dx);
    Ady = (long) abs (dy);
    if (Adx==0 || Ady==0)
        return ((Adx==0 && Ady==0) ? 0 :
                ((Adx==0) ?
                ((dy < 0) ? 12 : 4) :
                ((dx < 0) ?  8 : 0)));
    else{
        quo = (100*Ady) / Adx;
        phi = ((quo <  20) ? 0 :
              ((quo <  67) ? 1 :
              ((quo < 150) ? 2 :
              ((quo < 503) ? 3 : 4 ))));
        return ((dy > 0) ?
                ((dx > 0) ? phi   : 8-phi) :   /* 1.quad : 2.quad */
                ((dx < 0) ? 8+phi :            /* 3.quad */
                ((phi==0) ? 0     : 16-phi))); /* 4.quad */
} }
```

Figure B.4 C realization of the discrete inverse tangent.

This realization of the inverse tangent is easily extended to any angle range. Only the comparison algorithm needs to be changed. In the case of a range of 256 angle values (leading to 64 comparisons), this algorithm does not seem very elegant, but the approach is straightforward and yields a fast and robust solution.

B.5   Generation of a digital segment

The representation of an ideal segment by a discrete grid is not as simple as it seems. However, since this is a very basic problem of computer graphics, several algorithms for solving it are available. The realization of one of these algorithms is shown in Figure B.5. Its input values are the coordinates of the terminating points y0, x0, y1 and x1. Those pixels which represent the segment are collected by vector `Line`. The procedure returns the length of this vector. Note that the vector consumes memory which must be allocated at the right time (`GetMem(Line)`; Appendix B.2).

```
int GenLine (y0,x0,y1,x1, Line)
int  y0,x0,y1,x1;
LinTyp *Line;
{
   static int Step [2] = {-1,1};
   int XDiff, YDiff, XStep, YStep, Sum, i;

   XStep = Step [x0<x1]; XDiff = abs (x0-x1);
   YStep = Step [y0<y1]; YDiff = abs (y0-y1);
   GetMem (Line);
   Line[0].r = y0;
   Line[0].c = x0;
   i=1;
   if (XDiff > YDiff) {
      Sum = XDiff >> 1;
      while (x0 != x1) {
         x0 += XStep;
         Sum -= YDiff;
         if (Sum < 0) {
            y0 += YStep;
            Sum += XDiff;
         }
         GetMem (Line);
         Line[0].r = y0;
         Line[0].c = x0;
         i++;
      }
   }else{
      Sum = YDiff >> 1;
      while (y0 != y1) {
         y0 += YStep;
         Sum -= XDiff;
         if (Sum < 0) {
            x0 += XStep;
            Sum += YDiff;
         }
         GetMem (Line);
         Line[0].r = y0;
         Line[0].c = x0;
         i++;
      } }
   return (i++);
}
```

Figure B.5 C realization of segment generation. The procedure `GetMem` and the data type `LinTyp` are defined in Figure B.1.

Since the procedure is based on a standard algorithm, no further explanation concerning its details is given here. For more information, check the specialized literature about computer graphics.

Appendix C:
Calculus of variations

An important mathematical tool used, for instance, in image sequence analysis (Section 11.4) is the calculus of variations. The following sections offer a short and tool-oriented introduction to this topic.

A typical application of the well-known differential calculus is the search for maxima or minima of a function. Such a function may describe a system (of any kind), whose optimum states are represented by the extrema of the function. Unfortunately, we are frequently confronted with system optima which are not so simply defined. Assume a rocket is to transport a payload into orbit. The aim is to maximize the payload with regard to certain constraints. The optimum trajectory is not describable by simple extrema. It must be a *function*. The calculus of variations is a tool for finding such functions.

Our everyday experience tells us that a straight line is the shortest distance between two points. However, what is the correct formal proof of this experience? To answer this question, let us assume that two points $(x_0, y(x_0))$ and $(x_1, y(x_1))$ (with $x_0 < x_1$) are defined in a Cartesian system. As

351

Figure C.1 shows, these points can be connected by a smooth curve. This curve consists of infinitely short segments ds. The length l of the curve is:

$$l = \int_{x_0}^{x_1} ds$$

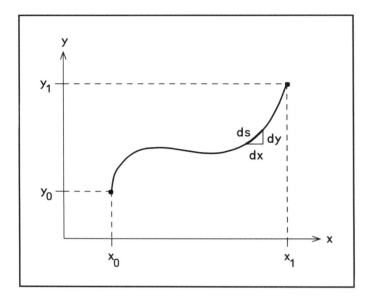

Figure C.1
On the determination of the minimum distance between two points.

With

$$ds = \sqrt{(dx)^2 + (dy)^2} = \sqrt{1 + \left(\frac{dy}{dx}\right)^2} \, dx$$

the length is:

$$l = \int_{x_0}^{x_1} \sqrt{1 + (y')^2} \, dx$$

Our aim is to find the function $y(x)$ for which the integral yields the minimum of l. In the context of calculus of variations such integrals are called *functionals I*:

$$I\left(y(x)\right) = \int_{x_0}^{x_1} \sqrt{1+ (y')^2}\ dx$$

Thus, a functional is a function depending on another function. Generally, an integral takes the form:

$$I\left(y(x)\right) = \int_{x_0}^{x_1} F(x, y, y', \ldots, y^{(n)})\ dx$$

Calculation of simple functionals

The procedure of finding the optimum function $y(x)$ is shown, as follows, with the aid of the simplest functional, namely:

$$I\left(y(x)\right) = \int_{x_0}^{x_1} F(x, y, y')\ dx$$

Let us assume that $y(x_0)$ and $y(x_1)$ are known. Now, we 'vary' the functional with a function $\bar{y}(x)$ in the 'neighborhood' of $y(x)$ which is defined as follows:

$$\bar{y}(x) = y(x) + \alpha n(x)$$

α is a parameter which may become infinitely small. $n(x)$ is a continuous differentiable function which is defined in the interval $x_0 \le x \le x_1$. The values $\bar{y}(x_0)$ and $\bar{y}(x_1)$ must be identical to $y(x_0)$ and $y(x_1)$. Imagine the function $y(x)$ as a string in a neutral position which is fixed at its terminating points $(x_0, y(x_0))$ and $(x_1, y(x_1))$. In terms of this example, the neighborhood function $\bar{y}(x)$ is a string which is plucked gently and not released.

The functional of the neighborhood function is:

$$I\left(\bar{y}(x)\right) = \int_{x_0}^{x_1} F(x, \bar{y}, \bar{y}')\ dx$$

$$= \int_{x_0}^{x_1} F(x, y + \alpha n(x), y' + \alpha n'(x))\ dx$$

Suppose the optimum function $y(x)$ is already known. Furthermore, assume the function $\bar{y}(x)$ is in such close proximity to $y(x)$ that the functional $I(\bar{y}(x))$ is simply describable as a function of α:

$$I\,(\bar{y}(x)) = \Phi(\alpha)$$

Due to this 'trick', the variation problem is reduced to the well-known optimization problem, namely the minimization of the function $\Phi(\alpha)$. For this purpose we need the first derivative as follows:

$$\frac{d\Phi(\alpha)}{d\alpha} = \frac{d}{d\alpha}\int_{x_0}^{x_1} F(x,\bar{y},\bar{y}')\,dx$$

According to the rules of the differentiation of integrals (Appendix D), we are allowed to put the differential quotient into the integral:

$$\frac{d\Phi(\alpha)}{d\alpha} = \int_{x_0}^{x_1} \frac{d}{d\alpha} F(x,\bar{y},\bar{y}')\,dx$$

Shortening $F(x,\bar{y},\bar{y}')$ to F, the according total differential (Appendix E) is:

$$dF\sqrt{\frac{\partial F}{\partial x}}\,dx + \frac{\partial F}{\partial y}\,d\bar{y} + \frac{\partial F}{\partial \bar{y}'}\,d\bar{y}'$$

and:

$$\frac{dF}{d\alpha} = \frac{\partial F}{\partial x}\frac{dx}{d\alpha} + \frac{\partial F}{\partial \bar{y}}\frac{d\bar{y}}{d\alpha} + \frac{\partial F}{\partial \bar{y}'}\frac{d\bar{y}'}{d\alpha}$$

Due to $F(x,\bar{y},\bar{y}') = F(x, y, + \alpha n(x),\ y', + \alpha n'(x))$, we get:

$$\frac{dF}{d\alpha} = \frac{\partial F}{\partial y} n(x) + \frac{\partial F}{\partial y'} n'(x)$$

Thus, the integral becomes:

$$\frac{d\Phi(\alpha)}{d\alpha} = \int_{x_0}^{x_1} \frac{\partial F}{\partial y} n(x)dx + \int_{x_0}^{x_1} \frac{\partial F}{\partial y'} n'(x)dx$$

With the aid of partial integration (Appendix D), the second integral is:

$$\int_{x_0}^{x_1} \frac{\partial F}{\partial y'} n'(x)dx = \left[\frac{\partial F}{\partial y'} n(x) \right]_{x_0}^{x_1} - \int_{x_0}^{x_1} \frac{d \frac{\partial F}{\partial y'}}{dx} n(x)dx$$

The term

$$\left[\frac{\partial F}{\partial y'} n(x) \right]_{x_0}^{x_1}$$

is zero, since $n(x_0) = n(x_1) = 0$. Thus, the whole integral becomes:

$$\frac{d\Phi(\alpha)}{d\alpha} = \int_{x_0}^{x_1} n(x) \left(\frac{\partial F}{\partial y} - \frac{d}{dx} \left(\frac{\partial F}{\partial y'} \right) \right) dx$$

At the optimum point, $d\Phi(\alpha)/d\alpha$ is zero. If, at the same time, α is forced to zero, we get (due to $\bar{y} = y + \alpha n(x)$ and $\bar{y}' = y' + \alpha n'(x)$):

$$\int_{x_0}^{x_1} n(x) \left(\frac{\partial F}{\partial y} - \frac{d}{dx} \left(\frac{\partial F}{\partial y'} \right) \right) dx = 0 \qquad (C.1)$$

Now, the Trojan horse α has served its purpose. However, the neighborhood function $n(x)$ must also be eliminated. This elimination is based on the *fundamental lemma of the calculus of variation*:

Let $n(x)$ be a continuously differentiable function with $n(x_0) = n(x_1) = 0$ and let $G(x)$ be another continuous function which is defined in the interval $x_0 \leq x \leq x_1$. If the integral

$$\int_{x_0}^{x_1} n(x)G(x)\,dx$$

becomes zero, then $G(x)$ becomes zero too.

The proof of this lemma is given in [C.1]. Applied to Integral (C.1), the lemma means that the integral vanishes. The remaining part is:

$$\frac{\partial F}{\partial y} - \frac{d}{dx}\left(\frac{\partial F}{\partial y'} \right) = 0 \qquad\qquad (C.2)$$

The solution to this differential equation optimizes the functional $I(y(x))$ with respect to the constraints $y(x_0)$ and $y(x_1)$. The application of the total differential (Appendix E) to the term $(\partial F/\partial y')$ yields:

$$d\left(\frac{\partial F}{\partial y'} \right) = \frac{\partial}{\partial y'}\left(\frac{\partial F}{\partial y'} \right) dy' + \frac{\partial}{\partial y}\left(\frac{\partial F}{\partial y'} \right) dy + \frac{\partial}{\partial x}\left(\frac{\partial F}{\partial y'} \right) dx$$

Thus, the differential equation (C.2) takes the following form:

$$\frac{\partial F}{\partial y} - \frac{\partial^2 F}{\partial y'^2}\, y'' - \frac{\partial^2 F}{\partial y' \partial y}\, y' - \frac{\partial^2 F}{\partial y' \partial x} = 0$$

This equation is known as the *Euler equation*. It is one of the most important tools of the calculus of variations. To familiarize ourselves with this tool, let us apply it to the example of the search for the shortest distance between two points. The functional corresponding to this problem was:

$$I\,(y(x)) = \int_{x_0}^{x_1} \sqrt{1 + (y')^2}\, dx$$

Thus:

$$F(x, y, y') = \sqrt{1 + (y')^2} \; dx$$

Since this equation only depends on y' the following terms become zero:

$$\frac{\partial F}{\partial y} = \frac{\partial^2 F}{\partial y' \, \partial y} = \frac{\partial^2 F}{\partial y' \, \partial x} = 0$$

The remaining differential quotient is:

$$\frac{\partial^2 F}{\partial y'^2} = \frac{1}{(1+(y')^2)^{\frac{3}{2}}}$$

Thus, the Euler equation reduces to:

$$\frac{1}{(1+(y')^2)^{\frac{3}{2}}} y'' = 0$$

So it is sufficient to solve the differential equation $y'' = d^2y/dx^2 = 0$. As expected the solution is obvious:

$$y = c_1 x + c_2$$

Calculation of functionals with several functions

The calculation of functionals with several functions

$$I \, (y_1(x), y_2(x), \ldots, y_p(x)) = \int_{x_0}^{x_1} F(x, y_1, y_2, \ldots, y_p, y'_1, y'_2, \ldots, y'_p) \; dx$$

whose limits $(y_1(x_0), y_1(x_1), y_2(x_0), y_2(x_1)$, and so on) are known, proceeds by variation of the single functions:

$$\bar{y}_1(x) = y_1(x) + \alpha_1 n_1(x)$$
$$\bar{y}_2(x) = y_2(x) + \alpha_2 n_2(x)$$
...

...
$$\bar{y}_p(x) = y_p(x) + \alpha_p n_p(x)$$

Function Φ depends on $\alpha_1, \alpha_2, ..., \alpha_p$. So:

$$\Phi(\alpha_1, \alpha_2, ..., \alpha_p) = \int_{x_0}^{x_1} F(x, \bar{y}_1, \bar{y}_2, ..., \bar{y}_p, \bar{y}'_1, \bar{y}'_2, ..., \bar{y}'_p) \, dx$$

Thus, we must realize p partial derivatives of Φ and force them to zero. In the end, we get p Euler equations ($i = 1,2,...,p$):

$$\frac{\partial F}{\partial y_i} - \frac{\partial^2 F}{\partial y_i'^2} y_i'' - \frac{\partial^2 F}{\partial y_i' \partial y_i} y_i' - \frac{\partial^2 F}{\partial y_i' \partial x} = 0 \quad i = 1, 2, ..., p$$

Calculation of functionals with two independent functions

Let the function y depend on two independent variables x_1 and x_2. Now, the functional is:

$$I(y(x_1, x_2)) = \iint_R F(x_1, x_2, y, y_{x_1}, y_{x_2}) \, dx_1 dx_2$$

with $y_{x_1} = \partial y/\partial x_1$, $y_{x_2} = \partial y/\partial x_2$ and the limits determined by region R. The variation takes the form:

$$\bar{y}(x_1, x_2) = y(x_1, x_2) + \alpha n(x_1, x_2)$$

Except for a few details, the remaining procedure is equivalent to those discussed above. This procedure yields the Euler equation:

$$\frac{\partial F}{\partial y} - \frac{d}{dx_1}\left(\frac{\partial F}{\partial y_{x_1}}\right) - \frac{d}{dx_2}\left(\frac{\partial F}{\partial y_{x_2}}\right) = 0$$

or:

$$F_{y_{x_1}y_{x_1}}\frac{\partial^2 y}{\partial x_1^2} + 2F_{y_{x_1}y_{x_2}}\frac{\partial^2 y}{\partial x_1 \partial x_2} + F_{y_{x_2}y_{x_2}}\frac{\partial^2 y}{\partial x_2^2} + F_{y_{x_1}y}\frac{\partial y}{\partial x_1} + F_{y_{x_2}y}\frac{\partial y}{\partial x_2} + F_{y_{x_1}x_1} + F_{y_{x_2}x_2} - F_y = 0$$

C.1   References

[C.1]   Miller, M.: *Variationsrechnung* (In German). Leipzig: Teubner 1959

[C.2]   Pike, R.W.: *Optimization for engineering systems.* New York: Van Nostrand Reinhold 1986

[C.3]   Salvadori, M.G.; Baron M.L.: *Numerical methods in engineering.* Englewood Cliffs, N.J.: Prentice-Hall 1961

[C.4]   Weinstock, R.: *Calculus of variations.* New York: Dover Publications 1974

Appendix D:
Rules for integration

For your convenience, here are some integration rules which are applied in Appendix C.

Differentiation of an integral

The differentiation of an integral according to the rule of Leibnitz:

$$\frac{d}{dx} \int_{a(x)}^{b(x)} f(x,\, t)\; dt = \int_{a(x)}^{b(x)} \frac{\partial}{\partial x}\; f(x,\, t)\; dt + \frac{b(x)}{dx} f(x,\, b(x)) - \frac{a(x)}{dx}\; f(x,\, a(x))$$

If the limits are constant, the last two terms vanish. There remains:

$$\frac{d}{dx} \int_{a}^{b} f(x,\, t)\; dt = \int_{a}^{b} \frac{\partial}{\partial x}\; f(x,\, t)\; dt$$

Partial integration

Partial integration is based on the rule:

$$\int u(x)v'(x)dx = u(x)v(x) - \int u'(x)v(x)dx$$

Appendix E:
Taylor series expansion/total differential

To understand the calculus of variations described in Appendix C, basic knowledge of the Taylor series expansion is required. This mathematical tool is widely known, but to aid understanding, the following description is adapted to the descriptive style used in Appendix C.

Taylor series expansion

A function $f(\eta)$ is approximated at point η_0 by the following Taylor polynomial:

$$f(\eta) = f(\eta_0) + \frac{f'(\eta_0)}{1!}(\eta - \eta_0) + \frac{f''(\eta_0)}{2!}(\eta - \eta_0)^2 + \dots + R$$

R is the remainder of the approximation. Assume the following example: the function $f(x+\delta x)$ is to be approximated at point x using the Taylor polynomial to the first derivative. In this case, we get $\eta = x+\delta x$, $\eta_0 = x$ and $f'(\eta_0)$ $= f'(x) = df(x)/dx$. The desired approximation is:

$$f(x + \delta x) = f(x) + \delta x \, \frac{df(x)}{dx} + R$$

In the case of a function which depends on multiple variables $f(\underline{\eta}) = f(\eta_1,$ $\eta_2, ..., \eta_n)$, we approximate at point $f(\underline{\eta}) = f(\eta_{1_0}, \eta_{2_0}, ..., \eta_{n_0})$:

$$f(\underline{\eta}) = f(\underline{\eta}_0) + \sum_{i=1}^{n} (\eta_i - \eta_{i_0}) \frac{\partial f(\underline{\eta}_0)}{\partial \eta_i} + \frac{1}{2!} \left[\sum_{i=1}^{n} (\eta_i - \eta_{i_0})^2 \frac{\partial}{\partial \eta_i} \right]^2 f(\underline{\eta}_0) + ... + R$$

Take the function $f(x+\delta x, y+\delta y, t+\delta t)$ as an example. This function is to be approximated at point (x,y,t). Now, we get $\eta_1 = x + \delta x$, $\eta_2 = y + \delta y$, $\eta_3 = t + \delta t$, $\eta_{1_0} = x$, $\eta_{2_0} = y$, $\eta_{3_0} = t$ and:

$$\frac{\partial f(\eta_{1_0}, \eta_{2_0}, \eta_{3_0})}{\partial \eta_{1_0}} = \frac{\partial f(x, y, t)}{\partial x} = \frac{\partial f}{\partial x}$$

We get $\partial f/\partial y$ and $\partial f/\partial t$ in a similar way. The result of the approximation is:

$$f(x + \delta x, y + \delta y, t + \delta t) = f(x, y, t) + \delta x \frac{\partial f}{\partial x} + \delta y \frac{\partial f}{\partial y} + \delta t \frac{\partial f}{\partial t} + R$$

Total differential

In some cases, it is sufficient to base the approximation merely on the first derivative of the Taylor polynomial:

$$f(\underline{\eta}) = f(\underline{\eta}_0) + \sum_{i=1}^{n} (\eta_i - \eta_{i_0}) \frac{\partial f(\underline{\eta}_0)}{\partial \eta_1} + R$$

Of special interest is the difference between the values $f(\underline{\eta})$ and $f(\underline{\eta}_0)$:

$$\Delta u = f(\underline{\eta}) - f(\underline{\eta}_0)$$

$$\Delta \eta_i = \eta_i - \eta_{i_0}$$

Thus:

$$\Delta u = \sum_{i=1}^{n} \Delta \eta_i \, \frac{\partial f(\underline{\eta}_0)}{\partial \eta_1} + R$$

The transition from differences to differentials and a vanishing remainder R leads to the *total differential*:

$$\Delta u = \sum_{i=1}^{n} d\eta_i \, \frac{\partial f(\underline{\eta}_0)}{\partial \eta_1}$$

As application example, assume that the total differential has the function $u = f(\eta_0, \eta_1, \eta_2)$:

$$\Delta u = \frac{\partial u}{\partial \eta_0} \, d\eta_0 + \frac{\partial u}{\partial \eta_1} \, d\eta_1 + \frac{\partial u}{\partial \eta_2} \, d\eta_2$$

Interpreting the differentials $d\eta_0$, $d\eta_1$, $d\eta_2$ as unit vectors of a Cartesian system, we get the gradient:

$$\text{grad } u = \frac{\partial u}{\partial \eta_0} \, \vec{e}_x + \frac{\partial u}{\partial \eta_1} \, \vec{e}_y + \frac{\partial u}{\partial \eta_2} \, \vec{e}_z$$

Appendix F:
Gauss-Seidel iteration

The Horn and Schunk procedure for the analysis of image sequences is based on a linear system (Chapter 11.4). A well-known method for a numerical solution is the Gauss-Seidel iteration. It is characterized by a robust convergence and insensitivity to computational errors. However, it suffers from a serious drawback: it is known that, in some cases, the iteration does not converge.

Fortunately, the convergence is secure if the system is *diagonal* [F.1]. The following example illustrates the procedure (adapted from [F.1]):

$$10x_1 + x_2 + x_3 = 12$$

$$2x_1 + 10x_2 + x_3 = 13$$

$$2x_1 + 2x_2 + 10x_3 = 14$$

The system is solved starting with the equation possessing the greatest coefficient:

$$x_1 = 1.2 - 0.1x_2 - 0.1x_3$$

$$x_2 = 1.3 - 0.2x_2 - 0.1x_3$$

$$x_3 = 1.4 - 0.2x_2 - 0.2x_3$$

To solve the first equation, we start the iteration with any start value for x_2 and x_3. With $x_2 = x_3 = 0$, x_1 is 1.2. With $x_1 = 1.2$ and $x_3 = 0$, the second equation yields $x_2 = 1.06$. x_3 is then calculated to be 0.95. Thus, the whole procedure is carried out according to the following scheme:

$$x_2 = x_3 = 0 \; \rightarrow \; x_1 = 1.20$$

$$x_1 = 1.2 \quad x_3 = 0 \; \rightarrow \; x_2 = 1.06$$

$$x_1 = 1.2 \quad x_2 = 1.06 \; \rightarrow \; x_3 = 0.95$$

These values are then the basis for the second iteration:

$$x_2 = 1.06 \quad x_3 = 0.95 \; \rightarrow \; x_1 = 0.99$$

$$x_1 = 0.99 \quad x_3 = 0.95 \; \rightarrow \; x_2 = 1.00$$

$$x_1 = 0.99 \quad x_2 = 1.00 \; \rightarrow \; x_3 = 1.00$$

The third iteration proceeds accordingly and yields $x_1 = 1$, $x_2 = 1$ and $x_3 = 1$. The differences of these results compared with those of the second iteration are slight. Thus, the iteration procedure can now be stopped.

F.1   References

[F.1]   Salvadori, M.G.; Baron M.L.: *Numerical methods in engineering.* Englewood Cliffs, N.J.: Prentice-Hall 1961

Appendix G:
Multivariate normal distribution

The parametric classifiers discussed in Section 10.4 use normal distribution to describe feature spaces. The one-dimensional normal distribution is well-known:

$$f(x) = \frac{1}{\sqrt{2\pi}\sigma} \exp{\frac{(x - \mu)^2}{2\sigma^2}}$$

Since feature spaces are usually multi-dimensional, we need a corresponding normal distribution:

With

$x \rightarrow \underline{x}$	: Vector of independent variables
$\mu \rightarrow \underline{\mu}$	: Mean vector
$\sigma^2 \rightarrow \underline{C}$	: $n*n$ – Covariance matrix
$\sqrt{2\pi} \rightarrow (2\pi)^{m/2}$	: Normalizing factor

the one-dimensional normal distribution becomes m-dimensional:

$$f(\underline{x}) = \frac{1}{(2\pi)^{m/2}\sqrt{\det\underline{C}}} \exp{-\frac{1}{2}(\underline{x}-\underline{\mu})^T \underline{C}^{-1}(\underline{x}-\underline{\mu})}$$

The multivariate normal distribution is a fairly specialized topic and might not be found in basic mathematical literature. However, a detailed discussion is offered by Moran [G.1].

G.1   References

[G.1]   Moran, P.A.P: *An introduction to probability theory.* Oxford, England: Oxford University Press 1984

Appendix H:
Solutions to exercises

Chapter 1   Introduction

1.1   A pixel represents an area of 20*20 m.

1.2   512*512*8 = 2,097,152 bits have to be sent. Thus, the transmission takes 218 seconds. Note that, in practice, the transmission protocol of the serial link consumes additional time.

1.3   A single image has 1280*1024*24 = 31,457,280 bits. The transmission of 25 such images per second requires 786,432,000 baud (750 Mbits/second or approximately 100 Mbytes. Note that in practice the transmission protocol of the serial link consumes additional time.

1.4   Figure H1.1 and Figure H1.2 show the sampling grids and digitized images with a resolution of 8*8 and 16*16 pixels.

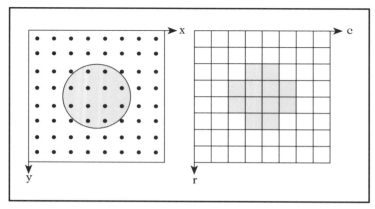

Figure H1.1 Sampling grid and digitized image with a resolution of 8*8 pixels.

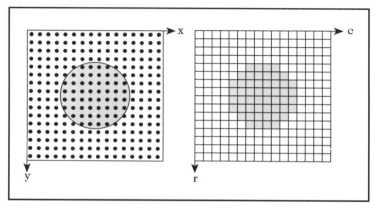

Figure H1.2 Sampling grid and digitized image with a resolution of 16*16 pixels.

1.5   Figure H1.3 shows that a structure which is finer than the sampling grid disappears.

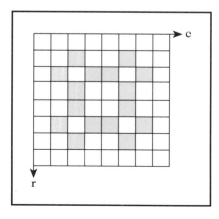

Figure H1.3
The answer to the question posed in Figure 1.29 is that the structure disappears.

1.6   Figure H1.4 shows the complete sample and tile representation.

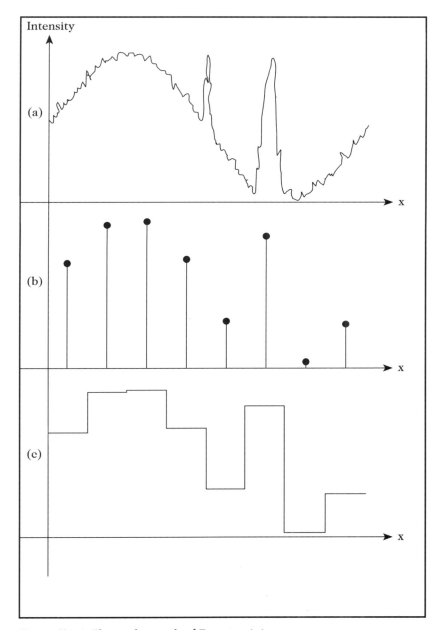

Figure H1.4 This is the result of Exercise 1.6.

Chapter 2   Point operations

2.1   The mapping function is shown in Figure H2.1, the look-up table in Figure H2.2, the resulting image in Figure H2.3 and the two histograms in Figure H2.4 and Figure H2.5.

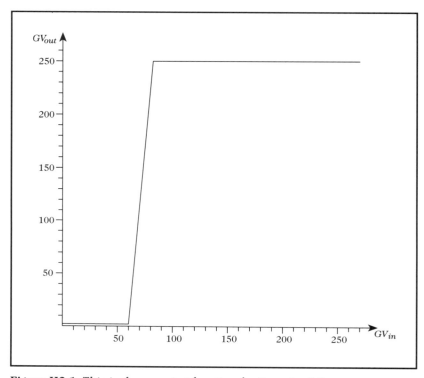

Figure H2.1 This is the mapping function for Exercise 2.1.

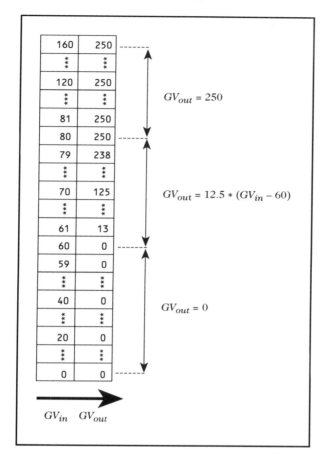

Figure H2.2
This is the look-up table for Exercise 2.1.

0	0	0	0	0	0	0	0
0	0	0	0	0	0	0	0
0	0	125	125	125	125	0	0
0	0	125	250	250	125	0	0
0	0	125	250	250	125	0	0
0	0	125	125	125	125	0	0
0	0	0	0	0	0	0	0
0	0	0	0	0	0	0	0

Figure H2.3
This is the resulting image for Exercise 2.1.

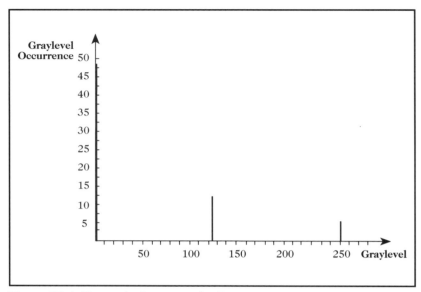

Figure H2.4 This is the histogram for Exercise 2.1.

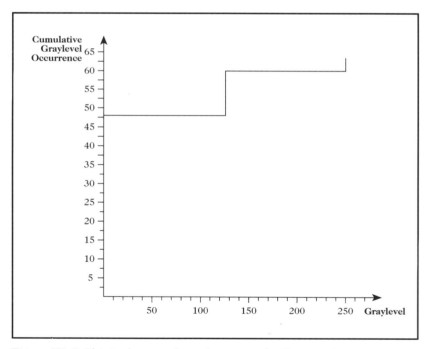

Figure H2.5 This is the cumulative histogram for Exercise 2.1.

2.2   The mapping function is shown in Figure H2.6, the look-up table in
Figure H2.7, the resulting image in Figure H2.8 and the two histograms
in Figure H2.9 and Figure H2.10.

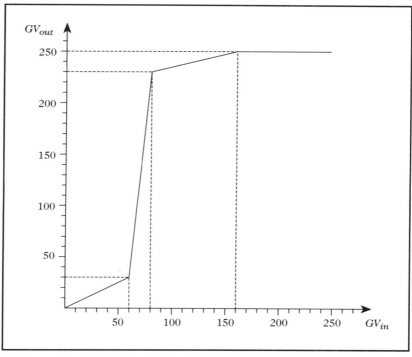

Figure H2.6 This is the mapping function for Exercise 2.2.

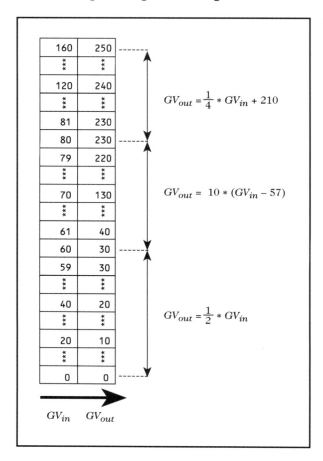

Figure H2.7
This is the look-up table for Exercise 2.2.

10	10	10	10	10	10	10	20
250	30	30	30	30	30	30	20
250	30	130	130	130	130	30	20
250	30	130	230	230	130	30	20
250	30	130	230	230	130	30	20
250	30	130	130	130	130	30	20
250	30	30	30	30	30	30	20
250	240	240	240	240	240	240	240

Figure H2.8
This is the resulting image for Exercise 2.2.

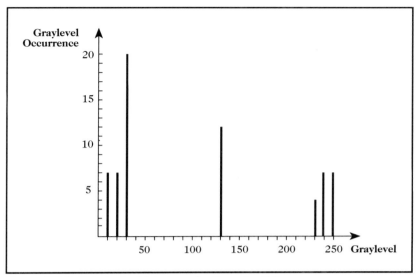

Figure H2.9 This is the histogram for Exercise 2.2.

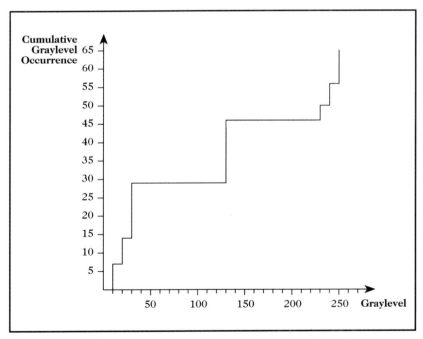

Figure H2.10 This is the cumulative histogram for Exercise 2.2.

2.3   The mapping function is shown in Figure H2.11, the look-up table in Figure H2.12, the resulting image in Figure H2.13 and the two histograms in Figure H2.14 and Figure H2.15.

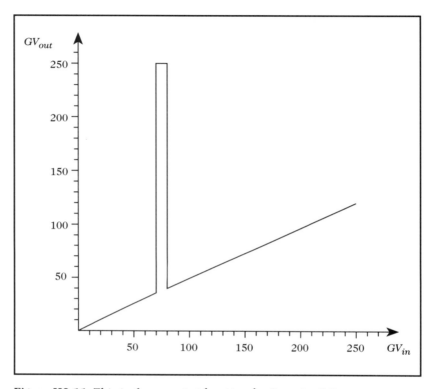

Figure H2.11 This is the mapping function for Exercise 2.3.

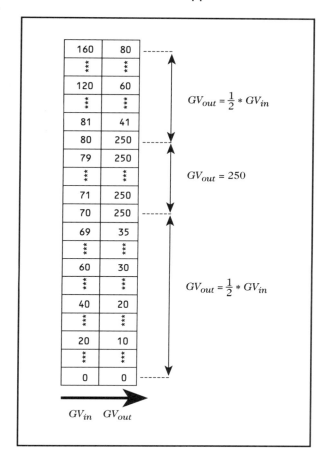

$$GV_{out} = \frac{1}{2} * GV_{in}$$

$$GV_{out} = 250$$

$$GV_{out} = \frac{1}{2} * GV_{in}$$

GV_{in} GV_{out}

Figure H2.12
This is the look-up table for Exercise 2.3.

10	10	10	10	10	10	10	20
80	30	30	30	30	30	30	20
80	30	250	250	250	250	30	20
80	30	250	250	250	250	30	20
80	30	250	250	250	250	30	20
80	30	250	250	250	250	30	20
80	30	30	30	30	30	30	20
80	60	60	60	60	60	60	60

Figure H2.13
This is the resulting image for Exercise 2.3.

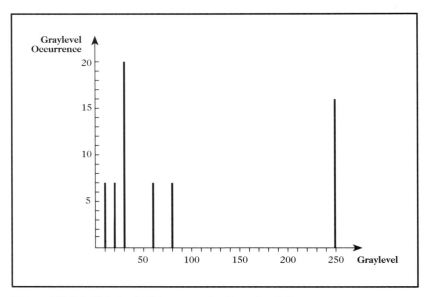

Figure H2.14 This is the histogram for Exercise 2.3.

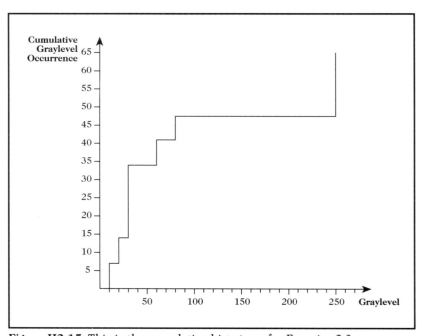

Figure H2.15 This is the cumulative histogram for Exercise 2.3.

2.4   The cumulative histogram (Figure 2.3) of the source image (Figure 2.1) yields the first mapping step:

$20 \rightarrow 7$
$40 \rightarrow 14$
$60 \rightarrow 34$
$70 \rightarrow 46$
$80 \rightarrow 50$
$120 \rightarrow 57$
$160 \rightarrow 64$

Since the graylevels should range from 0 to 250 the mapping is as follows:

$7 \rightarrow 0$
$14 \rightarrow 31$
$34 \rightarrow 118$
$46 \rightarrow 171$
$50 \rightarrow 189$
$57 \rightarrow 219$
$64 \rightarrow 250$

The resulting image and its histograms are shown in Figure H2.16, Figure H2.17 and Figure H2.18.

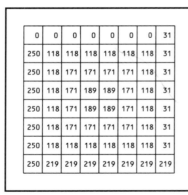

0	0	0	0	0	0	0	31
250	118	118	118	118	118	118	31
250	118	171	171	171	171	118	31
250	118	171	189	189	171	118	31
250	118	171	189	189	171	118	31
250	118	171	171	171	171	118	31
250	118	118	118	118	118	118	31
250	219	219	219	219	219	219	219

Figure H2.16
This is the resulting image for Exercise 2.4.

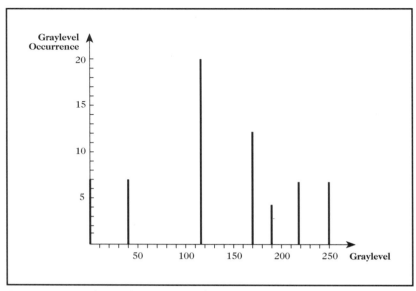

Figure H2.17 This is the histogram for Exercise 2.4.

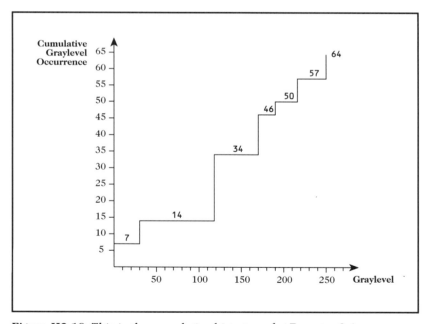

Figure H2.18 This is the cumulative histogram for Exercise 2.4.

2.5   The complete slices are shown in Figure H2.19.

Slice 3

0	0	0	0	0	0	0	0
0	0	0	0	0	0	0	0
0	0	1	1	1	0	0	0
0	0	1	1	1	0	0	0
0	0	1	1	1	0	0	0
0	0	0	0	0	0	0	0
0	0	0	0	0	0	0	0
0	0	0	0	0	0	0	0

Slice 2

0	0	0	0	0	0	0	0
0	0	0	0	0	0	0	0
0	1	0	0	0	1	0	0
0	1	0	0	0	1	0	0
0	1	0	0	0	1	0	0
0	1	1	1	1	1	0	0
0	0	0	0	0	0	0	0
0	0	0	0	0	0	0	0

Slice 1

0	0	0	0	0	0	0	0
0	0	0	0	0	0	0	0
0	0	0	0	0	0	1	0
0	0	0	0	0	0	1	0
0	0	0	0	0	0	1	0
0	0	0	0	0	0	1	0
0	1	1	1	1	1	1	0
0	0	0	0	0	0	0	0

Slice 0

0	0	0	0	0	0	0	0
0	1	1	1	1	1	1	0
0	0	0	0	0	0	0	0
0	0	0	0	0	0	0	0
0	0	0	0	0	0	0	0
0	0	0	0	0	0	0	0
0	0	0	0	0	0	0	0
0	0	0	0	0	0	0	0

Figure H2.19 These are the complete slices of the image shown in Figure 2.16.

2.6   The graylevel mapping results are shown in Figure H2.20. Figure
      H2.21 depicts the corrected image.

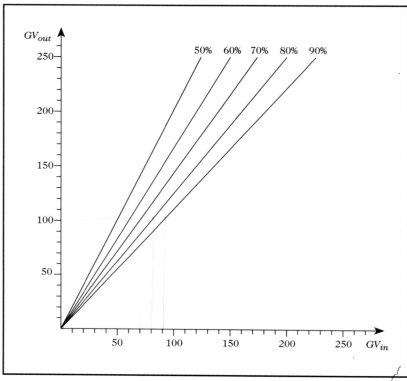

Figure H2.20 These are the graylevel mappings to correct the
inhomogeneous illumination shown in Figure 2.17.

10	10	10	10	10	10	10	10
10	10	10	10	10	10	10	10
10	10	100	100	100	100	100	100
10	10	100	100	100	100	100	100
10	10	100	100	100	100	100	100
10	10	10	100	100	100	100	100
10	10	10	10	100	100	100	100
10	10	10	10	10	100	100	100
10	10	10	10	10	10	100	100
10	10	10	10	10	10	100	100
10	10	10	10	10	10	100	100
10	10	10	10	10	10	100	100
10	10	10	10	10	10	100	100
10	10	10	10	10	10	100	100
10	10	10	10	10	10	10	10
10	10	10	10	10	10	10	10

Figure H2.21
This is the result of applying the mappings shown in Figure 2.51 to the source image shown in Figure 2.29.

2.7   The resulting images are shown in Figure H2.22 and Figure H2.23.

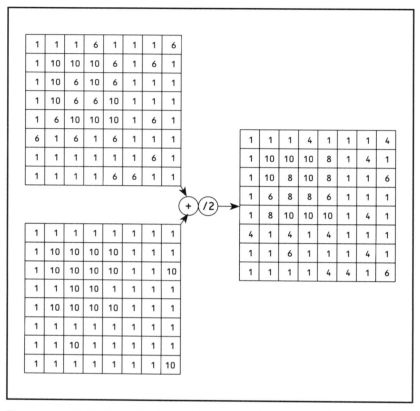

Figure H2.22 On the right-hand side, the result is shown of adding the noisy image in Figure 2.30 to the resulting image in Figure 2.18.

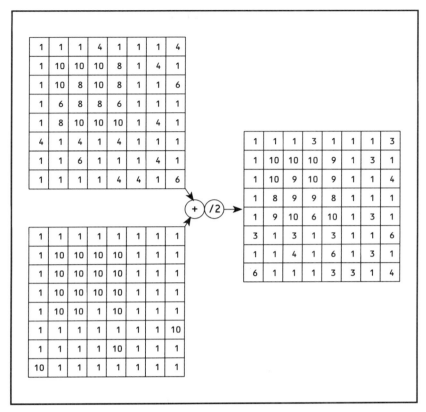

Figure H2.23 On the right-hand side, the result is shown of adding the noisy image in Figure 2.31 to the resulting image in Figure H2.22.

Chapter 3   Local operations

3.1   The output image resulting from the application of a Gaussian mean is shown in Figure H3.1.

0	0	0	0	0	0	0	0
0	2	2	4	7	9	8	0
0	2	2	3	7	9	8	0
0	1	1	3	7	9	10	0
0	1	1	3	7	9	9	0
0	2	2	4	8	9	8	0
0	2	2	6	9	9	9	0
0	0	0	0	0	0	0	0

Figure H3.1
Result of the application of a 3*3 Gaussian low-pass filter to the input image shown in Figure 3.2.

3.2   The result of the max operator is shown in Figure H3.2.

0	0	0	0	0	0	0	0
0	6	6	8	10	10	10	0
0	6	6	9	10	10	10	0
0	3	3	10	10	10	10	0
0	4	4	10	10	10	10	0
0	4	4	10	10	10	10	0
0	4	4	10	10	10	10	0
0	0	0	0	0	0	0	0

Figure H3.2
Complementary to the min operator (Figure 3.5) is the 3*3 max operator. It cleans the light region of the input image (Figure 3.2), but destroys the dark region.

3.3   The result of the median operator is shown in Figure H3.3.

0	0	0	0	0	0	0	0
0	1	1	1	9	10	10	0
0	1	1	2	8	9	10	0
0	1	1	1	9	10	10	0
0	1	1	2	9	10	10	0
0	1	1	2	10	10	10	0
0	1	1	2	10	10	10	0
0	0	0	0	0	0	0	0

Figure H3.3
The median operator has cleaned both the dark and the light regions of the input image (Figure 3.2) without flattening the steep graylevel step between these regions. The median operator is especially successful at removing black and white spots (salt-and-pepper noise) from an image.

3.4   The result of the nearest neighbor operator ($k=6$) is shown in Figure H3.4.

0	0	0	0	0	0	0	0
0	1	2	2	10	10	8	0
0	1	1	2	9	9	10	0
0	1	1	1	9	10	10	0
0	1	1	2	9	10	10	0
0	2	1	2	10	10	9	0
0	1	1	7	10	10	10	0
0	0	0	0	0	0	0	0

Figure H3.4
This is the result of a 3*3 nearest neighbor operator with $k=6$ (including the current pixel) applied to the input image shown in Figure 3.2. Compared to the result for $k=3$ (Figure 3.7), the smoothing effect is enhanced without the corresponding disadvantage of a flattened graylevel step.

3.5   Figure H3.5 shows the result of applying min and max operations to emphasize graylevel steps.

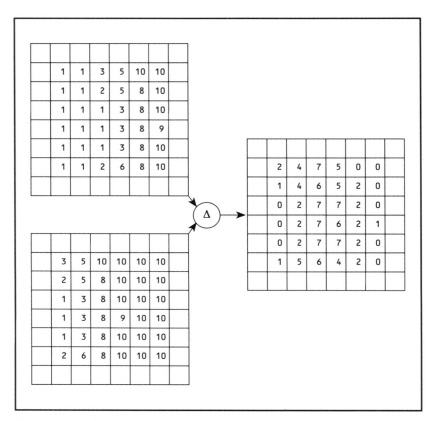

Figure H3.5 This is an alternative to the procedure shown in Figure 3.13. *Left:* results of a second lowest (*top*) and a second highest (*bottom*) operation applied to the source image (Figure 3.8). *Right:* the absolute difference between the second lowest and the second highest graylevels yields the emphasized graylevel step between the dark and the light regions.

3.6   Figure H3.6 shows the result of the second iteration of the closest of min and max operator.

1	1	1	1	10	10	10	10
1	1	1	1	10	10	10	10
1	1	1	10	10	10	10	10
1	1	1	1	1	10	10	10
1	1	1	1	10	10	10	10
1	1	1	1	10	10	10	10
1	1	1	10	10	10	10	10
1	1	1	10	10	10	10	10

Figure H3.6
The second iteration of the 3*3 closest of min and max operator (applied to the result of the first iteration shown in Figure 3.15) yields the steepest possible graylevel step between the dark and the light region.

3.7   Figure H3.7 shows the application of a 5*5 closest of min and max operator. Apart from a small peak, the 5*5 operator provides a good result. The peak may be removed by a median operator (Section 3.1.1).

1	1	1	1	10	10	10	10
1	1	1	1	1	10	10	10
1	1	1	1	1	10	10	10
1	1	3	1	1	10	10	10
1	1	3	1	1	10	10	10
1	1	1	1	1	10	10	10
1	1	1	1	1	1	10	10
1	1	1	1	1	1	1	10

Figure H3.7
This is the result of a 5*5 closest of min and max operator applied to the new input image (Figure 3.16).

Chapter 4   Global operations

4.1   In Section 4.4, the DFT was separated into its real and imaginary part as follows:

$$A_k = \frac{1}{M} \sum_{m=0}^{M-1} a_m \cos \frac{2\pi mk}{M} + b_m \sin \frac{2\pi mk}{M}$$

$$B_k = \frac{1}{M} \sum_{m=0}^{M-1} b_m \cos \frac{2\pi mk}{M} - a_m \sin \frac{2\pi mk}{M}$$

To simplify the equations, we first use real input signals only (b_m=0). Furthermore only 8 samples (M=8) are used. Hence:

$$A_k = \frac{1}{8} \sum_{m=0}^{M-1} a_m \cos \frac{2\pi mk}{M}$$

$$B_k = -\frac{1}{8} \sum_{m=0}^{M-1} a_m \sin \frac{2\pi mk}{M}$$

4.2   The spectrum representing the second harmonic is shown in Figure H4.1.

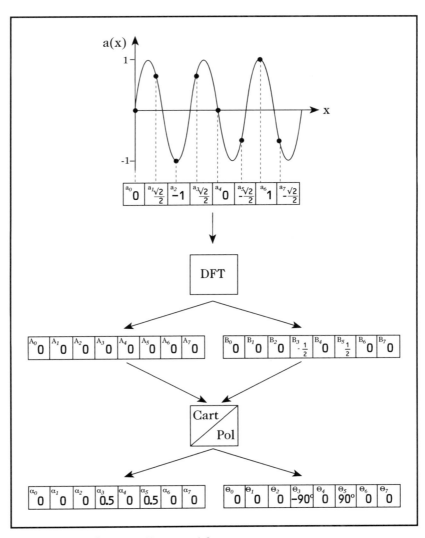

Figure H4.1 Solution to Exercise 4.2.

4.3   The spectrum representing the cosinusoidal signal is shown in Figure H4.2.

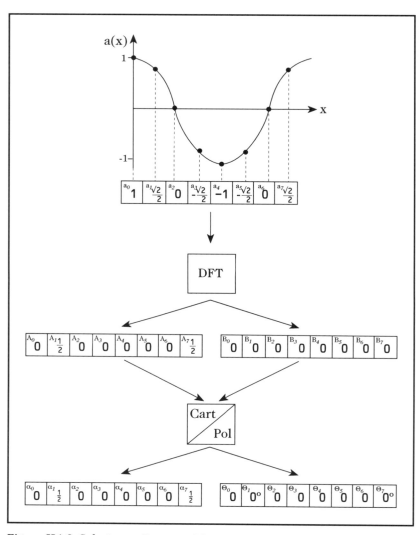

Figure H4.2 Solution to Exercise 4.3.

4.4   The spectrum representing the DC signal is shown in Figure H4.3.

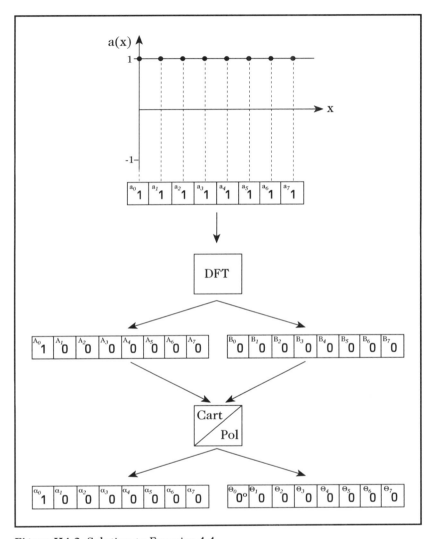

Figure H4.3 Solution to Exercise 4.4.

4.5   The spectrum representing the pulse is shown in Figure H4.4.

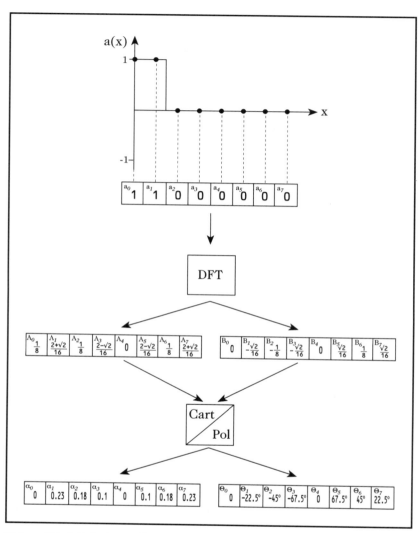

Figure H4.4 Solution to Exercise 4.5.

4.6   Figure H4.5 shows the 2-dimensional sinusoidal signal (first harmonic) and its spectrum.

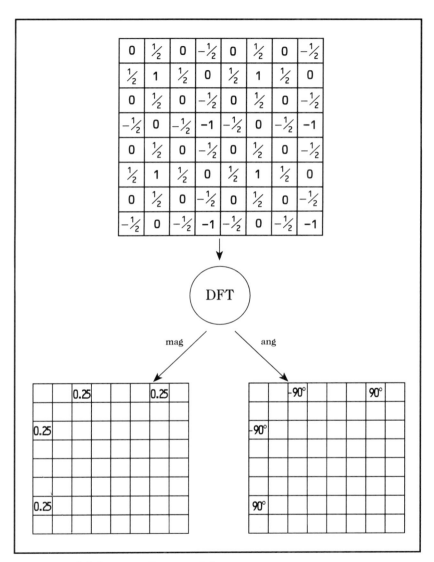

Figure H4.5 Solution to Exercise 4.6.

4.7 Figure H4.6 shows the 2-dimensional sine signal (second harmonic) and its spectrum.

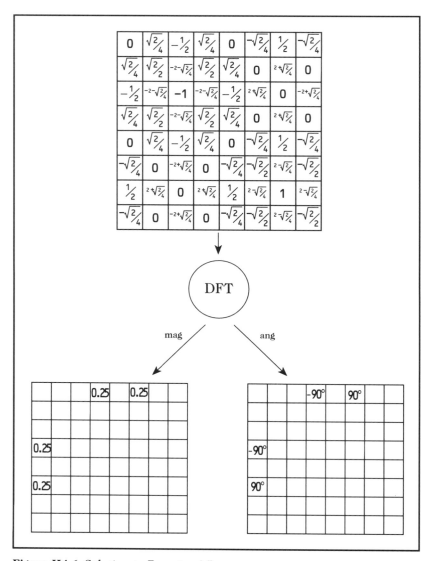

Figure H4.6 Solution to Exercise 4.7.

4.8   Figure H4.7 shows the superposition of a sinusoidal signal (second harmonic) and a cosinusoidal signal, as well as the spectrum of the 2-dimensional signal.

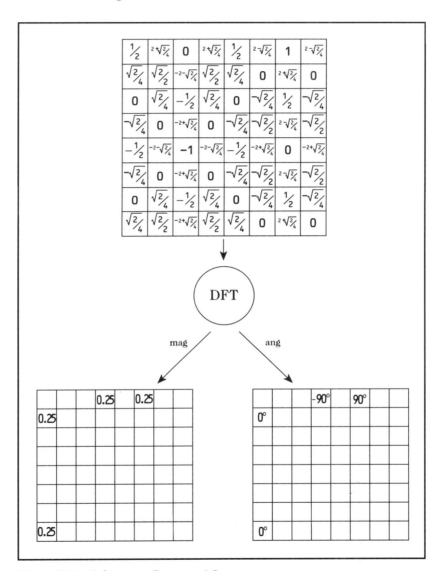

Figure H4.7 Solution to Exercise 4.8.

4.9   Figure H4.8 shows the 2-dimensional sinusoidal signal (second harmonic) and its spectrum.

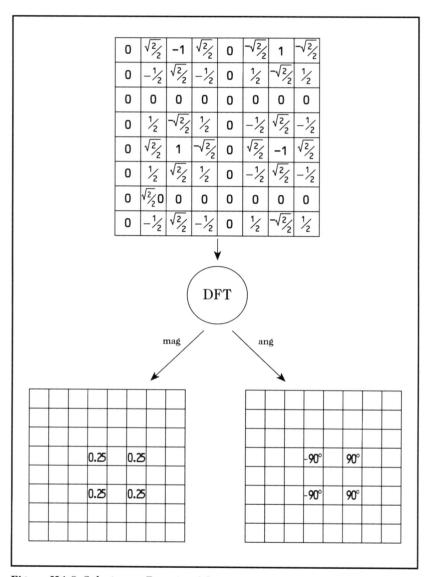

Figure H4.8 Solution to Exercise 4.9.

4.10   The 4 resulting images are shown in Figure H4.9.

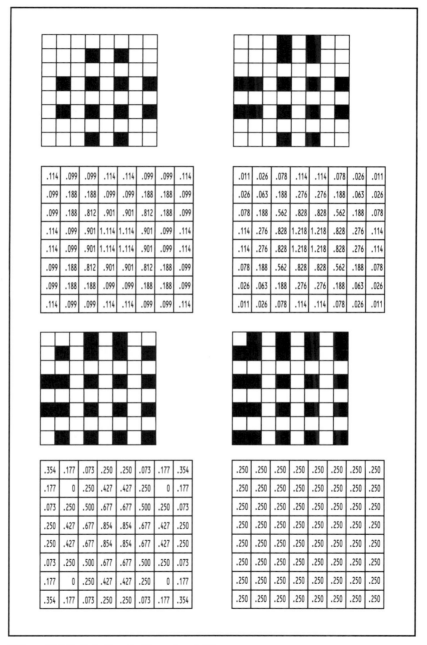

Figure H4.9 Solution to Exercise 4.10.

4.11   No, as Figure H4.10 shows, the magnitude is not invariant to rotation.

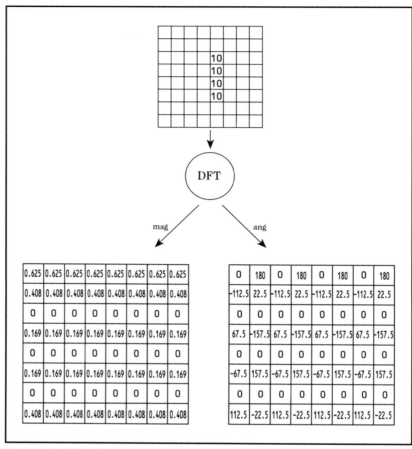

Figure H4.10 Solution to Exercise 4.11.

4.12   No, as Figure H4.11 shows, the magnitude is not invariant to rotation.

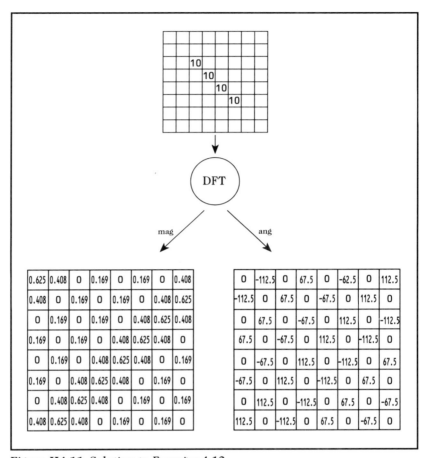

Figure H4.11 Solution to Exercise 4.12.

Chapter 5   Region-oriented segmentation

5.1   The results of applying the 'wrong' thresholds 2.5 and 8.5 are shown
        in Figure H5.1 and Figure H5.2.

0	0	0	1	1	1	1	1
0	0	0	1	1	1	1	1
0	0	0	1	1	1	1	1
0	0	0	1	1	1	1	1
0	0	0	1	1	1	1	1
0	0	0	1	1	1	1	1
0	0	0	1	1	1	1	1
0	0	0	1	1	1	1	1

Figure H5.1
A threshold of 2.5 applied to the
source image shown in Figure 5.2
yields a '1' region which is larger
than that obtained by the threshold
defined by the procedure shown in
Figure 5.2.

0	0	0	0	0	1	1	1
0	0	0	0	0	1	1	1
0	0	0	0	0	1	1	1
0	0	0	0	0	1	1	1
0	0	0	0	0	1	1	1
0	0	0	0	0	1	1	1
0	0	0	0	0	1	1	1
0	0	0	0	0	1	1	1

Figure H5.2
A threshold of 8.5 applied to the
source image shown in Figure 5.2
yields a '1' region which is smaller
than that obtained by the threshold
defined by the procedure shown in
Figure 5.2.

5.2   The manipulated histogram is shown in Figure H5.3. Figure H5.4
shows the new label image.

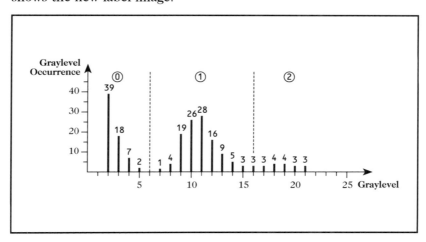

Figure H5.3 Averaging the original histogram shown in Figure 5.4 fills the
valley at graylevel 19 up. Thus, only two thresholds have to be applied.

0	0	0	0	0	0	0	0	0	0	0	0	0	0	0	0
0	0	0	0	0	0	0	0	0	0	0	0	0	0	0	0
0	0	1	1	1	1	1	1	1	1	1	1	1	1	0	0
0	0	1	1	1	1	1	1	1	1	1	1	1	1	0	0
0	0	1	1	1	1	1	2	2	2	1	1	1	1	0	0
0	0	1	1	1	1	2	2	2	2	2	1	1	1	0	0
0	0	1	1	1	1	1	2	2	2	2	1	1	1	0	0
0	0	1	1	1	1	2	2	2	2	1	1	1	1	0	0
0	0	1	1	1	1	2	2	2	2	1	1	1	1	0	0
0	0	1	1	1	1	1	1	1	1	1	1	1	1	0	0
0	0	1	1	1	1	1	1	1	1	1	1	1	1	0	0
0	0	1	1	1	1	1	1	1	1	1	1	1	1	0	0
0	0	1	1	1	1	1	1	1	1	1	1	1	1	0	0
0	0	0	0	0	0	0	0	0	0	0	1	0	0	0	0
0	0	0	0	0	0	0	0	0	0	0	0	0	0	0	0
0	0	0	0	0	0	0	0	0	0	0	0	0	0	0	0

Figure H5.4 The thresholds found in the manipulated histogram (Figure
H5.3) applied to the source image (Figure 5.3) yield the correct
segmentation.

5.3   Figure H5.5 shows the label and mark image.

3	3	2	1	1	1	2	2
3	3	2	1	1	1	2	2
3	3	2	1	1	1	2	2
2	2	2	1	1	1	2	2
1	1	1	1	1	1	2	2
1	1	1	1	1	2	2	2
0	0	0	0	0	2	1	1
0	0	0	0	0	2	1	1

Label image

a	a	b	c	c	c	d	d
a	a	b	c	c	c	d	d
a	a	b	c	c	c	d	d
b	b	b	c	c	c	d	d
c	c	c	c	c	c	d	d
c	c	c	c	c	d	d	d
–	–	–	–	–	d	e	e
–	–	–	–	–	d	e	e

Mark image

Figure H5.5 This is the result of Exercise 5.3. The label image is obtained segmenting the source image shown in Figure 5.35 using the thresholds 8, 13 and 17. The connectivity analysis yields five different regions plus background. Note that region 'b' is superfluous if we interpret its original graylevel (Figure 5.35) as transition between regions 'a' and 'c'.

Chapter 6   Contour-oriented segmentation

6.1   The results of the application of the gradient masks shown in Figure
        6.35 to the source image (Figure 6.3) are shown in Figure H6.1 and
        Figure H6.2.

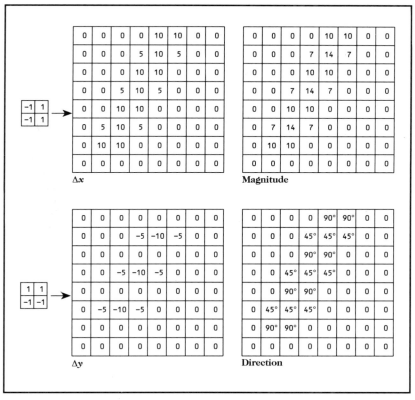

Figure 6.39 In comparison with the result of the simple gradient operator
shown in Figure 6.4, the improvement of this 2*2 mask is negligible.

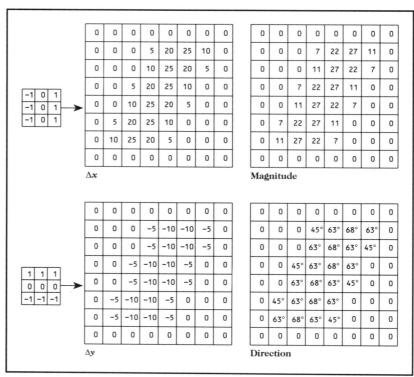

Figure H6.2 Compared to the results shown in Figure 6.4 and Figure H6.1, this 3*3 gradient operator yields superior results.

6.2   The neighborhood relations and the local maxima are shown in Figure H6.3, the results of the similarity check are depicted in Figure H6.4.

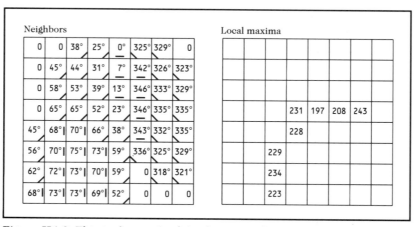

Figure H6.3 This is the result of the first step of a non-maxima suppression applied to the source image shown in Figure 6.36.

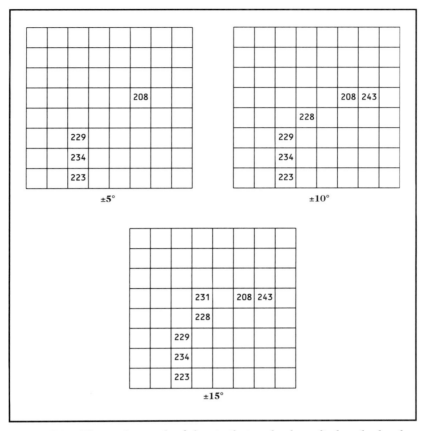

Figure H6.4 This is the result of the similarity check applied to the local maxima image shown in Figure H6.3.

6.3   Figure H6.5 shows the result of the 4-to-8 transform starting bottom right.

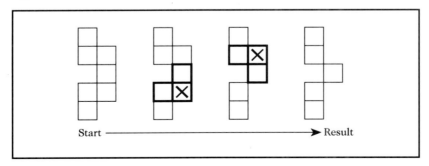

Figure H6.5 In this variation of the example shown in Figure 6.13, the processing starts bottom right. Note that the results differ.

6.4   Figure H6.6 shows the result of the refined 4-to-8 transform applied
       to the chain of contour points shown in Figure 6.37.

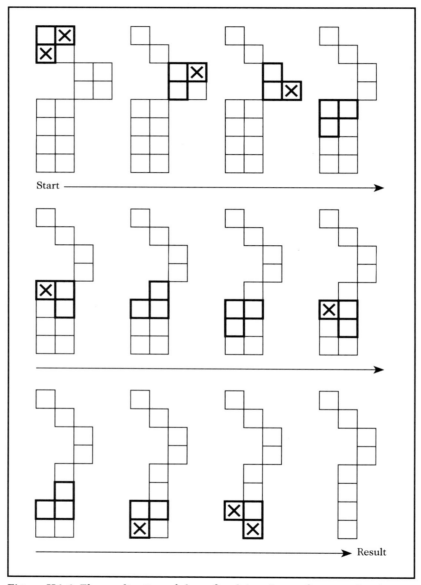

Figure H6.6 The application of the refined 4-to-8 transform on the chain
shown in Figure 6.37 yields a convincing result.

6.5   The result of the linking procedure is shown in Figure H6.7.

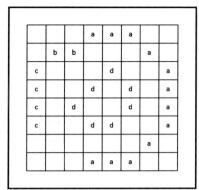

Figure H6.7
This is the result of the linking
procedure applied to the image
shown in Figure 6.38.

Chapter 7   Hough transform

7.1   Because in the accumulator parallel lines are indicated by equal θ values.

7.2   The accumulator resulting from the application of the Hough transform to Figure 7.18 is shown in Figure H7.1.

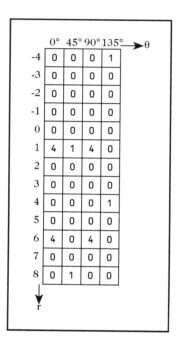

Figure H7.1
This is the result of the Hough transform applied to the gradient image shown in Figure 7.18. The four 4-entries are caused by the 16 vertically and horizontally oriented contour points representing the borders of the square, while the four 1-entries represent its corners.

7.3   Figure H7.2 shows the straight lines obtained from the accumulator shown in Figure H7.1.

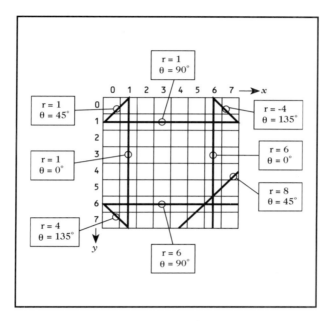

Figure H7.2
The diagonal straight lines extracted from the accumulator (Figure H7.1) are displaced by one pixel. This is due to the quantization effects calculating r and the intersection points at the image border.

7.4   The correctly placed straight lines are shown in Figure H7.3.

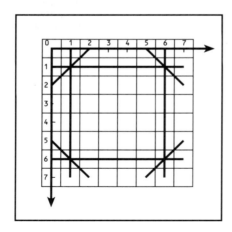

Figure H7.3
Avoiding quantization leads to an exact placement of the straight lines.

Chapter 8   Morphological image processing

8.1   The result shown in Figure H8.1 demonstrates the duality of erosion and dilation.

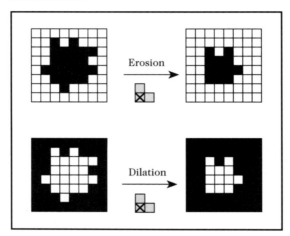

Figure H8.1
The solution to Exercise 8.1 demonstrates the duality of erosion and dilation.

8.2   The procedure is depicted in Figure H8.2.

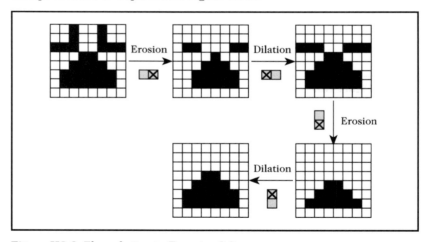

Figure H8.2 The solution to Exercise 8.2.

8.3   The result of contour extraction is shown in Figure H8.3.

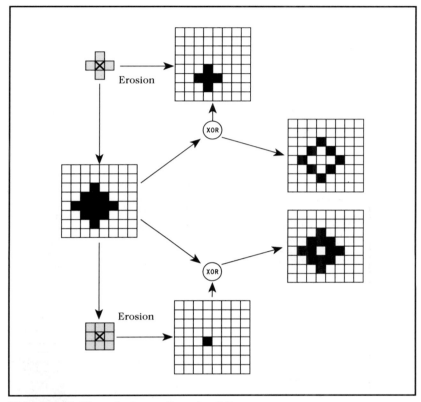

Figure H8.3 The solution to Exercise 8.3.

8.4   The results shown in Figure H8.4 and Figure H8.5 demonstrate that
       the skeleton procedure described in this chapter has to be applied
       carefully, since it may be destructive.

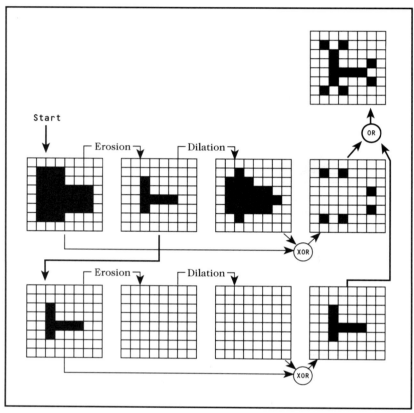

Figure H8.4 This is the first part of the solution to Exercise 8.4. *See also*
Figure H8.5.

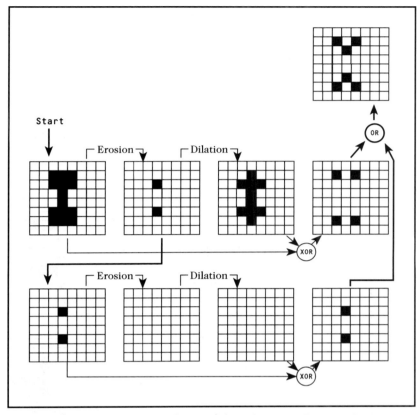

Figure H8.5 This is the second part of the solution to Exercise 8.4.

Chapter 9   Texture analysis

9.1   The graylevel mean (5) and variance (25) are identical for both images.

9.2   The results of the local graylevel mean and variance operations are shown in Figure H9.1.

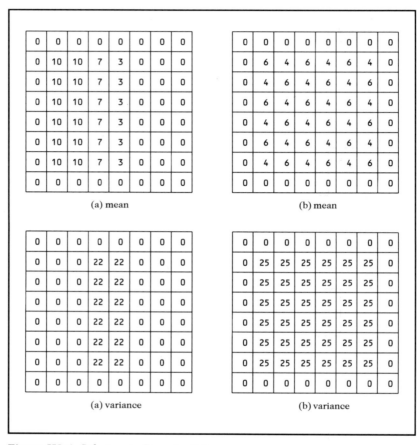

Figure H9.1 Solution to Exercise 9.2.

9.3   The co-occurrence matrices are shown in Figure H9.2, Figure H9.3 and Figure H9.4.

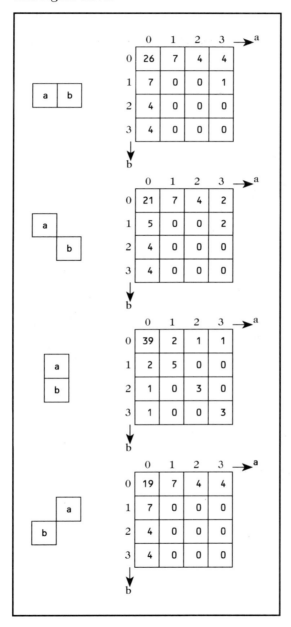

Figure H9.2
Solution to Exercise 9.3(a).

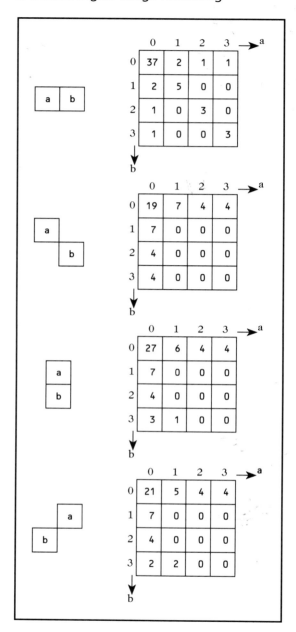

Figure H9.3
Solution to Exercise 9.3(b).

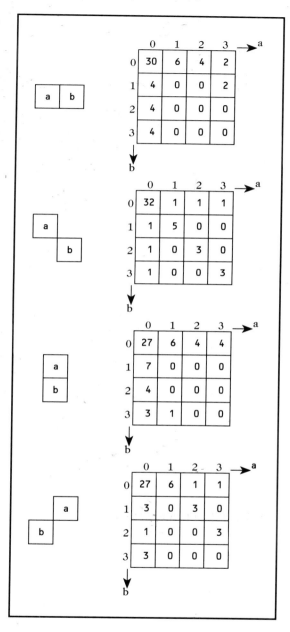

Figure H9.4
Solution to Exercise 9.3(c).

Chapter 10   Pattern recognition

10.1   For rejection level 2, the class centers are z = {10 Francs, 5 Marks, 1 Pound, 2 Francs, 1 Krone, 1 Mark, 5 Cents, 10 Pfennigs, 1 Pence, 10 Øres}. The following classes were generated:

k_0 = {10 Francs}
k_1 = {5 Marks}
k_2 = {1 Pound}
k_3 = {2 Francs, 2 Marks}
k_4 = {1 Krone, 1 Franc}
k_5 = {1 Mark, 1 Quarter}
k_6 = {5 Cents, 1/2 Franc}
k_7 = {10 Pfennigs, 25 Øres, 20 Centimes}
k_8 = {1 Pence, 10 Centimes}
k_9 = {10 Øres, 1 Cent}

For rejection level 3, the class centers are z = {10 Francs, 5 Marks, 1 Pound, 2 Francs, 1 Krone, 1 Mark, 5 Cents, 10 Pfennigs, 10 Øres}. The following classes were generated:

k_0 = {10 Francs}
k_1 = {5 Marks}
k_2 = {1 Pound}
k_3 = {2 Francs, 2 Marks}
k_4 = {1 Krone, 1 Franc}
k_5 = {1 Mark, 1 Quarter}
k_6 = {5 Cents, 1/2 Franc}
k_7 = {10 Pfennigs, 25 Øres, 20 Centimes, 1 Pence}
k_8 = {10 Øres, 10 Centimes, 1 Cent}

For rejection level 4, the class centers are z = {10 Francs, 2 Francs, 1 Franc, 5 Cents, 25 Øres, 10 Øres}. The following classes were generated:

k_0 = {10 Francs, 5 Marks, 1 Pound}
k_1 = {2 Francs, 2 Marks, 1 Krone}
k_2 = {1 Franc, 1 Mark, 1 Quarter}
k_3 = {5 Cents, 1/2 Franc, 10 Pfennigs, 1 Pence}
k_4 = {25 Øres, 20 Centimes}
k_5 = {10 Øres, 10 Centimes, 1 Cent}

For rejection level 5, the class centers are z = {10 Francs, 2 Francs, 1 Franc, 5 Cents, 20 Centimes, 10 Øres}. The following classes were generated:

---

k_0 = {10 Francs, 5 Marks, 1 Pound}
k_1 = {2 Francs, 2 Marks, 1 Krone}
k_2 = {1 Franc, 1 Mark, 1 Quarter}
k_3 = {5 Cents, 1/2 Franc, 10 Pfennigs, 25 Øres, 1 Pence}
k_4 = {20 Centimes}
k_5 = {10 Øres, 10 Centimes, 1 Cent}

For rejection level 6, the class centers are z = {10 Francs, 2 Marks, 1 Mark, 1 Pence}. The following classes were generated:

---

k_0 = {10 Francs, 5 Marks, 1 Pound, 2 Francs}
k_1 = {2 Marks, 1 Krone, 1 Francs}
k_2 = {1 Mark, 1 Quarter, 5 Cents, 1/2 Franc, 10 Pfennigs, 25 Øres, 20 Centimes}
k_3 = {1 Pence, 10 Øres, 10 Centimes, 1 Cent}

10.2(a) The center for the sample class 'a' is (x=4.7, y=11.3), the radius of its close border is 2.3, whereas the radius of the wider border is 4.3. Sample class 'b' is positioned at (x=11.7, y=4.0). The borders are 3.0 and 6.3.

Chapter 11   Image sequence analysis

11.1   Table H11.1 shows the movement of the pixels, while the needle image is shown in Figure H11.1.

r0	c0	r1	c1	r0	c0	r1	c1
2	2	8	8	5	2	10	8
2	3	8	9	5	3	10	9
2	4	8	10	5	4	10	10
2	5	8	10	5	5	10	10
2	6	2	11	5	6	10	12
2	7	2	12	5	7	10	13
3	2	9	8	6	2	12	8
3	3	9	9	6	3	12	9
3	4	9	10	6	4	12	10
3	5	9	10	6	5	12	10
3	6	3	11	6	6	4	11
3	7	3	12	6	7	4	12
4	2	10	8	7	2	13	8
4	3	10	9	7	3	13	9
4	4	10	10	7	4	13	10
4	5	10	10	7	5	13	10
4	6	10	12	7	6	13	11
4	7	10	13	7	7	13	12

Table H11.1
This table shows the movement of the pixels asked for in Exercise 11.1.

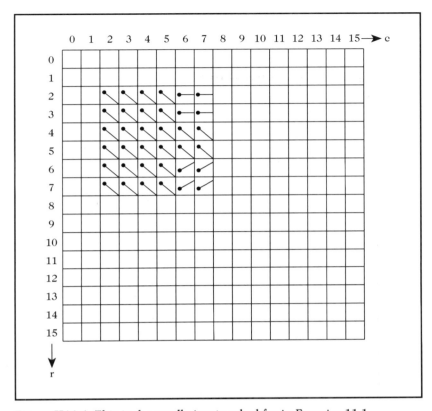

Figure H11.1 This is the needle image asked for in Exercise 11.1.

Index

Books from

International Thomson Publishing

On The Internet

PIECING TOGETHER MOSAIC
Navigating the Internet and the World Wide Web
Steve Bowbrick, 3W Magazine

Mosaic is the most widely used browser for the Internet's World Wide Web and runs on UNIX, Macintosh and Microsoft Windows. Providing a multimedia interface to the Internet, Mosaic helps the user navigate the Internet and the World Wide Web, and explore the information superhighway. This title provides a user-friendly introduction to Mosaic. Fully illustrated throughout, this invaluable guide explains what Mosaic is and how it works, including: a quick start session for those people who already have a browser set up; details of how to obtain Mosaic from the Internet and configure it for your platform; Web navigation and search strategies; how to use Internet tools and services via Mosaic; an appendix listing useful World Wide Web sites; a glossary of terms; beyond Mosaic – how to set up a Web server and write HTML documents.
Spring 1995/300pp/1-850-32142-6/paper

SPINNING THE WEB
How to Provide Information on the Internet
Andrew Ford

An indispensable guide for all those who provide or intend to provide information on the World Wide Web, or want to make the most of their existing services, this book for the first time draws together all of the most up to date information and details of contemporary resources into one essential volume. Providing exclusive coverage of Web features, the book includes an overview of Web facilities, how to create hypertext documents, security issues, how to set up a server and the selection and evaluation of software. A variety of examples from current Web sources are included.
December 1994/250pp/1-850-32141-8/paper

On CompuServe

COMPUSERVE FOR EUROPE
Roelf Sluman

CompuServe, the world's largest personal on-line service, allows access to a world of information and services – plus a gateway to the Internet, the information super highway. News, financial reports, hobbies, travel, entertainment, interest groups, forums and electronic mail are just a few of the range of services available on-line via CompuServe. Written with the European user in mind, this is the ideal guide to this on-line service. Whether an existing member or a first-time user, it provides help and advice in a readable, accessible way. It also provides a WinCIM disk free, a key program for CompuServe access – plus $15* credit for new and existing users.
CompuServe is an international service and is priced in $US. Billing is in local currency at the prevailing rate.
December 1994/448pp/1-850-32121-3/paper

Where to purchase these books?
Please contact your local bookshop, in case of difficulties, contact us at one of the addresses below -

ORDERS
International Thomson Publishing Services Ltd
Cheriton House, North Way, Andover, Hants SP10 5BE, UK
Telephone: 0264 332424/Giro Account No: 2096919/
Fax: 0264 364418

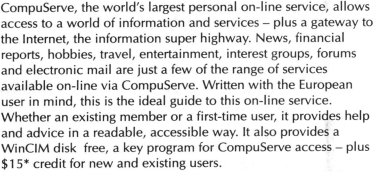

SALES AND MARKETING ENQUIRIES
International Thomson Publishing
Berkshire House, 168/173 High Holborn, London WCIV 7AA,UK
Tel: 071-497 1422 Fax: 071-497 1426
e–mail: Info@ITPUK.CO.UK

MAILING LIST
To receive further information on our Networks books, please send the following information to the London address –
Full name and address (including Postcode)

Telephone, Fax Numbers and e-mail address

Ad Oculos Digital Image Processing 2.0 Licence Agreement